JOURNAL FOR THE STUDY OF THE OLD TESTAMENT SUPPLEMENT SERIES
379

Sheffield Academic Press
A Continuum imprint

Understanding Dan

An Exegetical Study
of a Biblical City,
Tribe and Ancestor

Mark W. Bartusch

Journal for the Study of the Old Testament
Supplement Series 379

Published by Sheffield Academic Press Ltd
The Tower Building, 11 York Road, London SE1 7NX
15 East 26th Street, Suite 1703, New York, NY 10010

www.continuumbooks.com

British Library Cataloguing-in-Publication Data
A catalogue record for this book is available from the British Library

Typeset by Sheffield Academic Press
Printed on acid-free paper in Great Britain by Bookcraft Ltd, Midsomer Norton, Bath

ISBN 0-8264-6657-5

CONTENTS

ACKNOWLEDGMENTS

Many members of the Biblical Division at the Lutheran School of Theology at Chicago have been influential on my development as a scholar and teacher of the Church, and for each of them I am thankful. Professor of New Testament David M. Rhoads first introduced me to new ways of studying the Bible by using the resources of cultural anthropology and the social sciences in a Graduate Seminar on the Gospel of Mark. David is a gifted teacher, and I have had the privilege of being one of his teaching assistants. *Emeritus* Professor of New Testament Edgar M. Krentz encouraged me and others at the start of our graduate program by reminding us, in an aphorism, that if you have chosen a way that is without difficulties, you will find that it leads nowhere. I can honestly say, on the basis of the challenges encountered, that I am well along the way from where I was eight years ago. Wesley J. Fuerst, now *Emeritus* Professor of Old Testament, is a rare individual: solid scholar, excellent teacher, and faithful servant of the Church. I thank him for his kindness, friendship, and constant support along the way. Professor Walter L. Michel has taught (pushed?) me to look beyond the historical interpretations of the biblical text to which I seem naturally inclined, and for this I am grateful. Walter's Graduate Seminar on Biblical Hebrew Poetry was one of the finest courses I took during my graduate studies career; I intend to continue research in this area of scholarship, convinced that close attention to the variety of poetic devices promises the reward of deeper understanding of the biblical text. Thanks also to Professor Theodore Hiebert of McCormick Theological Seminary for graciously agreeing to serve on my dissertation committee.

Special thanks are due to my advisor and dissertation supervisor, Christ Seminary-Seminex Professor of Old Testament Ralph W. Klein. His work ethic and commitment to his students is worthy of emulation. Even during his busy years as Academic Dean at LSTC, Ralph always had time not only to meet with me to discuss my progress in the program, but also to supervise independent studies and read critically whatever I submitted to him. Ralph has been my teacher, mentor, constant motivator, source of encouragement in moments of uncertainty and disappointment, and friend.

I share a word of thanks also for Professor Walter E. Rast of Valparaiso University, who is now my senior colleague but who was my first teacher of Biblical Hebrew, and the one who first encouraged me to consider pursuing graduate work in Hebrew Bible.

Finally, I am grateful for the careful attention and helpful suggestions of Dr Duncan Burns, the production editor who guided the final preparation of this project.

Mark W. Bartusch
Valparaiso University
Valparaiso, IN
May 2003

ABBREVIATIONS

AASOR	Annual of the American Schools of Oriental Research
AB	Anchor Bible
ABD	David Noel Freedman (ed.), *The Anchor Bible Dictionary* (New York: Doubleday, 1992)
AJBA	*Australian Journal of Biblical Archaeology*
ANEP	James B. Pritchard (ed.), *Ancient Near East in Pictures Relating to the Old Testament* (Princeton: Princeton University Press, 1954)
ANET	James B. Pritchard (ed.), *Ancient Near Eastern Texts Relating to the Old Testament* (Princeton: Princeton University Press, 1950)
AnOr	Analecta orientalia
ATD	Das Alte Testament Deutsch
BA	*Biblical Archaeologist*
BAGD	Walter Bauer, William F. Arndt, F. William Gingrich and Frederick W. Danker, *A Greek–English Lexicon of the New Testament and Other Early Christian Literature* (Chicago: University of Chicago Press, 2nd edn, 1958)
BASOR	*Bulletin of the American Schools of Oriental Research*
BDB	Francis Brown, S.R. Driver and Charles A. Briggs, *A Hebrew and English Lexicon of the Old Testament* (Oxford: Clarendon Press, 1907)
BHK	R. Kittel (ed.), *Biblia hebraica* (Stuttgart: Württembergische Bibelanstalt, 1937)
BHS	*Biblia hebraica stuttgartensia*
Bib	*Biblica*
BKAT	Biblischer Kommentar: Altes Testament
BR	*Bible Review*
BTB	*Biblical Theology Bulletin*
BZ	*Biblische Zeitschrift*
BZAW	Beihefte zur *ZAW*
CBQ	*Catholic Biblical Quarterly*
DDD	Karel van der Toorn, Bob Becking and Pieter W. van der Horst (eds.), *Dictionary of Deities and Demons in the Bible* (Leiden: E.J. Brill, 1995)
DH	Deuteronomistic History

Dtr	The Deuteronomistic Historian
EncJud	*Encyclopaedia Judaica*
FOTL	The Forms of the Old Testament Literature
FRLANT	Forschungen zur Religion und Literatur des Alten und Neuen Testaments
GBS	Guides to Biblical Scholarship
GKC	*Gesenius' Hebrew Grammar* (ed. E. Kautzsch, revised and trans. A.E. Cowley; Oxford: Clarendon Press, 1910)
HALOT	Koehler, Ludwig, and Walter Baumgartner, *The Hebrew and Aramaic Lexicon of the Old Testament* (Leiden: E.J. Brill, rev. edn, 1994)
HAT	Handbuch zum Alten Testament
HSM	Harvard Semitic Monographs
ICC	International Critical Commentary
IEJ	*Israel Exploration Journal*
ISBE	Geoffrey Bromiley (ed.), *The International Standard Bible Encyclopedia* (4 vols.; Grand Rapids: Eerdmans, rev. edn, 1979–88)
JBL	*Journal of Biblical Literature*
JNES	*Journal of Near Eastern Studies*
JPOS	*Journal of the Palestine Oriental Society*
JSNT	*Journal for the Study of the New Testament*
JSOT	*Journal for the Study of the Old Testament*
JSOTSup	*Journal for the Study of the Old Testament*, Supplement Series
JSS	*Journal of Semitic Studies*
NCB	New Century Bible
NEAEHL	Ephraim Stern (ed.), *The New Encyclopedia of Archaeological Excavations in the Holy Land* (New York: Simon & Schuster, 1993)
NICOT	New International Commentary on the Old Testament
NJPS	*Tanakh: The Holy Scriptures, the New JPS Translation Accordinging to the Traditional Hebrew Text* (New York: Jewish Publication Society of America, 5748/1988)
NRSV	New Revised Standard Version
OBO	Orbis biblicus et orientalis
OTL	Old Testament Library
PJ	*Palästina-Jahrbuch*
RB	*Revue biblique*
RSV	Revised Standard Version
SBLDS	SBL Dissertation Series
SBLMS	SBL Monograph Series
SBLSCS	SBL Septuagint and Cognate Studies
SBT	Studies in Biblical Theology
ScrHier	*Scripta Hierosolymitana*
SHANE	Studies in the History of the Ancient Near East

ST	*Studia theologica*
TBü	Theologische Bücherei
TDOT	G.J. Botterweck and H. Ringgren (eds.), *Theological Dictionary of the Old Testament*
TLOT	Ernst Jenni and Claus Westermann (eds.), *Theological Lexicon of the Old Testament* (3 vols.; trans. Mark E. Biddle; Peabody, MA: Hendrickson, 1997)
UBL	Ugaritisch–Biblishe Literatur
UF	*Ugarit-Forschungen*
UT	Cyrus H. Gordon, *Ugaritic Textbook* (Analecta orientalia, 38; Rome: Pontifical Biblical Institute Press, 1965)
VT	*Vetus Testamentum*
VTSup	*Vetus Testamentum*, Supplements
WBC	Word Biblical Commentary
ZAW	*Zeitschrift für die alttestamentliche Wissenschaft*
ZDPV	*Zeitschrift des deutschen Palästina-Vereins*
ZTK	*Zeitschrift für Theologie und Kirche*

Chapter 1

INTRODUCTION

The word 'Dan' occurs in each portion of the Hebrew Canon: Torah, Prophets, and Writings. Some readers may think immediately of the city of Dan in the northern part of the land of Canaan, while the son of Jacob and eponymous ancestor of the Danites, or the tribe of Dan (and its territory), may come first to the mind of others. The fact is that Dan is unique in the Hebrew Bible because it alone refers not only to an ancestor and tribe of Israel (as well as the territory of the tribe of Dan, as do the other sons of Jacob), but also to a city. That is, Dan is the only ancestor, the only Israelite tribe, to share the name of a city in Palestine. Put simply, the overarching interest of the present study is to examine the entire Dan/Danite tradition in the Hebrew Bible in order to determine not only what the Bible, in fact, tells us about Dan, but also the degree to which traditions associated with one representation of Dan may have influenced the characterization of another.

The Hebrew Bible itself is unclear in places as to whether the intended referent is the ancestor or the tribe bearing his name. For example, the framework of the Blessing of Jacob (Gen. 49.1-2, 28) makes reference to both the 'sons of Jacob' and the 'tribes of Israel'. Are the individual sayings contained within this poem characterizations of the ancestor or the tribe ostensibly descended from him, and how might this contribute to one's reconstruction of early Israelite history? More importantly and, I think, more interesting, is the question: In what ways have events or traditions connected with the city of Dan, especially traditions associated with Jeroboam I, influenced the other texts about Dan and/or the Danites in the Hebrew Bible?

A survey of traditions from the end of the biblical period shows that the city traditions have indeed influenced material about the ancestor, or tribe, of Dan, in the rabbinic literature (Midrash), the New Testament, the *Testament of the Twelve Patriarchs*, and the writings of certain early church fathers.

1. *Revelation 7*

There is no mention of Dan in the text of Revelation 7, where there is included an enumeration of the other tribes of the 'sons of Israel' (v. 4). The tribes are listed in the following order, which nowhere appears in the Hebrew Bible: Judah, Reuben, Gad, Asher, Naphtali, Manasseh, Simeon, Levi, Issachar, Zebulun, Joseph, and Benjamin.[1] However, two textual variants indicate that in a distinct minority of manuscripts 'Dan' appears either in place of Gad (v. 5), or as a substitute for Manasseh (v. 6).[2] The question is: Why was Dan omitted from this list of Israelite tribes? The consensus among commentators on the book of Revelation is that the omission of Dan was intentional and not the result of textual corruption.[3] While several scholars assume that 7.1-8 is based on an earlier Jewish tradition, as Bauckham points out nothing of the sort is known.[4] Thus, most

1.   Besides the omission of Dan, the other unusual features of this list are the relatively high placement of Gad and Asher (the sons of Leah's maidservant, Zilpah), and the inclusion of both Joseph and one of the sons of Joseph, Manasseh (but not the other son, Ephraim).

2.   According to the critical apparatus in Nestle–Aland[27], Dan appears in the place of Gad in the eleventh-century manuscript 1854, as well as in a few other manuscripts. The Bohairic Version (Coptic) substitutes Dan for Manasseh. Thus, it seems clear that some in the early Christian community recognized the omission of Dan from and the most unusual addition of Manasseh to this list of the tribes of Israel and sought to correct the text. It is interesting to observe that in the *Testament of Judah* (7.2), while the text reads 'I, therefore, and Dan feigned ourselves to be Amorites...' there is a variant tradition (Greek and Slavonic) which substitutes Gad for Dan (see R.H. Charles, *The Apocrypha and Pseudepigrapha of the Old Testament in English, with Introductions and Critical and Explanatory Notes to the Several Books*. II. *Pseudepigrapha* [2 vols.; Oxford: Clarendon Press, 1913], p. 317).

3.   R.H. Charles, *A Critical and Exegetical Commentary on the Revelation of St. John* (ICC; Edinburgh: T. & T. Clark, 1920), pp. 207-208; J. Massyngberde Ford, *Revelation: Introduction, Translation and Commentary* (AB, 38; Garden City, NY: Doubleday, 1975), p. 118; G.R. Beasley-Murray, *The Book of Revelation* (NCB; Grand Rapids: Eerdmans, rev. edn, 1978), p. 143; Gerhard A. Krodel, *Revelation* (ACNT; Minneapolis: Augsburg, 1989), p. 183. Christopher R. Smith ('The Portrayal of the Church as the New Israel in the Names and Order of the Tribes in Revelation 7.5-8', *JSNT* 39 [1990], pp. 111-18 [117 n. 15]) makes reference to G.V. Sanderson's study ('In Defence of Dan', *Scripture* 3/4 [1948], pp. 114-15), in which the latter proposes that Manasseh appears as the result of a scribal error, namely the confusion of an earlier abbreviation ('Man[asseh]' for 'Dan'). Charles, however, notes that such an abbreviation is improbable (*Revelation of St. John*, p. 208).

4.   Richard Bauckham ('The List of the Tribes in Revelation 7 Again', *JSNT* 42 [1991], pp. 99-115 [100]) writes that 'the tradition that Antichrist would come from the

scholars assume that Judah was placed at the top of the tribal list in ch. 7 because the Messiah was believed to come from this tribe.[5] It is reasonable, then, to speculate that Dan was omitted and replaced by Manasseh by the early Christian community, which may have been aware of the traditions of Danite idolatry which grew out of the narratives about Micah, the Levite, and the Danite migration in Judges 17–18; and of Jeroboam I in 1 Kings 12.

2. *Irenaeus and Hippolytus*

The idea that Dan was intentionally omitted from the list of Israelite tribes in Revelation 7 for specifically theological reasons, however, emerges in the writings of the early Church Fathers Irenaeus and Hippolytus, who see in the tribe of Dan the origin of Antichrist. Irenaeus, citing Jer. 8.16, writes concerning Antichrist:

> And Jeremiah does not merely point out his sudden coming, but he even indicates the tribe from which he shall come, where he says, 'We shall hear the voice of his swift horses from Dan; the whole earth shall be moved by the voice of the neighing of his galloping horses: he shall also come and devour the earth, and the fulness thereof, the city also, and they that dwell therein'. This, too, is the reason that this tribe is not reckoned in the Apocalypse along with those which are saved.[6]

Of course, Irenaeus's interpretation of Jeremiah 8 is subject to question. As I will suggest in my own analysis of Jeremiah 8, Irenaeus's interpretation tells us much about Irenaeus, but has nothing to do with the context in Jeremiah. While Irenaeus understands Dan in this text as a reference to the

tribe of Dan is first found in Irenaeus, *Against Heresies* 5.30.2 (translations from Irenaeus are from Alexander Roberts and James Donaldson [eds.], *The Ante-Nicene Fathers: Translations of the Writings of the Fathers down to A.D. 325* [10 vols.; Grand Rapids: Eerdmans, 1981 (1885)], I, pp. 315-562 [559]) and Hippolytus, *De Antichristo* 14; it is found in no Jewish text and is very unlikely to be pre-Christian. The "Antichrist" figures of Jewish apocalyptic are always Gentiles.' On this, see also Charles, *Revelation of St. John*, p. 209, who refers to his earlier work on *The Testament of Dan* in *The Testaments of the Twelve Patriarchs: Transated from the Editor's Greek Text and Edited with Introduction, Notes, and Indices* (London: A. & C. Black, 1908).

5.   Charles, *Revelation of St. John*, pp. 193-94, 207-208; Beasley-Murray, *The Book of Revelation*, p. 144; Krodel, *Revelation*, p. 183; Henry Barclay Swete, *The Apocalypse of St John: The Greek Text with Introduction, Notes, and Indices* (New York: MacMillan, 2nd edn, 1907), p. 98.

6.   Irenaeus, *Against Heresies* 5.30.2. Cf. n. 4, above.

tribe, in fact Jer. 8.16 refers to the city of Dan on the northern boundary of the land of Israel (cf. 'from Dan as far as Beersheba'), over which the invading army crossed to enter Palestine from Syria/Mesopotamia. Since the Jeremiah text does not lend itself easily to the use Irenaeus makes of it, the question of the source of his tradition about Dan, with which he combined the curious absence of Dan in Revelation 7, must remain open.

More fascinating still is the appearance of Dan in the work of Hippolytus, a student of Irenaeus. Hippolytus interprets the metaphorical mention of Dan in Genesis 49 ('a serpent by the way') as a reference to the Pharisees and scribes 'who fastened like snakes upon Christ'.[7] Elsewhere, he identifies this 'serpent' (Dan) with 'the deceiver from the beginning, he who is named in Genesis, he who deceived Eve, and bruised Adam in the heel'.[8] It is also in Hippolytus that the origin of Antichrist is explicitly identified as the tribe of Dan. Seizing on the fact that, in the Hebrew Bible, both the tribe of Judah and the tribe of Dan are referred to as a 'lion's whelp' (Judah, in Gen. 49.9; Dan, in Deut. 33.22), Hippolytus draws a clear parallel between the descent of Christ from the tribe of Judah and Antichrist from the tribe of Dan:

> By thus naming the tribe of Dan as the one whence the accuser is destined to spring, he made that matter in hand quite clear. For as Christ is born of the tribe of Judah, so Antichrist shall be born of the tribe of Dan. And as our Lord and Saviour Jesus Christ, the Son of God, was spoken of in prophecy as a *lion* on account of His royalty and glory, in the same manner also has the Scripture prophetically described the accuser as a lion, on account of his tyranny and violence... For in every respect that deceiver seeks to make himself appear like the Son of God. Christ is a lion, and Antichrist is a lion.[9]

There can be little question that the works of Irenaeus and Hippolytus are examples of early Christian exegesis of the Danite traditions in the Hebrew Bible. In part, perhaps, their evaluation (demonization?) of Dan and the Danites was conditioned by their understanding of the apostasy of Jeroboam I at the city of Dan, and by the omission of any reference to Dan in the New Testament writings.

7.   Hippolytus, 'Fragments from Commentaries on Various Books of Scripture', in Roberts and Donaldson (eds.), *The Ante-Nicene Fathers*, V, pp. 163-203 (166).

8.   Hippolytus, 'Appendix to the Works of Hippolytus, Containing Dubius and Spurious Pieces', in Roberts and Donaldson (eds.), *The Ante-Nicene Fathers*, V, pp. 242-58 (246 §XVIII).

9.   Hippolytus, 'Appendix to the Works of Hippolytus', pp. 246-47 §§XIX-XX.

3. Testament of Twelve Patriarchs

According to the *Testament of Dan*, the ancestor Dan addresses his sons and speaks to them of their departure 'from the Lord' in the last days (5.4-8). One may speculate that the author of this *Testament* has set this notice in parallel with the tribe of Dan's earlier apostasy (Judg. 17–18; see also 1 Kgs 12). In addition, not only does Dan confess his own league with Beliar (*T. Dan* 1.7) in the fraternal plot against Joseph (Gen. 37), he further identifies Satan as his sons's 'prince' (ὁ ἄρχων).[10] As de Jonge notes, 'this notion [namely, the association of Satan with the sons/tribe of Dan] is not found in rabbinic or other Jewish literature. The rabbis denounce the tribe of Dan as especially idolatrous, but do not go so far as to declare that the Danites were led by Satan himself'.[11] This connection was made explicit, however, later in the writings of Irenaeus and Hippolytus.

4. *Rabbinic Literature/Jewish Legends*

The tribe of Dan is also negatively portrayed in several texts in rabbinic midrash and other Jewish legends.[12] The following sketch of the most important occurrences of Dan in this material provides a good impression of how the rabbis interpreted certain references to Dan in the Bible.

According to Genesis 14, Abram pursued the Eastern kings 'as far as Dan'. The Midrash of this text reads: 'Idolatry smites both before it comes and after it has departed. It smites in anticipation, as it is written, "and pursued as far as Dan". It smites retrospectively, as it is written, "The snorting of his horses is heard from Dan" (Jer. VIII, 16).'[13]

10. M. de Jonge, *Testamenta XII Patriarcharum* (Pseudepigrapha Veterii Testamenti, 1; Leiden: E. J. Brill, 2nd edn, 1970), p. 50.

11. M. de Jonge, *The Testaments of the Twelve Patriarchs: A Study of Their Text, Composition and Origin* (Assen: Van Gorcum, 2nd edn, 1975), p. 119.

12. See, e.g., the Soncino translation of the *Midrash Rabbah* (10 vols.; London: Soncino Press, 1939), edited by H. Freedman and Maurice Simon; also Louis Ginzberg, *The Legends of the Jews* (7 vols.; Philadelphia: Jewish Publication Society of America, 1909–38).

13. H. Freedman and Maurice Simon (eds.), *Midrash Rabbah, Genesis*. I. *Translated in English with Notes, Glossary and Indices* (London: Soncino Press, 1939), p. 353. The editors' note to this interpretation is helpful: 'The meaning is that the evil effects of idolatry are felt both before and after it is actually practised. Because Jeroboam was destined to set up a golden calf at Dan (I Kings XII, 19), Abraham was weakened now when he came to that place and so could pursue them no further. Similarly, even after it was destroyed Jeremiah speaks of terror raging in Dan.'

Three passages provide a negative appraisal of the tribe of Dan during Israel's wilderness years. First, the quality of the stone representing Dan in the breastplate of Aaron—there were twelve stones on Aaron's breastplate, corresponding to the twelve tribes of Israel (Exod. 28.15-21; 39.8-14)—is accounted for in this way:

> The twelve stones differed not only in color, but also in certain qualities peculiar to each, and both quality and color had especial reference to the tribe whose name it bore… Dan's stone was a species of topaz, in which was visible the inverted face of a man, for the Danites were sinful, turning good to evil, hence the inverted face in their stone.[14]

Second, the arrangement of the Israelite tribes's encampment in the wilderness (Num. 2) is explained in this way:

> The tribes of Dan, Asher, and Naphtali formed the last group, and for the following reason were united in this way. The tribe of Dan had already at the time of the exodus from Egypt been possessed of the sinful thought to fashion an idol. To counteract this 'dark thought' Asher was made its comrade, from whose soil came 'the oil for lighting'; and that Dan might participate in the blessing, Naphtali, 'full with the blessing of the Lord', became its second companion.[15]

Third, the tribe of Dan was one of the four standard-bearers in the wilderness (Num. 2.25-31; 10.25-27), and associated with the North:

> Dan, the tribe 'from which emanated dark sin', stood at the left side of the camp with his standard, corresponding to the angel Uriel, 'God is my light', for God illuminated the darkness of sin by the revelation of the Torah, in the study of which this angel instructed Moses, and devotion to which is penance for sin… From the North comes the darkness, and so from the tribe

---

14. Louis Ginzberg, *The Legends of the Jews*. III. *Bible Times and Characters from the Exodus to the Death of Moses* (Philadelphia: Jewish Publication Society of America, 1968 [1911]), pp. 169-71; cf. H. Freedman and Maurice Simon (eds.), *Midrash Rabbah, Numbers*. I. *Translated in English with Notes, Glossary and Indices* (London: Soncino Press, 1939), pp. 28-29. Ginzberg refers to his collection as Jewish, rather than Rabbinic legends, since 'the sources from which [he has] levied contributions are not limited to Rabbinic literature' (*The Legends of the Jews*. I. *Bible Times and Characters from the Creation to Jacob* [Philadelphia: Jewish Publication Society of America, 1909], p. xi). Among the sources he has used are included Talmudic and Midrashic literature, the Targums, medieval Bible commentators and homilists, the Kabbalah, and certain apocrypha and pseudepigrapha of the Christian Church (*The Legends of the Jews*, I, pp. xi-xiii). The reader is directed to the fifth and sixth volumes of Ginzberg's collection for detailed references to primary sources.

15. Ginzberg, *The Legends of the Jews*, III, p. 223.

of Dan will come the darkness of sin, for this tribe alone will declare itself willing to accept the idols of Jeroboam, hence its place to the North of the camp.[16]

Thus, many traditions of Dan at the close of the biblical period seem to evaluate the ancestor and the tribe of Dan of the Hebrew Bible in a wholly negative way.[17] My contention is that some of this is already going on in the biblical material. In particular, the political and theological interests reflected in the relatively late work of the Deuteronomistic Historian have cast a shadow over some other traditions concerning Dan in the Hebrew Bible which, in their origin, were more neutral or even positive.

The purpose of this study is a comprehensive investigation of the Danite traditions in the Hebrew Bible. This objective is uniquely complicated by the fact that Dan is used in reference to an eponymous ancestor, a tribe, a tribal territory, and a city on the northern frontier of Israel. In addition, there are several stories about individual Danites. Certain questions guide the study. In general: (1) What does the Hebrew Bible, in fact, tell us about Dan—the ancestor, the tribe, the city? (2) How have the (Judean) criticisms of Jeroboam's cult center at the city of Dan affected the judgment on the ancestor and/or the tribe? What can be said about the effect of the relationship between the city, the tribe (and its territory), and the ancestor as preserved in the Hebrew Bible? (3) How do the narratives about individual members of the tribe of Dan contribute to one's appraisal of the tribe generally? (4) Finally, What is there in the Hebrew Bible that led to such an entirely unflattering appraisal of Dan in the later Jewish and Christian traditions? To what degree is this latest, post-biblical Danite material shaped by the tribal traditions in the Hebrew Bible? That is, how do these late materials cohere with the biblical texts themselves?

5. *Statement of Thesis*

In this study I provide a thorough investigation of the Danite traditions in the Hebrew Bible. Given my interest in the possible interconnections, at

16. Ginzberg, *The Legends of the Jews*, III, pp. 231-33; Freedman and Simon (ed.), *Midrash Rabbah, Numbers*, I, pp. 38-39.

17. Josephus is an exception since, in his *Antiquities*, he essentially paraphrases the biblical material. Significant, also, is the fact that Josephus omits the disparaging story of Micah and his image in Judg. 17–18 (see Josephus, *Ant.* 5.276-317 [Samson], 318-37 [Ruth] [translation following *Josephus with an English Translation by H.St.J. Thackeray and Ralph Mareus, in Eight Volumes* [LCL; Cambridge, MA: Harvard University Press, 1934]).

some level, between the ancestral, tribal, and city stories (in what ways might certain traditions influence the interpretation of references to Dan in other parts of the Bible), none of the occurrences of Dan can be excluded if one anticipates reconstructing as complete a picture as possible of 'Dan in the Hebrew Bible'. While others have studied particular elements of the tradition (the history of the tribe of Dan, the material culture of Tell Dan, and literary analyses of individual Danite narratives), none takes into account the entire 'Dan' corpus.

In this study I focus on the biblical traditions of Dan, recognizing, on the one hand, their literary quality/character and, on the other hand, accepting that they reflect a 'real world' of persons, events, and cultural values and meanings. It is my thesis that by combining social-science models with the more traditional historical-critical methodologies in the exegesis of the biblical material, one is better able to understand the more original meaning of several of the traditions about Dan, meanings which have been obscured—in some cases—by the theological agenda of later editors. The conclusion put forward here is that the evidence from the Hebrew Bible does not completely support the negative portrayal of Dan in the later traditions; rather, the overall picture of Dan in the Hebrew Bible is ambivalent.

6. *Review of Recent Research and Methodology*

No one has conducted as thorough an examination of the Danite tradition in the Hebrew Bible as that offered in the present study.[18] Two investigations of Dan have, however, appeared since the mid-1980s, although neither approaches the material from the broad perspective of the present work. First, *Die Daniten: Studien zur Geschichte eines altisraelitischen Stammes*, by Hermann Michael Niemann, comes closest to one of the goals of this study, although his focus is on the *tribe* of Dan.[19] As the subtitle of

18. In this study, 'Danite tradition' is understood as the complete assemblage of the occurrences of 'Dan' in the Hebrew Bible. (This assemblage includes, in addition, 2 Sam. 20.18 where Dan, although absent from the MT, appears in the LXX as a geographical reference [city], and 1 Chron. 7.12, where mention of Dan has been omitted for textual reasons.)

19. Hermann Michael Niemann, *Die Daniten: Studien zur Geschichte eines altisraelitischen Stammes* (FRLANT, 135; Göttingen: Vandenhoeck & Ruprecht, 1985). See now, however, his 'Zorah, Eshtaol, Beth Shemesh and Dan's Migration to the South: A Region and its Traditions in the Late Bronze Age and Iron Ages', *JSOT* 86 (1999), pp. 25-48.

his work indicates, Niemann set for himself the task of reconstructing the *history* of this Israelite *tribe*. In fact, the book is arranged according to Niemann's chronology of the events narrated in the biblical tradition. Thus, he begins with the notice about the expulsion of the Danites by the Amorites from the coastal plain (Judg. 1.34-35; Josh. 19.47-48), which Niemann dates to a time before 1200 BCE. Next, he examines the mention of Dan in the Song of Deborah (Judg. 5.17), which, according to Niemann, presupposes the northward migration (Judg. 17–18) and settlement of the Danites. He dates this movement to the north to the first third of the twelfth century BCE.[20] Niemann concurs with those other scholars who propose that when the Danites journeyed northward, a remnant remained in the south, and that it was among these southern Danites that the Samson tradition circulated (Judg. 13–16; the hero Samson, a historical figure for Niemann, is dated to the period from about 1125 to 1075 BCE). The last biblical traditions that Niemann studies in any detail are the tribal sayings about Dan in Gen. 49.16-17 and Deut. 33.22, both of which he dates to the mid-twelfth century BCE, after the northward migration. The latter chapters of his book consider, in order: (1) the question of a westward wandering of the Danites into Cisjordan and the possible relationship of the Danites to other tribes; (2) the excavations at Tell el-Qāḍī; and (3) the hypotheses which identify the biblical Danites with various other Mediterranean groups (Denyen, Danuna, Danaoi) known from extra-biblical sources. Niemann concludes with a summary sketch of the history of the Danites.

While Niemann's is a commendable effort, the writing of a *history* of Israel (and of *early* Israel in particular) is today recognized by many scholars as an enterprise fraught with difficulty and uncertainty.[21] In addition, since his focus is the *tribe* of Dan and its history, other references to Dan in the Hebrew Bible are either entirely omitted (e.g. Gen. 14.14; Jer. 8.16; Amos 8.13-14) or treated only minimally (1 Kgs 12). Niemann's monograph is, then, by design, something less than an exhaustive study of 'Dan' in the Hebrew Bible. As has already been observed in the earlier-cited

20. Chapter 3 of his monograph, 'The Sanctuary of Micah and the Danites', is a detailed analysis of Judg. 17–18.

21. See, e.g., William H. Irwin, Review of *Die Daniten: Studien zur Geschichte eines altisraelitischen Stammes*, by Hermann Michael Niemann, *CBQ* 51 (1989), pp. 724-25; Rainer Albertz, review of *Die Daniten: Studien zur Geschichte eines altisraelitischen Stammes*, by Hermann Michael Niemann, *BZ* 31 (1987), pp. 299-301. In essence, Niemann is perhaps overly confident in reconstructing the history of the Danite tribe largely on the basis of the biblical evidence.

reference from Irenaeus, more than obvious references to the *tribe* of Dan
have helped to shape the overall Danite tradition. In particular, Jeroboam's
cultic activity at the city of Dan has exercised a significant influence on
certain biblical and post-biblical traditions. It is also significant that
Niemann does not make use of even the earlier 'social world' studies of
Mendenhall, Gottwald, and the like, a weakness already noted by H. Engel
in his review.[22] In no way does Niemann utilize the insights derived from a
social-scientific analysis of the biblical evidence (as the present study
does, where appropriate) in his reconstruction of Danite history.

Second, Avraham Biran, whose primary interest is in the *city* of Dan,
has provided the interested public with a readable, semi-popular book
which summarizes the excavations at Tell Dan, carried out since 1966
under his direction.[23] The first section of the book traces the archaeological
history of the site from the Neolithic Period to the Iron Age and the conquest and settlement of the city by the migrating tribe of Dan. The latter
part of the book examines particular phenomena associated with the site:
metallurgy, the 'sacred precinct', and the Israelite fortifications. The last
chapter describes the character of the city after the fall of the Northern
Kingdom in the eighth century through the Roman Period. A postscript
introduces the reader to the first of the fragments of an Aramaic inscription
discovered since 1993 at Tell Dan.

Since his primary goal is the reporting and interpretation of the material
remains uncovered at the site, Biran's treatment of the Danite tradition in
the Hebrew Bible is even more limited than that of Niemann. It is also the
case, one suspects, that the biblical material and Biran's parochial commitment to it lies just beneath the surface of his archaeological interest. That
is, it is apparent that the biblical story about Dan and the Danites has
greatly influenced Biran's interpretation of the archaeological record at
Tell Dan. The careful reader will notice that his remark about how 'the
insatiable intellectual curiosity and the search for knowledge are prime
movers in the advancement of science in general and archaeological research in particular' is followed immediately by the comment that 'for
those of us who were brought up on the Bible there is an urge to visualize,
to touch, to reconstruct the past and its material culture'.[24]

22. Helmut Engel (Review of *Die Daniten: Studien zur Geschichte eines altisraelitischen Stammes*, by Hermann Michael Niemann, *Bib* 67 [1986], pp. 292-95)
describes this shortcoming as 'painfully obvious' (*schmerzlich spürbar*).
23. Avraham Biran, *Biblical Dan* (Jerusalem: Israel Exploration Society, 1994).
24. Biran, *Biblical Dan*, p. 21.

Although a full evaluation of Biran's archaeological fieldwork and publication is beyond the scope of the present study, it is clear that some of Biran's conclusions correlating the results of archaeology with the biblical record call for closer examination and, perhaps, reconsideration. It appears as though Biran is at times overly zealous to associate specific material remains unearthed at Tell Dan with the traditions preserved in the Hebrew Bible. For example, Biran seems too ready to identify the inhabitants of Stratum VI (Iron I), with their distinctive settlement pattern and lifestyle (nomadic or semi-nomadic), cisterns, and collared-rim jars with the biblical Danites.[25] It is only in passing that Biran notes that the theory identifying the collared-rim storage jars with the Israelites, originating with his teacher W.F. Albright in the 1930s, is today a matter of much debate. What is more, whether the early Israelites were a nomadic or semi-nomadic group, or whether they were the first to make use of (plastered) cisterns, are likewise lively questions among archaeologists and biblical scholars at the present time.[26] While it may be true that there exists a dramatic caesura, together with a change in settlement pattern and material culture, between Strata VII and VI at Tell Dan (even accompanied by a destruction layer), archaeologists are less inclined to attribute a phenomenon such as this automatically to a new population group. It seems at least possible that, as a result of the conflagration, the (Canaanite) resident population of Laish temporarily adopted a less urban and more pastoral mode of existence.[27] Throughout his book Biran makes helpful reference to the nature of this population at Tell Dan on the basis of the material evidence. Thus, some of his remarks approach what is sometimes referred to as 'social history/social description'.[28]

25. Biran, *Biblical Dan*, pp. 128-32.

26. Israel Finkelstein and Nadav Na'aman (eds.), *From Nomadism to Monarchy: Archaeological and Historical Aspects of Early Israel* (Washington: Biblical Archaeology Society, 1994), p. 11; Lawrence E. Stager, 'The Archaeology of the Family in Ancient Israel', *BASOR* 260 (1985), pp. 1-35; David C. Hopkins, 'Life on the Land: The Subsistence Struggles of Early Israel', *BA* 50 (1987), pp. 178-91.

27. Biran himself notes (*Biblical Dan*, p. 135) that 'it did not take the tribe of Dan too long to shed its seminomadic character. Our next level of occupation, Stratum V, represents an urbanized community.' This might suggest instead either that Biran's 'Israelite' inhabitants of Stratum VI were not so closely tied to pastoral pursuits as he would lead us to believe, or that these were neither 'Israelites' nor (semi-)nomads in the first place.

28. See Dale B. Martin, 'Social-Scientific Criticism', in Steven L. McKenzie and Stephen R. Haynes (eds.), *To Each Its Own Meaning: An Introduction to Biblical Criticisms and Their Application* (Louisville, KY: Westminster/John Knox Press,

In addition to the larger works of Niemann and Biran, several shorter studies have appeared which analyze individual parts of the biblical Danite tradition from the perspective of the 'new literary criticism'. An especially profitable Danite tradition has been that of Samson in Judges 13–16.[29] Ordinarily in biblical studies literary criticism is defined as source criticism (e.g. JEDP in Pentateuchal research). In fact, the 'new literary criticism' is, as Krentz observes, a return to its 'classical sense', where it refers to 'the study and evaluation of literature as artistic production. It treats the rhetorical, poetic, and compositional devices used by an author to structure his thought and embellish it with suitable language'.[30] The method has been used profitably in both Hebrew Bible and New Testament research.

Two of the fundamental tenets of this new literary criticism are (1) the analysis of the text as it stands now, in its final form (apart from concern with the question of sources or of the possible redaction history of the narrative), and (2) the recognition of the importance of the 'literary world', the 'world in the story' created by the author, a world distinct from the 'real' world of actual persons and events.[31] In their book on the Gospel of Mark, Rhoads and Michie write:

1993), pp. 103-19 (103); see also Carol Meyers, *Discovering Eve: Ancient Israelite Women in Context* (New York: Oxford University Press, 1988), p. 48; John H. Elliott, *What is Social-Scientific Criticism?* (GBS; Minneapolis: Fortress Press, 1993), p. 20; and Carolyn Osiek, *What Are They Saying About the Social Setting of the New Testament?* (New York: Paulist Press, rev. and exp. edn, 1992), pp. 4, 108.

29. Joseph Blenkinsopp, 'Structure and Style in Judges 13–16', *JBL* 82 (1963), pp. 65-76; H. Steinthal, 'The Legend of Samson', in Ignaz Goldhizer (ed.), *Mythology Among the Hebrews and Its Historical Development* (New York: Cooper Square Publishers, 1967), pp. 392-446; James L. Crenshaw, *Samson: A Secret Betrayed, A Vow Ignored* (Atlanta: John Knox Press, 1978); J. Cheryl Exum, 'Promise and Fulfillment: Narrative Art in Judges 13', *JBL* 99 (1980), pp. 43-59; Stanislav Segert, 'Paronomasia in the Samson Narrative in Judges 13–16', *VT* 34 (1984), pp. 454-61; Mieke Bal, *Death and Dissymetry: The Politics of Coherence in the Book of Judges* (Chicago: University of Chicago Press, 1988); Lillian R. Klein, *The Triumph of Irony in the Book of Judges* (JSOTSup, 68; Sheffield: Almond Press, 1988), pp. 109-39.

30. Edgar Krentz, *The Historical-Critical Method* (GBS; Philadelphia: Fortress Press, 1975), pp. 49-50. David Rhoads and Donald Michie (*Mark as Story: An Introduction to the Narrative of a Gospel* [Philadelphia: Fortress Press, 1982], p. 2) speak of the 'formal features of narrative, such as the role of the narrator, point of view, style, plot, settings, and characters'.

31. Rhoads and Michie, *Mark as Story*, p. 3; see also Norman K. Gottwald, *The Hebrew Bible—A Socio-Literary Introduction* (Philadelphia: Fortress Press, 1985), p. 22; David M. Gunn, 'Narrative Criticism', in McKenzie and Haynes (eds.), *To Each Its Own Meaning*, pp. 171-95 (171).

Although the author of the Gospel of Mark certainly used some sources rooted in the historical events surrounding the life of Jesus, the final text is a literary creation with an autonomous integrity... One can read and interpret Mark's gospel as a story independent from the real people and events upon which it is based... Thus, Mark's narrative contains a closed and self-sufficient world with its own integrity, its own imaginative past and future, its own sets of values, and its own universe of meaning.[32]

Literary criticism shares some characteristics with the newer social-scientific criticism, although each methodology nevertheless maintains its distinctive qualities. While social-scientific criticism tends also to treat the final form of the text as *the* text to be interpreted, it does not postulate a clear distinction between the 'story world' and the world of the author/reader. That is, the social science critic does not see the world of the story as an entirely 'fictive world' utterly and intentionally independent from the 'real world' of actual persons and events. I concur with Gottwald who points out this drawback of the literary-critical method *for someone who is interested in the history of early Israel* thus:

The disadvantage of this [new literary criticism] is that it ignores the social and historical substrata or contexts out of which the literature arose, genre by genre, source by source, writing by writing, collection by collection, until it reached its end form. The literary world is real enough, as literary critics remind us, but its writers lived in an everyday world of their own and many of the topics and interests of biblical texts reflect the conditions and events of that everyday biblical world which it is folly to ignore if we want a well-rounded understanding of ancient Israel.[33]

32. Rhoads and Michie, *Mark as Story*, pp. 3-4. So also Gottwald (*Hebrew Bible*, pp. 22-23) writes about 'the Hebrew Bible as a literary production that creates its own fictive world of meaning and is to be understood first and foremost, if not exclusively, as a literary medium, that is, as words that conjure up their own imaginative reality... For [many biblical literary critics] literature is not, in the first place, a means to something else, such as historical or religious understandings of the writers and their everyday world. Literature is a world all its own, in and of itself, biblical literature included.' Later he observes: 'The literary critic of the Hebrew Bible seems often to be most clearly distinguished by disinterest either in the historical reconstruction of early Israel or in the coherence or validity of its religious claims, both of which appear immaterial to "literary truth"' (p. 30)

33. Gottwald, *Hebrew Bible*, p. 32. Similarly, Elliott (*What is Social-Scientific Criticism?*, p. 8) writes that 'social-scientific criticism...studies the text as both a reflection of and a response to the social and cultural settings in which the text was produced. Its aim is the determination of the meaning(s) explicit and implicit in the text, meanings made possible and shaped by the social and cultural systems inhabited by both authors and intended audience.'

Recent historical-critical research has noted both the value and limitations of the Bible as a historical source, recognizing that although the Bible contains what Miller calls 'authentic historical memory', it is, at the same time, 'heavily influenced by theological and nationalistic interests'.[34] It has been suggested that the rise of the new literary criticism is due, in part, to the perception among some biblical critics that the sub-disciplines of historical-critical investigation have contributed what they are able to contribute to the exegetical enterprise, and that new methodologies are required to answer the newer questions currently addressed to the biblical material.[35] It may also be the case that the rise in popularity of this new literary criticism in biblical study is simply due to the current interests of contemporary exegetes, interests which may grow out of the greater interdisciplinary study of the Bible, and which seem to be more interested in historiography and historical literature than in historical reconstruction. One must also consider the possibility that this new literary approach to the Bible is a conscious reaction against a perceived misuse of the biblical evidence in previous reconstructions of Israelite history.

Methodologically, I intend to be as broad or eclectic as necessary in the present study to accomplish my stated goal of interpreting Dan in the biblical traditions. In addition to the classical historical-critical methodologies (including archaeology), I am attentive to the literary and social concerns of the texts. I share with the newer literary critics an acknowledgment and appreciation of the literary character of the biblical material (some of it is very sophisticated), but I prefer not to dissociate it completely from a 'real world' of actual persons, events, cultural values, and meanings. At the same time, while recognizing the degree of probability that elements in the biblical traditions (as well as the traditions themselves) can be located within the early history of Israel, I understand it to be imprudent to pro-

---

34. J. Maxwell Miller, 'Reading the Bible Historically: The Historian's Approach', in McKenzie and Haynes (eds.), *To Each Its Own Meaning*, pp. 11-28 (16). On the one hand, one of the underlying interests of the present study is an attempt to move beyond a narrow, historical fixation that is reflected in many interpretations of this biblical material. On the other hand, I do not propose to reject outright the significance of history, even early history, presupposed in these texts, as some prefer to do today. While I recognize the historical character of the material, I am interested in pursuing the question of what, in addition to history, may be going on in these texts. If one is not limited to the genre of history, how else might one understand what is related in a particular story?

35. Gottwald, *Hebrew Bible*, p. 21.

pose absolute historical reconstructions on the basis of a literal reading of this biblical material alone. The Bible is literature, to be sure, but it is more than 'just a story'. The Bible preserves historical memories (or agendas) about historical events, and one must exercise care in moving from the poetic and historical literature of the Bible to making definitive historical claims.[36]

In the last 30 years, use of the social science method has been an emerging trend especially in New Testament research, although scholarly articles have appeared in which one or more interpretive models borrowed from the fields of sociology and cultural anthropology have been applied to texts from the Hebrew Bible.[37] In addition, even in the New Testament

36. See David Noel Freedman's balanced remarks concerning reconstructable history in his 'Early Israelite History in the Light of Early Israelite Poetry', in *idem* (ed.), *Pottery, Poetry, and Prophecy: Studies in Early Hebrew Poetry* (Winona Lake, IN: Eisenbrauns, 1980), pp. 131-66 (132).

37. I distinguish social-scientific criticism from the social history/description method with Martin ('Social-Scientific Criticism', p. 103) who writes: 'Some scholars are content to define themselves as social historians, seeing their own work as a continuation of traditional historical criticism of the Bible, except that they explore social aspects of biblical issues that have traditionally been analyzed from a theological point of view. Other scholars explicitly call their work "social-scientific," indicating that they self-consciously appropriate concepts and models from sociology and anthropology and attempt to explain ancient Israelite and early Christian developments by use of those models.' On the conscious use of models in the study of antiquity, see Chapter 1, 'Models: What are They and What Do They Do?', in T.F. Carney, *The Shape of the Past: Models and Antiquity* (Lawrence, KS: Coronado, 1975), pp. 1-43. Among the most important New Testament publications are included: Jerome H. Neyrey (ed.), *The Social World of Luke–Acts: Models for Interpretation* (Peabody, MA: Hendrickson, 1991); Bruce J. Malina and Richard L. Rohrbaugh, *Social-Science Commentary on the Synoptic Gospels* (Minneapolis: Fortress Press, 1992); Elliott, *What is Social-Scientific Criticism?*; Bruce J. Malina, *The New Testament World: Insights from Cultural Anthropology* (Louisville, KY: Westminster/John Knox Press, rev. edn, 1993); John J. Pilch and Bruce J. Malina (eds.), *Biblical Social Values and Their Meanings: A Handbook* (Peabody, MA: Hendrickson, 1993); Richard Rohrbaugh (ed.), *The Social Sciences and New Testament Interpretation* (Peabody, MA: Hendrickson, 1996); David J. Chalcraft (ed.), *Social-Scientific Old Testament Criticism: A Sheffield Reader* (The Biblical Seminar, 47; Sheffield: Sheffield Academic Press, 1997). Articles dealing with texts from the Hebrew Bible include: Lyn M. Bechtel, 'Shame as a Sanction of Social Control in Biblical Israel: Judicial, Political, and Social Shaming', *JSOT* 49 (1991), pp. 47-76; Ken Stone, 'Gender and Homosexuality in Judges 19: Subject—Honor, Object—Shame?', *JSOT* 67 (1995), pp. 87-107; Saul M. Olyan, 'Honor, Shame, and Covenant Relations in Ancient Israel and Its Environment', *JBL*

studies there are numerous passages from the Hebrew Bible to which reference is made.

The suitability of interpretive models from the social sciences for the exegesis of the Hebrew Bible is demonstrated not only by the publication of the previously cited articles, but also by the following presumption: namely, that the social world of the Hebrew Bible is continuous with that of the New Testament and of the modern Mediterranean 'diffusion sphere' (a phrase used by anthropologists to identify a particular geographical region 'sharing a set of common cultural institutions that have persisted over long periods of time').[38] Regarding the use of such models in biblical interpretation Elliott writes:

> The social and cultural models most appropriate for the analysis of the Bible and its environment, it is presumed, are those constructed on the basis of research and data pertaining to the geographical, social, and cultural region inhabited by the biblical communities, that is, the area of the Circum-Mediterranean and ancient Near East. Just as historical criticism insists on situating the biblical documents within their respective time frames, so social-scientific criticism insists on situating them within their appropriate geographical, social, and cultural contexts. Thus social-scientific critics read the biblical writings as products of the *preindustrial, advanced agrarian society of the Circum-Mediterranean region.*[39]

Of special significance is the last remark. This preindustrial, advanced agrarian social system appears to have emerged sometime between 4000–3000 BCE, and had persisted until the industrial revolution of the latter eighteenth and early nineteenth century of the common era.[40] Thus the

115 (1996), pp. 201-18; and Ronald A. Simkins, '"Return to Yahweh": Honor and Shame in Joel', *Semeia* 68 (1996), pp. 41-54. A particularly useful contribution of Olyan's article is his identification of vocabulary in the Hebrew Bible pertinent to the topic of honor/shame (p. 203 n. 6). See also Lawrence E. Stager, 'Archaeology, Ecology, and Social History: Background Themes in the Song of Deborah', in J.A. Emerton (ed.), *Congress Volume 1986, Jerusalem* (VTSup, 40; Leiden: E.J. Brill, 1988), pp. 221-34.

   38. Malina and Rohrbaugh, *Social-Science Commentary on the Synoptic Gospels*, p. 3. On this expression see also Richard L. Rohrbaugh, 'Introduction', in *idem* (ed.), *The Social Sciences and New Testament Interpretation*, pp. 1-15 (7).

   39. Elliott, *What is Social-Scientific Criticism?*, p. 49 (emphasis added).

   40. Malina and Rohrbaugh, *Social-Science Commentary on the Synoptic Gospels*, pp. 3-6; see also Richard Rohrbaugh, 'Agrarian Society', in Pilch and Malina (eds.), *Biblical Social Values and Their Meaning*, pp. 4-8. Social-scientific critics of the New Testament have made use of these models from social and anthropological studies of

world of ancient Israel can be understood as such a social system, and the application of these models is not only appropriate, but promises to be a worthwhile endeavor.

Elliott distinguishes social-scientific criticism and its models from the various historical-critical analyses of biblical texts, but sees the former not as replacing the latter, but as complementing them. Indeed, he understands a significant dimension of the social-scientific method to be exegetical in nature, directed to the interpretation of biblical texts:

> social-scientific criticism supplements the other methods of critical interpretation with the aim of elucidating the structure, content, strategy, and intended rhetorical effect of the text within its social context. The text is analyzed as a vehicle of communication whose genre, structure, content, themes, message, and aim are shaped by the cultural and social forces of the social system and the specific historical setting in which it is produced and to which it constitutes a specific response.[41]

I share with Elliott this view on the relationship of social-scientific criticism to the other historical-critical subdisciplines of the exegetical enterprise. To make this clear, in this study my approach will combine both historical-critical and social-scientific methodologies. That is, the results of the classical historical-critical method (involving textual, philological, source, literary, form, redaction, and historical criticism) will be paired, where appropriate, with readings of the texts utilizing various interpretive models derived from the social sciences. Given the nature of social-science research, which is designed to look chiefly at the 'big picture', not every part of the Dan/Danite tradition can be examined with these models. In several cases, there is simply insufficient data in the biblical material to accommodate the profitable application of an abstract model. Where such models can be applied, one must ask: Which social or cultural methodolo-

the modern Mediterranean world. According to Malina and Rohrbaugh, 'given the persistence over time, the modern Mediterranean is far closer to the world of the Bible than North America has been during any period of its history. The societies of the present-day circum-Mediterranean area offer the closest living analogue we possess to the value sets and social structures that characterized daily human interaction in the Bible' (*Social-Science Commentary on the Synoptic Gospels*, p. 4; see also Malina, *New Testament World*, p. 25). See Gerhard Lenski, *Human Societies: A Macrolevel Introduction to Sociology* (New York: McGraw–Hill, 1970), pp. 237-89.

41. Elliott, *What is Social-Scientific Criticism?*, p. 33, also pp. 7-8, 15. See also Gottwald's remarks about 'sociological exegesis' in his *Hebrew Bible*, pp. 28-29; Jerome H. Neyrey, 'Preface', in *idem* (ed.), *The Social World of Luke–Acts*, pp. ix-xviii (xi).

gies contribute to a fuller understanding of the story? How does the use of
social-science models broaden and/or deepen our understanding of the
biblical material? What new light can this method shed on these old texts,
composed and handed down in a social world fundamentally different
from our own? What new meaning can be brought to light?

The following social-science models or cultural interests appear to be
well-suited to the task of interpreting the Danite traditions in the Hebrew
Bible.

Honor and shame are recognized as fundamental values in the ancient
Mediterranean world.[42] Honor, which can be either ascribed (inherited) or
acquired (gained or lost), is a claim to worth or status, *together with* the
social acknowledgment of that stature or standing. Moxness provides this
most succinct definition: 'Honor is fundamentally the *public* recognition of
one's social standing'.[43] Both the claim and the recognition are important,
since a claim to worth that is not publicly acknowledged is shame. Honor
which is acquired may be gained or lost in the ongoing social dynamic
known as 'challenge/riposte'. In this public exchange, the winner defends
his honor and may even enhance his standing, while the loser experiences
shame and injury to his public standing. I examine carefully two stories
about Samson in Judges 14–16 in order to determine the degree to which
this literary complex might be interpreted in terms of challenge/riposte.
Other texts which show a special interest in the categories of honor/shame
include Gen. 30.1-6, Lev. 24.10-23, Judges 1 and 17–18.

Halvor Moxness defines *patronage* thus:

> Patron–client relations are social relationships between individuals based on
> a strong element of inequality and difference in power. The basic structure
> of the relationship is an exchange of different and very unequal resources.
> A patron has social, economic, and political resources that are needed by a
> client. In return, a client can give expressions of loyalty and honor that are
> useful for the patron.[44]

42. Malina (*New Testament World*, p. 28) refers to them as 'pivotal values'; Joseph
Plevnick ('Honor/Shame', in Pilch and Malina [eds.], *Biblical Social Values and Their
Meaning*, pp. 95-104 [95]) calls them the 'core values in the Mediterranean world in
general and in the Bible as well'. Thus, each of the texts to be investigated could be
addressed in light of this broad-reaching model.

43. Halvor Moxness, 'Honor and Shame', in Rohrbaugh (ed.), *The Social Sciences
and New Testament Interpretation*, pp. 19-40 (20).

44. Halvor Moxness, 'Patron-Client Relations and the New Community in Luke–
Acts', in Neyrey (ed.), *The Social World of Luke–Acts*, pp. 241-68 (242).

Previous studies have interpreted גר/גור as 'to serve as client/one who serves as client'.[45] The appearance of this root in both Judg. 5.17 (concerning the tribe of Dan) and 17.7 (the wandering Levite) invites the use of this patron–client model in the present exegetical task. The father–son language used to characterize the relationship between Micah and the Levite appears to correspond to the 'family feeling' which marked the patron–client relationship (patron = father, client = child[ren]).[46] The notion that this relationship was ordinarily an enduring one (for life) is significant in light of the disloyalty and dishonor shown Micah by the Levite (Judg. 17–18).[47]

Kinship encompasses (social) relationships based on either birth or marriage. Under the broad heading of kinship, this study will investigate such areas of interest as family, marriage, barrenness, and genealogy as appropriate to the biblical material at hand. The following Danite texts are fruitful ground for study in light of these cultural interests: Genesis 29–30 (birth stories of the sons of Jacob); Joshua 13–19 and 21 (allotment of land to the tribes; levitical cities); Judges 13 (birth of Samson); the genealogical/tribal lists (scattered throughout Genesis, Exodus, Numbers, and 1 Chronicles); and those texts containing accounts of intermarriage (Lev. 24; Judg. 14–16; 2 Chron. 2).

Coalitions and *factions* are typically set in contrast to 'corporate groups'. Malina and Rohrbaugh define a coalition as a 'type of impermanent group gathered for specific purposes over a limited period of time'. A faction is understood by them as a

> type of coalition formed around a central person who recruits followers and maintains the loyalty of a core group. Factions share the common goal of the person recruiting the faction. Membership is based on a relationship with that central personage... More loosely connected peripheral members often have indistinct, fluid, and incidental relationships with the faction. Peripheral members sometimes divide their loyalty with other factions and their leaders and thus can threaten a faction's effectiveness. Rivalry with other groups is basic; hence hostile competition for honor, truth (an ideological justification), and resources is always present.[48]

45. Stager, 'Archaeology, Ecology, and Social History'.
46. Bruce J. Malina, 'Patronage', in Pilch and Malina (eds.), *Biblical Social Values and Their Meaning*, pp. 133-37 (133-34).
47. John H. Elliott, 'Patronage and Clientage', in Rohrbaugh (ed.), *The Social Sciences and New Testament Interpretation*, pp. 144-56 (149).
48. Malina and Rohrbaugh, *Social-Science Commentary on the Synoptic Gospels*, p. 86.

The record of the troops that joined with David in Hebron (1 Chron. 12) includes mention of a Danite contingent. Of greater significance for the study of Dan is the possibility that, at some level of abstraction, the account of Jeroboam's rebellion and the establishment of a separate, Northern Kingdom (Israel, as distinct from the kingdom of Judah in the south) may also be interpreted in terms of factional activity.

Finally, in this study I will be attentive to the agrarian world setting, and the importance of *land*. Similar to honor and shame, this reality of the social system is a broad category encompassing numerous aspects of life. Oakman writes that 'the chief productive factor in agrarian economies is land. Control of land is one of the central political questions of agrarian societies.'[49] As with honor/shame, then, most Danite texts could be interpreted in light of this model. However, two texts in particular stand out: Josh. 19.40-48 (allotment of Danite territory) and Judges 1 (occupation of the land). Significant is the fact that Judges 1 has been interpreted as the first steps in the Danites's loss of their land, which necessitated their migration to the north.[50]

Other social interests include: folklore analysis (Judg. 13–16), anthropological study of tribal society (Josh. 13–19), the embeddedness of religion in both kinship (domestic) and political systems in the ancient world, and labeling theory (Lev. 24).

As a part of the present analysis, I will remark on the evaluation of 'Dan' in each text (positive, negative, neutral/ambivalent), in order to determine any possible coherence with the negative portrayal of Dan in the latest biblical and post-biblical traditions.

7. Arrangement of Chapters

A goal of this study is to provide a comprehensive investigation of the Danite traditions in the Hebrew Bible. Without question, certain Danite texts are more significant than others for the task at hand; thus, while every Danite text will be cited, not every text will receive the same detailed analysis. The present study is organized around the biblical texts

49. Douglas E. Oakman, 'The Countryside in Luke–Acts', in Neyrey (ed.), *The Social World of Luke–Acts*, pp. 151-79 (154).

50. On the critical importance of the control and maintenance of one's land, see Mark McVann, 'Family-Centeredness', in Pilch and Malina (eds.), *Biblical Social Values and Their Meaning*, pp. 70-73 (72).

to be investigated, so that the chief object of interest, namely, the Danite traditions, remains in focus, and the interpretive methods and models are clearly seen as exegetical tools.

It is not assumed that the Danite traditions in this study are arranged chronologically, since a growing number of critical biblical scholars recognizes that we are no longer able to assign absolute (nor, in some opinions, even relative) dates to the biblical traditions with any degree of confidence. That is, while several years ago, according to a scholarly consensus dating, it may have seemed quite appropriate to begin with the poetry of Judges 5 (the Song of Deborah, frequently dated to the twelfth century BCE), move on to the pre-deuteronomistic pentateuchal traditions (J and E of the tenth–ninth centuries BCE), the Deuteronomistic History (seventh–sixth centuries BCE), the Priestly Tradition of the sixth century BCE, and finally to the books of Chronicles (fourth–third centuries BCE), this is no longer an unchallenged chronological scheme. A further drawback to such a supposed chronological arrangement is that it is misleading, suggesting a single Danite tradition whose development over time may be chronicled. Instead, there seem to be multiple Danite traditions, some negative while others quite positive in character, and, while some of these may be related, others stand independently. In the end, however, when the entire tradition is investigated, one is left with an ambivalent picture of the Danites in the Hebrew Bible.

The present study follows the canonical order of the Hebrew Bible.[51] Chapter 2 examines Pentateuchal texts about Dan, Chapters 3 and 4 provide analyses of Danite passages in the Former and Latter Prophets (respectively), and Chapter 5 discusses the occurrences of Dan in the Writings (limited to 1–2 Chronicles). Chapter 6 summarizes the results of the present study and articulates my conclusions about interpreting Dan in the Hebrew Bible.

---

51. This arrangement does not correlate, however, with a 'canonical' reading of the texts (cf. Brevard S. Childs, *Introduction to the Old Testament as Scripture* [Philadelphia: Fortress Press, 1979]). That is, I do not presume that the interpreter of texts appearing later in the Hebrew canon was familiar with the content of earlier texts.

Chapter 2

INTERPRETING DAN IN THE PENTATEUCH

Dan occurs in each book of the Pentateuch and in a variety of literary genres: poetry, narrative, and Priestly lists. Dan occurs as a reference to the city in the north (Gen. 14.14; Deut. 34.1); as the son of Jacob and the eponymous ancestor of the Danites (Gen. 29–30; 35, 49; Exod. 1); and as (ostensibly) a reference to the tribe of Dan (Deut. 33, although my conclusion is that the character of the later city of Dan has influenced the saying about the tribe in this passage). In addition, there are stories about individual members of the tribe of Dan: the craftsman, Oholiab, who worked on the tabernacle in the wilderness (Exod. 31–40); and an anonymous 'blasphemer' in Leviticus 24. Dan occurs in the Pentateuch most frequently in the book of Numbers (ten times), where it refers to the tribe. However, these occurrences are in late Priestly lists which are a limited source of information peculiar to the Danites.

1. *The Book of Genesis*

Dan occurs in four passages in the book of Genesis: as the name of the northern city in the enigmatic story about Abram and the eastern kings (ch. 14); as the eponymous ancestor of the Danites in the story of the births of the children of Jacob (chs. 29–30); as one of the sons of Jacob in the priestly lists (35.22b-26 and 46.8-27); and in the Blessing of Jacob (ch. 49).

a. *Genesis 14*
The first mention of Dan in the biblical tradition is a reference to the city in the north (formerly Laish, cf. Judg. 18), in the heroic story of Abram's victory over four eastern kings. According to the narrative in Genesis 14, the rulers of four eastern kingdoms advanced westward against the rulers of five Canaanite city-states who had rebelled against their Mesopotamian

suzerains (vv. 1-9). In the course of the battle the kings of the city-states fled, and the eastern armies plundered the unprotected cities of Sodom and Gomorrah. They also took Lot, Abram's kinsman, who had settled in Sodom (cf. Gen. 13.12), together with his property, and left. The narrative continues:

> [13] Now a fugitive came and announced [the news] to Abram the Hebrew, who was dwelling among the terebinths of Mamre the Amorite, his kinsman Eshkol, and his kinsman Aner (now these were confederates of Abram). [14] When Abram heard that his kinsman was taken captive, he assembled his armed retainers, born of his household—318—and he went in pursuit as far as Dan. [15] And he divided his force against them at night, he and his servants, and he attacked them. And he pursued them as far as Hobah, which is north of Damascus. [16] And he brought back all the property; and also Lot, his kinsman, and his property, he brought back, and also the women and the [rest of the] people.[1]

[Notes on the MT:

Verse 13: For 'Aner', the name of one of Mamre's kinsmen, the Samaritan Pentateuch reads עַנְרֻם, 1QGenesis Apocryphon reads *'rnm*, and the LXX reads Αυναν.

Verse 14: For 'And he assembled' (= 'mustered', from hiphil רִיק = 'to empty out, make empty'), Eissfeldt (the editor of the book of Genesis in *BHS*) suggests reading with the Samaritan Pentateuch וַיְּדֶק, apparently from דּוק (cf. BDB, p. 189); so perhaps the LXX, which reads 'and he numbered, counted (out)' (ἠρίθμησεν).]

The phrase 'as far as Dan' in Gen. 14.14 contains the first occurrence of Dan in the Hebrew Bible. There is no scholarly agreement on either the date of the composition of this narrative, or of its constituent parts, although many critical scholars have determined that this story is, in its final form, quite possibly among the latest compositions in the Old Testament.[2] There is a consensus among scholars who subscribe to some notion of Pentateuchal sources that Genesis 14 does not fit into any of the usual sources: J, E, or P.[3] Borrowing an image from archaeology, Skinner writes

1.   Unless otherwise noted, all translations in the present study are my own.

2.   This is not the place for an in-depth analysis of this enigmatic passage; the secondary literature is extensive. See, e.g., the lengthy bibliographies in Gordon J. Wenham, *Genesis 1–15* (WBC, 1; Waco, TX: Word Books, 1987), pp. 301-302; Claus Westermann, *Genesis 12–36: A Commentary* (Minneapolis: Augsburg, 1985 [German original 1981]), pp. 182-85.

3.   John Skinner, *A Critical and Exegetical Commentary on Genesis* (ICC; New York: Charles Scribner's Sons, 1910), p. 256; Samuel Rolles Driver, *An Introduction to the Literature of the Old Testament* (New York: Charles Scribner's Sons, rev. edn, 1931 [1913]), p. 15; Ephraim Avigdor Speiser, *Genesis: Introduction, Translation, and*

of Genesis 14 metaphorically as 'an isolated boulder in the stratification of the Pent., a fact which certainly invites examination of its origin, but is not in itself an evidence of high antiquity'.[4]

A related, and prior issue concerns the question of the chapter's literary unity. Genesis 14 is ordinarily divided into two distinct parts: vv. 1-11 and vv. 12-24, with the Melchizedek episode in vv. 18-20 recognized as a separate piece. For example, Westermann traces the first part (vv. 1-11, the report of the battle between the eastern kings and the rulers of the Canaanite city-states) to a type of royal inscription used by Assyrian and Babylonian kings, and he situates vv. 12-24, which he characterizes as a 'savior narrative' (although without the name Abram), in the period of the judges. The conversation between Abram and Melchizedek, according to Westermann, reflects the interests of the time of David. In Westermann's estimation, the final form of the chapter was not reached until the 'late postexilic period' and is to be compared 'with other late Jewish writings'.[5] Similar (though by no means identical) literary conclusions are reached by Gunkel, Van Seters and, most recently, Soggin.[6] On the basis of the literary analysis of

Notes (AB, 1; Garden City, NY: Doubleday, 1964), p. 105; Otto Eissfeldt, *The Old Testament: An Introduction* (trans. Peter R. Ackroyd; Oxford: Basil Blackwell, 1965), p. 211; Georg Fohrer, *Introduction to the Old Testament* (trans. David Green; Nashville: Abingdon Press, 1968), p. 187; Gerhard von Rad, *Genesis: A Commentary* (OTL; Philadelphia: Westminster Press, rev. edn, 1972), p. 170; Martin Noth, *A History of Pentateuchal Traditions* (trans. with an Introduction by Bernhard W. Anderson; Scholars Press Reprints and Translations Series, 5; Atlanta: Scholars Press, 1981 [1972]), p. 154; Westermann, *Genesis 12–36*, p. 188; Richard Elliott Friedman, *Who Wrote the Bible?* (New York: Harper & Row, 1987), p. 247; Wenham, *Genesis 1–15*, pp. 304-307.

4. Skinner, *Genesis*, p. 256.

5. Westermann, *Genesis 12–36*, pp. 189-93. Cf. the books of Daniel, Esther, and Judith.

6. Hermann Gunkel, *Genesis* (trans. Mark E. Biddle; Mercer Library of Biblical Studies; Macon: Mercer University Press, 1997), pp. 283-85; John Van Seters, *Abraham in History and Tradition* (New Haven: Yale University Press, 1975), pp. 296-308; J.A. Soggin, 'Abraham and the Eastern Kings: On Genesis 14', in Ziony Zevit, Seymour Gitin and Michael Sokoloff (eds.), *Solving Riddles and Untying Knots: Biblical, Epigraphic, and Semitic Studies in Honor of Jonas C. Greenfield* (Winona Lake, IN: Eisenbrauns, 1995), pp. 283-91. Significantly, Van Seters argues for the literary unity of the chapter, although he concedes that certain parts of it are modeled after other, more ancient literary forms (see esp. pp. 300-302). Cf., however, Wenham (*Genesis 1–15*, pp. 306-307), who defends the literary unity of the narrative, and further maintains the antiquity of the entire chapter. He concludes (against those who prefer a postexilic date for the final form of the text) that Gen. 14 'consists largely of pre-J material'.

the text, and since there is no extra-biblical evidence corroborating the events narrated in Genesis 14, the historical veracity of its contents is almost universally doubted.

I concur with those scholars who understand the final form of Genesis 14 to be a late, postexilic composition whose purpose is to glorify Abram on the scene of world history. At a time when Judah was an inferior and powerless province in Syria-Palestine, this portrayal of Abram as a hero figure would have been intended to inspire the Jewish community re-establishing itself in its homeland. Thus, while in the biblical tradition Abram is ordinarily situated in the Middle Bronze Age (early second millennium BCE), the reference to Dan in this chapter in fact occurs in a composition that dates from the Persian period. Several interpreters note the anachronistic use of Dan in a narrative about events in the days of the patriarch Abram.[7] Therefore, while the mention of Dan in Genesis 14 is anachronistic with respect to content (since, according to biblical tradition [Judg. 18], the city in the north was known by the name Laish until the early Iron Age), it is not anachronistic with respect to the composition of this chapter. That is, the final form of the text comes from a time when the city was known by the name Dan, not Laish. The significance of this reference to Dan for the present study is that it represents the ideal boundary of the Israelite territory, remembered from the 'Golden Age' of David and Solomon, and later (perhaps) during the reign of Josiah (2 Chron. 34.6-7). In this postexilic story of the heroic Abram, it is intimated that Israel's historic (and now ideal), northern boundary was in the vicinity of the city of Dan in Upper Galilee. Thus, this mention of Dan may be compared with the mention of Dan in the expression 'from Dan as far as Beersheba' in the Deuteronomistic History (DH), which was used to describe the traditional northern and southern limits of the promised land of Israel.

b. *Genesis 29–30*
Dan occurs next in the book of Genesis in the birth stories of Jacob's children born at Haran to his wives and their maidservants. Here Dan appears as the eponymous ancestor of the Danites. The proper interpretation of the individual births depends on the broader context of the Jacob story, especially the remark in Gen. 29.30 that Jacob loved Rachel, the

---

7. Gunkel, *Genesis*, p. 278; Skinner, *Genesis*, p. 267; Westermann, *Genesis 12–36*, p. 201; Nahum M. Sarna, *The JPS Torah Commentary: Genesis, The Traditional Hebrew Text with the New JPS Translation* (Philadelphia: Jewish Publication Society of America, 5749/1989), p. 108.

younger sister, more than Leah, the older sister and his first wife. Robert Wilson rightly observes that

> it is important to notice that this interpretation is impossible unless the entire context of the genealogy is taken into account. The genealogy itself only groups the various sons of Jacob, but to correctly interpret the significance of these groupings, one must be familiar with the Yahwist's story of Jacob and his wives (Gen. 29.1-30), for only here does one learn that Rachel is the favored wife. This piece of information is essential for the proper interpretation of the genealogy, and as a result the genealogy is in a sense dependent on its context for its correct interpretation.[8]

It is the passionate rivalry between the sisters that drives the narrative. Rachel is the beloved wife, but is barren, while Yahweh observes that Leah is unloved by her husband and opens her womb. The order of births alternates between Leah and Rachel. First, Leah bears Reuben (Jacob's firstborn, evidently an old tradition; cf. Gen. 49), Simeon, Levi, and Judah.[9] In desperation Rachel demands that Jacob 'give [her] children'. However, since she is infertile, she must acquire children through her maidservant, Bilhah, whom she gives to Jacob 'as a wife'. Bilhah bears Dan and Naphtali. Leah, having stopped bearing children, likewise gives her maidservant, Zilpah, to Jacob 'as a wife'. Zilpah bears Gad and Asher. Next, Leah bears Issachar, Zebulun, and a daughter, Dinah.[10] Finally, the narrator tells the reader that 'God remembered Rachel' (cf. 8.1) and opened Rachel's womb (cf. 29.31, where it was Yahweh who opened Leah's womb). She becomes pregnant and bears a son, whom she names Joseph.[11] Thus the order of births is: Leah, Rachel's maidservant, Leah's maidservant, Leah, and Rachel (or, schematically, Leah–Rachel–Leah–Rachel). There can be no question that the primary interest of the narrator is in Rachel, the younger of the sisters and Jacob's favorite wife, who is,

---

8.   Robert R. Wilson, *Genealogy and History in the Biblical World* (Yale Near Eastern Researches, 7; New Haven: Yale University Press, 1977), pp. 185-86.

9.   The vast majority of source and form critics attribute this passage to J, chiefly due to the divine name, Yahweh, in Gen. 29.31, 32, 33, 35. See Skinner, *Genesis*, p. 385; Gunkel, *Genesis*, p. 321; Noth, *A History of Pentateuchal Traditions*, pp. 25, 29; Friedman, *Who Wrote the Bible?*, p. 248; cf. Westermann, *Genesis 12–36*, p. 472; Wenham, *Genesis 16–50*, p. 242.

10.   It is likely that the mention of Dinah here is a later interpolation (note that no etymology is given for her name) based on the narrative in Gen. 34.

11.   It is worth noting that the order of the sons of Jacob in Gen. 29–30 is unique in the Hebrew Bible; cf. Gen. 35; 46; 49; Exod. 1; Deut. 33; Josh. 13–19; Judg. 5.

however, childless as the story begins. Some of the narrative tension is lightened when Rachel's maidservant bears a son 'on [Rachel's] knees' (30.3), but is only relieved when Rachel herself gives birth to Joseph that the narrative climax is attained.

The birth of Dan is narrated in Gen. 30.1-6, a passage usually divided between the Pentateuchal sources J and E, although the concession is often made that the basis of this passage is E.[12]

(1) *Genesis 30.1-6*

[1] When Rachel saw that she did not bear children to Jacob, Rachel became jealous of her sister. So she said to Jacob, 'Give me sons; if not, I shall die!' [2] But Jacob's anger was kindled at Rachel, and he said, 'Am I in the place of God, who has withheld from you the fruit of the womb?' [3] Then she said, 'Here is my maidservant, Bilhah. Go into her, and she will give birth upon my knees, so that I shall be built up—even I—from her'. [4] So she gave to him Bilhah her maid as a wife, and Jacob went into her. [5] And Bilhah became pregnant, and she bore to Jacob a son. [6] Then Rachel said, 'God has vindicated me, and also he has heard my voice and has given me a son'. Therefore she called his name Dan.

If it is accepted that the basic narrative of 30.1-6 is from the northern Pentateuchal document, E, then the unique status of Dan in this text is more easily understood: the city of Dan, associated in Judg. 18.29 with the eponymous ancestor of the Danites, was a leading city of the Northern Kingdom and the site of one of Israel's royal sanctuaries (1 Kgs 12.25-33). Outside of the book of Genesis, Dan is nowhere else associated with Bilhah in the biblical tradition (cf. the Priestly lists of the sons of Jacob in Gen. 35 and 46; however, it is likely that these passages are dependent on the narrative in Gen. 29–30). While many of the tribal lists in the Hebrew Bible tend to group the maidservant tribes together, significantly, Dan is never in the biblical tradition singled out and disparaged for being the son of a maidservant rather than of a wife of Jacob.[13] But why is Dan presented

---

12. The sudden absence of the divine name, Yahweh, which was so prevalent in the preceding verses, is readily apparent, as is the occurrence of 'God' (אלהים) in 30.2, 6. See Friedman, *Who Wrote the Bible?*, p. 248; Gunkel, *Genesis*, p. 321; Skinner, *Genesis*, p. 385; Noth, *A History of Pentateuchal Traditions*, pp. 29, 35; cf. Wenham, *Genesis 16–50*, pp. 241-42; Westermann, *Genesis 12–36*, p. 472.

13. Note, however, the arrangement of the tribes in Ezekiel's vision of restored Israel, where the tribes descended from Jacob's wives take precedence over the tribes descended from the handmaids, Bilhah and Zilpah. In this case, Dan is recognized as descended from Bilhah. A recent study of the tribal lists and genealogies that probes

as the firstborn of Rachel's maidservant, born 'on [Rachel's] knees?' It is possible that this is no more than the way the birth story was preserved in the tradition available to the narrator of Genesis 29–30.[14] It may, however, be that while Dan was traditionally associated with Bilhah, Rachel's maid-servant, the later status of the city of Dan in the north may have influenced the position of Dan in the birth order of the sons of Jacob, namely, as the firstborn of Bilhah, as well as the remark that Dan was 'born on [Rachel's] knees'.

A number of elements in this passage are important for understanding the mention of Dan in this biblical tradition. At the point of the Danite pas-sage (Gen. 30.1-6), Leah has already given birth to four sons, while Rachel remains childless. According to 30.1, it is a matter of life and death: 'Give me sons', Rachel pleads, 'if not, I shall die'. Rachel's demand of Jacob is more than hyperbole. In the ancient Mediterranean world, a childless woman was in a most precarious and vulnerable position. At marriage a woman was disembedded from her father's household and embedded in the household of her husband. However, as Malina and Rohrbaugh note, 'a wife remained for the most part on the periphery of her new husband's family'.[15] Until she gave birth to a son, the wife would be regarded by her husband's family as an outsider, a stranger—an identification that kept her at some distance from other members of the household. Thus, the birth of a son was critical for Rachel. Even though the matter of inheritance was also important for the family in the ancient world, an heir for Jacob is not the central issue in this passage since Leah has already given Jacob heirs (29.32-35). Rather, Rachel's son would be his mother's ally, and the advocate of her interests even against his father.[16]

However, since she is barren, Rachel (like Sarah before her [Gen. 16]), gives her maidservant to her husband *as a wife* in order that she might 'be built up...from her'.[17] According to 30.3, Rachel proposes that her

the relationship between the birth stories of the eponymous ancestors and the tribal territory allotment and settlement traditions in the Hebrew Bible is Zecharia Kallai's 'The Twelve-Tribe Systems of Israel', *VT* 47 (1997), pp. 53-90.

14. In most tribal/ancestral lists, Dan precedes Naphtali (cf. Josh. 19).

15. Malina and Rohrbaugh, *Social-Science Commentary on the Synoptic Gospels*, p. 241.

16. Malina and Rohrbaugh, *Social-Science Commentary on the Synoptic Gospels*, p. 242.

17. The phrase has also been translated as 'that through her I too may have chil-dren' (see the NJPS translation in Sarna, *Genesis*, p. 208). For the suggestion that this custom was for the benefit of the wife, not the husband, see John Van Seters, 'The

maidservant, Bilhah, 'bear on [her] knees'. There is no clear understanding of what is intended by this expression. It has been suggested that an adoption ceremony is meant; others refer to some ritual of legitimation, whereby the child is acknowledged as one's own.[18] Skinner suggests that the origin of this 'primitive ceremony of adoption' is to be traced

> to a widespread custom, according to which, in lawful marriage, the child is actually brought forth on the father's knees (cf. Jb. 3[12]; *Il.* ix. 455f.; *Od.* xix. 401ff); then it became a symbol of the legitimation of a natural child, and finally a form of adoption generally.[19]

However, given the clearly delineated and separated spheres of men and women in the ancient Mediterranean world, it is more probable that birth was an event that took place within the female domain, and was attended by women rather than by men. Thus, it is more likely that a custom originally practiced among women was later transferred to the sphere of men.

Whether or not adoption was practiced in ancient Israel depends in part on how 'adoption' is understood. Knobloch observes that some scholars, arguing that adoption occurs only 'where a person under paternal authority (patria potestas) is transferred to the authority of a third (free) individual and appointed heir', conclude that adoption did not exist in pre-exilic Israel.[20] Others have come to the conclusion that although biblical law is silent about adoption, certain stories in the Hebrew Bible (particularly from the patriarchal age), taken together with ancient Near Eastern adoption

Problem of Childlessness in Near Eastern Law and the Patriarchs of Israel', *JBL* 87 (1968), pp. 401-408 (403). Interestingly, the narrator does not use the technical term for concubine (פילגש) in reference to Bilhah. Perhaps the intention was to minimize the distinction between maidservants and wives in the matter of childbirth. Nevertheless, it is likely that one is still to distinguish between primary and secondary wives.

18. Commentators who prefer the language of adoption include Gunkel, *Genesis*, p. 325; Skinner, *Genesis*, p. 386; Wenham, *Genesis 16–50*, p. 244. Westermann (*Genesis 12–36*, p. 474) and Sarna (*Genesis*, pp. 207-208) leave the adoption/legitimation question open.

19. Skinner, *Genesis*, pp. 386-87. However, it must be noted that Skinner's references to Job and Homer do not necessarily place the father at the child's birth. The Job text, for example, more likely intends a woman than a man or father (knees//breasts). In the *Iliad* reference cited by Skinner, the image is of a father playfully bouncing a child up and down on his knees—not something that happens at the moment of birth. Finally, in the *Odyssey* passage, not only is the male the child's grandfather (cf. Gen. 48.12-20), but unless Autolycos is a most fortunate man, some time apparently passes between Odysseus' birth and his being placed upon Autolycos' knees.

20. Frederick W. Knobloch, 'Adoption', in *ABD*, I, pp. 76-79 (79).

documents, point to the practice of adoption in early Israel.[21] Especially
noteworthy are two passages which may suggest a formula of adoption. In
Exod. 2.10 the grown Moses is brought to Pharaoh's daughter, who makes
him her son (ויהי־לה לבן). According to Esth. 2.7, Mordecai adopted
Esther (his niece) as his own daughter (לקחה מרדכי לו לבת). Whether
or not Rachel formally adopted Bilhah's child cannot be unequivocally
demonstrated in Gen. 30.1-6. Genesis 30.3 reads as a part of a simple
narrative, unencumbered by the legal trappings of notions about adoption.[22] It seems better to interpret this passage as Rachel merely regarding
the child to be born of Bilhah as her own. The reference to 'bearing on
[Rachel's] knees' may, in this case, have been included as a way to under-
score Rachel's passionate longing to have a child (son), and the important
relationship between Rachel and this son, Dan.[23]

It is Rachel who names the child born to Bilhah, not Bilhah (cf. 16.15,
where the father [Abram] names the maidservant's child [Ishmael]). The
act of naming is recognized as the expression of authority over another
(whether this implies that Rachel has authority over the child because she
has authority over its mother [30.4] is not stated). Since in the birth stories
in Genesis 29–30 the mothers name the children, the impression given is
that Rachel regards herself as the mother of the child. It is Rachel who
exclaims, 'God has vindicated me...' (דנני אלהים); on account of her
vindication, she names the child Dan. As is the case elsewhere in the story
of the birth of Jacob's children, the popular etymology and paronomasia
surrounding this name in no way reflects the history of the later tribe
presumably descended from this Dan.[24] The name, Dan, is associated here

21. Knobloch, 'Adoption', p. 79; Jeffrey H. Tigay, 'Adoption', *EncJud*, II, pp.
298-301. For the ancient Near Eastern documents, see John Van Seters, *Abraham in
History and Tradition*, pp. 68-71; *idem*, 'The Problem of Childlessness', pp. 401-408;
Thomas L. Thompson, *The Historicity of the Patriarchal Narratives: The Quest for the
Historical Abraham* (BZAW, 133; New York: W. de Gruyter, 1974), pp. 252-69.

22. Whether Rachel, as a woman, would have been legally able to adopt a child is
also evidence against 'adoption' being the transaction that transpires here.

23. The possibility that this statement indicates Rachel's intention to act as midwife
for Bilhah cannot be ruled out. Does Rachel somehow hope to overcome her
barrenness by participating in the birth of Bilhah's child, so that she, too, might
eventually conceive? See the controversial article by Samson Kardimon, 'Adoption as
a Remedy for Infertility in the Period of the Patriarchs', *JSS* 3 (1958), pp. 123-26.
Nevertheless, nowhere in the biblical text is Dan identified as a son of Rachel. In Gen.
35.25 and 46.23, Dan is recognized as Bilhah's son.

24. See Gen. 49.16, where another play on the root דין occurs ('Dan shall judge his
people...').

with the circumstances of his birth. In the birth of this child God has acted in such a way as to render a legal verdict that overcomes the shame of childlessness Rachel has endured (cf. 30.23, where Rachel's reproach/ shame/dishonor [חרפה] is removed with the birth of Joseph).[25]

Rachel is the key figure in the story of the birth of the children of Jacob at Haran, and the narrator has preserved in Gen. 30.1-6 the basic form of a northern tradition about the birth of Dan. Since Dan is important to Rachel, and since Rachel is important to the narrator, it follows that Dan is also important to the narrator. Simply put, this is a positive text with regard to the characterization of Dan. There is nothing negative about Dan in this text: he is associated with Rachel, the favorite/beloved wife of Jacob, who claims him as her own; he is born on Rachel's knees by Rachel's maidservant, thus establishing the closest of relationships with Rachel. Indeed, nowhere in the patriarchal traditions is Dan referred to negatively, even in those texts which explicitly mention his matriarchal origin, namely, Rachel's maidservant, Bilhah.

c. *Genesis 35 and 46*

According to most source-critical scholars, the next two occurrences of Dan in the book of Genesis appear in Priestly lists: 35.22b-26 and 46.8-27. The first is a list of the sons of Jacob situated at the end of the Abraham–Jacob cycle of narratives (ch. 36 is a genealogy of Esau's descendants, and chs. 37–50 comprise the Joseph story). In this case, the twelve sons of Jacob (Leah's daughter, Dinah, is omitted) are arranged according to matriarchal origin in the following scheme: first, all the sons of Leah (Reuben, Simeon, Levi, Judah, Issachar, and Zebulun); second, the two sons of Rachel (Joseph and Benjamin); third, the sons of Rachel's maidservant, Bilhah (Dan and Naphtali); and finally, the sons of Leah's maidservant, Zilpah (Gad and Asher). The form is thus chiasmic: Leah (A)–Rachel (B)–Rachel's maidservant (B')–Leah's maidservant (A').

The second list (Gen. 46), which is of the descendants of Jacob who went into Egypt, includes the children of Jacob (Dinah is included) in addition to their offspring. Since the editor must arrive at the number 70, the number of totality (46.27), there are certain peculiarities present.[26] In the case of Rachel's maidservant, Bilhah, vv. 23-25 count as her sons not only Dan and Naphtali (cf. 30.1-8), but also Dan's son, Hushim, and

---

25. For the forensic character of the root דין, see V. Hamp and G.J. Botterweck, 'דין *dîn*', in *TDOT*, III, pp. 187-94.

26. The LXX has 75; cf. Acts 7.14.

Naphtali's sons Jahzeel, Guni, Jezer, and Shillem (אלה בני בלחה—it is likely that 'sons of' here is to be understood more broadly as 'descendants of'). As in ch. 35, the children are listed according to matriarchal origin; that is, children of the same mother are grouped together. However, the order of mothers is not the same here as in ch. 35. The order in ch. 46 is: first, all the children of Leah (Reuben, Simeon, Levi, Judah, Issachar, Zebulun, and Dinah [without descendants]); second, the sons of Leah's maidservant, Zilpah (Gad and Asher); third, the sons of Rachel (Joseph and Benjamin); and finally, the sons of Rachel's maidservant, Bilhah (Dan and Naphtali). Thus the form is no longer that of a chiasm; instead the children of the first wife of Jacob (the older sister, Leah) and her maidservant (Zilpah) are listed before the children of the second wife of Jacob (the younger sister, Rachel) and her maidservant (Bilhah). The criterion, therefore, appears to be a hierarchy of age and/or marriage.

d. *Genesis 49*
Genesis 49 is ordinarily referred to as the Blessing of Jacob.[27] The poetic text (49.2-27) is set within a narrative framework, by which it is joined into the already interwoven ancestral stories of Jacob and Joseph. The final form of the text is ambiguous on the question of whether the recipients of the blessings are the twelve sons of Jacob (49.1-2) or the twelve tribes of Israel (49.28). Source critics are inclined, on the one hand, to assign the introduction to the chapter, which mentions the sons (v. 1a; cf. vv. 28b-33), to the later Priestly redactor of the Pentateuch. On the other hand, they treat v. 28a ('all these are the twelve tribes of Israel') as the conclusion to the earlier Yahwistic poem, and so conclude that the earlier form of the blessing had the tribes as the object.[28] This judgment is sound. Under-

27. Gen. 49.28b. Since not all of the individual sayings are favorable in character, some commentators prefer the designation 'Testament of Jacob' (see Speiser, *Genesis*, p. 370; Wenham, *Genesis 16–50*, p. 468; Sarna, *Genesis*, p. 331). However, according to BDB (p. 139), the verb usually translated 'bless' (ברך) may, in certain circumstances, carry instead the antithetical meaning '*curse*...from the greeting in departing, saying adieu to, taking leave of; but rather a blessing overdone and so really a curse as in vulgar English as well as in the Shemitic cognates' (see 1 Kgs 21.10, 13; Job 1.5, 11; 2.5, 9; Ps. 10.3). The traditional title is satisfactory.

28. Noth, *A History of Pentateuchal Traditions*, p. 14; see also the critics cited in Wenham, *Genesis 16–50*, p. 461. It is by no means universally acknowledged that the Yahwist is responsible for the poem as it now appears in Gen. 49. It is even less likely that J created the individual tribal sayings. The possibility exists that the Yahwist may have been the one to gather the individual tribal sayings together in the present text.

standing the twelve-tribe scheme as a creation of the monarchic period (rather than a tradition grounded in authentic ancestral traditions, i.e., twelve sons of Jacob [see the discussion below in Chapter 3, in the section on the distribution of tribal territories in Josh. 13–19]), it seems reasonable to conclude that the notion of an eponymous ancestor is a further development from the tribal tradition.

The saying about Dan is actually comprised of multiple statements, the first of which begins with a play on the name, Dan (v. 16); the second saying includes an animal metaphor similar to those that occur elsewhere in the poem (v. 17; cf. vv. 9, 14, 21, 22, 27). The Dan saying, containing multiple elements, is not unique in Genesis 49, since the same appears to be the case for the extensive sayings about Judah and Joseph, two tribes that predominate in Israel's history. This may suggest that Dan, too, was, at the time of the composition of this poem from earlier traditions, a significant group.

It is likely that the Blessing of Jacob, while set in the ancestral period before Israel's sojourn in Egypt, in reality was composed during the period of the United Monarchy. While the order of the first four tribes follows the order of birth in Genesis 29, the attention falls to Judah, the tribe descended from the fourth-born son of Jacob by Leah and the tribe from which David rose to power. Judah is the first tribe in the list in ch. 49 to receive any kind of 'blessing'; Reuben, Simeon, and Levi are all censured.[29] It is also interesting to note that by the time of the United Monarchy, these three tribes are no longer vital forces in Israel: the tribe of Levi was scattered throughout the land, some of whose members likely administered the boundaries of the kingdom in the special levitical cities (Josh. 21); the tribe of Simeon had been absorbed into Judah (Josh. 19.1-9; Judg. 1.1-3); and the tribe of Reuben seems mysteriously to have disappeared (cf. 2 Sam. 24.5-6).[30] Several earlier scholars preferred a date in the late premonarchic period, and suggested as a setting some sort of tribal ceremony at which representatives of all twelve tribes would assemble and share

---

29. The saying concerning Reuben relates to the incident recorded briefly in Gen. 35.22; the saying about Simeon and Levi follows from the narrative in Gen. 34.

30. For the subsequent history of the Reubenites, see also the Mesha Inscription (Moabite Stone), which notes the habitation of 'the men of Gad' in Transjordan, but which is silent about the Reubenites (W.F. Albright, 'The Moabite Stone', in *ANET*, pp. 320-21). See also Frank Moore Cross, Jr, 'Reuben, First-Born of Jacob', *ZAW* 100 (1988), pp. 46-65.

news.[31] However, it is difficult to imagine three tribes being regularly censured at such events. Rather, Genesis 49 comes from a time when Reuben, Simeon, and Levi played more marginal roles in Israel's life. The supremacy of Judah in this poem points to a time in the United Monarchy.

The positive sayings about Dan also suggest this time period before the division of the kingdom of David and Solomon. After the separation of the ten northern tribes from united Israel, and with the inauguration of Jeroboam I as the Northern Kingdom's first monarch, Dan is usually depicted—under the influence of the Deuteronomistic movement—in light of the illicit sanctuary established at the city of Dan. Thus, elsewhere Dan is negatively portrayed. However, this is not the case in Genesis 49.

(1) *Genesis 49.16-17*

[16] דן ידין עמו כאחד שבטי ישראל׃
[17] יהי־דן נחש עלי־דרך שפיפן עלי־ארח
הנשך עקבי־סוס ויפל רכבו אחור׃

> [16] Dan shall judge his people,
>> like the One (he shall judge) the tribes of Israel.
> [17] Let Dan be a serpent upon the road,
>> a horned snake upon the way;
>> who bites the horse's heels,
>>> so that its rider falls backwards.

It is apparent that there are two, originally independent, sayings about Dan in this text. The first, in v. 16, depicts Dan as an executor of judgment and justice in Israel. The second, in v. 17, includes an animal metaphor in the description of Dan's character. Each saying is a unified whole in its own right; the two verses are discontinuous. In the first place, the present translation of each colon in v. 16 includes the verb 'to judge' (דין) which, in the MT, only appears in the first line. This technique is called ellipsis, a common poetic device, and in this specific case one may say that the verb in the first colon does 'double-duty'. While it is written only in the first half of the verse, with Dan as the subject ('Dan shall judge'), it is intended

---

31. Westermann compares such gatherings to those described in Josh. 24 and Judg. 20 (*Genesis 37–50: A Commentary* [Minneapolis: Augsburg, 1986 (German original 1982)], p. 222). A.H.J. Gunneweg proposed a national covenant festival ('Über den Sitz im Leben der sogenannten Stammessprüche [Gen 49 Dtn 33 Jdc 5]', *ZAW* 76 [1964], pp. 245-55; cited in Wenham, *Genesis 16–50*, p. 470). See also Frank Moore Cross, Jr, and David Noel Freedman, *Studies in Ancient Yahwistic Poetry* (SBLDS, 21; Missoula, MT: Scholars Press, 1975), p. 69.

to describe the identical activity of the same (implied) subject in the second half of the verse: 'Like the One (divine epithet; cf. Deut. 6.4) he (Dan) shall judge the tribes of Israel'.[32] Thus, the two cola of v. 16 are inextricably bound together. In the second place, a careful structural analysis of v. 17 reveals clear evidence of this verse also being an originally independent saying, whose cola are closely interrelated. There are at least five points of linkage between the four lines of the quatrain (the first two may be more obvious than the others, since the former are instances of the better known poetic device known as synonymous parallelism): (1) 'upon the road' (A)// 'upon the way' (B); (2) 'serpent' (A)//'horned snake' (B); (3) 'serpent' (A [נחש]) corresponds to 'who bites' (C [הנשך]); (4) 'way' (B [אֹרַח]) rhymes with 'backwards' (D [אָחוֹר]); and (5) 'heels' (C [עִקְבֵי]) is similar in sound to 'its riders/charioteers' (D [רֹכְבוֹ]).

According to Gen. 49.16,

> Dan shall judge his people,
> like the One (he shall judge) the tribes of Israel.[33]

The first line of this bicolon begins with an etymological pun on the name 'Dan'. The first two words in the MT derive from the same root. While it is, of course, possible that this line preserves an ancient tradition joining the members of the tribe of Dan with the execution of justice in Israel (cf. 2 Sam. 20.18-19, LXX, where, however, 'Dan' signifies the city by that name), the *poetic* linkage between Dan and judgment at least suggests an alternative possibility, namely, that the tribe of Dan's activity is fabricated based on its name. 'Dan' *judges* (יָדִין) his people (Israel) because that is what one would expect *Dan* (דָּן) to do.

Commentators are divided about whether 'his people' in v. 16 refers to the tribe of Dan or to the whole of the people Israel.[34] I prefer the latter,

---

32. See Wilfred G.E. Watson, *Classical Hebrew Poetry: A Guide to Its Techniques* (JSOTSup, 26; Sheffield: Sheffield Academic Press, 2nd edn, 1995), pp. 303-304; see also Mitchell J. Dahood's 'The Grammar of the Psalter', in his *Psalms. III. 101–150: Introduction, Translation, and Notes, with an Appendix, The Grammar of the Psalter* (AB, 17A; Garden City, NY: Doubleday, 1970), p. 435.

33. The suggestion has been made (Ralph W. Klein, private communication) that instead of 'tribes' (שבטי), perhaps one should read 'judges' (שפטי), as in Num. 25.5 and 1 Chron. 17.6. However, while in both of these latter texts the alternative ('tribes') occurs in the LXX and is noted in the critical apparatus to *BHS*, in the case of Gen. 49.16 the LXX agrees with the MT.

34. Those who prefer the members of the tribe of Dan only include Gunkel, *Genesis*, p. 459; Skinner, *Genesis*, p. 527; von Rad, *Genesis: A Commentary*, p. 426; and

largely on the basis of the parallelism with the next line. Ordinarily this second colon is translated 'like one of the tribes of Israel', and much debate has focused on the intention of the prefix-preposition כ (as 'like'). There seem to be two chief interpretations of this line. According to the first explanation, while Dan was in reality a social unit smaller than a typical tribe (according to Judg. 13.2 and 18.2 the Danites were a 'clan'), he shall, nevertheless, judge his people in the same way as any of the other tribes of Israel.[35] The second interpretation is more imaginative and highly speculative. A minority of scholars recognizes in this expression evidence of an extra-Israelite origin for the tribe of Dan. Yigael Yadin is responsible for the original statement of the argument that the biblical Danites were, if not identical with, then at least associated with, an eastern Mediterranean group known variously as the Danai (= Danoi), the Dan(n)una, or the Denyen, whose members spread throughout the Mediterranean world as far as Greece.[36] A part of this group also appeared among the Sea Peoples, in Egyptian sources by the name Denyen (= Dan[n]una), along with the Philistines and the Tjeker. For example, in the reliefs at the Temple of Medinet Habu all three groups are depicted similarly clad.[37] Yadin proposes that since the Philistines settled along the southern Mediterranean coast of Canaan, and the Tjeker were located farther north, in the vicinity of Dor, the Danuna presumably settled in the area between (that is, between Dor and the northern border of Philistia). He concludes that the biblical Danites were, in ancient times, marginally related to the

Westermann, *Genesis 37–50*, p. 234. Wenham (*Genesis 16–50*) interprets 'his people' as a reference to all Israel, while Sarna (*Genesis*, p. 340) allows for both possibilities.

35. Niemann, *Die Daniten*, p. 255. See also Skinner, *Genesis*, pp. 527-28; Gunkel, *Genesis*, p. 459; and Westermann, *Genesis 37–50*, pp. 234-35.

36. Yigael Yadin, '"And Dan, why did he remain in Ships?": Judges, V, 17', *AJBA* 1 (1968), pp. 9-23. Yadin's conclusion has been met by approval from Trude Dothan and Moshe Dothan (*People of the Sea: The Search for the Philistines* [New York: Macmillan, 1992], pp. 215-18) and Othniel Margalith (*The Sea Peoples in the Bible* [Wiesbaden: Otto Harrassowitz, 1994], p. 117); see also the debatable monograph by Allen H. Jones, *Bronze Age Civilization: The Philistines and the Danites* (Washington: Public Affairs Press, 1975).

37. For a description of the reliefs and translation of the texts, see William F. Edgerton and John A. Wilson, *Historical Records of Ramses III: The Texts in Medinet Habu, I and II* (Studies in Ancient Civilization; Chicago: University of Chicago Press, 1936), esp. pp. 46-53, and n. 24a on p. 48: 'In dress and headdress the captives of these three registers are not distinguishable from one another. See Pl. 43, n. 19a'. For the Plates, see H.H. Nelson, *Medinet Habu I: Early Historical Records of Ramses III* (Chicago: University of Chicago Press, 1930).

association of the tribes of Israel but not fully part of the Israelite confederation. It should be noted that Yadin does not go so far as to insist on
the identification of the Danites with the Danai/Danuna/Denyen. At the
conclusion of his study Yadin writes:

> either there were two different tribes (the Danites and the Danai) with an
> identical name and similar characteristics which operated in the identical
> geographical region and period, or...there is a link between the Tribe of
> Dan and the Tribe of the Danai, and possibly even a certain measure of
> identity. The former case would constitute an exceedingly peculiar and
> remarkable concatenation of circumstances; whereas the second case, which
> appears more realistic, enables us to explain various phenomena linked with
> the Danai themselves, and particularly, all that affects the Tribe of the
> Danites. From this we may feel entitled to conclude that Dan was an ancient
> tribe which spread throughout the east, and that at the most ancient period it
> already had some link with the Tribes of Jacob. Certain sections settled in
> Palestine and at the beginning of the twelfth century drew near to the Tribes
> of Israel (again?) and were admitted to the Amphyctionic Covenant and
> given the status of *one of the Tribes of Israel*. At an early stage of their
> settlement (that is, at the time of the Song of Deborah) they dwelt on the
> seashore—between the Tjeker and the Philistines—and were engaged with
> shipping as of old; but after they were forced inland from the coast (by the
> other Peoples of the Sea) apparently about the end of the twelfth century,
> when the Kingdom of Sidon began to weaken, they wandered northwards.[38]

There are several debatable points in Yadin's presentation which call into
question his conclusion. First, his interpretation of the mention of Dan in
the Judg. 5.17—that, as an element of the Sea Peoples, it is understandable
that the Danites were early-on located along the Mediterranean coast and
engaged in seafaring—has been persuasively opposed by Stager's more
recent study.[39] Second, Yadin himself admits that there is 'no document...describing the history of the Danuna or their place of settlement'.
Thus, it is only speculation that they settled between the Philistines and the
Tjeker on the Mediterranean coast.[40] Third, his proposed solution to the
word כאחד in the MT ('and were admitted to the Amphyctionic Covenant
and given the status of *one of the Tribes of Israel*') has lost at least some
of its distinction with the demise of the 'amphyctiony hypothesis'. Since it
now seems less certain that there was a formal confederation of all the

---

38. Yadin, '"And Dan, why did he remain in Ships?"', p. 22 (emphasis added).

39. Stager, 'Archaeology, Ecology, and Social History'. See also the discussion of
Judg. 5, below.

40. Yadin, '"And Dan, why did he remain in Ships?"', pp. 17-18.

Israelite tribes antecedent to the rise of the monarchy in Israel, there would have been no already existing association to which Dan was subsequently admitted. Fundamental to this argument is the understanding of the prefix-preposition metaphorically, that is, as joining two otherwise distinct and unrelated objects. In this case the two objects are 'Dan' and the 'tribes of Israel', and the comparison is made between Dan the deity (Yahweh; 49.18).

I prefer an interpretation of כאבד which follows from certain remarks of the early rabbis, who compared the Danites with Israel's God.[41] While many of the rabbinic comments about Gen. 49.16-17 in the *Genesis Rabbah* (Midrash) relate the sayings about Dan to the tribe of Judah and/or the Danite judge, Samson, it is possible to understand the phrase in question as a reference to Yahweh. Commenting on 49.16, the rabbinic tradition reads:

> R. Joshua b. Nehemiah said: Had he not been coupled with the most distinguished of the tribes, he would not have produced even the one judge that he did produce; and who was that? Samson the son of Manoah. Another interpretation of AS ONE; he—Samson—was like the Unique One of the world; as the Unique One of the world required no assistance, so did Samson the son of Manoah require no assistance...[42]

I do not interpret the sayings about Dan in Genesis 49 as the rabbis did, namely, as clear references to Samson.[43] However, the mention of the 'Unique One of the world' in the context of 49.16 would seem to permit the comparison of Dan with the God of Israel. Elsewhere in the Hebrew Bible, Yahweh is portrayed judging his people (עמו), Israel, in language identical to that used in Genesis 49 with Dan as the subject: Deut. 32.36;

---

41. Cf. Deut. 6.4.

42. H. Freedman and Maurice Simon (eds.), *Midrash Rabbah, Genesis*. II. *Translated in English with Notes, Glossary and Indices* (trans. H. Freedman; New York: Soncino Press, 1983), p. 962, cf. p. 985.

43. H. Freedman and Maurice Simon (eds.), *Midrash Rabbah, Numbers: Translated into English with Notes, Glossary and Indices* (trans. Judah J. Slotki; 2 vols.; London: Soncino Press, 1983), II, p. 604. In their comments on the offering made by Dan's leader (Ahiezer son of Ammishaddai) in Num. 7, the rabbis wrote: 'Observe that this prince presented his offering in allusion to Samson, for Jacob's blessing to Dan was entirely in reference to Samson'. Only the sayings in Gen. 49 regarding Reuben, Simeon, and Levi (who are all censured with negative statements) are explicitly related to corresponding stories in the Hebrew Bible. Since not all of the sayings in Gen. 49 refer to other parts of the Bible, it is not *necessary* that the sayings about Dan be understood with clear reference to Samson.

Ps. 135.14 (cf. v. 12; Ps. 72.2). Therefore, it is possible to interpret this saying of Dan thus: 'Like the One, he (Dan) will judge the tribes of Israel'.[44] If this interpretation is accepted, then this would be the most positive saying about Dan in the biblical tradition, comparing Dan's activity among the rest of the tribes of Israel with that of Israel's God.[45]

According to Gen. 49.17,

Let Dan be a serpent upon the road,
   a horned snake upon the way;
who bites the horse's heels,
   so that its rider falls backwards.

This saying about Dan shares with several other of the tribal sayings in Genesis 49 the character of being an animal metaphor (נחש).[46] As a metaphor, that is, as a literary figure which has a single point of comparison to be highlighted, the interpreter is left to decide what it is about Dan that is being compared to a serpent and horned snake.[47] It is possible that the parallel term, 'horned snake' (שפיפן), is intended to help locate the point of comparison. However, the helpfulness of this term is suspect not only because this is the only occurrence of this word in the Hebrew Bible, but also because the LXX omits any term parallel to 'serpent' (apparently the LXX translator did not know this *hapax legomenon*) and instead reads 'lying couched upon the beaten path'. It is better, it seems, to focus attention on 'serpent', which, however, commentators seldom do. Most previous commentators have seemed to focus on the character of the 'horned snake' which, while a *hapax legomenon*, is identified with *Pseudocerestes fieldi* on the basis of its description in this single text.[48] As this type of serpent

44. While this interpretation assumes a different vocalization of the MT, the consonantal text is maintained.

45. Of course, whether this saying reflects the historical role of the Danites (as judge) cannot be determined from this text alone. As previously noted, the idea of Dan's judging may simply be the result of the Semitic root from which both the name, Dan, and judge/judgment derive.

46. So also Judah (lion's whelp, v. 9), Issachar (strong-boned ass, v. 14), Naphtali (hind, v. 21), Joseph (wild ass, wild colts, v. 22), Benjamin (ravenous wold, v. 27). The only being in the Bible (metaphorically) associated with 'serpent' is Satan/Devil in Rev. 20.2 (cf. 12.9). See Patrick D. Miller, Jr, 'Animal Names as Designations in Ugaritic and Hebrew', *UF* 2 (1970), pp. 177-86.

47. See G.B. Caird, *The Language and Imagery of the Bible* (Philadelphia: Westminster Press, 1980), p. 145.

48. Wenham, *Genesis 16–50*, p. 481 (note his reference to H.B. Tristram, *The Natural History of the Bible* [New York: Pott, Young & Co., 1867]).

was relatively small and venomously lethal, so is Dan to be characterized. Westermann writes:

> Dan is a small, though dangerous, serpent, referring to the smallness of the tribe; it has at its disposal all too few warriors to be able to engage its Canaanite enemies in open battle. Now and again it can risk a surprise attack, an ambush, as the metaphor describes it; the weaker resorts to a stratagem against the stronger...[49]

The fact that the depiction of 'serpent' in the Hebrew Bible is generally negative, may lead one to conclude that here Dan is negatively portrayed. While such an interpretation is, of course, possible, there is insufficient corroborating evidence about the tribe of Dan in the biblical tradition to rest assured (while Judg. 13.2 does refer to Dan as a 'clan' rather than as a tribe, the exodus tradition depicts Dan as one of the largest tribes coming out of Egypt; cf. Num. 2.31), and the unique occurrence of 'horned snake' in the Bible is perhaps strong reason against basing one's interpretation of this passage on a single word. It is also possible that the occurrence of 'serpent' in this text is not negative. Rather, there is sufficient reason to conclude that, like v. 16, the portrayal of Dan in this verse may be in praise of this Israelite tribe. The likelihood is that this tradition about Dan originated in the north, was connected with the Mosaic tradition, and may possibly have left some trace in the material culture at Tell Dan/Laish.

A number of Mosaic elements in this text suggest a northern provenance for this saying; such an origin is suggested by the explicit and implicit references to the Moses tradition which is usually located in the north.[50] First, the use of 'serpent' calls to mind the etiological narrative in Numbers 21. According to this story, while in the wilderness the people rebelled against God and Moses and, in response, God sent הנחשים השרפים ('fiery serpents'?) against them. Many people died on account of the bites of these serpents. Moses interceded on behalf of the people, and God commanded him to construct a 'seraph figure' (שרף), mounted on a pole, to which those who had been bitten were to turn for healing. Instead of constructing this specific image, Moses made a נחש נחשת, a bronze serpent, which he obediently set on a standard.[51] This was the figure whose destruction is ascribed by the Deuteronomistic Historian (Dtr) to King

49. Westermann, *Genesis 37–50*, p. 235.
50. Friedman, *Who Wrote the Bible?*, pp. 70-83.
51. For the identification of this as an E story, see Friedman, *Who Wrote the Bible?*, p. 253.

Hezekiah as part of his religious reform.[52] 2 Kings 18 implies that this serpentine figure (Neḥushtan) had been an object of worship in the Jerusalem temple for some time ('until those days', 18.4, which seems to refer to older religious practices). However, nowhere in the Deuteronomistic story of the earlier kings of Judah is this serpent mentioned.[53] The possibility must be entertained, then, that Neḥushtan was only recently (in the time of Hezekiah) erected in the Temple in Jerusalem, having perhaps been brought from a northern Israelite shrine/cult center after the collapse of the Northern Kingdom in 722 BCE. Another Mosaic element in Gen. 49.17 is the reference to 'rider' (רכבו = 'charioteer'?), intended perhaps to call to mind the exodus event and the pursuit of the liberated Hebrews by Egyptian forces (Exod. 15.1, 21; cf. 14.25). It is conceivable that a northern tradition, in which the character of Moses figured prominently, and with whom the serpent is associated, had some measure of positive evaluation for this creature and so used this figure metaphorically as a reference to the northern tribe of Dan.[54] Finally, storage jars with serpentine decoration have been recovered in the excavations at Tell Dan, supplying further evidence for the positive regard given to this figure at the site.[55] As a tradition originating in the north, this saying about Dan is intended to praise the tribe. A similar conclusion may be drawn from the saying about Dan in Deuteronomy 33, to which we shall turn shortly.

52. While this reform cannot be precisely located in time, it must be admitted that 2 Kgs 18.1-4 envisions Hezekiah initiating religious reform immediately after ascending the throne, to which Miller and Hayes (for example) assign a date of 727 BCE (on the reign of Hezekiah and its chronological difficulties, see J. Maxwell Miller and John H. Hayes, *A History of Ancient Israel and Judah* [Philadelphia: Westminster Press, 1986], pp. 346-63). An alternate chronology for Hezekiah's reign (715–697 BCE) is given in Gwilym H. Jones, *1 and 2 Kings* (2 vols.; NCB; Grand Rapids: Eerdmans, 1984), II, p. 561.

53. Or are we to understand that references to divination (based on the same Hebrew root) are associated with the bronze serpent of Moses? See 2 Kgs 17.17; 21.6; 2 Chron. 33.6.

54. In the Pentateuch, 'serpent' (נחש) appears as a negative figure in the J source (see Gen. 3.1-2, 4; Exod. 4.3; 7.15), while it is positively portrayed by in the E strand (Num. 21.8-9). The ambiguous character of the serpent in the biblical tradition is reflected in the broader ancient Near Eastern literary and mythological context.

55. Biran, *Biblical Dan*, pp. 165-77.

2. *The Book of Exodus*

Dan occurs in two sections in the book of Exodus: in ch. 1, Dan refers to the son of Jacob who went down into Egypt; in chs. 31–40 an individual Danite, Oholiab, is mentioned. All references to Dan in Exodus come from the Priestly tradition in the Pentateuch which, while probably utilizing older material, dates to the exilic period.

a. *Exodus 1*

Most source critics agree that the list of the sons of Jacob who accompanied Jacob into Egypt in Exod. 1.1-7 comes from P.[56] As in Genesis 35, the eleven sons (Joseph, Rachel's firstborn, is omitted from this list since he is already in Egypt [Gen. 37.28-36; 39.1]) are arranged schematically (and chiasmically) according to matriarchal origin: first, all the sons of Leah (Reuben, Simeon, Levi, Judah, Issachar, and Zebulun); second, the second son born to Rachel (Benjamin); third, the sons of Rachel's maidservant, Bilhah (Dan and Naphtali); and finally, the sons of Leah's maidservant, Zilpah (Gad and Asher).

b. *Exodus 31–40*

While interrupted by chs. 32–34, which narrate the golden calf episode, the command of Moses to leave Sinai, and the second carving of the covenant tablets, the primary interest of Exodus 31–40 is the construction of the wilderness tabernacle and its related furnishings. An unnumbered host of artisans participate in the project, although two are singled out by name: Bezalel, son of Uri, son of Hur, of the tribe of Judah (31.2; 35.30; 36.1-2; 38.22), and Oholiab, son of Ahisamach, of the tribe of Dan (31.6; 35.34; 36.1-2; 38.23). Of some interest for the present study is the association of a Judahite and a Danite, tribes elsewhere associated with each other (for better or for worse—see, e.g., Judg. 15). The Judahite, Bezalel, is pre-eminent, a phenomenon which may preserve a historical memory (contra the Graf–Wellhausen hypothesis, according to which the wilderness tabernacle was a 'pious fraud' from the Second Temple period), or, at least, the partisan interests of a Judean author (P). The Danite, Oholiab, son of Ahisamach, is of secondary importance in these chapters, and is always, and only, mentioned together with Bezalel of the tribe of Judah (note, however, that Bezalel appears separately in 37.1). In Exodus 31, the

---

56. See, e.g., Noth, *A History of Pentateuchal Traditions*, p. 14.

skills of Bezalel are listed, then it is simply noted that Oholiab was appointed by Yahweh 'with him' (נתתי אתו את אהליאב). While Bezalel appears in postexilic works (1 Chron. 2.20; 2 Chron. 1.5; Ezra 10.30), which may indicate that a leading family in the postexilic community lent its name to an ancestral character, mention of the Danite Oholiab is limited to the latter part of Exodus.[57] His name occurs nowhere else in the Hebrew Bible, and thus one cannot be absolutely certain of his origin.[58]

In reality Bezalel is the only independent character (in addition to Moses) in Exodus 31–40, since, apart from his name and ancestry, the Danite Oholiab for the most part blends in with the other workers. For example, in Exod. 31.1-11, Bezalel is portrayed as possessing a divine spirit, and is endowed with skill ('wisdom'), ability, knowledge, and every kind of service. No such introduction accompanies the initial mention of Oholiab, who is otherwise indistinguishable from all the other skilled workers to whom Yahweh had given skill for the manufacture of all the things commanded through Moses (31.6b). In the chapters narrating the construction of the tabernacle (chs. 36–38), there is alternation between the work of Bezalel (cf. 37.1) and the work of the assembled artisans (note the interchange of singular and plural verb forms). The contribution of Oholiab to the effort is not specified. More explicit is 35.34-35, where both Bezalel and Oholiab are inspired to teach (v. 34 is difficult and perhaps fragmentary), and are filled with 'skill of heart ("ability")' to do every work of the metal worker and inventive workman, and weaver in violet, and in purple, and in scarlet thread, and in fine twisted linen'. It is only with the final mention of Oholiab in Exod. 38.23 that a clear portrait of the Danite emerges, and this corresponds almost exactly with the list of abilities ascribed to both craftsmen in Exodus 35. In this text he is described as 'a metal worker and inventive workman, and a weaver in violet, and in purple, and in scarlet threads, and in fine twisted linen'.[59] Thus, Oholiab son of Ahisamach, of the tribe of Dan, is most specifically associated with the textiles connected with the tabernacle and its furnishings.[60]

57. Noth, *A History of Pentateuchal Traditions*, pp. 187-88.

58. An intriguing observation whose significance cannot be fully understood is that the feminine form of this name, Oholibah, occurs in Ezek. 23 as a metaphor for adulterous Jerusalem. Ezekiel is also a Priestly work (1.3), from the time of the Exile.

59. According to BDB (p. 360), the word here translated 'metal worker' may have the connotation of 'idol-maker'.

60. Contra Biran (*Biblical Dan*, p. 151), who highlights Oholiab's metal working.

With minor exceptions (chiefly confined to chs. 32–34), source critics attribute Exodus 31–40 to the P tradition.[61] At issue, then, is the date of this P material. The hypothesis associated with the names Graf and Wellhausen supposed that the tabernacle description in the book of Exodus was actually a literary fiction from the postexilic period, fabricated by Priestly writers in order to undergird the religious interests of this later era.[62] If this was the case, then the mention of a Danite in such a prominent role is significant although difficult to account for, since Dtr (preceding the Priestly tradition by a century or more) not only evaluated Dan and the Danites in a wholly negative way, but may even have suppressed mention of a Danite in connection with the erection of Solomon's temple (according to 1 Kgs 7.14, the mother of Hiram from Tyre was a widow from the tribe of Naphtali; in 2 Chron. 2.12-13, his mother was a Danite woman). This postexilic date for this material in P held sway into the twentieth century. In the middle of the last century, however, Frank M. Cross, Jr, re-examined the tabernacle tradition in the Bible and concluded that it was not a 'pious fraud' from the postexilic period, but was rather a priestly creation based on elements of the Davidic tent shrine.[63] If this is the case, namely, that the priestly tabernacle tradition goes back to sources/material from the time of David in the tenth century BCE, then it is easier to understand the positive mention of the Danite Oholiab. The tradition used by the Priestly Writer was antecedent to the division of the monarchy after the death of Solomon,

61. Noth, *A History of Pentateuchal Traditions*, pp. 17-18, 271; Friedman, *Who Wrote the Bible?*, pp. 251-52.

62. Julius Wellhausen, *Prolegomena to the History of Israel* (Scholars Press Reprints and Translations Series; Atlanta: Scholars Press, 1994 [1885]), pp. 37-51.

63. Frank M. Cross, Jr, 'The Tabernacle: A Study from an Archaeological and Historical Approach', *BA* 10 (1947), pp. 45-68. A similar conclusion was reached by Menahem Haran (*Temples and Temple-Service in Ancient Israel: An Inquiry into Biblical Cult Phenomena and the Historical Setting of the Priestly School* [repr., Winona Lake, IN: Eisenbrauns, 1985 (1978)], pp. 189-204). Cross has been followed by, e.g., his student Richard Elliott Friedman, who argues that the tabernacle structure described in the book of Exodus would have fit perfectly beneath the outstretched wings of the cherubim in the holy of holies in the First Temple ('The Tabernacle in the Temple', *BA* 43 [1980], pp. 241-48). Presuming that P's emphasis on sacrifice exclusively at the Tabernacle must have arisen at a time when the Solomonic Temple still stood, he locates the literary activity of the Priestly Writer(s) in the years prior to the Babylonian destruction of Jerusalem (see also Friedman, *Who Wrote the Bible?*, pp. 186-87). While the present writer is not convinced of this date, and prefers instead an exilic or early postexilic date for the composition/redaction of P, it seems clear that the Priestly Writer(s) made use of sources from the period of the United Monarchy in Israel.

and well before Dtr's anti-Dan program. While Oholiab from the tribe of Dan is clearly subordinate to the Judahite Bezalel, the fact that a Danite is mentioned by name at all seems significant.

Whether or not the figures of Bezalel and Oholiab were historical persons whose memories have been preserved in this tabernacle tradition is a question we are unable to answer. Their names do not occur in other contemporary records and, as previously noted, only Bezalel occurs elsewhere in the Hebrew Bible—and that is in the postexilic books of Chronicles and Ezra. The critical consensus today is that the earliest period of Israel's history, prior to the rise of the Israelite monarchy, is shrouded in uncertainty and largely uncorroborated by extra-biblical evidence.

An interesting question is that of the possible relationship between Oholiab in Exodus 31–40, and the Hiram/Huram-abi mentioned in 1 Kgs 7.13-14 and 2 Chron. 2.12-13, respectively. According to the parallel stories in the historical books, an artisan by the name of Hiram (1 Kings) or Huram-abi (2 Chronicles) from the coastal city-state of Tyre came to Jerusalem to lead the construction of the furnishings for Solomon's Temple (in 1 Kgs 7.13 Solomon sent for and brought Hiram from Tyre [the impression is that the craftsman was known to Solomon]; in the parallel account in 2 Chron. 2.12 the King of Tyre independently sends Huram-abi to Solomon in response to the latter's request for a skilled artisan). According to 1 Kgs 7.14, Hiram was the 'son of a "widow woman/wife" who was from the tribe of Naphtali, and his father was a man of Tyre, a worker in bronze' (בן־אשה אלמנה הוא ממטה נפתלי ואביו איש־צרי חרש נחשת). The description of the craftsman Huram-abi in 2 Chron. 2.13 is slightly but significantly different. In this text, he is 'the son of a woman from the daughters of Dan, and his father is a man of Tyre' (איש־צרי בן־אשה מן־בנות דן ואביו). Two differences are obvious: first, in one account the mother is a widow, while in the other she appears as married to a living husband;[64] second, in 1 Kings the mother is descended from the

---

64. It is unclear why she is portrayed by Dtr as a widow in this text, or even how the designation 'widow' is to be understood. Ordinarily in the ancient world, a widow was a woman whose husband had died and who had no male from her husband's family (i.e. brothers-in-law, sons) to assume responsibility for her (Paula S. Hiebert, '"Whence Shall Help Come to Me?": The Biblical Widow', in Peggy L. Day [ed.], *Gender and Difference in Ancient Israel* [Minneapolis: Fortress Press, 1989], pp. 125-41; John Rook, 'When Is a Widow Not a Widow? Guardianship Provides an Answer', *BTB* 28 [1998], pp. 4-6). In Hebrew, this woman is referred to as אשה אלמנה, which I have translated 'widow woman'. This descriptor occurs in the Hebrew Bible only in the DH, and in every text it refers to a woman whose husband has died but who does have a

tribe of Naphtali, whereas in 2 Chronicles she is a Danite. It is impossible to draw indisputable conclusions about which text is the earlier in this case. Ordinarily, it is assumed that the Chronicler used the books of Samuel and Kings as the chief source for his history of Israel. In this case, preference would go to the text in 1 Kings, and the form of the passage in Chronicles would be understood as a change made by the Chronicler. However, one must ask whether it is likely that Dan would have been substituted in a text after the work of Dtr. It is, in the mind of the present writer, more likely that Dan stood originally in the common tradition about the construction of the temple known both to Dtr and the Chronicler.[65] The Chronicler, then, has more faithfully represented this earlier tradition.[66] Dtr, however, expunged the mention of Dan in this important religious tradition, most probably in light of Jeroboam's establishment of an illicit shrine at the city of Dan following the division of Solomon's Kingdom (1 Kgs 12). In 1 Kings 7, the Danite ancestry of the artisan, Hiram, is sup-

living son. (In 2 Sam. 14.1-11 and 1 Kgs 11.26, the son[s] in question are apparently old enough to be able to provide and assume responsibility for the mother; the age of the 'son/child' in 1 Kgs 17.9-10, however, is uncertain. He is called בֵּן [vv. 12-13, 17-20] and יֶלֶד [vv. 21 (twice), 22-23] in the MT, and variously τέκνον [plural, vv. 12, 13, 15], παιδάριον [vv. 21 (twice), 22], or υἱός [vv. 17-20, 23] in the LXX; a range of meanings from little boy to child to youth to son of unspecified age to fully grown persons is possible for each Hebrew or Greek word [cf. BDB and BAGD]). It is thus possible (as Rook suggests [p. 5]), that during the monarchic period in Israel the meaning of 'widow' was expanded to include women with adult/grown sons. It is tempting to suspect that the mother as 'widow' was an invention of Dtr, given the unprotected, and thus vulnerable widows' frequent association with deities and/or their temples in the ancient world (Karel van der Toorn, 'Torn Between Vice and Virtue: Stereotypes of the Widow in Israel and Mesopotamia', in Ria Kloppenborg and Wouter J. Hanegraaff [eds.], *Female Stereotypes in Religious Traditions* [Studies in the History of Religions, 65; Leiden: E.J. Brill, 1995], pp. 1-13 [7-10]). That is, it would have served to enhance Hiram's credentials/character as potential temple-builder to know that his Israelite mother was a widow.

65. One can only speculate that this tradition was that preserved in the Priestly material in Exod. 31–40 (which became part of the basic Priestly document dating to the exilic period [Pᵍ]; see Karl Elliger, 'Sinn und Ursprung der priestlichen Geschichtserzählung', *ZTK* 49 [1952], pp. 121-43 [121-22]). It is also possible that a record of the construction of the Temple was preserved in a Temple archives, and that this would have constituted the common tradition known to both Dtr and the Chronicler (see, e.g., G.H. Jones, *1 and 2 Kings*, I, pp. 57, 151-52).

66. While the account in 2 Chronicles will be examined in more detail later in the present study, suffice it for now to say that it preserves better the earlier tradition than does 1 Kgs 7.

pressed due to Dtr's systematic effort to portray all things Danite in a negative way. It would have been at odds with Dtr's purpose of negatively criticizing the Northern Kingdom to reproduce a tradition in which a Danite was so closely aligned with the manufacture of accessories for the temple of Yahweh in Jerusalem. Thus the ancestry of the craftsman is shifted from Dan to Naphtali, an old tribal territory in the northern part of the Israelite kingdom, not far from the region of Tyre. This was deemed a reasonable alternation.

Many scholars have noticed the similarity between the leaders in the construction of the wilderness tabernacle and the construction of the Solomonic temple. Is Oholiab in Exodus 31–40 a prototype for Hiram/ Huram-abi? Or is the latter a model on whom the former was artificially created? The majority of contemporary commentators allow for the historical precedence of at least the *tradition* of Bezalel and Oholiab.[67] That is, even if one cannot demonstrate historical continuity—it is beyond the evidence to conclude that, in fact, a Danite by the name of Oholiab, actually existed and was instrumental in the production of the tabernacle and its accoutrements in the wilderness—it is reasonable to assume continuity of tradition: the tradition about a Danite in connection with the tabernacle is clearly linked in 2 Chronicles with the Danite Huram-abi and the temple. Several commentators even suggest an intention on the part of the Israelite historians to associate the tabernacle and the temple by means of the primary leaders.[68]

---

67. H.G.M. Williamson, *1 and 2 Chronicles* (NCB; Grand Rapids: Eerdmans, 1982), pp. 197-201 ('temple-tabernacle typology'); S. Japhet, *I and II Chronicles: A Commentary* (OTL; Louisville, KY: Westminster/John Knox Press, 1993), pp. 541-45; G.H. Jones, *1 and 2 Kings*, I, p. 179; Leslie C. Allen, 'The First and Second Books of Chronicles: Introduction, Commentary, and Reflections', in Leander E. Keck *et al.* (eds.), *New Interpreter's Bible* (Nashville: Abingdon Press, 1999), III, pp. 297-659 (478).

68. See especially Raymond B. Dillard's introductory remarks about 'Solomon and Huram-abi as the new Bezalel and Oholiab' in his *2 Chronicles* (WBC, 15; Waco, TX: Word Books, 1987), pp. 4-5, cf. pp. 18-23. His highlights are impressive: (1) Bezalel and Oholiab, and Solomon and Huram-abi, are the only named individuals in their respective stories; (2) Bezalel (the prominent artisan in the Exodus account) and Solomon are both from the tribe of Judah, while Oholiab and Huram-abi are Danites (Dillard understands the reference to Dan to be the contribution of the Chronicler); (3) the more extensive list of Huram-abi's skills more closely matches those abilities enumerated for the chief craftsmen in Exod. 31–40 (cf. 1 Kgs 7.14, which focuses on Hiram's metal-working skill).

Whether the tradition accurately preserves historical reality is an unanswerable question. Nevertheless, at the time of the construction of Solomon's temple (or, possibly, at the time of the composition of Dtr's account of the construction of Solomon's Temple [each is centuries later than the wilderness period]), there was known a tradition of a Judahite and a Danite participating as leading figures in the construction of the wilderness tent-shrine. It is my conclusion that Exodus 31–40 preserves an early tradition about the tabernacle construction project which includes a relatively positive mention of the Danite Oholiab. This tradition gets replicated in 2 Chronicles 2, while such an affirmative mention of Dan is expectedly expunged from the work of Dtr and replaced with a reference to the tribe of Naphtali (1 Kgs 7).

3. *The Book of Leviticus*

a. *Leviticus 24*

The single reference to Dan in the book of Leviticus occurs in 24.10-23, in the narrative of the so-called 'blaspheming son'. There are numerous critical questions surrounding these verses, but most significant for the present study is the lineage of the blasphemer: his mother is a Danite.

[10] Now the son of an Israelite woman went out (and he was the son of an Egyptian man) into the midst of the sons of Israel; and they struggled with each other in the camp—the son of the Israelite woman and a certain Israelite. [11] And the son of the Israelite woman cursed the Name and he treated it as contemptible; so they brought him to Moses (now the name of his mother was Shelomith daughter of Dibri, belonging to the tribe of Dan). [12] They placed him in the camp's guard house until the decision of Yahweh was declared to them. [13] Then Yahweh spoke to Moses saying: [14] 'Bring out the blasphemer outside the camp, and let all who heard lay their hands upon his head. Then let the entire congregation stone him to death'. [15] And to the sons of Israel you shall speak saying: 'Anyone who blasphemes his God shall bear the punishment of his sin. [16] And the one who curses the name Yahweh shall surely be put to death, the entire congregation shall stone him to death. The client and native alike, when he curses the Name, shall be put to death. [17] And if a man slays any/another human being, he shall surely be put to death. [18] But the one slaying a beast shall make compensation, life for life. [19] And if a man should maim his fellow, just as he has done thus it shall be done to him: [20] fracture for fracture, eye for eye, tooth for tooth. Just as he has maimed another person, thus it shall be given to him. [21] Now the one slaying a beast shall make compensation; but the one slaying another person shall be put to death. [22] One sentence there shall be for you, (for) the client and the native alike it shall be; for I

am Yahweh your God.' [23] So Moses spoke to the sons of Israel. Then they brought out the blasphemer outside the camp and they stoned him to death with stones. The sons of Israel did just as Yahweh commanded Moses.

[Notes on the MT:

Verse 10: The Samaritan Pentateuch reads the masculine singular form of adjective 'Israelite' at the end of the verse without the definite article (see GKC, 126ʳ).

Verse 11: For 'the Name', the LXX[59] (Ethiopic Version, Targum[Ms]) read 'the name of the Lord' (cf. v. 16). Even with this additional phrase, vv. 11 and 16 are not identical. It is apparent that these Versions sought to make explicit an identification which was implicit in the Hebrew text. Read the MT.

Verse 15: The LXX Codices Vaticanus and Alexandrinus read simply 'God' in place of 'his God', quite possibly for apologetic reasons: there is, in the theology of these LXX translators, only one God, not a host of personal deities.

Verse 16: At the second occurrence of 'the Name' in this verse, the LXX (the Vulgate) reads 'the name of the Lord' (cf. v. 11 note a). This may represent an attempt to harmonize this occurrence with the antecedent mention of 'the Name' in this verse and in v. 11. On the other hand, it is equally plausible that the Tetragrammaton has dropped out at this point due to homoeoarchton with the word following ('he shall be put to death'). The present translation reflects the MT.

Verse 17: After 'human being', the LXX adds 'and he dies'; likewise v. 18 note b and v. 21 note b.

Verse 18: The word נֶפֶשׁ before 'beast' is absent from a reading from the Cairo Genizah and several medieval manuscripts of the Hebrew Old Testament, the LXX, and the Vulgate. After 'beast', the LXX adds 'and it dies'.

Verse 21: 'Now the one slaying a beast shall make compensation' is absent from the LXX, thereby damaging the chiasm in vv. 15-22. Read the MT. After 'human being', the LXX adds 'and he dies'.

Verse 22: The editor of the book of Leviticus in *BHS* (G. Quell) suggests revocalizing the word for 'sentence' with Num. 15.16. This emendation of the vocalizaion is reasonable (see GKC, 134d).

Verse 23: After 'with stones', the Syriac Version of the Old Testament adds *wmjt* = וַיָּמָת ('and he died').]

The main interest of the present study in this passage is to ascertain the historical reliability of the report that the mother of the blasphemer was from the tribe of Dan. That is, what is the degree of probability that this narrative preserves a historical memory of an event that occurred in Israel's wilderness period? Some scholars suggest that the seemingly poor fit of this story in the book of Leviticus generally, and in ch. 24 in particular (it is entirely unrelated to its present context), is evidence of the accuracy of this report: this narrative is located where it is in the book of Leviticus because it preserves an event which actually occurred immediately after

Moses's instructions about the lamps and the bread offering.[69] Of course, this only begs the question. There is, rather, sufficient reason to doubt the historical reliability and pre-settlement provenance of this narrative. Instead, Lev. 24.10-23, probably better reflects the interests of the post-exilic community in Judah. In this case, while the mention of Dan seems significant, its precise meaning remains unclear.

Among source critics, Leviticus 24 is attributed to the Priestly Writer(s). Those who would identify an original, exilic edition of P, and a postexilic supplement, tend to locate vv. 10-23, with its chiefly legal interest, in the supplementary material.[70] The narrative opens with the introduction of a certain 'son of an Israelite woman' whose father was an Egyptian.[71] The books of Ezra and Nehemiah relate the Israelite concerns about intermarriage with people in the land in the sixth–fifth centuries BCE. According to Ezra 9.1-2, a report is brought to Ezra that numerous Israelites, including priests and Levites, have intermarried with the 'peoples of the land whose idolatrous practices are like those of the Canaanites, the Hittites, the Perizzites, the Jebusites, the Ammonites, the Moabites, the Egyptians, and the Amorites'.[72] As commentators have rightly pointed out, intermarriage is not express prohibited in the Pentateuchal Law.[73] There are numerous ancestral stories of intermarriage (Joseph, Moses—also, Elimelech), as well as the long list of Solomon's foreign wives (1 Kgs 11.1-2). This

69. See Gordon J. Wenham, *The Book of Leviticus* (NICOT, 3; Grand Rapids: Eerdmans, 1979), pp. 308-309. A highly speculative proposal for the events leading up to this incident is offered by H. Mittwoch, 'The Story of the Blasphemer Seen in a Wider Context', *VT* 15 (1965), pp. 386-89. For a recent reassessment of Lev. 24.10-23, interpreting this text within its literary context, see Rodney R. Hutton, 'Narrative in Leviticus: The Case of the Blaspheming Son (Lev 24, 10-23)', *Zeitschrift für Altorientalische und Biblische Rechtsgeschichte* 3 (1997), pp. 145-63.

70. Elliger, 'Sinn und Ursprung'.

71. See H. Freedman and Maurice Simon (eds.), *Midrash Rabbah: Leviticus* (London: Soncino Press, 1939), p. 412, where the Egyptian father of the blasphemer is identified as a taskmaster who 'misconducted himself' with the wife of one of his Israelite officers. The rabbis understand this one to be the Egyptian whom Moses slew (Exod. 2.12).

72. Whether the 'peoples of the land' were neighboring peoples, foreigners re-settled in Judah during the exile, or perhaps Judeans who had not been in Babylonian captivity, is unclear. Regardless, they were outside the community of returned exiles and to be feared (Ezra 3.3).

73. H.G.M. Williamson, *Ezra, Nehemiah* (WBC, 16; Waco, TX: Word Books, 1985), p. 130; D.J.A. Clines, *Ezra, Nehemiah, Esther* (NCB; Grand Rapids: Eerdmans, 1984), p. 116.

traditional list of nations in Ezra 9 hearkens back to the list of the indigenous nations in Canaan at the time of the settlement. Intermarriage with *these* nations is expressly forbidden (see Deut. 7.1-2). It is true that at least superficially the concern in Ezra and Nehemiah is over Israelite men who have married foreign women. However, in both books it is stated that neither should Israelite women be given in marriage to men of such foreign nations (Ezra 9.12; Neh. 13.25). Thus the marriage of an Israelite woman to an Egyptian man, as noted in Lev. 24.10, is reflected in the concerns of the postexilic community.[74] It is possible, in fact, that the narrative in Leviticus has its origin in the postexilic period.

Another detail in Lev. 24.10-23 that may point to a period later than the wilderness period is the concern of 'the Name' (הַשֵּׁם־אֶת).[75] The only other verse in the Hebrew Bible where this word occurs in this absolute form (with the definite article) is Deut. 28.58, part of the Deuteronomic Code. Just as intermarriage with foreign nations in the land was prohibited in the postexilic period, based in part on Deut. 7.1-2, so, too, does the occurrence of 'the Name' in Lev. 24.11 indicate the persistence of Deuteronomic influence after the exile.[76]

The name of the mother of the blasphemer may also point to a late date.[77] The only other passages where this name, Shelomith, occurs are in the postexilic works of the Chronicler (1 Chron. 3.19, among the descendants of the Judahite, Solomon; 23.18, a male among the descendants of Levi; 26.28, a male; 2 Chron. 11.20, gender unknown]), and Ezra (8.10, a male; cf. 1 Esd. 8.36). There is no text in the Hebrew Bible that corroborates the narrative in Leviticus 24.

It is possible, on literary-critical grounds, to conclude that the identification of the mother of the blasphemer as a Danite is a secondary addition

74. It is also noteworthy that Egyptians are included in the list of peoples of the lands to whom Israelite men and women are not to marry.

75. For the discussion of the Deuteronomic/Deuteronomistic 'Name Theology', see Gerhard von Rad, 'Deuteronomy's "Name" Theology and the Priestly Document's "Kabod" Theology', in his *Studies in Deuteronomy* (SBT, 9; London: SCM Press, 1953), pp. 37-44; Ernest W. Nicholson, *Deuteronomy and Tradition* (Philadelphia: Fortress Press, 1967), pp. 55-56, 71-73.

76. Joseph Blenkinsopp, *Ezra–Nehemiah: A Commentary* (OTL; Philadelphia: Westminster Press, 1988), p. 185.

77. It is unclear why the mother's name was remembered in the tradition, but not the name of the blasphemer himself. Is this to be associated with the notion of one's memory being blotted out in Israel (cf. Exod. 32.33; Deut. 9.14; 29.19; 1 Macc. 12.53)?

to a postexilic text. In the opening verse of the narrative, she is introduced simply as an Israelite woman who happens to be married to an Egyptian, who is also the father of her son. It is only in the wake of her son's blasphemous crime that her lineage is mentioned. It may be supposed that this apparently secondary addition is an instance of 'delayed identification', a literary device more common in poetry (but which occurs also in narrative, a hallmark example being Gen. 22.2 [MT; the NRSV and the NJPS are two translations that unfortunately obscure this literary device]).[78] The primary purpose of delayed identification is to build suspense.[79] This is not, however, what is achieved in Leviticus 24. That she (and so the blasphemer himself) is a Danite does not effect uneasiness or anxiety in the reader. Rather, this mention of lineage seems an afterthought, a remark not well integrated into the text (note that it breaks up the action of the son being taken 'to Moses' and his subsequent confinement 'in the camp's guard house'). The connection of the blasphemer's mother with the tribe of Dan has no further significance in the text; none of the legal decisions enumerated in vv. 15-22 have to do specifically with the Danites or with Danites that are intermarried with foreigners.

This text is, then, of doubtful historical significance. It does not contribute anything incontrovertible to our understanding of the tribe of Dan in the period before the Israelite settlement in Canaan. Nevertheless, the question remains: What does this text indicate about the way other (later) traditions interpreted Dan? It is likely that an editor, later in the postexilic period, inserted the mention of Dan in this text and thereby introduced a particular characterization of the Danites in the earlier period.

Previous scholarship has focused on either the historical or theological questions raised by this narrative which apparently intends to answer, in its present form, the question: Does the Law, given specifically to the children of Israel, apply equally to foreigners or to residents of mixed parentage?[80] The 'labeling and deviance theory' model from the social sciences

78. The MT of Gen. 22.2a is translated: 'And (God) said, "Take your son, your only son, whom you love, Isaac, and go to the land of Moriah"'. The proper identity of the son is not revealed until, finally, after a most benign 'your son', and the more intriguing descriptors 'your only son' and 'whom you love', the name is given: Isaac (not Ishmael).

79. Watson, *Classical Hebrew Poetry*, pp. 336-37.

80. For example, attempts have been made to determine the identity of the characters involved, the relationship between the framing narrative (vv. 10-14, 23) and the legal material (vv. 15-22), and the precise nature of the crime involved by probing

is an additional resource for interpreting this narrative. Deviant behavior is ordinarily defined, in the social science literature, as whatever 'thought, feeling, or action that members of a social group judge to be a violation of their values or rules'.[81] However, this caveat must be noted: deviance is a relative concept; what is considered to be deviant is dependent on the perceptions (values, rules) of the labeling group.[82] Since the son in this narrative is brought before Moses, the pre-eminent mediator between Yahweh and the people, and then imprisoned pending the divine judgment, the behavior described in vv. 10-11 is understood by the storyteller (or his group) as deviant, socially out of place.[83] It is the values and world-structures of this group that are threatened by the blasphemous outburst in the camp.[84]

In Lev. 24.14, 23, the primary subject of the narrative, the son of the Israelite woman and Egyptian man, is plainly labeled a 'blasphemer' (המקלל). Malina and Neyrey note that 'names are social labels by means of which the reader/hearer comes to evaluate and categorize the persons presented in the story both negatively and positively'.[85] These interpreters go on to indicate that 'in the mouths of influential persons, [labels] can inflict genuine injury when they succeed in defining a person as radically out of social place'.[86] There is no more influential character in this text for

---

deeply into the meanings of נקב and קלל. On the basis of the latter Hebrew word (meaning 'to diminish, dishonor'), this text may also be profitably interpreted using the anthropological model of honor/shame (see the list of honor/shame vocabulary in Olyan, 'Honor, Shame, and Covenant Relations', pp. 203-204).

81. Jack D. Douglas and Frances Chaput Waksler, *The Sociology of Deviance: An Introduction* (Boston: Little, Brown & Co., 1982), p. 10. A more recent introduction to and the development of labeling theory can be found in Ronald L. Akers, *Criminological Theories: Introduction and Evaluation* (Los Angeles: Roxbury, 2nd edn, 1997), pp. 99-113. See Bruce J. Malina and Jerome H. Neyrey, 'Conflict in Luke–Acts: Labeling and Deviance Theory', in Neyrey (ed.), *The Social World of Luke–Acts*, pp. 97-122 (100), for an application of the theory in biblical studies.

82. Douglas and Waksler, *The Sociology of Deviance*, p. 15; Akers, *Criminological Theories*, pp. 99-100; see also Carney, *The Shape of the Past*, p. 3.

83. Insofar as 'the Name' is central to the crime committed, it is plausible to characterize the narrator's group as sympathetic to the Deuteronomic/Deuteronomistic program.

84. Cf. Exod. 22.27 (ET v. 28). For blasphemy as deviant behavior, see Table 2 in the Appendices to Bruce J. Malina and Jerome H. Neyrey, *Calling Jesus Names: The Social Values of Labels in Matthew* (Sonoma: Poleridge, 1988), pp. 152-54. Particular texts in Matthew which refer to Jesus as a blasphemer are Mt. 9.3 and 26.65.

85. Malina and Neyrey, 'Conflict in Luke–Acts', p. 99.

86. Malina and Neyrey, 'Conflict in Luke–Acts', p. 99.

Israel than the deity, and it is Yahweh who speaks first, in the imperative
mood, to label the son a deviant: 'Bring out the blasphemer outside the
camp' (24.14; cf. v. 13). Without question, the audience is expected to
give ready assent to this negative label, thereby implicitly aligning themselves with the interests of the narrator and his group.

The deviant label also is a statement about the person's social status. It
is possible to interpret the son's lineage (he is the product of an ethnically
and religiously mixed marriage) as an indicator of his 'ascribed deviant
status' (status over which he has no control). That his father is from among
one of the groups with which Israelites are prohibited from intermarrying
(cf. Ezra 9.1) functions to diminish the son's standing within the Israelite
community (note the repeated references to the whole of the Israelite community in Lev. 24.10-23). It is more certainly the case that the deviant
status of the son in the text is dependent on his having said what he ought
not to have said ('acquired deviant status', 24.11).[87]

A final part of this social-science analysis to consider is the phenomenon known as 'retrospective interpretation'.[88] Malina and Neyrey discuss
retrospective interpretation as an understanding of a person's entire life in
light of the deviant label which the person has received:

> When a person is successfully declared a deviant, people who knew the per-
> son begin to see connections between the deviant condemnation and all that
> they knew about that deviant's past life, often from infancy... Retrospective
> interpretation often takes place by subjecting alleged deviants to biographi-
> cal scrutiny and character reconstruction. Analysis begins with the present
> and looks back for information to clarify the present: some unrecognized
> character defect present in a person's biography, some events symbolic of a
> character consistent with the current deviant episode... Retrospective inter-
> pretation then seeks new facts or the interpretation of old ones in an effort to
> establish consistency between the actor's current deviant behavior and char-
> acter in order to explain the discreditable conduct and legitimize the label.[89]

One of the primary goals of retrospective interpretation is to provide evidence in support of the deviant label given the person, with the result that
the person becomes recognized by the community as an 'outsider'. This
reality is represented in Leviticus 24 by the references to that area 'outside
the camp' (24.10, 14, 23). This, I suggest, is the essence of the addition of
the remark detailing the lineage of the blasphemer's mother (24.11b). An

87. Malina and Neyrey, 'Conflict in Luke–Acts', p. 101.
88. Malina and Neyrey, 'Conflict in Luke–Acts', p. 105.
89. Malina and Neyrey, 'Conflict in Luke–Acts', p. 105.

editor late in the postexilic period added this note in light of the legacy of the Deuteronomistic criticism of the sanctuary erected by Jeroboam I at the city of Dan in the last quarter of the tenth century BCE (see 1 Kgs 12 and the final form of Judg. 17–18). The slogan of Jeroboam, 'Here is/are your god(s), O Israel, who brought you up from the land of Egypt' (1 Kgs 12.28), referring to the golden calves at Bethel and Dan, may be construed as a blasphemous exclamation. The effect of this editor's addition to the narrative in Leviticus 24 (probably made under the influence of 1 Kgs 12) is to link it with another case of blasphemy also associated with mention of Dan.

In the final analysis, the historical reliability of the event reported in Lev. 24.10-23 remains in doubt. The degree of probability that an actual historical occurrence is preserved in these verses is low. There is, to the contrary, significant reason to understand this narrative as an originally postexilic text, to which the reference to Dan was inserted at a still later time. Canonically speaking, Leviticus 24 is the first negative evaluation of Dan in the Hebrew Bible. However, this conclusion must recognize that the material in this chapter is of a later date than other occurrences of Dan elsewhere in the Hebrew Bible (i.e. the DH). While there is little in this text one can confidently use in the reconstruction of the history of the tribe of Dan, this text nevertheless is significant for understanding the legacy of Dan in the Hebrew Bible influenced by the Deuteronomistic movement/ theology in which Dan is evaluated in a wholly negative way.

4. *The Book of Numbers*

In the Pentateuch, the word 'Dan' occurs most frequently in the book of Numbers, either as a reference to the tribe by that name, or to an individual leader of the tribe of Dan. Every mention of Dan appears in material associated with the Priestly tradition, material which tends to take the form of lists. Numbers 1 refers both to the tribe of Dan and to a certain leader, Ahiezer son a Ammishaddai (1.12). This same Danite leader appears in chs. 7 and 10. Other individual Danites named in the book of Numbers include the leader/scout Ammiel son of Gemalli (13.12), Shuham (26.42), and Buqqi son of Yogli (34.22).

a. *Numbers 1*
Numbers 1 contains two distinct lists in which mention of Dan occurs. Verses 5-15 are a list of tribal representatives designated to assist Moses

and Aaron in conducting a census of 'the whole congregation of the sons of Israel'; included in this roster is the Danite, Ahiezer son of Ammishaddai. The purpose of the census is military conscription, and thus the Levites (whose responsibilities are cultic rather than military) are excluded.[90] A few observations about the list of tribal leaders in 1.5-15 are in order.[91] First, all the Leah tribes are listed at the top of the list, in an order corresponding to not only the other Priestly lists of the sons of Jacob (Gen. 35; 46; Exod. 1) but also to the J(E) tradition in Genesis 29–30. Next in order are listed the Rachel tribes: Ephraim and Manasseh (from Joseph), and Benjamin (cf. Gen. 35; 46). Finally, there is an *inclusio* arrangement of the maidservant tribes: Dan (Bilhah [Rachel's maidservant]), Asher and Gad (Zilpah [Leah's maidservant]), and Naphtali (Bilhah [Rachel's maidservant]).[92]

There is no scholarly consensus on the probable age of this list of tribal leaders. On the one hand, some interpreters suggest that the absence of Yahwistic names, in conjunction with those formed with El or Shaddai elements, indicates an early date.[93] On the other hand, others regard the list of names as more ambiguous, pointing to either an earlier or a later date.[94] While the evidence is inconclusive, the arguments in favor of a later date (exilic/postexilic) appear preferable. The representative of the tribe of Dan is Ahiezer son of Ammishaddai (1.12; see also 2.25; 7.66, 71; 10.25).[95] He only appears in lists of other tribal leaders, and nothing more than his name is specifically reported about him.

Numbers 1.20-46 is a census of Israelites, 'from the age of twenty years up, all those in Israel who are able to bear arms' (NJPS), listed by tribe. The order of the tribes in this list corresponds with the list of tribal leaders in 1.5-15, with the exception of the location of Gad. In 1.5-15, Gad appears near the end of the list, among the other maidservant tribes. In 1.20-46,

90. Jacob Milgrom, *The JPS Torah Commentary: Numbers, The Traditional Hebrew Text with the New JPS Translation* (Philadelphia: Jewish Publication Society of America, 5750/1990), p. 336.

91. Notice that Martin Noth proposes that the list of names has been secondarily inserted into the narrative (*Numbers: A Commentary* [London: SCM Press, 1968], p. 18); see also Eryl W. Davies, *Numbers* (NCB; Grand Rapids: Eerdmans, 1995), p. 5.

92. Note the similar *inclusio* in Gen. 49.16-21 (although the Zilpah tribes [Asher and Gad] appear in reverse order).

93. Noth, *Numbers*, pp. 18-19; Milgrom, *Numbers*, p. 6.

94. E.g. Davies, *Numbers*, pp. 12-14.

95. A Benjaminite kinsman of Saul of the same name (Ahiezer, with the 'son of Ammishaddai') appears in 1 Chron. 12.3.

however, Gad appears higher in the list, between Simeon and Judah, thus interrupting the list of Leah tribes. There is no satisfactory explanation for this change in position for the tribe of Gad.[96] Dan is still located near the end of the list of tribes, along with Asher and Naphtali, and is reported to have 62,700 males over the age of 20 years, making it one of the largest tribes coming out of Egypt (1.38-39).[97]

The chief issue pertaining to the census in Num. 1.20-46 is the totals given for each tribe and the total population of Israel in the wilderness period these totals require. According to 1.46, all who were numbered in this census of only a portion of the Israelite community totaled 603,550. On the basis of this figure, the total Israelite population has been estimated to have been in excess of two million.[98] This assumes, of course, that one understands the figures to be taken literally. Scholars, rightly troubled by the possibility that over two million Israelites would have survived in the inhospitable Sinai wilderness for some 40 years, have sought other interpretations of these numbers.[99] The present writer is convinced that the

96. See, however, Milgrom (*Numbers*, p. 8), who suggests both geography and the influence of Num. 2 as possible reasons for the order of tribes in 1.20-46.

97. Only the tribe of Judah is larger, with a total of 74,600 men of fighting age (1.26-27). Whether this reflects the actual historical situation cannot be determined. It may be the case that the tribe of Judah was regarded by the Priestly Writer as the pre-eminent tribe, and thus is accorded the highest number. It is interesting to observe that the tribes from which the two named artisans in the Priestly tabernacle material in Exod. 31–40 (Bezalel and Oholiab) originate are the two largest tribes according to Num. 1: Judah and Dan. Further, the pre-eminent artisan, Bezalel, comes from Judah (the larger tribe), while the subordinate craftsman, Oholiab, comes from the tribe second in size, namely, Dan. Contrast this Priestly depiction of Dan in Exodus and Numbers with the Deuteronomistic portrayal of Dan (and Judah) in, e.g., Judg. 1 (see Chapter 3, below). It is tempting to consider the possibility that the Priestly Writer, at work in the exilic period, focused attention on the tribes of Judah and Dan in his stories of the wilderness period as a way to portray 'all Israel' in the nation's life during and after exile.

98. Milgrom, *Numbers*, pp. 338-39; Norman K. Gottwald, *The Tribes of Yahweh: A Sociology of the Religion of Liberated Israel, 1250–1050 B.C.E.* (Maryknoll, NY: Orbis Books, 1979), p. 51; cf. Exod. 12.37.

99. See Eryl W. Davies' article, 'A Mathematical Conundrum: The Problem of the Large Numbers in Numbers I and XXVI', *VT* 45 (1995), pp. 449-69, for a helpful summary and critique of these scholarly proposals. The proposal that has, perhaps, been most widely accepted is that which originated with Sir W.M. Flinders Petrie (*Egypt and Israel* [London: SPCK, 1911], pp. 42-46) but which has received renewed interest in the work of George E. Mendenhall ('The Census Lists of Numbers 1 and

603,550 census figure (and the more than two million total population figure extrapolated from this number) is not historically reliable. However, I am persuaded that these totals are to be understood literally; that is, the Priestly Writer meant what he wrote. So, for example, when the Priestly Writer gives the total 62,700 for the Danites 20 years of age and older, the reader is to take this literally, and not suppose that a significantly lesser number of military units is intended (contra Mendenhall). While the extremely large population number strikes the reader as not historically accurate, similar exaggerations occur elsewhere in the Hebrew Bible and in the ancient Near East.[100] Eryl Davies notes not only the rhetorical but also the theological significance of such large numbers in Numbers 1 and 26:

> The aim of the Priestly writer was almost certainly to demonstrate the miraculous power of Yahweh who was able to sustain such a large throng during the trials and tribulations of the wilderness wanderings. But his purpose was also to emphasize the fact that the promise of abundant progeny made by Yahweh to the patriarchs (Gen. xxii 1-3, etc.) was already in the process of being fulfilled during the period of Israel's desert sojourn.[101]

Significantly, the tribe of Dan is second only to Judah in size coming out of Egypt.

b. *Numbers 2*
Numbers 2 depicts the Israelite tribes encamped in the wilderness of Sinai, in a square-shaped (or rectangular?) arrangement around the Tent of

26', *JBL* 77 [1958], pp. 52-66) is that אֶלֶף in this text means not 'thousand', but 'family' or 'tent group' (Petrie), or 'subsection of a tribe/contingent of troops under its own leader' (Mendenhall).

100. E.g., the relatively small number of Israelite warriors compared to the superior force of Israel's enemy (Josh. 23.10; Judg. 1.4; 3.29). On the other hand, there are other biblical texts which most likely exaggerate the large number of Israelites troops: Judg. 20.1-2; 1 Sam. 15.4; 2 Chron. 13.3; 14.8; 17.14-18 (see recently Ralph W. Klein, 'Reflections on Historiography in the Account of Jehoshaphat', in David P. Wright, David Noel Freedman and Avi Hurvitz [eds.], *Pomegranates and Golden Bells: Studies in Biblical, Jewish, and Near Eastern Ritual, Law, and Literature in Honor of Jacob Milgrom* [Winona Lake, IN: Eisenbrauns, 1995], pp. 643-57 [646]; *idem*, 'How Many in a Thousand?', in M. Patrick Graham, Kenneth G. Hoglund and Steven L. McKenzie [eds.], *The Chronicler as Historian* [JSOTSup, 238; Sheffield: Sheffield Academic Press, 1997], pp. 270-82). In other ancient Near Eastern texts, one notes, for example, the exaggerated reigns of Sumerian kings (see *ANET*, pp. 265-66).

101. Davies, 'A Mathematical Conundrum', p. 468.

Meeting.[102] The order of the tribes in the second half of the list corresponds with the list of tribes in 1.20-46 (including the relocation of Gad to a position in the upper portion of the list). However, there is a slight reorganization of the first half of the list (2.1-16; cf. 1.20-30). The triad, Judah–Issachar–Zebulun (in 1.20-46, these are tribes four, five, six), has been moved to the top of the list, ahead of the triad Reuben–Simeon–Gad. Two observations: first, with this shift all of the Leah tribes are listed in primary position (Gad no longer interrupts the Leah group; cf. 1.20-30). It may be significant that Gad, here located immediately after the Leah tribes, was the first son of Zilpah, the maidservant of Jacob's first wife, Leah. Thus, Gad here occupies a position of prominence.[103] Second, the change in order between 1.20-46 and ch. 2 serves to locate Judah at the top of the list. While not the firstborn son of Jacob, the tribe descended from Judah rose to prominence in the time of the United Monarchy in Israel, and the name continued on as the name of the pre-eminent kingdom after the division. This order no doubt reflects the interests of the Priestly Writer.

Four division leaders are designated in Numbers 2, one at each point of the compass. It is possible to offer probable explanations for why certain tribes appear more prominently than other tribes. Moving clockwise from the east around to the north side of the camp, one moves in order of descending importance.[104] On the east side of the Tent of Meeting is the tribe of Judah. In Num. 3.38-39, the reader learns that at this same side are Moses, Aaron and his sons (the priests). The entrance to the Tent of Meeting is also found on the east side (3.38; cf. Ezek. 47.1). In this way the Priestly Writer has brought together the priests, the tribe of Judah, and the preferred side of the camp. This is the most important part of the Israelite camp in the wilderness. Continuing on in a clockwise direction, on the south side is the tribe of Reuben, recalling that the eponymous ancestor of the Reubenites was Jacob's firstborn (Gen. 29.31-32). Ephraim,

102. See Milgrom (*Numbers*, pp. 340-41), who suggests a late second-millennium Egyptian parallel to this rectangular (as opposed to the circular) formation of the war camp.

103. The arrangement of the tribes in the Priestly lists is inconsistent. On the one hand, in the P list in Gen. 46.8-27, the order of tribes is: Leah, Zilpah, Rachel, Bilhah. On the other hand, in the P lists of Gen. 35 and Exod. 1, the order is chiastic: Leah, Rachel, Bilhah, Zilpah. Thus, the order in Num. 2 most likely serves a particular purpose.

104. Davies, *Numbers*, pp. 20-23; Baruch A. Levine, *Numbers 1–20: A New Translation with Introduction and Commentary* (AB, 4; New York: Doubleday, 1993), pp. 142-44; Milgrom, *Numbers*, pp. 340-41.

descended from Joseph, the firstborn son of Rachel, Jacob's favorite wife, is the division leader on the west side of the Tent of Meeting. Although the younger of two brothers, Ephraim apparently ascended to a position of superiority over Manasseh, a reality reflected in the Hebrew Bible (Gen. 46.20; 48.12-20). It should also be remembered that Ephraim was one of the names for the Northern Kingdom (Israel). Finally, the tribe of Dan is named as the division leader on the north side of the Tent of Meeting (2.25-31). While Dan occupies the side of least relative importance, this does not seem to reflect negatively on the tribe. That is, Dan's northern location here in Numbers 2 is unrelated to the later establishment of an illicit sanctuary at the city of Dan in the north (1 Kgs 12.25-33; cf. the Midrash). The tribe of Dan's position of relative unimportance in Numbers 2 has to do, rather, with the Priestly Writer's concern for the earlier traditions (Gen. 29–30). Each of the other division leaders had to take precedence over Dan, as previously noted. Dan's prominence in this chapter probably is the result of the tradition (Gen. 30.1-6) according to which this tribe's eponymous ancestor was the son of Rachel's maidservant, Bilhah.[105] It is significant that Dan is mentioned at all in this text, and there can be no question that it is a positive remark.

c. *Numbers 7*

The Danite chieftain, Ahiezer son of Ammishaddai, appears again among the other tribal chiefs in Numbers 7. (The chieftains are identical with those listed in Num. 1.5-15; their order of appearance, however, follows the ordering of the tribes in ch. 2. Thus, the chieftain of the tribe of Judah is the first to make his offering.) Numbers 7 is divided into two unequal parts. In the first part, vv. 1-9, the chiefs collectively bring draught carts and oxen for the service of the Levites (7.5). The latter portion of the chapter, vv. 10-89, is a repetitive list of the dedication offerings presented by each chieftain on successive days.[106] On each of twelve successive days, one tribal leader offers a gift identical to that of his colleagues:

---

105. Rachel was Jacob's favorite wife, but because she was barren Bilhah was given to Jacob in order to 'give birth upon [Rachel's] knees'. Ultimately, it is Rachel who names the child, Dan. In the birth stories in Gen. 29–30, it is the mother who names the children as they are born. Since Rachel names the child born of Bilhah, the impression given is that Rachel regards herself as the mother of the child.

106. Milgrom (*Numbers*, p. 54) prefers 'initiation offering'. Regardless of precise meaning, it appears to be used (nominal form) only by P and Chr (see Phillip J. Budd, *Numbers* [WBC, 5; Waco, TX: Word Books, 1984], p. 83).

one silver bowl weighing 130 shekels and one silver basin of 70 shekels by
the sanctuary weight, both filled with choice flour with oil mixed in, for a
meal offering; one gold ladle of 10 shekels, filled with incense; one bull of
the herd, one ram, and one lamb in its first year, for a burnt offering; one
goat for a sin offering; and for his sacrifice of well-being: two oxen, five
rams, five he-goats, and five yearling lambs. (Num. 7.13-17 [NJPS])[107]

Ahiezer son of Ammishaddai, of the tribe of Dan, made his offering on
the tenth day. It is doubtful that the tenth day holds any special significance in this case, since this is little more than the place of Dan in the
order of the tribes arranged around the Tent of Meeting, at the head of
which is Judah. His gift is identical to that of the other tribal leaders, so
that the stereotypical form of the gift-list does not allow conclusions to be
drawn about the individual wealth or social standing of the respective
tribal leaders. As a Priestly document from a later era, the intent of Numbers 7 may have been to encourage generosity on the part of the people
toward the religious establishment in the postexilic period. The conformity
of the tribal gifts with each other may further suggest equality of standing
among members of the later community.

d. *Numbers 10*

In Numbers 10, the Israelite tribes break camp in the Wilderness of Sinai
and begin their march to the Wilderness of Paran. The order of the tribes
for the march is given in vv. 11-28: the names of the tribal leaders are in
accordance with 1.5-15 (cf. 7.12-83); the order of the tribes, however,
follows the register of divisions given in ch. 2. Thus, the division of Judah
goes first, while the division of Dan (Dan, Asher, Naphtali) goes last and
serves as the 'rear guard' (מאסף). In the midst of the roll-call of tribes by
division, the Tent of Meeting is disassembled (10.17) and the Tent,
together with its related objects, also goes out (10.21). The significance of
the leadership role of the tribe of Dan—at the head of the north division—
has already been discussed (see Num. 2, above). The only item of interest
with regard to the Danites and their fellow tribesmen on the north side of

---

107. Budd (*Numbers*, p. 84) sounds a note of caution to those who would attempt
to reconstruct pre-settlement history on the basis of this gift-list when he writes that
'no attention is given to the historical problem about where in the wilderness such a
wealth of gifts, including those of precious metals, was to be found. The sole objective
was the encouragement of generosity and commitment among the post-exilic laity.'
(See also Davies, *Numbers*, p. 70, for a similar interpretation of the overwhelming
generosity of the *laity* depicted in this text.)

the camp is their service as 'rear-guard'. The Hebrew word, מְאַסֵּף, is a piel participle used as a substantive. According to BDB, this is the only occurrence of this form (meaning 'rear-guard') in the Priestly Writing; the word otherwise occurs with this meaning in Josh. 6.9, 13, and, interestingly, in Isa. 52.12, where it refers to the God of Israel going both before and behind the people.

e. *Numbers 13*

In ch. 13, leaders from each of the tribes are sent to 'scout, seek out' (תור) the land.[108] However, the names of these leaders in vv. 4-15 are not the same as those in Num. 1.5-15. The fact that the names are different in ch. 13, while the leaders are still identified as נשׂיא (cf. 1.16), seems to suggest, on the one hand, that there was a diversified leadership in early Israel. On the other hand, the suggestion has been made that this list of leaders (13.3b-16) has been inserted secondarily into P, and that originally in the P material v. 3b was followed immediately by v. 17.[109] This theory may account for the fact that the order of tribes in Num. 13.4-15 is unusual, corresponding to none of the other tribal registers in the book of Numbers. The list begins with the tribe of Reuben (cf. 1.5-15, 20-46), but then one notices numerous differences. For example, the tribes of Issachar and Zebulun are here separated (13.7-10); they are otherwise always listed together (1.8-9, 28-31; 2.5-7 [10.14-16]; 7.18-24; 26.23-27; 34.25-26). A similar breakup occurs with Ephraim and Manasseh (13.8-11; cf. 1.10, 32-35). This distinctive order led Gray to conclude that 'the text is not only dislocated, but corrupt'.[110] However, given the literary possibility that the list of names is an insertion, and the uniqueness of almost all 24 of the personal names in this group, it is better simply to suppose that this is a list enumerating the tribes in a different order from those otherwise encountered in the book of Numbers. There is insufficient evidence to warrant the

---

108. Milgrom (*Numbers*, p. 100) draws attention to the different vocabulary used by the Priestly Writer and the Deuteronomistic tradition to describe the mission: Num. 13 speaks of 'to scout, seek out', while Deut. 1 uses the verb meaning 'to spy out' (חפר). He concludes: 'but this is not surprising since in its (DH) view, the reconnaissance was initiated by the people, not God (v. 22)'.

109. See Noth, *Numbers*, p. 103; he is followed by Davies, *Numbers*, p. 133; cf. Levine, *Numbers 1–20*, p. 352. See also already George Buchanan Gray, *A Critical and Exegetical Commentary on Numbers* (ICC; New York: Charles Scribners Sons, 1903), p. 135.

110. G.B. Gray, *Numbers*, p. 136.

conclusion that the present text is dependent on Numbers 1 (for example) but has been damaged.

The scholarly consensus on the date of this list of names seems to be that it is a late creation, in which the compiler made use of names that had an archaic ring to them.[111] In his study of the names in Num. 13.4-15, Davies observes that

> of the twenty-four names listed…eleven do not occur elsewhere in the Old Testament; of the remaining thirteen names, some are found in early passages (e.g., Shaphat; cf. 1 Kg. 19.16) while others are confined to late texts (e.g., Zaccur; cf. Neh. 3.2)… It is altogether probable that the list is an artificial construction composed at a relatively late date, and this seems to be confirmed by the occurrence of a Persian name, Vophshi, in v. 14…and by the presence of other names which betray a Persian influence.[112]

Ammiel son of Gemalli is the leader from the tribe of Dan sent to scout the land (13.12). This Danite is ninth in the list of twelve scouts. The name Ammiel, with his father's name, occurs only here in the Hebrew Bible (Gemalli appears nowhere else). Ammiel, by itself, however, occurs in 2 Sam. 9.4-5; 17.27; 1 Chron. 3.5; 26.5. In none of these texts is he identified with the tribe of Dan (in 1 Chron. 26.5 he is identified as the sixth son of Obed-edom and a gatekeeper at the house of Yahweh during the reign of David). There is nothing more known about the Danite leader.

f. *Numbers 26*

Numbers 1 purports to be a census of the Israelite militia taken in the Wilderness of Sinai soon after the exodus from Egypt (1.1). Numbers 26, near the end of the book of Numbers, is a second census (26.2; cf. 1.2), this time taken on the steppes of Moab in Transjordan just before the Israelites's entry into, and settlement of, Canaan. Thus the two censuses form an *inclusio* around the years of Israel's wilderness sojourn. The expressed purpose of this census is to determine the total number of persons in each tribe in preparation for the just apportionment of the land. Each tribe is to be allotted a share in the land according to its relative size: a larger share for larger tribes, a smaller share for smaller tribes (26.52-56). The order of the tribes in ch. 26 is nearly identical to that in 1.20-46, with the only exception being that Ephraim and Manasseh are in reverse order. The census numbers are also similarly exaggerated in both chapters (the

---

111. Noth, *Numbers*, pp. 103-104.
112. Davies, *Numbers*, p. 133.

total figure in ch. 26 is 601,730). The tribe of Dan is once again among the largest in number, second only to Judah in size (26.43; cf. 26.22). The principal difference between the two censuses is that the second census enumerates the able-bodied men in Israel over the age of 20 years by tribal clans, *which are named.*[113]

The registration of the tribe of Dan appears in Num. 26.42-43:

> [42] These are the sons of Dan, by their clans: of Shuham, the clan of the Shuhamites. These are the clans of Dan by their clans. [43] All the clans of the Shuhamites, those numbered: 64,400.[114]

It is frequently pointed out in the commentaries that the Danites's remarkable size is attributed to a single clan, the clan of the Shuhamites.[115] According to Davies,

> Dan is represented as having only one clan, Shuham (Hushim in Gen. 46.23), which perhaps suggests that at one time this tribe was regarded as comparatively small (cf. Jg. 18.2). The incongruously high census figure for this tribe (64,400) confirms the suspicion that the clan list originally existed independently of the census results.[116]

The Priestly Writer is, however, consistent on the question of descendants of Dan, since Gen. 46.23 similarly records a single Danite group under the name Hushim (חֻשִׁים).[117] In addition, when it is to be recognized that the census figures in the book of Numbers are likely artificial—and exaggerated—constructions of the Priestly Writer (see the discussion of the census totals in Num. 1, above), then the remarkably high number reported for the tribe of Dan in particular poses no additional historical or textual difficulty. In addition, the figure for *every* tribe in Numbers 26

---

113. Note, however, that already in Num. 1 the Israelite community is registered 'by their clans, by their ancestral houses' (למשפחתם לבית אבתם; 1.2; cf. 26.12, 15, 20, 23, 26, 28, 35, 37-38, 42, 44, 48, 50).

114. The repetition in these verses has led the editor of the book of Numbers in *BHS* to propose that 'by their clans. All the clans of the Shuhamites' has been added. This is, however, without any support in the versions.

115. Noth, *Numbers*, p. 208; Davies, *Numbers*, pp. 291-95; Timothy R. Ashley, *The Book of Numbers* (NICOT; Grand Rapids: Eerdmans, 1993), pp. 537-38.

116. Davies, *Numbers*, p. 295.

117. A comparison of these two proper names, שׁוּחָם and חֻשִׁים, leads one to recognize the possibility that they refer to the same familial group, and that the first two consonants have simply been transposed in the transmission of the text (the yod in the latter name may easily have been lost independently). The LXX has Σαμι in Num. 26.42, while Ασομ appears in Gen. 46.23 (metathesis similar to that in the MT).

appears equally remarkable when one considers the relative size of the clan in an agrarian society.[118] Instead, the large census figures in this chapter have the rhetorical effect of highlighting the Priestly Writer's belief in the extraordinary power of Yahweh to sustain the Israelite throng over the course of their years of wandering in the harsh wilderness, in addition to his perception that in the remarkable Israelite population the promise of Yahweh to the ancestors of abundant offspring was already in the process of fulfillment.[119]

g. *Numbers 34*

In Numbers 34 there is a list of tribal chieftains who are designated to assist Eleazar the priest, and Joshua son of Nun, in the apportionment of the land (34.17). Literarily, this list corresponds with the tribal leaders named in 1.5-15 as assistants to Moses and Aaron. Similar correspondences can be noted elsewhere in the book of Numbers. In many ways the census list in ch. 26 corresponds to the census list in 1.20-46. In addition, the list of tribal chieftains in 4.16-29, through whom the land of Canaan would be apportioned, compares with the leaders named in 1.5-15.[120] It is possible that both lists of tribal leaders (1.5-15; 34.16-29) are secondary insertions into the narrative. They could easily be removed without significantly damaging the storyline.[121] The tribal leaders here named are those who will lead the new generation of Israelites, which is permitted to enter and take possession of the land (see Yahweh's judgment on the exodus generation in 14.26-35).[122]

The ordering of the tribes anticipates their eventual settlement in the land of Canaan, moving roughly from south to north. Numbers 34.1-12 looks forward to this geographical scheme by tracing the boundaries of the

---

118. The clan is larger than the ancestral house, but smaller than the tribe. An ancestral house might vary in size between about 50 and 100 persons; see Gottwald, *The Tribes of Yahweh*, p. 285; cf. S. Bendor, *The Social Structure of Ancient Israel: The Institution of the Family (Beit 'Ab) from the Settlement to the End of the Monarchy* (Jerusalem Biblical Studies, 7; Jerusalem: Simor, 1996), p. 53.

119. Davies, *Numbers*, p. 468.

120. Except that in ch. 34 only the ten Cisjordanian tribes are represented; see ch. 32 and 34.13-15 regarding the Transjordanian tribes.

121. Noth, *Numbers*, p. 18; Davies, *Numbers*, p. 5.

122. The careful reader will notice that the first three individuals (representing Judah, Simeon, and Benjamin) are not designated נשיא. The LXX confirms the MT. The present writer concurs with Milgrom's conclusion that there is no satisfactory explanation for this apparent oversight (*Numbers*, p. 288).

land Israel is to inherit. Judah, however, because of its prominence in Israelite history, is listed in first position, ahead of Simeon which was, in reality, the southernmost tribe.[123] The tribe of Dan is depicted in its southern location, in the vicinity of Judah and Benjamin (cf. Josh. 19.40-48; Judg. 18.1-2). It may simply be the case that the Priestly Writer was well aware of the tradition of a Danite holding in the southern part of the land. It may also be possible that even after the so-called 'migration of Dan' (Judg. 18) a significant Danite population remained in the south.

There seems to be a scholarly consensus that the list of the names of these tribal leaders is late, although some of them give the impression of being very old.[124] The name of the Danite chieftain is Buqqi son of Yogli (Num. 34.22). This full name does not otherwise occur in the Hebrew Bible. The name Buqqi, however, occurs in 1 Chron. 5.31, 6.36 (ET 6.5, 51), and Ezra 7.4; in these texts, Buqqi is listed as the son of Abishua in the Priestly line going back to Aaron. It is beyond doubt that these are two different individuals.

5. *The Book of Deuteronomy*

References to Dan occur in the book of Deuteronomy in the proclamation of blessings and curses in ch. 27, in the Blessing of Moses in ch. 33, and in the survey of the land given by Yahweh to Moses immediately prior to Moses's death (ch. 34). While the first two occurrences refer ostensibly to the tribe of Dan, the characterization of the Danites in 33.22 is probably dependent on the leading role of the city of Laish/Dan centuries after the Israelite settlement. In ch. 34, the reference is indisputably to the city at the northern boundary of the land promised to Israel.

a. *Deuteronomy 27*
In Deuteronomy 27, Moses and the elders of Israel instruct the people concerning what they are to do 'as soon as [they] have crossed over the Jordan into the land that Yahweh [their] God is giving to [them]' (27.1-2). Among the ritual activities in which the people are to participate is the proclamation of blessings and curses; for this event the Israelite tribes are to divide themselves between the mountains that flank the city of Shechem. The following tribes are to assemble atop Mt Gerizim (south of Shechem)

123. Simeon was eventually absorbed into the territory of Judah; see Josh. 19.1.
124. Noth, *Numbers*, p. 251; Budd, *Numbers*, pp. 365-66.

for the proclamation of the blessings: Simeon, Levi, Judah, Issachar, Joseph, and Benjamin. The tribes of Reuben, Gad, Asher, Zebulun, Dan, and Naphtali speak the curses from the summit of Mt Ebal (north of Shechem).

Generally speaking, it is possible that the division of the tribes is related to geography.[125] On the one hand, the tribes associated with Mt Gerizim and blessing are southern tribes (Issachar stands out, however, as a northern tribe). On the other hand, the tribes related to northern Mt Ebal and the curses are northern tribes (the exception is Reuben in Transjordan, which is latitudinally equivalent to Judah in Cisjordan). Another possibility is that Dtr has utilized the birth narratives of the sons of Jacob preserved in the older epic tradition (chs. 29–30; 35).[126] Accordingly, the tribes assembled on Mt Gerizim for the proclamation of the blessings are those descended from the sons born to Jacob's wives, Leah (Simeon, Levi, Judah, Issachar) and Rachel (Joseph, Benjamin).[127] Atop Mt Ebal and responsible for the proclamation of the curses are the tribes whose eponymous ancestors were born to the *maidservants* of Jacob's wives, Zilpah (Gad and Asher) and Bilhah (Dan and Naphtali), *and* the tribes of Reuben and Zebulun (tribes descended from sons born to Jacob's first wife, Leah). Perhaps these latter two tribes have been separated from the other Leah tribes for the following reasons: Reuben, although he was the firstborn son of Jacob, lost favor and position because of his inappropriate relationship with Bilhah (35.22); and Zebulun was Jacob's last-born son (30.19-20). It is also possible that Dtr simply wanted to balance the number of tribes atop Mt Gerizim and Mt Ebal, and the (perhaps arbitrary) relocation of these last named tribes allowed him to accomplish his goal.

Beyond noting the distinction that seems to have made between tribes descended from the sons of Jacob's wives and those descended from the sons of their maidservants, there is little to assert about the occurrence of Dan in this text. The Danites's association with Mt Ebal and the curse is almost certainly due to their eponymous ancestor's birth to a maidservant

125. Jeffrey H. Tigay, *The JPS Torah Commentary: Deuteronomy, The Traditional Hebrew Text with the New JPS Translation* (Philadelphia: Jewish Publication Society of America, 5756/1996), pp. 252-53.

126. See, e.g., Samuel Rolles Driver, *A Critical and Exegetical Commentary on Deuteronomy* (ICC; New York: Charles Scribner's Sons, 1895), p. 298; A.D.H. Mayes, *Deuteronomy* (NCB; Grand Rapids: Eerdmans, 1979), p. 344.

127. The arrangement follows the birth-order of the sons of Jacob (see Gen. 29.31-35; 30.14-18).

rather than to a full wife of Jacob.[128] One may only speculate that Dtr exploited this distinction (between birth mothers) in light of the city of Dan's association with the sins of Jeroboam, and thereby intended to imply a negative judgment on the tribe in this text. There is no explicit judgment rendered on any of the tribes in ch. 27.

b. *Deuteronomy 33*

According to Deut. 33.1, what follows is the 'blessing with which Moses, the man of God, blessed the sons of Israel before his death'. A preliminary question is, however, whether this collection of sayings antedates the time of Moses and was placed in his mouth at a later time, or whether it originated in a period subsequent to the so-called biblical 'conquest' tradition. While some of the sayings appear to have in mind the eponymous ancestors of the tribes of Israel (for example, regarding Asher in v. 24), most of the sayings can reasonably be interpreted as referring to the situations of the tribes themselves after their settlement in the land. In addition, the reference to Moses in the third person in 33.1, together with a similar reference in v. 4, indicates that this Blessing probably did not originate with Moses, but has been secondarily attributed to this 'man of God'.[129] Thus, the collection of sayings almost certainly comes from a time after the Mosaic period.

The saying concerning Dan in 33.22 is customarily translated:

ולדן אמר דן גור אריה יזנק מן־הבשן:

> And about Dan he said:
> Dan is a whelp of a lion/young lion;
> (And) he shall leap/who leaps forth from Bashan.

[Notes on the MT:

For גור, the Samaritan Pentateuch reads גר; compare the Targum.

Instead of simply יזנק, the Samaritan Pentateuch reads ויזנק (with the addition of the waw consecutive). There is a narrative quality to the variant reading, which seems to point to a completed, past event—namely, Dan's attack on the city of Laish.

The editor of the book of Deuteronomy in *BHS* (J. Hempel) suggests possibly reading מבשן (where the word following the prefix preposition, [ן]מן, בש is equivalent to Ugaritic *btn*, 'serpent/snake'). See Cross and Freedman, *Studies in Ancient Yahwistic*

---

128. According to the interpretation of the birth of Dan in Gen. 30.1-6 offered in the present study, Dan is there evaluated positively in the epic (E) tradition.

129. Tigay, *Deuteronomy*, p. 523; Mayes (*Deuteronomy*, p. 396) suggests that the framework of Deut. 33 (vv. 2-5, 26-29) possibly existed as a single unit, originally independent of the tribal sayings now incorporated into it.

Poetry, pp. 29, 74; followed by Peter C. Craigie, *The Book of Deuteronomy* (NICOT; Grand Rapids: Eerdmans, 1976), p. 401; Mayes, *Deuteronomy*, p. 409.]

This saying is always (and correctly) interpreted as referring to the character of the tribe of Dan rather than the ancestor. Of course, in the biblical tradition the tribe of Dan appears in two geographical locations: a southern location (Josh. 19.40-48; Judg. 13.1, 25; 18.1-2) and a northern location (Judg. 18.27-31). To which location does Deut. 33.22 point? Traditionally, it is understood that the northern situation is intended.[130] The text seems sufficiently straightforward: the tribe of Dan is here compared, metaphorically, to a young lion (cf. Judah in Gen. 49.9), and either the lion and/or the tribe leaps forth from the region of Bashan in Transjordan.[131] This is the preferred interpretation. Nevertheless, several questions have been raised about this passage which call for a brief response. These issues arise chiefly from the Hebrew text; nearly every word *could* be translated differently, providing a very different meaning.

For example, the phrase 'a lion's whelp/young lion' may, on the basis of Ugaritic, be rendered something like 'client-kinsman' (*gr 'ary*).[132] The words 'young/whelp' (גּוּר) and 'client' (גֵּר) are derived from the same triliteral root, גור. It is noteworthy that elsewhere in the biblical tradition about Dan the members of the tribe are depicted as clients of superior patrons (see Judg. 5.17). Against this proposal is the reality that this same phrase, 'a lion's whelp/young lion', occurs of Judah in Gen. 49.9, and that context makes it clear that the lion-like metaphor is correct.[133] Thus, it

130. Driver, *Deuteronomy*, p. 412.

131. Some scholars, in light of the Bible's silence regarding Danites in Bashan, prefer to limit the 'leaping forth' portion of the saying to the lion metaphor. That is, they do not understand it as a reflection of the history of the tribe of Dan (see, e.g., Driver, *Deuteronomy*, p. 412; Tigay, *Deuteronomy*, p. 332). It is assumed that at one time lions were numerous in the region of Bashan, although they have completely disappeared from the Middle East. No evidence of lions has yet appeared in the faunal remains uncovered at Tell Dan (see Paula Wapnish, Brian Hesse and Anne Ogilvy, 'The 1974 Collection of Faunal Remains from Tell Dan', *BASOR* 227 [1977], pp. 35-62). The fact that sheep, goats, cattle, deer, dogs, and a few (wild) pigs are attested at the site, but no lions, may simply be because these were either domesticated or sacrificial animals (or both), while lions remained unrestrainable wild animals.

132. *UT*, pp. 366, 379. See also the Samaritan Pentateuch.

133. Gen. 49 is ordinarily granted chronological priority over Deut. 33 (Skinner, *Genesis*, pp. 509-10; Speiser, *Genesis*, p. 371; Westermann, *Genesis 37–50*, p. 221; cf. William Foxwell Albright, *Yahweh and the Gods of Canaan: A Historical Analysis of Two Contrasting Faiths* [Winona Lake, IN: Eisenbrauns, 1990 (1968)], pp. 13-20).

should probably here be translated in the same way: Dan is a young lion/lion's whelp.

Second, it could be argued that the meaning of the word here translated 'leaps forth' is not certain, since this is a *hapax legomenon* in the Hebrew Bible. Perhaps something very different was intended originally by the Hebrew poet, but has since been lost. However, while the root זנק does not otherwise occur in the Hebrew Bible, the word is known from post-biblical Hebrew, Arabic, and Syriac sources (the root is so far unattested in the Ugaritic texts), where it has a similar meaning.[134] In addition, the LXX translator rendered יזנק as ἐκπηδήσεται (from ἐκπηδάω, 'rush or leap out; start up, get up quickly').[135] The usual translation is acceptable.

The last phrase in the Hebrew text of v. 22, מן־הבשן, has generated more interest, particularly since the discovery of the Ugaritic texts from Ras Shamra. Basing their work on a suggestion of their teacher, W.F. Albright, Frank Moore Cross, Jr, and David Noel Freedman read מִבָּשָׁן instead of the MT for both metrical and orthographic reasons.[136] Following Albright, these scholars translated בָּשָׁן not as the place name, Bashan, but as 'serpent, viper', as in Ugaritic.[137] This alternate reading eliminates any reference to the region of Bashan in the north, east of the Jordan River and north of the Yarmuk River. The significance of this understanding of the text is that is dissociates the tribe of Dan from its northern location. Although this reading, based on the Ugaritic evidence, has received favorable response from several scholars, the more traditional reading and interpretation of this phrase as the end of Deut. 33.22 is to be preferred for the following reasons. First of all, the usual reading ('from Bashan') is the plain meaning of the MT. The phrase מִן־הַבָּשָׁן occurs nowhere else in the Hebrew Bible. However, wherever the word בָּשָׁן occurs, the meaning is 'Bashan', referring to the geographical locale in Transjordan (*passim*).

134. HALOT, p. 276.

135. BAGD, p. 243.

136. Cross and Freedman, *Studies in Ancient Yahwistic Poetry*, p. 119. Omitting the definite article before 'viper' (for metrical and orthographic reasons) they translate the text: 'Dan is a lion's whelp who shies away from a viper'.

137. Ugaritic *bṯn* can be translated as 'serpent' (see *UT*, p. 378). This proposal is adopted more recently by Craigie, *The Book of Deuteronomy*, p. 401; and Mayes, *Deuteronomy*, p. 409. Cross and Freedman (*Studies in Ancient Yahwistic Poetry*, p. 119) suggest that the same word occurs in Ps. 68.23 with this meaning. In this, they are followed by Mitchell J. Dahood (*Psalms*. II. *51–100: Introduction, Commentary, and Notes* [AB, 17; Garden City, NY Doubleday, 2nd edn, 1973], p. 145).

Second, those commentators who prefer 'serpent' point out that in Gen. 49.17 Dan is compared with a 'serpent/horned snake'.[138] However, such a reading essentially pits the two depictions of Dan against each other. According to Genesis 49 Dan *is* (at least metaphorically) a serpent/horned snake, while in the alternate reading of Deut. 33.22, Dan is portrayed as if fleeing *from* such a dangerous creature! It is difficult to imagine that such divergent sayings have the same tribe in mind.

The northern location of Dan, in the vicinity of Bashan, is frequently defended on the basis of the order of the tribes in the Blessing of Moses. The order of the tribes given in Deuteronomy 33 is unique in the Hebrew Bible.[139] It is often supposed that the tribes are arranged geographically, following, roughly, a south to north orientation.[140] While this is possible, it is not certain. The evidence is inconclusive. Simeon, the southernmost tribe, is omitted altogether. The list of tribes begins in Transjordan with Reuben, Jacob's firstborn, followed by Judah.[141] Next is Levi, a tribe to whom no territory is allotted (Josh. 14.3-4), then Benjamin and Joseph (Ephraim and Manasseh). The northward progression continues with Zebulun, but then the movement turns southeast to Issachar, and then still further southeast (into Transjordan) to Gad. Dan comes next (presumably the tribal territory of Dan in the north was centered around the city of Laish/Dan), then a westward movement covers Naphtali and Asher, in order.

Although the south to north arrangement is imperfect, the plain mention of Bashan in the saying about Dan leads me to conclude that in the mind of the final redactor of the Blessing of Moses, Dan is located in the north of the land. This corresponds to a particular part of the biblical tradition about the tribe of Dan, namely, the migration narrative in Judges 18. It is likely that the present remark about Dan, while appearing canonically prior to Judges 18, is, in fact, dependent on the later narrative. It is argued below that the final form of Judges 17–18, including the (earlier) narrative about

138. The vocabulary is different (see the discussion of Gen. 49.16-17, above).

139. In terms of matriarchal origin, the order is: Leah (3)–Rachel (2)–Leah (2)–Bilhah–Zilpah (2)–Bilhah. There is an envelope structure in both the lists of sons of wives and maidservants, although for the wives it is Leah–Rachel–Leah, while for the maidservants it is Rachel–Leah–Rachel.

140. Most recently Tigay, *Deuteronomy*, p. 332.

141. A supposed 'southern priority' is questioned by the limited remarks about Judah, the pre-eminent tribe, compared to the lengthy sayings about Joseph/Manasseh–Ephraim = Israel, one of the names of the Northern Kingdom.

the so-called migration of Dan, may come from after the time of Jeroboam I; thus, a date probably in the ninth century or later is in order for Deut. 33.22.[142] It is occasionally assumed, due to the connection between Dan and Bashan in this text, that the migrating Danites used the region of Bashan as a staging ground from which to attack the city of Laish (Judg. 18).[143] It must be stated, however, that this assumption of a Transjordanian base of operations for the Danite incursion is uncorroborated by the other biblical evidence. No strategy of the sort is preserved in the Hebrew Bible. While the major north–south trade route through Transjordan, known popularly as the 'King's Highway', does pass through Bashan and its capital city, Ashtaroth, the clear impression given in the Judg. 18 narrative is that the Danites's route was confined to Cisjordan.

The appraisal of Dan in this passage is positive. However, there is here, in all likelihood, essentially nothing of significance about either the history or character of the tribe of Dan. Simply put, the early history of the Danites cannot be reconstructed confidently on the basis of this single verse. In addition, the presence of the lion metaphor cautions against historical reconstruction on the basis of such poetic language. The appearance of such a metaphor with both royal and religious associations for Dan, when packaged together with such a brief and enigmatic saying about Judah in Deut. 33.7, suggests a northern, Israelite provenance for the final form of Deuteronomy 33.[144] (The supplication in 33.7, that Judah be restored to his people, may point to a time after the division of the United Monarchy of David and Solomon. This verse may indicate the hope—here articulated from the point of view of the leaders of the Northern Kingdom—of

142. It is possible that some of the sayings in Deuteronomy are significantly earlier than the one about Dan. However, the present collection in Deut. 33 may date to as late as the eighth century BCE (see D.A. Robertson, *Linguistic Evidence in Dating Early Hebrew Poetry* [SBLDS, 3; Missoula, MT: Scholars Press, 1972], pp. 49-55, followed by Mayes, *Deuteronomy*, p. 397).

143. Cf. Mayes, *Deuteronomy*, pp. 408-409 (although he himself does not adopt this interpretation, preferring instead the variant translation suggested by Cross and Freedman). If it was the case that Laish/Dan first became part of the Israelite kingdom during the reign of David (see the analysis of Judg. 17–18 in Chapter 3 of the present study), then the possibility exists that David's conquest of northern Transjordan allowed him to use that region in his advance against the territory surrounding Laish/Dan. This can, of course, only be offered as speculation.

144. Note also the relatively lengthy passage dedicated to Joseph (Ephraim and Manasseh), Deut. 33.13-17. Ephraim is one of the names for the Northern Kingdom of Israel in the Hebrew Bible.

Judah's eventual reunion with Israel.) What is more, the present evaluation of the tribe of Dan is possibly the result of a positive estimation of the city of the same name. It is the reflection of the city (from the time of Jeroboam I) that is seen here in the portrayal of the tribe.

Returning to the text of 33.22—'Dan is a whelp of a lion/young lion; (And) he shall leap/who leaps forth from Bashan'—in the ancient Near East, the lion was a popular symbol of royal and divine strength.[145] Kings and deities were often portrayed as lions or as possessing lion-like qualities. One need only consider, for example, the crouching lion images carved in ivory from Samaria, the so-called 'Shema seal' from Megiddo, and the famous images of lions (in enameled brick) along the procession street leading from the Ishtar gate at Babylon.[146] The city of Dan was the site of one of Jeroboam's national shrines, and thus a location (albeit decentralized) of the confluence of royal/political and religious authority. The characterization of Dan as a '*young* lion' may serve to distinguish this northernmost city of the Israelite kingdom from the capital city of Samaria. In fact, since the identical metaphor of young lion is used of Judah in Genesis 49, the tribe of Dan—by virtue of the name it shared with the city—is, in some way, comparable to this pre-eminent Israelite tribe.[147] While in several other places in the biblical tradition Dan is negatively evaluated (chiefly under the influence of Dtr), this is not the case with the reference to Dan in Deuteronomy 33. In this text, which is antecedent to the work of Dtr and which betrays the partisan perspective of the Northern Kingdom, the positive evaluation of the tribe of Dan may be understood as the reflection of a similar evaluation of the city of Dan.

Although variant translations and interpretations have been proposed for Deut. 33.22, the plain meaning of the MT is to be preferred; there is no compelling reason to stray far from the traditional interpretation of text. The primary contribution of the present analysis is the suggestion that the tribe of Dan in Deuteronomy 33 owes its portrayal to the characterization of the city of Dan. While this short saying ostensibly originated at the end of Israel's wilderness period and is supposedly about the tribe, in all

---

145. See, e.g., G. Johannes Botterweck, "אֲרִי *'arî*', in *TDOT*, I, pp. 374-88.

146. See *ANEP*, illustrations 129, 276, 760, and 762.

147. Stanley Gervitz ('Adumbrations of Dan in Jacob's Blessing on Judah', *ZAW* 93 [1981], pp. 21-37) argues that the metaphor originated with the Danites, and was only secondarily applied to Judah. The significance of the tribal name, Judah, occurring *after* the metaphor in Gen. 49, while in Deut. 33 the name, Dan, *precedes* the metaphor, is unclear.

likelihood this saying is from a later time and reflects instead the characterization of the city of Dan (formerly Laish).

c. *Deuteronomy 34*

The final mention of Dan in the Pentateuch is in Deuteronomy 34. Atop Mt Nebo in Transjordan, Yahweh shows Moses the whole of the land that Israel is about to enter. As in Genesis 14, where Dan occurs for the first time in the Pentateuch, the phrase 'as far as Dan' here refers to the city of Dan, formerly known as Laish (according to Judg. 18), at the northern limit of the land. The mention of Dan does not refer to an undetermined region, as Reider suggests.[148] Only two cities are indicated absolutely in Deut. 34.1-4: Dan (v. 1) and Zoar (v. 4). Both cities designate particular locations in relation to broader, geographical regions: Dan is associated with (literally) 'the Gilead'; Zoar is located relative to 'the valley of Jericho, the city of palm trees'. In this way, the mention of Dan and Zoar functions as an *inclusio*, enveloping the descriptive material between them.

There is no question that Dan is here located in the north of the land. This is the plain meaning of the review of the land given here. The land is described as if following the eyes of one viewing it from Mt Nebo, looking northward beginning from Transjordan, then moving west and southward to the southern boundary of Cisjordan. While the location of Zoar is disputed, most scholars understand it to have been situated somewhere near the southern end of the Dead Sea (cf. Gen. 14.2).[149] What is significant here is that with this mention of Dan, the northern limit of the land is envisioned. That this name, rather than Laish, is used is evidence that this tradition originated, according to biblical chronology, at a time during the controversial period of the Judges at the earliest (Judg. 18), when, in biblical tradition, the name of the city was changed with the arrival of a new population group.[150] Insofar as the city is portrayed as a

148. Joseph Reider, *The Holy Scriptures: Deuteronomy, with Commentary* (Philadelphia: Jewish Publication Society of America, 1937), p. 343: 'The chief city of northern Dan, formerly known as Leshem or Laish'.

149. Herbert G. May (ed.), *Oxford Bible Atlas* (New York: Oxford University Press, 3rd edn, 1984), p. 57; James B. Pritchard (ed.), *The Harper Atlas of the Bible* (New York: Harper & Row, 1987), p. 33. Cf. Walter E. Rast, 'Bab edh-Dhra and the Origin of the Sodom Saga', in Leo G. Perdue, Lawrence E. Toombs and Gary L. Johnson (eds.), *Archaeology and Biblical Interpretation: Essays in Memory of D. Glenn Rose* (Atlanta: John Knox Press, 1987), pp. 185-201.

150. The historical veracity of the ch. 18 narrative is, of course, subject to question. See the proposed interpretation of Judg. 17–18 in Chapter 3, below.

town on the boundary of the land, it is reasonable to infer that the tradition comes from the time of the monarchy in Israel (cf. the phrase 'from Dan as far as Beehsheba' in the DH) when Israel's control of the land extended to the northern frontier marked by the city of Dan.

6. *Summary: Dan in the Pentateuch*

Dan is unique in the Hebrew Bible insofar as it refers not only to one of the twelve tribes of Israel, descended from an eponymous ancestor (a son of Jacob), but also to a city on the northern boundary of the land. The word 'Dan' occurs as a reference to each of these (tribe, city, ancestor) in the Pentateuch. It is clear that the stories of the births of the sons of Jacob in Genesis 29–30 have, in large measure, determined the arrangement of the tribes of Israel in other Pentateuchal texts (Gen. 35; 46; Exod. 1; Num. 1; 2; 7; 10; 26; Deut. 27). Thus, the character of this ancestor, Dan, as a son of a maidservant and not of a full wife, has influenced the portrayal of the tribe of the Danites relative to the other tribes. Yet, Dan occupies a special place among the sons of Jacob born of maidservants because he was the first son born of a maidservant, and because his mother was the maidservant of Jacob's favorite wife, Rachel. In addition, there are two individual Danites about whom stories are preserved: the craftsman, Oholiab (Exod. 31–40), and an anonymous 'blasphemer' (Lev. 24).

In several texts, the tribe of Dan is portrayed exercising leadership in Israel. First, one of only two named craftsmen in the story of the construction of the wilderness Tabernacle and its furnishings is Oholiab of the tribe of Dan. Second, during the period of Israel's encampment around the Tent of Meeting in the wilderness of Sinai, the tribe of Dan is listed as one of four division leaders (along with Judah, Reuben, and Ephraim); as the tribes break camp and begin their journey to the Wilderness of Paran, Dan serves as the 'rear guard'. Finally, I have proposed an interpretation of the saying about Dan in Gen. 49.16 that likens the tribe of Dan's judicial activity among the rest of the tribes of Israel to that of Yahweh.

References to the city of Dan in the north appear in Genesis 14 and Deuteronomy 34, thus forming an *inclusio* around the Pentateuch. Unlike many of the references to the city of Dan later in the DH, neither of these is negative. In both texts, Dan appears as the marker of the northern boundary of the land promised to Israel. It may be noteworthy that these two occurrences of Dan, referring to the city, are connected with two of Israel's leading figures: Abra(ha)m and Moses.

Some suggest that Dan had become an insignificant tribe in Israel since only the shortest possible list of descendants (a single son or clan) is preserved for its eponymous ancestor (Gen. 46; Num. 26). Yet, according to the census figures in the book of Numbers, the tribe of Dan was second in size only to Judah. Rather than being troubled about such large population figures attributed to each of the tribes, regardless of the number of sons or clans listed, one should consider the rhetorical effect of these Priestly texts on readers and hearers through the years.

I conclude that the portrayal of Dan in the Pentateuch is fundamentally positive. The only negative reference to Dan (the tribe) occurs in the final form of the story of the blasphemer in Leviticus 24. However, I have shown that the mention of the Danite lineage of the mother is not integral to the narrative, and may be a secondary addition by an editor influenced by the negative appraisal of Dan in the DH.

Chapter 3

INTERPRETING DAN IN THE FORMER PROPHETS

Some of the most extensive biblical traditions concerning Dan and the Danites are situated in the canonical corpus known traditionally as the Former Prophets (Joshua–2 Kings), and generally referred to in critical scholarship (since the 1940s) as the Deuteronomistic History. Principal texts include the territorial allotments to the tribes in Joshua 13–19, the list of levitical cities in Joshua 21, the prelude to the book of Judges (1.1-36), the Song of Deborah in Judges 5, the Samson cycle in Judges 13–16, the integrated stories of Micah and the Danite conquest of Laish in Judges 17–18, and the establishment of a royal sanctuary at the city of Dan by Jeroboam I in the last third of the tenth century BCE (1 Kgs 12.25-33).[1]

In 1943 Martin Noth first published his *Überlieferungsgeschichtliche Studien*, in which he proposed a new hypothesis—namely, that instead of the continuation of the literary traditions isolated in the Pentateuch (J, E, P), the books of Deuteronomy, Joshua, Judges, 1–2 Samuel and 1–2 Kings (together) comprise a single literary unit which, in light of its dependence on the Deuteronomic Law as a means of evaluating Israel's history, is appropriately called the Deuteronomistic History.[2] According to Noth, the Deuteronomistic Historian

1. Other texts are: Deut. 27.11-14 (see Chapter 2, above); 2 Sam. 20.18 (LXX); 1 Kgs 15; 2 Kgs 10; the 'Dan to Beersheba' texts (1 Sam. 3.20; 2 Sam. 3.10; 17.11; 24.2, 15).
2. Martin Noth, *The Deuteronomistic History* (JSOTSup, 15; Sheffield: JSOT Press, 2nd edn, 1991 [trans. from the German 2nd edn = *Überlieferungsgeschichtliche Studien: Die sammelnden und bearbeitenden Geschichtswerke im Alten Testament* (Tübingen: Max Niemeyer Verlag, Zweite Unveränderte Auflage, 1957]). The first chapter of the German work bears the (translated) title 'The Deuteronomistic Work'; Chapter 2 is 'The Chronistic Work'; while an appendix takes up 'The "Priestly Writing" and the Redaction of the Pentateuch'.

was not merely an editor but the author of a history which brought together material from highly varied traditions and arranged it according to a carefully conceived plan. In general Dtr. simply reproduced the literary sources available to him and merely provided a connecting narrative for isolated passages.[3]

A key item in Noth's theory was that the DH was the work of a single author writing in Palestine in the middle of the sixth century BCE (shortly after the last event narrated by Dtr, Jehoiachin's release from prison in about 562 BCE [2 Kgs 25.27-30]).[4] In Noth's evaluation, the purpose of Dtr was wholly negative: to point out to his exilic audience that their sufferings were fully warranted as the just consequences of the nation's continual disloyalty to Yahweh. Again, Noth writes that

> Dtr. did not write his history to provide entertainment in hours of leisure or to satisfy a curiosity about national history, but intended it to teach the true meaning of the history of Israel from the occupation to the destruction of the old order. The meaning which he discovered was that God was recognizably at work in that history, continuously meeting the accelerating moral decline with warnings and punishments and, finally, when these proved fruitless, with total annihilation.[5]

Subsequent critical responses to Noth's hypothesis have challenged, in particular, his understanding of Dtr's purpose, and his notion that the DH was the product of a single, exilic author. Von Rad, writing soon after the publication of Noth's study, characterized the work of Dtr as 'a history of the creative word of Jahweh'.[6] The scheme von Rad utilized in his study was that of promise (word) and fulfillment (history). Arguing that Yahweh's word (law and gospel) must be fulfilled in history, von Rad seized upon the closing verses of the DH, 2 Kgs 25.27-30 (Jehoiachin's release from prison), as indicative of the historian's hopeful perspective. According to von Rad, writing during the exile Dtr ended his work on a note of hope, seeing in the release of Jehoiachin from prison an anticipation of the fulfillment of Yahweh's promise to David and the restoration of Judah.[7]

---

3.   Noth, *Deuteronomistic History*, p. 26.
4.   Noth, *Deuteronomistic History*, pp. 27, 130, 135.
5.   Noth, *Deuteronomistic History*, p. 134.
6.   Gerhard von Rad, 'The Deuteronomistic Theology of History in the Books of Kings', in his *Studies in Deuteronomy* (SBT, 9; London: SCM Press, 1953 [German original 1948]), pp. 74-91.
7.   Thus, while Noth's DH was an apology for Yahweh's rejection and the ensuing destruction of the Southern Kingdom, for von Rad hope persists in the yet/once more to be fulfilled promise made to David.

Wolff saw no such encouragement to hope and instead argued that the purpose of Dtr was to call the exiles to repent, to (re)turn to Yahweh. Wolff found the answer to the question of Dtr's purpose in the period of the Judges, in particular, in the cycle of apostasy, oppression by enemies, cry to Yahweh, and deliverance through the agency of a judge (Judg. 2.11-18).[8] According to Wolff, the destruction of Judah and Jerusalem was a necessary (and not totally unexpected) consequence of King Manasseh's apostasy. But he continued: 'that judgment, now carried out, and conclusive as it seems, is merely one more in the chain of historical reversals, and there is no reason to think that it, too, will not be reversed, if the people repent'.[9] To 'return' to Yahweh would have the effect of reversing the judgment already carried out. Wolff traced this theme of 'return' in the DH (e.g. during the reign of Josiah [2 Kgs 23.25]) and concluded that it 'appears at important highpoints of the Deuteronomic presentation of history, and it thereby demonstrates through different examples what Israel should hear and do under judgment in the exile'.[10] Thus, the community in exile is, through the DH, encouraged to repent, and turn once more to obedience to the word of Yahweh, contained pre-eminently in the instruction of Moses (the book of Deuteronomy).

Von Rad and Wolff did not challenge Noth's idea of a single author of the DH living in the middle of the sixth century BCE. On the question of whether the DH is the work of a single, exilic author, Rudolph Smend and his students have proposed, on the one hand, a theory of multiple, exilic redactions (Prophetic, Nomistic) of an original history (DtrG). On the other hand, Frank M. Cross has advanced the theory of a double redaction of the DH, according to which the first edition was composed as a piece of propaganda during the reign of Josiah; the second edition, the product of the exilic period, updated the history from the time of Josiah to the Exile, and situated the blame for the Exile squarely on Manasseh.[11]

However, it must be pointed out that most of the DH passages under investigation in the present study (Josh. 13–22; Judg. 1–2; 13–16; 17–18) are considered secondary additions to the DH by not only Noth, but also

---

8. Hans Walter Wolff, 'The Kerygma of the Deuteronomic Historical Work', in Walter Brueggemann and Hans Walter Wolff (eds.), *The Vitality of Old Testament Traditions* (Atlanta: John Knox Press, 1975 [German original 1961]), pp. 83-100.

9. Wolff, 'The Kerygma', p. 89.

10. Wolff, 'The Kerygma', p. 91.

11. For a summary of research on the DH, see Steven L. McKenzie, 'Deuteronomistic History', in *ABD*, II, pp. 160-68, and the literature cited there.

by the vast majority of his respondents.[12] So while it has become scholarly
convention to refer to the literary corpus spanning the books of Deuteronomy through 2 Kings as the Deuteronomistic History, it must be remembered that most of the material from this corpus considered in the present
study has been recognized by critical scholars as secondary to the work of
the sixth-century Dtr. While these passages may have been added to the
DH at a later date, and given their present shape by the later editor (who
was sympathetic to the Deuteronomistic agenda), it is possible and, in
some cases likely, that the individual traditions are much older. Thus, a
part of my investigation of each biblical tradition about Dan will be a
review of the question concerning its date and/or redaction history.

1. *The Book of Joshua*

References to Dan appear on two occasions in the book of Joshua: in the
long section describing the allocation by lot of tribal portions in the land of
Canaan under Joshua (chs. 13–19), and in the list of levitical cities in
Joshua 21. On both occasions, the reference is to Dan as a tribal territory
(19.40-48; 21.5, 23-24). The historical-critical issues associated with the
latter half of the book of Joshua are numerous and complex. It has already
been noted that Noth regarded both of these sections (chs. 13–19 and 21)
as secondary interpolations, and omitted them from his discussion of the
original work of Dtr in the sixth century.[13] For example, regarding the
chapters describing the allotment of tribal territories in the book of Joshua,
Noth writes:

> The long section on the settlement of the individual tribes (Josh. 13–22) is
> not originally part of Dtr.'s work... However, the language and attitude of
> this section are very akin to Dtr. One must assume that it was interpolated
> soon after the completion of Dtr.'s work, in keeping with his approach and
> spirit... Thus we conclude that a later writer augmented Dtr.'s version at
> this point with very valuable historical material, transforming a description
> based on two different documents of the possessions of the twelve Israelite

12. See Noth's *Deuteronomistic History* on the following texts (respective page
numbers supplied in brackets after the reference): Deut. 27.11-14 (p. 33); Josh. 13–22
(pp. 41 n. 1, 66); Judg. 1–2 (pp. 23-24); 13–16 (pp. 77, 84-85); 17–18 (p. 77). A noteworthy exception is Timo Veijola, a student of Smend, who includes Judg. 17–21 in
the DH (see his *Das Königtum in der Beurteilung der deuteronomistischen Historiographie: Eine redaktionsgeschichtliche Untersuchung* [Annales Academie Scientiarum
Fennicae, Series B, 198; Helsinki: Suomalainen Tiedeakatemia, 1977], pp. 15-29).
   13. Noth, *Deuteronomistic History*, pp. 66-67; cf. pp. 41 n. 1, 43 n. 1.

tribes after the conquest into a narrative of the distribution of the land to the tribes at the time to the conquest and integrating this into Dtr.'s account after Joshua 12.[14]

a. *Joshua 13–19*

Joshua 13–19 is an account of the division and occupation of the land by the Israelite tribes under the leadership of Joshua. The tribes settling in Transjordan are discussed in ch. 13; ch. 14 is concerned with the special inheritance of Caleb (Hebron). The allotment of the land in Cisjordan continues in ch. 15 with Judah, and with the Joseph tribes (Ephraim and Manasseh) in chs. 16–17. Chapters 18–19 deal with the remaining seven tribes, whose inheritance had not yet been allotted (18.2). Following a survey of the land (18.3-10), the land is allotted to the tribes in the following order: Benjamin, Simeon, Zebulun, Issachar, Asher, Naphtali, and Dan.

Form-critical study of this material in Joshua 13–19 originated in the mid-1920s with Albrecht Alt, who distinguished two types of literature in these chapters: boundary descriptions and lists of places (town- or city-lists).[15] He observed that boundary descriptions are preserved for all tribes except Simeon, Issachar, and Dan.[16] In Alt's analysis, 16.1-3 is a good example of a boundary description; the inheritance of Dan in 19.40-48 represents a city list. Martin Noth built on the results of Alt's work, and proposed that antecedent to the boundary *descriptions* were lists of boundary points (*Grenzfixpunkten*).[17] According to Noth, a redactor was responsible for connecting the points by inserting descriptive verbs and explanatory notes. The form-critical work of Alt and Noth continues to be accepted by many recent commentators.[18]

14. Noth, *Deuteronomistic History*, pp. 66-67.

15. Albrecht Alt, 'Judas Gaue unter Josia', *PJ* 21 (1925), pp. 100-16 (reprinted in *Kliene Schriften zur Geschichte des Volkes Israel* [3 vols.; Munich: C.H. Beck, 1959], II, pp. 276-88).

16. Some scholars have noted that 19.22 may preserve a fragmentary boundary description for Issachar (see Zecharia Kallai, *Historical Geography of the Bible: The Tribal Territories of Israel* [Leiden: E.J. Brill, 1986], p. 194; Nadav Na'aman, *Borders and Districts in Biblical Historiography: Seven Studies in Biblical Geographical Lists* [Jerusalem Biblical Studies, 4; Jerusalem: Simor, 1986], p. 77).

17. Martin Noth, *Das Buch Josua* (HAT, 7; Tübingen: J.C.B. Mohr [Paul Siebeck], 2nd edn, 1953), pp. 13-15. The original statement of this theory can be found in Noth's 'Studien zu den historisch-geographischen Dokumenten des Josuabuches', *ZDPV* 58 (1935), pp. 185-255.

18. Robert G. Boling and G. Ernest Wright, *Joshua: A New Translation with Notes and Commentary* (AB, 6; Garden City, NY: Doubleday, 1982); Trent C. Butler, *Joshua*

The question of the date of these distinct forms (boundary descriptions, lists of places) remains more unsettled.[19] Alt proposed separate dates for the two documents. On the one hand, he dated the boundary descriptions to the settlement period, before the rise of the monarchy in Israel and for the purpose of settling disputes about territorial claims. On the other hand, the town lists, which he further divided by geography into northern and southern lists (the tribes of Ephraim and Manasseh in the middle of the land are without town lists), belonged to the administrative organization of Josiah in the seventh century BCE.[20] Here also, Noth followed Alt.[21] Other scholars, however, have suggested different dates for all or part of the town lists. For example, while accepting the premonarchic date of Alt and Noth for the boundary descriptions, Frank M. Cross, Jr, and G. Ernest Wright dated the southern town list to the reign of Jehoshaphat in the first half of the ninth century BCE.[22] Near the opposite end of the chronological spectrum, Sigmund Mowinckel has proposed that Joshua 13–19 is the work of a postexilic author/historian living in Jerusalem, based on memory (in Mowinckel's opinion, no documents could have survived the destruction of Judah in the sixth century).[23]

Kallai and Na'aman are among those scholars who are less inclined to drive a chronological divider between the two literary forms identified by

(WBC, 7; Waco, TX: Word Books, 1983); Richard D. Nelson, *Joshua: A Commentary* (OTL; Louisville, KY: Westminster Press, 1997); J. Alberto Soggin, *Joshua: A Commentary* (OTL; London: SCM Press, 1972).

19. For a brief summary of recent research, see Butler, *Joshua*, pp. 142-44. See also Richard Hess, 'Tribes, Territories of the', *ISBE*, IV, pp. 907-13.

20. Alt, 'Judas Gaue unter Josia', pp. 106-11; *idem*, 'Das System der Stammesgrenzen im Buche Josua', in W.F. Albright (ed.), *Beiträge zur Religionsgeschichte und Archäologie Palestinas. Ernst Sellin zum 60. Geburtstage* (Leipzig: Deichert, 1927), pp. 13-24 (reprinted in *Kliene Schriften zur Geschichte des Volkes Israel* [Munich: C.H. Beck, 1959], I, pp. 193-202).

21. Noth, *Das Buch Josua*, pp. 13-14.

22. Frank M. Cross, Jr, and G. Ernest Wright, 'The Boundary and Province Lists of the Kingdom of Judah', *JBL* 75 (1956), pp. 202-26.

23. Sigmund Mowinckel, *Zur Frage nach dokumentarischen Quellen in Josua 13–19* (Oslo: I. Kommisjon hos J. Dybwad, 1946); *idem, Tetrateuch—Pentateuch—Hexateuch: Die Berichte über die Landmahme in den drei altisraelitischen Geschichtswerken* (BZAW, 90; Berlin: Alfred Töpelmann, 1964). However, Mowinckel fails to persuade on the question of the significance of tribal divisions in the postexilic period (cf. Ezra–Nehemiah, in which the ancestral houses/clans [אבות, Ezra 10.16; Neh. 7.70] appear as the more significant social unit). Even Ezekiel's exilic vision of the restored land in ch. 48 is more schematic and ideal than the product of historical memory.

Alt in Joshua 13–19, locating both the boundary descriptions and the town lists in the period of Israel's United Monarchy, at which time they reflected a historical reality.[24] Tracing the origin of the document comprising not only the boundary descriptions, but also the town lists to David's census (2 Sam. 24), Na'aman writes:

> A census had many uses: besides being a register for military service it was also the basis for labour conscription, for levying and collecting taxes, for the allotment of fields and the examination of land ownership rights. By inference, one may suggest that one of the main purposes of David's census was the exact delineation of territories in order to establish ownership rights. And it was in those areas where there were ownership disputes between neighbouring tribes that their territory had to be accurately demarcated and fully described. That was why the author of the boundary system was able to delineate those particular borderlines in such detail (e.g., Josh. 15.6-10; 16.1-3, 6-7; 17.7-9; 18.12-19; 19.10-14). This would fit very well with his main purpose, which was the proper allocation of the territories to the Israelite tribes. In regions where there were no demarcation problems, such as the recently conquered Canaanite area, presumably the censors recorded only towns and their inhabitants. This lack of precise delineation was an obstacle to the author of the boundary system. In the west, he resolved the problem by following river-beds to the sea, which necessarily led to a schematic description of borders. In other areas, he was obliged to use a combination of towns and borders, and sometimes merely a town list. By analysing the type of descriptions in the boundary system, we can learn what kind of records were made during the census in different parts of the country.
>
> We may conclude that the form of the boundary system is the direct result of the sources available to its author: the original records of David's census. *The varying descriptions do not justify tearing it to pieces.* It was the nature of the documents on which the system was based that dictated its final literary form.[25]

A date in the period of the United Monarchy in Israel is supported by other pieces of evidence. First, de Geus surveys the tribal lists in the Hebrew Bible and shows that 'in the time of the Judges the set of twelve nowhere appears, not even where it might reasonably be expected'.[26]

---

24. Kallai, *Historical Geography of the Bible*, pp. 331-32, 479; Na'aman, *Borders and Districts*, pp. 83-84, 98-107.

25. Na'aman, *Borders and Districts*, pp. 100-101 (emphasis added).

26. C.H.J. de Geus, *The Tribes of Israel: An Investigation into Some of the Presuppositions of Martin Noth's Amphictyony Hypothesis* (SSN, 18; Assen: Van Gorcum, 1976), p. 112.

Rather, as a designation of the totality of Israel, he concludes that the twelve-tribe system 'represents the situation of the United Monarchy'.[27] Similarly, Gottwald, who is unable to isolate any premonarchic setting for the land allocation traditions of Joshua 13–19, suggests that 'a firm beginning for the allotment traditions is best assigned to the rise of the monarchy, when the tribal holdings as the natural concomitants of the socioeconomic components of premonarchic Israel were transformed into administrative districts in David's kingdom'.[28] During the period of the United Monarchy, the twelve-tribe scheme served political or administrative functions: in the recruitment of the militia, the raising of taxes, and the imposition of corvée. After the division of the Davidic–Solomonic kingdom, the system of twelve tribes fulfilled a religious, symbolic function, representing the whole of Israel as a community related to Yahweh.[29]

Anthropological study of tribal societies supports Gottwald's sociological analysis which fails to uncover any function of a twelve-tribe system in the settlement period, but which instead emphasizes the political relevance of such a scheme for monarchic Israel. Marshall Sahlins defines a tribe as

> a body of people of common derivation and custom, in possession and control of their own extensive territory. But if in some degree socially articulated, a tribe is specifically unlike a modern nation in that its several communities are not united under a sovereign governing authority, nor are the boundaries of the whole thus clearly and politically determined.[30]

Unlike the picture of the Israelite tribes preserved in the biblical record, it is uncommon for tribal boundaries to be contiguous with those of a neighboring tribe. Rather, instead of clearly demarcated inter-tribal boundaries, there tends to exist a transitional zone, in which members of settlements peripherally associated with various tribes form relationships with one another. Where boundaries between tribes do in fact exist, these tend to follow naturally dividing features of the landscape such as coast/inland, hill country/valley, or forest/plain regions of habitation.[31] In addition, even

27. De Geus, *The Tribes of Israel*, p. 118.

28. Gottwald, *The Tribes of Yahweh*, p. 182; see also pp. 182-84, 362-75.

29. Gottwald, *The Tribes of Yahweh*, pp. 362-74. Gottwald does allow for the possibility that, politically, after the rupture of the Davidic–Solomonic kingdom, the notion of twelve tribes could express the claim of the kingdom of Judah on the northern, break-away kingdom (p. 372).

30. Marshall D. Sahlins, *Tribesmen* (Foundations of Modern Anthropology Series; Engelwood Cliffs, NJ: Prentice–Hall, 1968), pp. vii-viii.

31. Sahlins, *Tribesmen*, pp. 16-23.

in tribal societies, greater importance lies not in the tribe as a whole, but in the smaller kinship groups (household, local lineages, village). At these lower levels of social interaction one finds one's identity; here also resides the tribe's economic power. According to Sahlins, 'the tribe (as a whole) is often the weakest link in the segmentary chain'.[32] Thus, while it is not impossible that Joshua 13–19 preserves some notion of tribal Israel before the rise of the monarchy, with identifiable groups inhabiting particular parts of Canaan, the twelve-tribe scheme, which not only encompasses the whole of the land but also includes carefully delineated boundary lines, and by which the component parts of Israel are identified, poorly reflects the social character of tribal society as recognized by cultural anthropologists.

It is often assumed that smaller tribal societies developed over time into nations. Another anthropologist, Morton Fried, has gone so far as to suggest that, contrary to this popular understanding, most tribes do not comprise a stage on the evolutionary line toward state formation, but are, rather, better understood as a 'secondary phenomenon', the product of the newly developed state. In the Preface to his book, *The Notion of Tribe*, Fried writes:

> Although we are accustomed to think about the most ancient forms of human society in terms of tribes, firmly defined and bounded units of this sort actually grew out of the manipulation of relatively unstructured populations by more complexly organized societies. The invention of the state, a tight, class-structured political and economic organization, began a process whereby vaguely defined and grossly overlapping populations were provided with the minimal organization required for their manipulation, even though they had little or no internal organization of their own other than that based on conceptions of kinship. The resultant form was that of the tribe.[33]

Fried suggests that the structure of society prior to the rise of the state tended to be open rather than closed, loosely administered rather than tightly organized, and ordinarily devoid of precisely demarcated boundaries.[34]

32. Sahlins, *Tribesmen*, p. 16. See also Paula McNutt, *Reconstructing the Society of Ancient Israel* (Library of Ancient Israel; Louisville, KY: Westminster/John Knox Press, 1999), p. 84.

33. Morton H. Fried, *The Notion of Tribe* (Menlo Park: Cummings, 1975).

34. Fried, *The Notion of Tribe*, p. 76. Gottwald characterizes Fried's position as 'extreme' and insists that Fried's model must be modified if it is to be applied to early Israel. Thus, Gottwald proposes that Israel's tribalism is better understood as a 'retribalization movement', in conscious reaction against the centralization of power and wealth in Canaanite society (*The Tribes of Yahweh*, pp. 323-34). It is, nevertheless,

In light of the anthropological evidence, the twelve-tribe system re-corded in Joshua 13–19 is perhaps better understood as the administrative means of the Davidic–Solomonic state for managing the loosely arranged pre-monarchic population settled throughout Canaan.[35]

likely that Gottwald's suggestion also needs to be re-examined since the centralization of power and influence in Canaan that originated with the monarchy of David was proportionately different from (and superior to) the centralization exercised by the independent rulers of Iron I city-states in Canaan.

35. Nevertheless, Richard Hess ('Asking Historical Questions of Joshua 13–19: Recent Discussion Concerning the Date of the Boundary Lists', in A.R. Millard, James K. Hoffmeier and David W. Baker [eds.], *Faith, Tradition, and History: Old Testament Historiography in Its Near Eastern Context* [Winona Lake, IN: Eisenbrauns, 1994], pp. 191-205; *idem*, 'Late Bronze Age and Biblical Boundary Descriptions of the West Semitic World', in George J. Brooke, Adrian H.W. Curtis and John F. Healey [eds.], *Ugarit and the Bible: Proceedings of the International Symposium on Ugarit and the Bible, Manchester, September 1992* [UBL, 11; Münster: Ugarit-Verlag, 1994], pp. 123-38) has recently called for a positive reconsideration of Alt's hypothesis that the boundary descriptions in Josh. 13–19 originated in the premonarchic period. On the basis of comparative study of ancient Near Eastern documents from the Late Bronze Age (texts from Ugarit, Mari, Alalakh, including Hittite treaties), Hess argues that 'if one were to date Josh. 13–19 solely on the basis of the period in which the known political-geographical divisions most closely correspond to the boundary descriptions, the closest correspondence would be with the Late Bronze Age world of the Amarna correspondence' ('Asking Historical Questions', p. 197).

While noting that a premonarchic date for the boundary descriptions in the book of Joshua (based on what he calls 'formal similarity' with the ancient Near Eastern parallels) creates 'the problem of the unreality of these descriptions', Hess responds to this question by resurrecting Alt's suggestion that the descriptions represent Israel's ideal boundaries ('Asking Historical Questions', p. 203). A more significant problem, which Hess overlooks, is the fact that all of the Late Bronze Age parallels he cites concern political relations between established city-states or nations. None of his parallels deal with tribal boundaries, such as those ostensibly described in Josh. 13–19. If the boundary descriptions in Joshua delineated the borders of adjacent city-states or nations, then the ancient Near Eastern evidence would provide a suitable basis for dating Josh. 13–19 to the premonarchic period. However, given the sociological and anthropological data reviewed here, as well as the ancient Near Eastern evidence from Late Bronze Age nations studied by Hess, it is better to assign the material in the book of Joshua to the period in which their was a king in Israel, and when Israel had a national character (Iron II or later).

Hess's remarks that the treaty context of the Hittite documents provides an appropri-ate historical background for understanding Josh. 13–19 (Josh. 24 supplies the Israelite covenant context) are also unpersuasive. First of all, he fails to consider that ch. 24, while perhaps preserving an earlier (premonarchic) document, is most likely unrelated

Thus, the notion that pre-monarchic Israel was a unified tribal society is likely to be an artificial socio-political construct intended to ground in earlier history the territorial claim and political reality of the United Monarchy. As part of this scheme, the division of the land among the seven remaining tribes is reported in Joshua 18–19. The land is distributed in the following order: Benjamin, Simeon, Zebulun, Issachar, Asher, Naphtali, and Dan.[36] Form-critically, city-lists and passages of mixed forms (city-lists and boundary descriptions) make up the material about the territorial allotments to the seven remaining tribes. Those of mixed forms include the apportionments to the tribes of Benjamin, Zebulun, Issachar, Asher, and Naphtali. City-lists alone are given for the tribes of Simeon and Dan.[37] A common pattern is discernible in the descriptions of the tribal divisions, although no two are identical. Each section begins with the number of lot and the name of the tribe (e.g. 'to the tribe of the sons of Dan, for their clans, went out the seventh lot', 19.40); a geographical description of the territory follows. Next appears a summary statement noting the number of cities and dependent villages in the territory. Each section concludes with a remark such as: 'This was the portion of …by their clans—these cities and their villages' (הערים [האלה] וחצריהן).[38]

to chs. 13–19, having been connected to the preceding record of land division and possession by a later redactor (see, e.g., Boling and Wright, *Joshua*, pp. 66, 543-45). In addition, Hess overlooks the importance of the distinguishing character of the Israelite covenant as a covenant with God, rather than as a covenant between national leaders. Israel's covenant with God in Josh. 24 is qualitatively different from other covenants (treaties) between leaders of separate city-states or nations.

36. While the list has some similarity with the roster of tribes in Judg. 1, and less similarity with other tribal lists in the Hebrew Bible, there seems to be no rationale for the order given here in Josh. 18–19. A geographical scheme (south to north) fails under closer examination (while Benjamin is toward the south, it is not the southernmost tribe in the list [the tribe of Simeon occupies this position]; Dan is not located in the north, but in the Judean hill country west of the territory allotted to Benjamin [i.e. west of the city later called Jerusalem]).

37. Some scholars have suggested (partially on the basis of the LXX) that 19.46 preserves a fragment of a boundary description (see, e.g., Cross and Wright, 'Boundary and Province Lists', p. 210). Their arguments are not persuasive.

38. The phrase '(these) cities and their villages' occurs repeatedly in Josh. 18–19 and indicates that the proper social context for understanding this material is that of the agrarian society, in which the pre-industrial city exists in an interdependent relationship with its associated villages. The inhabitants of the pre-industrial city were dependent on the agriculturalists outside the city walls for their food, supplies, and other raw materials. In addition, the pre-industrial city served not only as the economic center for

Two significant concepts are mentioned in Joshua 18–19. The first is the fact that the apportionment of the land involves casting lots (גוֹרָל),

the surrounding villages, but also functioned as the political and religious center, insofar as the palace and the temple were included within it (the fundamental study is Gideon Sjoberg, *The Preindustrial City: Past and Present* [New York: Free Press, 1966]; see also Lenski, *Human Societies*, pp. 237-89; Eric R. Wolf, *Peasants* [Foundations of Modern Anthropology Series; Englewood Cliffs, NJ: Prentice–Hall, 1966]; Frank S. Frick, *The City in Ancient Israel* [SBLDS, 36; Missoula, MT: Scholars Press, 1977], p. 92). Perhaps the most fundamental distinction between city (עִיר) and village in the ancient Near Eastern world (and thus in the Hebrew Bible) is that the city was a permanent settlement surrounded by a defensive wall, while the village was an unwalled, less permanent settlement subsidiary to the city (Frick, *The City in Ancient Israel*, p. 30). While the term does not occur in these chapters, villages are occasionally referred to as 'daughters' (e.g. Josh. 15.45, 47; Judg. 1.27). Frick points out that the social status of women in the agrarian world illuminates this relationship between cities and villages. He writes: 'Both mother and daughter play a clearly subordinate, but nevertheless important role in the Hebrew family. The mother, while having the primary function of producing children, also had considerable authority over her daughters, hence the analogical control of a mother-city over the dependent daughter-villages. The mother had major responsibilities in caring for the children, and similarly, the city provided protection for its dependent daughter-villages' (p. 58). Although the city may have provided protection in times of emergency, at other times the city and its inhabitants were less 'motherly' (taxation, conscription, etc.). A piece of legislation in the Hebrew Bible (Lev. 25.29-31) also makes a distinction between houses within walled cities and those in villages: a house within a city, once sold, could only be redeemed within a period of one year. A house in a village, however, could always be redeemed. (See, e.g., Baruch A. Levine, *The JPS Torah Commentary: Leviticus, the Traditional Hebrew Text with the New JPS Translation* [Philadelphia: Jewish Publication Society of America, 5749/1989], pp. 176-77.) The Hebrew word used repeatedly throughout Josh. 13–19 for village is חָצֵר, which means either 'enclosure, court' or 'settled abode, settlement, village' (see BDB, pp. 346-47; V. Hamp, 'חָצֵר *ḥāṣēr*', in *TDOT*, V, pp. 131-33). Hamp notes that while these villages are without fortified walls (Lev. 25.31), they are, nevertheless, permanent settlements and are not to be identified with the temporary encampments of semi-nomads. Comparatively little is known about village life in the ancient world; this is due in part to the relatively less permanent nature of the villages' structures, and also due to archaeology's earlier preoccupation with the tell, urban life, and royal architecture. Socially, the village may be characterized as organized along kinship lines. Oakman ('The Countryside in Luke–Acts', p. 166) makes this observation about the character of village life in the first century CE, while Gottwald (*The Tribes of Yahweh*, p. 257) notes the same for the premonarchic period: 'all available evidence suggests that the *mishpāḥāh* lived together in the same village or neighborhood, a matter of great importance for plotting the location of the *mishpāḥāh* in a general anthropological typology of social organizational forms'. Unfortunately, Gottwald fails to identify the source(s) of 'all available evidence'.

although the details of this ceremony are unspecified.[39] While casting lots had a secular usage in the ancient world as an easily interpreted means of making unprejudiced decisions (and one which could not be easily misappropriated), the ceremony in the Hebrew Bible appears laden with heavy theological overtones. According to Dommershausen,

> The Old Testament gives particular consideration to casting lots 'before Yahweh'. In other words, Israel is convinced that God holds the fate of man in his hands, and reveals his will immediately and unambiguously through lot casting. Therefore, the people of God in the Old Testament regard lot casting as a sacral act... Along with dreams and prophetic oracles (cf. 1 S. 28.6) the lot is regarded as an answer and final decision of Yahweh, against which there is no appeal.[40]

Thus, the reader is to understand that, for Israel, the territorial allotments are an expression of the divine will, not subject to human interference. An important question surfaces when, in the final form of the text, as in the case of the tribe of Dan, the divinely appointed territory is lost and the Danites migrate north to defeat and occupy the city of Leshem (= Laish). Does this suggest that unnamed, presumably human forces, can overcome the will of Yahweh?[41] Or does this suggest that the Danites's loss of the territory allocated to them by Yahweh is, in some way, the consequence of their violation of their relationship with Yahweh? Or is the reader to understand that although, at a certain point in history, a portion of the tribe of Dan left (lost?) its divinely given territory, that former region remains its rightful possession?[42] That is, does the territory in the

---

39. Does the lot signify a tribe or a tribal territory? The text is ambiguous. It is not clear whether the tribes were first arranged in order and then the lot was cast to determine their particular territory, or whether seven lots (each lot representing a different tribe) were placed in a container and as each tribe's lot emerged, a territory was designated.

40. W. Dommershausen, 'גּוֹרָל *gôrāl*', in *TDOT*, II, pp. 450-56 (452); see also, H.H. Schmid, 'גּוֹרָל *gôrāl* lot', in *TLOT*, I, pp. 310-12 (311). A religious use of the term also occurs in Akkadian (*šīmtum*, meaning 'what is established, fixed, decreed [by the gods], fate, destiny; a euphemism for death' [John Huehnergard, *A Grammar of Akkadian* (HSS, 45; Atlanta: Scholars Press, 1997), p. 523]).

41. However, the MT simply states that the Danite territory 'went out from them'. No reason is given. Was it 'lost', 'taken (by an indigenous group)', or 'taken away (by Yahweh)?' The MT does not say (cf. the LXX and Judg. 1.34-35).

42. Cf. R.D. Nelson, *Joshua: A Commentary*, p. 220. Butler (*Joshua*, p. 206) goes beyond the evidence in the text when he identifies as the emphasis of this passage God's gift of 'an inheritance in the land' even when an original lot has been lost: 'Even

Judean highlands west of the territory of Benjamin remain the 'inheritance' of the tribe of Dan, to which its families may lay claim although,
according to the biblical story, a portion of the tribe resides within the
walls of the city of Dan in the territory of Naphtali in the north?

The second significant concept in Joshua 13–19 is that the tribal territories are defined as 'hereditary portions' or 'inheritances' (נחלה). For
example, the Dan section refers to the גבול נחלתם ('boundary [or terri-
tory] of their inheritance') and begins the conclusion with זאת נחלת
מטה בני־דן ('this is the inheritance of the tribe of the sons of Dan').
Building on the work of Dybdahl, Habel has argued that נחלה means
'inheritance' only in a minority of instances, namely, in the context of the
family. In the majority of other cases, a נחלה is 'a rightful share or allotment, an approved entitlement to land, property, or people'. A נחלה is not,
in the first place, 'something simply handed down from generation to generation, but the entitlement or rightful property of a party that is legitimized
by a recognized social custom, legal process, or divine charter'.[43] Therefore, in Joshua 13–19, the נחלה apportioned to each tribe is best understood as a share of the land, given to the tribe by Yahweh, to which the
tribe may lay claim. The sacral character of Joshua 13–19 suggests that
apart from social rules governing the inheriting of property, each of the
tribes of Israel possesses, by divine decision, an indisputable claim to the
land. Thus, although 19.47 narrates the movement of the tribe of Dan from
the Judean hills to the city of Leshem (= Laish), the tribe's 'rightful share'
remains in the south (as v. 48 makes clear) where, it has been suggested,
some of the Danites stayed.[44]

(1) *Joshua 19.40-48 (MT)*

[40] To the tribe of the sons of Dan, to their clans, the seventh lot went out.

[41] And the territory of their inheritance was Zorah and Eshtaol and Ir

when a tribe lost its original lot, God replaced it. This was of particular importance to
the readers of the Deuteronomistic history in exile. They had lost all their inheritance.
They had no more lot.' The role of God in the Danites's conquest of Leshem (= Laish)
is nowhere explicitly specified either here in Josh. 19, or in Judg. 1, or in Judg. 18 (see
below on these chapters).

43. Norman C. Habel, *The Land is Mine: Six Biblical Land Ideologies* (OBT; Minneapolis: Fortress Press, 1995), p. 35.

44. See, e.g., C.F. Burney, *The Book of Judges, with Introduction and Notes, and
Notes on the Hebrew Text of the Books of Kings, with an Introduction and Appendix*
(The Library of Biblical Studies; repr., New York: Ktav, 2nd edn, 1970 [1930]), p. 339;
Gottwald, *The Tribes of Yahweh*, p. 250.

Shemesh. [42] And Shaalabbin and Aijalon and Ithlah. [43] And Elon and Timnathah and Ekron. [44] And Eltekeh and Gibbethon and Baalath. [45] And Yehud and Bene-Berak and Gath-rimmon. [46] And Me Hayyarqon and Haraqqon, with the territory opposite Joppa. [47] And the territory of the sons of Dan went out from them; and the sons of Dan went up and they waged war with Leshem and they captured it, and they smote it to the mouth of the sword and they took possession of it and they inhabited it, and they called Leshem 'Dan', according to the name of Dan their ancestor. [48] This is the inheritance of the tribe of the sons of Dan, according to their clans; these cities and their villages.

[Notes on the MT:

Verse 41: For 'And Ir', a few medieval manuscripts of the Hebrew Old Testament, the Editions, read 'and En'; a few medieval manuscripts of the Hebrew Old Testament, Targum[f Ms], read 'And Beth'.

Verse 42: For 'Shaalabbin', a few medieval manuscripts of the Hebrew Old Testament, the Editions read 'Shaalbim', as Judg. 1.35 and 1 Kgs 4.9.

Verses 42-43: John Strange's proposal ('The Inheritance of Dan', *ST* 20 [1966], pp. 120-39 [122]) that Elon in v. 43 is a case of dittography is without textual support. In addition, its removal violates the scheme of grouping the place names for the Danite territory in threes. Thus, while the existence of a site by this name is not certain (cf. 'Appendix: Site Identifications', in R.D. Nelson, *Joshua: A Commentary*, the MT is the preferred reading.

Verse 43: For 'and Timnathah', the LXX [Mss] (the Syriac and the Vulgate) reads καὶ θαμνα, thus נה– (Timnah).

Verse 44: For 'And Eltekeh', the LXX [Mss] reads καὶ Ελθεκω (Akkadian *Altaqū*).

Verse 46: For 'Me', the LXX reads καὶ ἀπὸ θλάσσης. The editor of the book of Joshua in *BHS* (R. Meyer) suggests that the MT should probably be read ומים ('and from the sea'). 'And Haraqqon' is absent from the LXX, and the editor recognizes its presence in the Hebrew text as due to dittography, and suggests that it be deleted from the MT. For 'with the territory opposite Joppa', the editor of the book of Joshua in *BHS* suggests that, instead, the text be read as עד with one medieval manuscript of the Hebrew Old Testament and with the Syriac. The word in question is altogether absent from the LXX. At the end of v. 46 in the MT, the editor notes that at this point the LXX transposes v. 48 (that is, the LXX reverses the order of vv. 47 and 48).

Verse 47: For 'And the territory of the sons of Dan went out from them', the LXX reads otherwise; compare Judg. 1.34. For 'Leshem' (Judg. 18.7, 27, 29), read לְיִשׁ; it has been proposed that one read לְשָׁם. At the end of v. 47 (MT), the LXX adds many words; compare Judg. 1.35.

Verse 48: The adjective 'these', in reference to the enumerated cities of the territory of Dan, is absent from the LXX and the Vulgate; compare Josh. 19.16, critical note b.]

The tradition surrounding the allotment of territory to the Danites in 19.40-48 is, in several aspects, distinctive within the immediate context of Joshua 18–19. First, only in the case of the Danite text does the first verse begin with לְמַטֵּה and end with a phrase about the casting of lots (in all other instance the order is reversed; cf. 19.1). Second, a narrative, such as that about the Danite migration and conquest of Leshem (= Laish) in 19.47, is unparalleled in Joshua 18–19.[45] Third, the LXX of vv. 47-48 differs significantly from the MT: the verses are in reverse order and, according to the LXX, Judah—not Dan—journeys to conquer a *neighboring* city (in the LXX, the city is Lachish, not Leshem, and the new name given to the city is not Dan but Lasendak).

The territory apportioned by lot to the tribe of Dan was located in the hill country west of the territory of Benjamin (west/northwest of Jerusalem).[46] Whatever the date of the boundary descriptions and city-lists date—proposals range from the time of the United Monarchy to the post-exilic period—on the basis of this text there persisted a tradition of at least a Danite enclave in the southern part of the land after the so-called migration of Dan (according to the narrative in Judges 18, at least a portion of the tribe [18.11, 21] migrated northward and conquered Laish, renaming it Dan).[47] The following cities attributed to the tribe of Dan occur in other parts of the Danite tradition: Zorah and Eshtaol, in the stories of Samson (chs. 13–16), and Micah and the Danites (chs. 17–18); Eltekeh and Gibbethon, Aijalon and Gath-rimmon are designated levitical cities in Joshua 21; Timnathah, in the Samson story (Judg. 14); and Ir Shemesh, Shaalabbin, and Aijalon (or their equivalents) are given as Amorite cities in Judg.

45. The difference in place names—Laish/Leshem—remains unresolved. Is the equation Leshem = Laish accurate? The former occurs only in Josh. 19.47; the similarity between this verse and the narrative in Judg. 18 has lead to the equation of the two place names. While Laish does occur in a few ancient Near Eastern texts, there is no extra-biblical evidence for Leshem. Several pieces of evidence suggest that this verse is an interpolation. Notice, for example, that it occurs precisely where the other tribal traditions preserve a numerical summary of their cities and villages, just before the concluding statement about the tribal portion (inclusive of its cities and villages [הערים האלה וחצריהן]).

46. See, e.g., May (ed.), *Oxford Bible Atlas*, p. 61.

47. On the possible identification of the cities within the Danite territory, see the appendix in R.D. Nelson, *Joshua: A Commentary*, pp. 285-89. As Nelson's list indicates, several of the Danite sites have not yet been positively identified. The reader will observe that, according to Josh. 13–19, the tribal territories of Dan and Judah share certain cities. The tradition suggests that perhaps tribal boundary lines were more fluid than usually understood. However, to review the research into this question would move too far beyond the scope of the present study. It is sufficient at this point to note that this is one example among many of some relationship between Dan and Judah in the biblical tradition. This is an observation made repeatedly in the present study.

1.35. All of these biblical traditions assume a Danite inheritance and presence in the southern part of the land.

Joshua 19.47 is important in the interpretation of Dan in the biblical traditions. The verse is narrative in form (which is unique in Josh. 18–19) and describes the apparent 'loss' of the Danite territory (literally, 'the territory...went out from them') and the tribe's subsequent ascent against, and resettlement of, Leshem in the north. This narrative may be properly understood as a secondary addition to 19.40-48. First of all, its narrative form is striking, and is unparalleled in the immediate context (Josh. 18–19). In addition, the verse occurs precisely where the reader expects a statistical summary of the Danite inheritance; in the final form of the text, there is no concluding number of Danite towns and villages (cf. 18.28; 19.4-8, 15-16, 22-23, 30-31, 38-39), this part of the regular form perhaps having been lost when the migration narrative was added. Finally, the content of this verse has a parallel, in more extensive form, in Judges 18 (see below).[48]

Joshua 19.47 reports the Danites's loss of the land allotted to them. The exact meaning of the phrase 'went out' (יצא) is not altogether clear since this is a distinctive use of the word. Elsewhere in the Hebrew Bible, where this word is used with גבול, the description is of the extension of a boundary (Num. 34.9; Josh. 15.11; 18.11, 15). This is apparently not its use here. In an attempt to make sense out of this unusual text, Boling and Wright proposed emending the verb to ויאץ (from root אוץ), and thus read 'and their territory became too confining for them'. They write that 'this is the first clause of v 47 in MT and the last clause of v 47 in LXX. The Greek reflects wy'ṣ (cf. 17:15) which gave rise to the unintelligible wy'ṣ in MT.'[49] I share with Nelson the conclusion that this is an unnecessary

---

48. While each passage contains some unique language, the following vocabulary occurs in both texts, suggesting some literary relationship: לפי חרב, נכה, בני דן, עלה, קרא, ישב, and בשם דן אביהם (כשם). Cf. also Judg. 1.34-35 where, however, as in Josh. 19.47, there is no discussion of a Danite migration, only mention that the Amorites prohibited the Danites from entering the plain but instead forced (לחץ/θλίβω) them back into the hill country.

49. Boling and Wright, *Joshua*, p. 463. Martin Noth is responsible for the critical apparatus to the book of Joshua in *BHK* (3rd end), where he suggests emending the text to ויצר (from the root צרר?). However, the intended purpose is not evident. Marten H. Woudstra (*The Book of Joshua* [NICOT; Grand Rapids: Eerdmans, 1981], p. 295) interprets 'went out from them' to mean that the Danite territory was 'too small for them'. This cannot be supported by the MT.

emendation, and one whose support in the LXX is questionable.[50] In the LXX, the subject of the verb θλίβω ('press upon, oppress') is not 'the boundary of their portion' (cf. the MT), but 'the Amorites'. The LXX is perhaps better translated: 'Now the Amorites were not permitting them to descend into the valley, but they took by oppression/affliction from them the boundary of their portion'.[51] The point is that the LXX does not read 'For the territory of the Danites was too restricted for them' (wrong subject), and thus does not support the emendation of וַיֵּצֵא in the MT to וַיְאָץ.[52]

Aside from this obscure note about the loss of their territory, Josh. 19.47 gives no explicit motivation for the Danite migration to the north. Nevertheless, the narrative in this single verse has a parallel in Judg. 18.1-31, an extended narrative detailing the Danite migration northward and, ultimately, the conquest and resettlement of Laish. While it is scholarly convention to trace literary development from the shorter to the longer text, my conclusion is that this addition to Joshua 19 (v. 47) comes from the hand of a scribe who already knew Judges 18 (already an appendix to the book of Judges). On the basis of this longer text, a scribe formulated the brief statement in Josh. 19.47. This interpolation may thus be understood as perhaps one of the latest additions to the book of Joshua.

(2) *Joshua 19.47-48 (LXX)*

A very different narrative about Dan, probably an independent tradition, appears in the LXX version of this portion of Joshua 19. After the enumeration of the cities in the territory of Dan, the LXX is translated as follows:

> [47] This is the inheritance of the tribe of the sons of Dan, according to their families, their cities and their villages. [47a] And the sons of Dan did not squeeze out the Amorite who pressed them hard into the hill country; now the Amorites were not permitting them [the Danites] to descend into the valley, but they took by oppression/affliction from them the boundary of their portion. [48] And the sons of Judah went and made war upon Lachish,

50. Nelson, *Joshua: A Commentary*, p. 219.

51. The critical phrase is ἔθλιψαν ἀπ, which occurs nowhere else in the LXX. Is this a Semitism (i.e. comparative use of the preposition—cf. Hebrew מִן)? Or might θλίβω in this instance have the sense of 'to take by means of oppression/affliction?' Note also that in some LXX manuscripts ἐπι occurs for ἀπο. In this case, the sense may be that the Amorites pressed upon (rather than oppress/afflict) the Danite boundaries, thus effectively limiting the tribe's movement and eventually taking over the territory.

52. For this translation of the LXX, see John Gray, *Joshua, Judges, Ruth* (NCB; Grand Rapids: Eerdmans, 1986), p. 160.

and when they had overtaken it, then they smote it with the mouth of the sword, and they inhabited it and they called the name of it Lasendak [Lucianic LXX has 'Lesen Dan']. [48a] And the Amorite remained to dwell in Elōm and in Salamein; and the hand of Ephraim was heavy upon them, and they became to them as forced labor.

In comparing the MT and the LXX of this passage, the only observed similarity is the summary statement regarding the cities and villages within the inheritance of the 'tribe of the sons of Dan'. However, even this note occurs in a different place in the two versions. While in the MT this conclusion is located at the end of the passage, in the LXX it has been moved to a place immediately after the list of cities. Thus, the LXX reads or flows more logically to a twentieth century, Western reader: the list of cities, the summary remark about cities and their villages, and then the note about Dan and the Amorites.[53]

The first of two more significant variations in the LXX is the remark about the interaction between the Danites and the Amorites (vv. 47a, 48a). According to this version, the Danites, inhabiting the hill country, were not only unable to expand their holding into the valley, neither were they able to maintain their borders against Amorite aggression. This is entirely absent from the MT. At this point in the LXX the tradition about Dan breaks off; the lasting image is of the Danites and the Amorites locked in a tug of war at the boundary. Nothing is narrated about the tribe of Dan migrating northward, conquering Leshem, and renaming the city after their eponymous ancestor. Instead, the LXX describes certain actions of the sons of Judah against the city of Lachish.[54]

The fundamental question, of course, concerns the origin of this LXX tradition. On the one hand, it is possible that this is a text-critical matter alone. Thus, Lindars has suggested that the LXX text (v. 48), Ἰούδα, represents a missed reading of τοῦ δὰν '(sons) of Dan'. In addition, the presence of Lachish rather than Leshem (MT) may point to an attempt by the LXX translator to replace an obscure or otherwise unknown place name (it may be significant that Leshem occurs *only* in Josh. 19.47 [MT]) with a more common, well known, name.[55]

53. If it is recognized that the narrative about the migration of Dan in the MT (v. 47) is a secondary addition to the text, then the text of the MT (without v. 47) reads equally smoothly.

54. Some LXX Mss read Δαν and λεσεμ for Judah and Lachish, respectively.

55. Barnabas Lindars, *Judges 1–5: A New Translation and Commentary* (Edinburgh: T. & T. Clark, 1995), p. 87. The critical apparatus in the Cambridge LXX

On the other hand, it is also possible that this LXX text reflects an alternate Hebrew *Vorlage*. Thus, Tov argues that 'the LXX reflects many pluses, minuses, and differences which, when retroverted into Hebrew, present a book different from that contained in MT'.[56] He notes that Josh. 19.47 is one of the important pluses contained in the LXX. Tov concludes:

> The data adduced so far lead to the view that the MT and LXX do not reflect textual differences, but rather two different *editions* of the book... An analysis of the minuses of the LXX leads to the conclusion that the edition of MT expanded the shorter one reflected in the LXX. In other words, there is a genetic relationship between the two editions. The pluses of the LXX do not contradict this assumption, but they slightly complicate the description.[57]

includes several other place names, most of which suggest that the *Vorlage* read לשם. Boling and Wright (*Joshua*, p. 466) suggest that Laish and Leshem are really names for the same place. According to these scholars, in the case of Leshem the last consonant may be an enclitic-mem.

56. Emanuel Tov, 'The Growth of the Book of Joshua in the Light of the Evidence of the LXX Translation', *ScrHier* 31 (1986), pp. 321-39 (322). According to Tov (pp. 326, 328), the pluses to the LXX are 'Hebraistic in diction', such that the retroversion into Hebrew is done with relative ease (see also Emanuel Tov, 'Midrash-Type Exegesis in the LXX of Joshua', *RB* 85 [1978], pp. 50-61 [51]; and Harry M. Orlinsky, 'The Hebrew Vorlage of the Septuagint of the Book of Joshua', in the Board of the Quarterly [eds.], *Congress Volume, Rome 1968* [VTSup, 17; Leiden: E.J. Brill, 1969], pp. 187-95). While Frank M. Cross, Jr (see P. Benoit, 'Editing the Manuscript Fragments from Qumran', *BA* 19 [1956], pp. 75-96 [83-86]) reported in 1956 that the fragments of Joshua recovered from Cave 4 at Qumran 'follow the tradition of the *Vorlage* of the Greek text', more recent study of these two fragments (4QJosh[a] and 4QJosh[b]) has led scholars to propose that a third text is known to us from Qumran, a text which Leonard Greenspoon has characterized as 'an evolving (that is, expanding) form of the tradition eventually designated MT' (Leonard Greenspoon, 'The Qumran Fragments of Joshua: Which Puzzle are They Part of and Where Do They Fit?', in George J. Brooke and Barnabas Lindars [eds.], *Septuagint, Scrolls and Cognate Studies: Papers Presented to the International Symposium on the Septuagint and Its Relations to the Dead Sea Scrolls and Other Writings [Manchester 1990]* [SBLSCS, 33; Atlanta: Scholars Press, 1992], pp. 159-94 [179]).

57. Tov, 'The Growth of the Book of Joshua', p. 337. Samuel Holmes argues similarly that the LXX translator rendered faithfully the Hebrew text before him, except that for Holmes the LXX and the MT tradents likely used an identical Hebrew *Vorlage* (*Joshua: The Hebrew and Greek Texts* [Cambridge: Cambridge University Press, 1914], pp. 14-16, 70-71). He proposes that while the LXX reflects more completely (in this case) the Hebrew *Vorlage*, a Hebrew reviser is responsible for the omission of the account of the Danite failure (LXX Josh. 19.47a) from the MT. Unfortunately, Holmes does not account for the origin of the LXX tradition about the sons of Judah and their conquest of Lachish. Instead, he writes that, after omitting the part about the Danite

So one may reason, following Tov, that the variance between the MT and the LXX versions of Josh. 19.47-48 is not due to the translation technique (omissions) of the LXX scribe in the latter centuries of the period before the common era. Rather, the difference between the MT and the LXX is the result of the LXX following a different Hebrew *Vorlage* of uncertain date, perhaps one whose ideological interest was in the tribe of Judah. A pro-Judah scribe, perhaps in the early years of the Divided Monarchy, removed the positive mention of the 'sons of Dan' and their conquest of Leshem (which was then renamed, according to the biblical witness, Dan, the northern city at which Jeroboam I erected a royal sanctuary [cf. Judg. 18; 1 Kgs 12.25-33] and replaced it with a record of Judah's conquest of Lachish.[58] This variant tradition was eventually preserved in the LXX.[59]

failure, 'the section containing the account of the conquest of Laish by Dan he [the Hebrew reviser] retained but transferred it to a position before P's subscription' (pp. 16-17).

58. Ostensibly the story of the conquest of Lachish by Judah in Josh. 19.47-48 (LXX) is dated to the Iron I period, before the rise of the monarchy in Israel. It is possible that the city was not inhabited at this time. The archaeological evidence reveals that Lachish, the largest city in Canaan after the destruction of Hazor in the thirteenth century, was an unfortified city during the Late Bronze Age. Stratum VII was destroyed about 1200 BCE; Stratum VI, the last Canaanite city, was destroyed in a great conflagration in about 1150-1130 BCE—the site was abandoned and not resettled until the tenth century. Stratum V, the Iron II city, was also unfortified. This city was destroyed again in 925 BCE, presumably by Shishak (David Ussishkin, 'Lachish', in *NEAEHL*, III, pp. 897-911 [905]. It is possible that if the note about Judah's conquest of Lachish is not entirely a historical fiction, then perhaps the scribe was aware of a destruction of the city in the period before the rise of the monarchy in Israel. This destruction was then later attributed to the tribe of Judah.

Not all scholars agree with this understanding of the origins of the MT and the LXX of Josh. 19.47-48. Boling and Wright (*Joshua*, pp. 465-66) trace the differences not to different prototypes, but to the various interests of Dtr[1] (the shorter MT) and Dtr[2] (the longer LXX).

59. This LXX tradition in Josh. 19.47-48 has some correspondence with that preserved in Judg. 1.34-35, which I include here only in translation (MT and LXX) and which will be examined further below. The MT reads: 'And the Amorite pressed/squeezed the sons of Dan toward the hill country, for he did not permit [them = the sons of Dan?] to descend to the valley. And the Amorite undertook/determined to dwell in Har-Heres, in Aijalon and in Shaalbim; and the hand of the house of Joseph was heavy and they were as forced labor.' The LXX is slightly, although significantly, different: 'And the Amorite pressed the sons of Dan into the hill country, because they [the sons of Dan] did not permit him [the Amorite] to descend into the valley. And the Amorite began to dwell in the hill country of ostraca/shells, in which there are bears

b. *Joshua 21*

In its present form, Joshua 21 enumerates the cities assigned to the Levites by Eleazer, the priest, Joshua, and the heads of the ancestral houses of the Israelite tribes, according to Yahweh's command to Moses (Num. 35.1-8). The levitical cities are selected from those cities listed in the tribal inheritances in Joshua 13–19 (which accounts for the absence of certain cult cities such as Jerusalem, Dan, Bethel, and Shiloh, which some scholars have expected to be included among the levitical cities).[60] While the other

---

and in which there are foxes, in Mursinōn and in Thalabein; and the hand of the house of Joseph was heavy upon the Amorite, and he became to them as forced labor.' It is interesting to observe that the MT of Judg. 1.34, concerning the Amorite oppression and confinement of the sons of Dan to the hill country, corresponds more closely to the LXX tradition of Josh. 19.47 than it does to the MT of that Joshua text. This may well point to the complex textual history of the book of Joshua. The LXX of Judg. 1.34, on the basis of a careful reading of the Greek text, presents a confused characterization of the sons of Dan. In the first half of the verse, the sons of Dan appear as the object of the Amorite aggression, while in the second half of the verse the subject/object roles are reversed: the sons of Dan (as subject) prevent the Amorite (object) from descending into the valley. (The difficulty of this verse is supported by the textual variants included in the critical apparatus of the Cambridge LXX, where there are Mss in which the Amorite continues as subject in the second half of v. 47, and the sons of Dan continue as object.) The picture given in this text, then, is of two different groups (Danites and Amorites) inhabiting the same hill country, the Amorites ultimately being subjected to forced labor by the house of Joseph. If this is the case, then it fits well into the rest of the second part of Judg. 1, where several tribes of Israel are depicted as dwelling together with elements of the indigenous population of the land, often subjecting the latter to forced labor (cf. Judg. 1.21, 23, 27-28, 29-30, 31-32, 33).

A comparison of the LXX of Josh. 19.47-48 and Judg. 1.34-35 reveals the following commonalities: the Amorites press the Danites into the hill country; and the Amorites are subjected to forced labor by another Israelite tribe. The differences are more numerous: there is no mention in Josh. 19.47-48 of the sons of Dan not permitting the Amorites to expand into the valley (cf. Judg. 1.34); Judg. 1.34-35 reports nothing of the Judahite conquest of Lachish (cf. Josh. 19.48); the habitation of the Amorites in the hill country is variously described in the two texts; and, finally, the Israelite tribe whose hand was heavy upon the Amorite was Joseph in Judges, but Ephraim in Joshua.

Significant is the observation that neither of these versions reports on the Danite migration to the North and the tribe's conquest of Laish. Thus we are left with the fact that while the MT records the Danite migration in both Josh. 19 and Judg. 18, the LXX preserves this story only in Judg. 18.

60. Na'aman, *Borders and Districts*, p. 217, followed by Nelson, *Joshua: A Commentary*, p. 240. The absence of certain cult centers from the roster of levitical cities indicates that the Levites were involved, at least at some point in time, in more than religious affairs.

tribes were allotted cities 'and their villages', in the case of the Levites, their portion in the land consisted of cities and 'their pasture lands'.[61] From the territory allotted to the tribe of Dan (in its southern location, according to Josh. 19.41-46) are given the cities of Eltekeh and Gibbethon, Aijalon and Gath-rimmon, together with their pastures (21.23-24). Unfortunately, recent archaeology has been unable to provide conclusive identifications for these cities; for each of the four levitical cities of the Danite inheritance, two possible identifications have been suggested. Eltekeh has been associated with both Khirbet el-Muqenna' and Tell esh-Shalaf.[62] For Gibbethon, Tell Malat and Ras Abu Hamid have been proposed. However, if this is the same Gibbethon as occurs in 1 Kgs 16.17-18, Peterson prefers

61. This distinction is significant for understanding the social status of the Levites and their function in the history of Israel. It is not altogether clear why the Levites were granted these pasture lands (common land), although it is possible that these tracts of land were necessary for the keeping of the herds required by the Levites' sacrificial system in later years, during which time greater emphasis was placed on animal rather than cereal offerings. According to Num. 35.3, the pasturelands were intended for the Levites' cattle (לבהמתם), their livestock (ולרכשם), and all their beasts (ולצל חיתם). (Both 'cattle' and 'livestock' appear in several places in the Hebrew Bible as sacrificial offerings. 'Beasts', however, seem not to occur in the context of sacrifice. Note that in BDB [p. 312] there is another noun, formed from the same root, which means 'community' [= 'kinfolk']. Thus, should this part of the verse be translated: 'for their cattle, and for their livestock, and for their whole community?') The allotment of pasturelands for animals rather than fields suitable for agriculture/farming may have to do with the mandate that the Levites are to have no inheritance in the land, since Yahweh (or the priesthood) is their inheritance. From the perspective of the agrarian world, one could say that the Levites, as government officials, were not themselves involved in the work of the peasant farmers who worked the agricultural land (thus they had no need of fields for cultivation), but rather were concerned with the affairs of the urban elite who inhabited the pre-industrial city. (It is possible that the Levites were part of the retainer class. See Gerhard E. Lenski, *Power and Privilege: A Theory of Social Stratification* [New York: McGraw–Hill, 1966], pp. 243-48. Note Lenski's discussion on the retainers' role of mediating between the ruling class and the peasants [p. 246]; cf. 2 Chron. 24.10-11.)

62. Khirbet el-Muqenna' was suggested by Albright in the mid-1920s, and is maintained most recently by John L. Peterson ('Eltekeh', in *ABD*, II, pp. 483-84). However, the current excavators of the site (better known as Tel Miqne), Trude Dothan and Seymour Gitin ('Miqne, Tel [Ekron]', in *NEAEHL*, III, pp. 1051-59), identify it as biblical Ekron rather than biblical Eltekeh. On the suitability of Tel esh-Shalaf, see Benjamin Mazar, 'The Cities of the Territory of Dan', in Shmuel Ahituv and Baruch A. Levine (eds.), *The Early Biblical Period: Historical Studies* (Jerusalem: Israel Exploration Society, 1986), pp. 110-12.

Tell Malat, which is a significant, fortified site.[63] Aijalon has been identified as either Yalo or Tel Qoqa.[64] Finally, suggestions for the identification of Gath-rimmon include Tel Gerisa (= Tell Jerisheh) and Tell Abu Zeitun (among the sites in the Bene-Barak region).[65]

The date of this list of levitical cities has been the object of much scholarly interest. Suggestions range from the time before the monarchy in Israel to the postexilic period, although the former has been espoused most recently only by Kaufmann.[66] Proposed dates during the monarchic period include the tenth, eighth, and seventh centuries. Recognizing the twelve-tribe scheme to be a creation of the monarchic period, the tenth century, the time of the United Monarchy, is likely to be the earliest possible date for the system of levitical cities preserved in Joshua 21. Contrary to Kaufmann's notion of an 'ancient utopia', Albright assumed the list had a historical quality about it. According to Albright, 'the only systematic way in which to tackle the problem of the date of our list is to find a time, if possible, during which all the towns listed in it belonged to Israel'.[67] For Albright, that time was the end of the reign of David, or the beginning of the reign of Solomon (roughly the period 975–950 BCE).[68] Albright suggested that the levitical cities served an administrative function within the

63. John L. Peterson, 'Gibbethon', in *ABD*, II, pp. 1006-1007.

64. John L. Peterson, 'Aijalon', in *ABD*, I, p. 131.

65. Both sites have evidence of occupation from the Late Bronze Age through Iron Age II (occupation at Tel Gerisa begins in the Middle Bronze Age IIA). See Zeev Herzog, 'Gerisa, Tel', in *NEAEHL*, II, pp. 480-84, and Jacob Kaplan, 'Bene-Barak and Vicinity', in *NEAEHL*, I, pp. 186-87.

66. Yehezkel Kaufmann, *The Biblical Account of the Conquest of Palestine* (Jerusalem: Magnes Press/Hebrew University Press, 1953), pp. 40-46. Yet even he argues that the list is an 'ancient utopia', deriving from early in the conquest period, but never reflecting a historical reality. One of the keys to Kaufmann's argument is the absence of Jerusalem from the list. He cannot envisage that a list of cultic cities dating from the time after David's conquest of Jerusalem would omit the religious center of ancient Israel. Thus, according to Kaufmann, the list must come from a time before Jerusalem became a part of the Israelite nation. A second important part of Kaufmann's argument is his identification of the Levites as strictly religious functionaries, whom he cannot imagine ever inhabiting cities which did not include shrines. Since a number of the levitical cities in the list were not shrine cities, he concludes that the list cannot reflect a real situation at any point in history.

67. W.F. Albright, 'The List of Levitic Cities', in American Academy for Jewish Research, *Louis Ginzberg Jubilee Volume: On the Occasion of His Seventieth Birthday* (New York: American Academy for Jewish Research, 1945), pp. 49-73 (56).

68. Albright, 'The List of Levitic Cities', p. 58.

reorganization of the nascent Israelite kingdom.[69] Mazar and Aharoni follow Albright in dating the list to the time of the United Monarchy in Israel, the former preferring the reign of Solomon, the latter opting for the reign of David.[70]

However, the archaeological record may raise questions about a tenth-century date for this list. In his 1977 dissertation, Peterson attempted to identify the sites of the levitical cities in the land of Israel and, by means of surface surveys and excavation reports, sought to determine at what time all of these cities were inhabited. Peterson discovered that more than half of the sites identified as levitical cities show no evidence of tenth-century occupation. His conclusion is that the list of levitical cities must come from the eighth century, a century or two after David and Solomon.[71]

---

69. William Foxwell Albright, *Archaeology and the Religion of Israel* (Baltimore: The Johns Hopkins University Press, 1942), pp. 121-24. On this administrative function of the Levites and the levitical cities in the period of the United Monarchy, see also, Kallai, *Historical Geography of the Bible*, pp. 448-55.

70. B. Mazar, 'The Cities of the Priests and the Levites', in The Board of the Quarterly (eds.), *Congress Volume, Oxford 1959* (VTSup, 7; Leiden: E.J. Brill, 1960), pp. 193-205; Yohanan Aharoni, *The Land of the Bible: A Historical Geography* (Philadelphia: Westminster Press, rev. and enlarged edn, 1979), pp. 301-305. Mazar further develops the administrative duties of the Levites, which he proposes may have been instituted under the model of Egyptian governance in Canaan.

71. John L. Peterson, 'A Topographical Surface Survey of the Levitical "Cities" of Joshua 21 and 1 Chronicles 6: Studies in the Levites in Israelite Life and Religion' (unpublished ThD dissertation, Chicago Institute of Advanced Theological Studies and Seabury-Western Theological Seminary, 1977), p. 701. The results of his work have been accepted by Boling and Wright, and included in their Anchor Bible commentary (*Joshua*, pp. 492-97; see also Robert G. Boling, 'Levitical Cities: Archaeology and Texts', in Ann Kort and Scott Morschauser [eds.], *Biblical and Related Studies Presented to Samuel Iwry* [repr., Winona Lake, IN: Eisenbrauns, 1985], pp. 23-32). Regarding the purpose of the levitical cities, Peterson adopts Campbell's unsubstantiated thesis (which Campbell himself developed from the work of Wright) that the Levites were the 'story-tellers in the countryside', the 'theological educators of Israel'. Thus, Peterson is led to interpret the levitical cities as 'Yahweh teaching centers' ('outposts for the Mosaic teaching'), rather than as administrative/political centers ('A Topographical Surface Survey', pp. 707-708). Menahem Haran (*Temples and Temple-Service in Ancient Israel: An Inquiry into Biblical Cult Phenomena and the Historical Setting of Priestly Schools* [Winona Lake, IN: Eisenbrauns, 1985 (1978)], pp. 132-48) also finally dates the list of levitical cities to the time of Hezekiah in the eighth century. (In an earlier, two-part article ['Studies in the Account of the Levitical Cities', *JBL* 80 (1961), pp. 45-54, 156-65], Haran investigated the lists of levitical cities in light of the historical and utopian extremes of scholars in the first half of the twentieth century.)

Peterson's investigation seems to be, at first glance, irrefutable evidence against a date for this list in the period of the United Monarchy. However, two critical points must be made. First, not only is the identification of sites in Palestine with ancient Israelite cities (as recorded in the biblical text) not beyond question, but surface surveys are not always the most accurate representation of a given site. Second, Peterson's focus on pottery remains may be construed as a narrow criterion.[72] What is the other evidence of occupation in the tenth century BCE? Does the stratigraphy of a particular site (or the remains of a fortified wall, or burials), when correlated with other sites of known date, provide evidence of earlier habitation? *The New Encyclopedia of Archaeological Excavations in the Holy Land* (1993) reports evidence of tenth-century occupation for the following sites identified by Peterson: Hebron, Eshtemoa(?), Gibeon, Qibzaim, Elteqe (whether the remains are Israelite or not remains an open question), Jarmuth, Mishal, Qedesh (poorly represented), and Joqneam.[73] While, admittedly, some of the evidence is better than other, there is evidence of tenth-century occupation (to some degree) for each of these sites.

The traditio-historical scholars Alt and Noth have proposed still other dates for the list of levitical cities. On the basis of the geographical 'gaps' in the list (the hill country of Ephraim and Manasseh, which Alt under-

His thesis is that 'this account is not to be understood in terms of either of these possibilities, because it actually contains both the historical and the utopian elements'. The second part of his article notes how each of these elements occurs in the list. Haran categorizes the following items as utopian: (1) the measurements of the pastureland surrounding the cities as an exact square of 2000 cubits; (2) the uniformity of these dimensions for all 48 levitical cities; (3) the jubilee legislation, which is interwoven with the idea of the levitical cities; (4) the portrayal of these cities as the exclusive habitation of Levites; and (5) the differentiation between priests and Levites. According to Haran, these utopian features are balanced by five realistic elements: (1) the dispersion of the tribe of Levites throughout the land; (2) the settlement of Levites in cities without shrines; (3) the location of levitical cities beyond the ideal boundaries of the land of Israel (cf. Num. 34.1-12); (4) the lack of distinction between priests and Levites, such that 'the same legal status and the same social and economic position characterize all the forty-eight cities'; and (5) the greater number of Levites relative to the number of priests in the Priestly material. Haran initially concluded that the account of the levitical cities reflects an actual, historical situation (which he did not date), to which certain utopian characteristics have been added.

72. Cf. G.W. Ahlström, *Royal Administration and National Religion in Ancient Palestine* (SHANE, 1; Leiden: E.J. Brill, 1982), p. 53.

73. For publication details for Stern (ed.), *The New Encyclopedia of Archaeological Excavations*, consult the Abbreviations list—*NEAEHL*.

stood as the focus of Josiah's activity), which resulted from the Josianic reformation, Alt dated it to the time of Josiah's reform in the seventh century.[74] On the other hand, Noth argued for a post-Josianic, postexilic date for the list, partly on account of the organization of the Levites according to the families of Kohath, Gershon, and Merari—an organization which is not yet reflected in the books of Ezra and Nehemiah. More specifically, Noth locates the list of levitical cities in the time just before the restoration in the Persian period.[75]

Additional scholars have located the composition of this list of levitical cities in the postexilic period. At the end of the nineteenth century, Wellhausen argued that the list of levitical cities represents an 'artificial construction' whose origin is not the tenth century or earlier, but the postexilic period, the period of Judaism.[76] In part, his conclusion is based on the observation that several of the levitical cities were not under Israelite control during the pre-monarchic and early monarchic periods. Also understanding the Levites strictly in religious terms, Wellhausen writes:

> The theocratic ideal was from the exile onwards the centre of all thought and effort, and it annihilated the sense for objective truth, all regard and interest for the actual facts as they had been handed down… Judaism is just the right soil for such an artificial growth as the forty-eight priestly and Levitical cities.[77]

More recently, the catalog of those assigning a postexilic date to the system of levitical cities depicted in Joshua 21 includes Spencer, Ahlström, and Nelson.[78] For each of them, the archaeological record (which I have

---

74. Albrecht Alt, 'Bemerkungen zu einigen judäischen Ortslisten des Alten Testaments', in *idem, Kliene Schriften zur Geschichte des Volkes Israel* (3 vols.; Munich: C.H. Beck, 1959), II, pp. 289-305. So also, Na'aman (*Borders and Districts*, pp. 203-36), who notes that one of the reasons that the period of the United Monarchy is to be dismissed is that 'many of the cult centres of that time are not included among the Levitical cities' (p. 207). The chief problem with this remark is that it assumes that the Levites had a cultic or religious function alone. It is more likely that the Levites had both political-administrative and cultic responsibilities. The sharp distinction between things political and religious is a much more modern phenomenon (see Malina and Rohrbaugh, *Social-Science Commentary on the Synoptic Gospels*, pp. 256-57).

75. Noth, *Das Buch Josua*, pp. 131-32.

76. Wellhausen, *Prolegomena*, pp. 159-61.

77. Wellhausen, *Prolegomena*, p. 161.

78. John R. Spencer, 'The Levitical Cities: A Study of the Role and Function of the Levites in the History of Israel' (unpublished PhD dissertation, University of Chicago, 1980); *idem*, 'Levitical Cities', in *ABD*, IV, pp. 310-11; Ahlström, *Royal Administra-*

suggested is equivocal) is strong evidence against a tenth-century date for the list. As an artificial creation by a literary figure in the postexilic period (perhaps on the basis of an earlier city-list and a recollection of an old administrative system involving Levites), the purpose of Joshua 21 was to help explain where the Levites came from, and to justify Israel's claim on the land of Canaan.

Critical biblical scholarship in the twentieth century, then, has been unable to arrive at a consensus on the date of the list of levitical cities in Joshua 21. The current trend, judging by the most recent commentary on the book of Joshua (Nelson) and study on the levitical cities (Ben Zvi), is to understand the list in ch. 21 as an artificial construction dating from the postexilic period.[79] This is, in part, due to the archaeological evidence; it also has to do with a focus on the question of the relative status of various levitical families, and almost exclusive attention to the cultic/religious functions of the Levites in ancient Israel. While it is, perhaps, most likely that the *particular system* of the levitical cities recorded in Joshua 21 dates from the postexilic period, I have already indicated that the archaeological evidence marshaled against a tenth-century date for the list is not incontrovertible. Even the ideal characteristics of this list do not necessarily rule out the time of the United Monarchy. As previously noted (see the discussion of Josh. 13–19, above), there is good reason to understand the twelve-tribe scheme as a literary product of the period of the United Monarchy, formulated as part of the administrative organization of the nascent kingdom. If this is accepted as plausible, then the notion of an idealized arrangement of levitical cities from the same period cannot automatically be dismissed (although such an idealized arrangement could also come from many later periods; cf. 1 Chron. 1–9). Thus, whether the final form of the list of levitical cities in Joshua 21 is best dated to the tenth or eighth or sixth century (or later) remains an open question. There is no

---

tion, pp. 52-55; Nelson, *Joshua: A Commentary*, pp. 238-41. See also, Ehud Ben Zvi, 'The List of the Levitical Cities', *JSOT* 54 (1992), pp. 77-106.

79. Japhet (*I and II Chronicles*, p. 147) maintains the traditional position that the Chronicler's version of the list of levitic cities is dependent on that in the book of Joshua. She notes (p. 164) that the Davidic context of the list of levitical cities in 1 Chron. 6 is a context different from that in Josh. 21 (the time of Joshua) and may be closer to historical fact. Nevertheless, she includes this caveat: 'Whether or not the list was promulgated at the time of David (or, for that matter, at any point in the history of Israel) should be decided without the benefit of the Chronicler's testimony on the matter' (p. 164).

question, however, about the location of the levitical cities assigned from
the territory of the tribe of Dan: they are in the south. Further, if this
particular list originated in the exilic period, then it is evidence of the
persistence of the tradition (if not the actual settlement) of Danite territory
in the south.

The levitical cities owe their name to the Levites who are, in the biblical
traditions, associated with them. There is some evidence that the Levites
may have functioned as part of the administrative structure of the central
government during the reigns of David and Solomon. A key passage is
1 Chron. 26.30, according to which a family of Levites from Hebron was
appointed by David for 'every public affair of Yahweh and every service
of the king' (לכל מלאכת יהוה ולעבדת המלך). This union of cultic and
political/administrative functions where Levites are concerned suggests
that the popular premise that these two spheres of service are mutually
exclusive originates in an anachronistic reading of ancient Israelite culture.
Neither an exclusively political, nor an exclusively religious understanding of the role of the Levites is satisfactory. Rather, politics and religion
were more closely associated in antiquity, so that it is likely that the
Levites not only fulfilled certain priestly functions, but also carried out
other responsibilities as servants of the state.[80] Ahlström argues that
understanding the Levites as governmental officials accounts for their
lack of an 'inheritance' in the land: 'As officials at national shrines they
could not [inherit the land]. Their employer, the state or state sanctuary,

---

80. It is, indeed, anachronistic to suggest that in ancient Israel there was a separate
religious institution run by exclusively 'religious' personnel. Malina and Rohrbaugh
(*Social-Science Commentary on the Synoptic Gospels*, p. 396) write that 'though it is
common in the contemporary world to think of politics, the economic system, and
religion as distinct social institutions (and to make arguments about keeping them
separate), no such pattern existed in antiquity. In the world of the New Testament only
two institutions existed: kinship and politics. Neither religion nor economics had a
separate institutional existence or was conceived of as a system on its own.' Instead,
religion was 'embedded' in the two principle institutions of the ancient world: politics
and kinship. Religion in antiquity was either political religion (administered by political
personnel) or domestic religion (run by family personnel). The objection that this
social description of the New Testament world does not apply to the social world of
early Israel is rendered ineffective by the realization that both 'worlds' were agrarian
societies, the characteristics of which persist over time. Ahlström also argues that the
union of temple and palace makes up 'the essence of the state' (*Royal Administration*,
pp. 3-4). Note also the confluence of 'religious' and 'political' responsibilities associated with Israel's earliest monarchs.

owned land outside the cities where they lived.'[81] Further, the Levites's status as royal appointees, owing loyalty to the king, contributes to an understanding of their association with the גרים, who are better understood as dependent clients rather than 'sojourners'. According to Ahlström, 'the word *lwy* meant client. As government appointees they were not members of the clans of the district where they lived; they were clients of the government.'[82]

What later came to be systematized as 'levitical cities' were at an earlier date cities throughout the land where Levites were stationed as government officials. It was from these cities that they administered areas newly incorporated into the kingdom of Israel, instructed the people in the 'law of Yahweh' (2 Chron. 17.9), and assisted in the collection of taxes (24.9-11). While the list in Joshua 21 may, in fact, date from a later period, since the role of the Levites was well-known already from the tenth century (and since the compiler made use of a tenth-century document [Josh. 13–19]), the list has a certain ring of authenticity about it.

This picture of the Levites (in whom are combined religious and civil functions), derived from the biblical evidence, is corroborated by what anthropologists have ascertained about administration in preindustrial society, that societal type which characterized early Israel. In his study of human societies, Lenski suggests that it is only with the emergence of *advanced* agrarian society some time in the eighth century BCE (characterized materially by the more widespread use of iron for ordinary tools) that there is 'increasing separation of religion and political institutions'.[83] Still, Lenski goes on to write that 'despite the growing organizational separation of politics and religion, the two systems continued to work closely to-

81. Ahlström, *Royal Administration*, p. 50.
82. Ahlström, *Royal Administration*, p. 51. Ahlström proposes that 'the label "Levite" was a technical term for priests and government officials stationed at different locations in the kingdom. This supports a derivation of the word from לוה (*lāwāh*), "to accompany", in niph. "to attach oneself to", or "to be bound". These persons were, thus, associated with, or bound, to the central government as its employees... Any royal employee, either in Israel or in Judah, may have been called a Levite' (pp. 48-49).
83. Lenski, *Human Societies*, p. 283. Note that according to this chronological scheme, the United Monarchy (tenth century) is to be located within a *simple* agrarian society, characterized by a greater association of the political and religious institutions. The dominant image of the Levites in the Hebrew Bible as religious officials may be the result of the superimposition of a later role (eighth century and later) over an earlier one. 'Increasing separation' suggests that a complete division was not necessarily a *fait accompli* at any point in Israel's history.

gether, and political and religious leaders were normally allied'.[84] Among other things, the religious functionaries defended the elite class against the peasants, and served to provide divine legitimation for the actions of the ruling class. In return for their service, the clergy would receive from their agrarian rulers land grants and special tax exemptions.[85]

This model for understanding the function of the Levites from cultural anthropology is reflected in the picture of the Levites preserved in the biblical tradition. The reference to both political/administrative and religious functions in 1 Chronicles 26 has already been noted. In addition, the political/administrative role of the Levites in the early years of the monarchy in Israel may be detected in their expulsion from the north by Jeroboam I (1 Kgs 12). Toews argues persuasively in his monograph that, in light of the political influence exercised by those also responsible for religious activities (priests), it was necessary for Jeroboam I to dismiss some Levites and appoint new leaders. He writes that

> one could surmise that at the time of Israel's secession from the United Monarchy one of Jeroboam's administrative priorities will have been to install priests loyal to himself for official religious service in the new state. Probably Jeroboam also had to expel certain of the priests already in office because he could not count on their loyalty to his kingship since they had previously served the interests of the Davidic monarchy in Jerusalem.[86]

This close relationship between the ruler and the Levites is further supported by the phenomenon of the levitical cities. In return for their loyal service, the Levites received certain benefits, such as land grants. In *Peasants*, Wolff outlines three types of domain (ultimate ownership or control over the use of a given area): patrimonial, prebendal, and mercantile. Most immediately applicable is Wolff's definition of prebendal domain:

> *Prebendal domain* over land differs from patrimonial domain in that it is not heritable, but granted to officials who draw tribute from the peasantry in their capacity as servants of the state. Such domains are not lineage domains, then; rather they represent grants of income—*prebends*—in return for the exercise of a particular office. The term *prebend*, used in this way by Max Weber, originally referred to stipends, or 'livings,' granted the European

---

84. Lenski, *Human Societies*, p. 284.

85. Lenski, *Human Societies*, p. 285. Cf. 2 Chron. 24.9-11.

86. Wesley I. Toews, *Monarchy and Religious Institution in Israel under Jeroboam I* (SBLMS, 47; Atlanta: Scholars Press, 1993), p. 90. See also Ahlström, *Royal Administration*, p. 57.

clergy. This form of remuneration is characteristically associated with strong-
ly centralized bureaucratic states... The political organization...attempted to
curtail heritable claims to land and tribute, and asserted instead the eminent
domain of a sovereign, a despot, whose claims overrode all inferior claims to
domain. Any inferior domain was granted to officials in their capacities as
servants of the sovereign.[87]

By applying the prebendal domain model, the following picture of the
Levites and the levitical cities in ancient Israel may be constructed. In
addition to the religious functions, which are well documented in the
biblical tradition (and which came to dominate the office of Levite later),
the Levites performed an administrative function. The Levites were governmental officials, servants of the state, to whom were granted by the
king cities throughout the land (prebendal domains) in which to live and
fulfill their prescribed duties. The location of the levitical cities in regions
beyond the immediate influence of the capital suggests that a part of the
Levites's function was to represent the king, extend the authority of the
central government, and bolster support for the state in problem areas/
territories in need of strengthening.

The need for Jeroboam I to reorganize the administrative officials in the
north indicates that this organization was not an innovation, but rather an
expected reorganization of a system of administration which he inherited,
one that was likely to have been already in place during the time of
Solomon.[88] That the Levites appear in the latest traditions and redactional
layers of the Hebrew Bible as simply religious leaders is due, in part, to
the developing separation of the religious and political institutions in
advanced agrarian society and, in part, due to the collapse of the state, first
in the north (722 BCE) and later in the south (586 BCE).[89]

While religious functions dominate the picture of the Levites in the
biblical tradition, there is sufficient reason (textual and comparative/social
science) for arguing that they were politically aligned at some earlier point
in their history.

87. Wolff, *Peasants*, p. 51.
88. For this date, see also J. Maxwell Miller, 'Rehoboam's Cities of Defense and
the Levitical City List', in Leo G. Perdue, Lawrence E. Toombs and Gary L. Johnson
(eds.), *Archaeology and Biblical Interpretation: Essays in Memory of D. Glenn Rose*
(Atlanta: John Knox Press, 1987), pp. 273-86 (282).
89. Note, however, the re-emergence of a confluence of cultic and civic functions
in what has been termed the 'Citizen–Temple Community' in the theocratic government led by religious officials in the postexilic period (see Joel Weinberg, *The Citizen–
Temple Community* [JSOTSup, 151; Sheffield: JSOT Press, 1992]).

2. *The Book of Judges*

Turning to Judges, references to Dan occur throughout the book in a variety of literary contexts: in the report of the Israelites settlement of Canaan (1.34-35); in the Song of Deborah (5.17—recognized as one of the oldest texts in the Hebrew Bible); in the Samson narrative (13.2, 25; 16.31); and in the story of the Danites's northward migration to, and conquest of, Laish (ch. 18). Since Noth included only Judges 5 from among these Dan texts in the original edition of the DH, a part of the present study must be to address the question of provenance of these other texts.[90] Thus, while the book of Judges is included in the final form of the DH, it is likely that most of the occurrences of Dan in Judges occur in texts that do not come from the hand of Noth's sixth-century Dtr. Each text must be investigated individually, with some attention to its origin, in order to determine what it contributes to our understanding of Dan in the book of Judges.

a. *Judges 1*

Dan first appears in the book of Judges in 1.34-35, at the end of a report describing the Israelite tribes's settlement of Canaan 'after the death of Joshua' (1.1). According to this report, Yahweh directs the tribe of Judah to go up first, with its brother-tribe, Simeon, against the Canaanite inhabitants of the land, in order to take possession of the inheritance allotted to Judah. A litany of Judahite victories follows (vv. 4-20), interspersed with a discrete narrative about the defeat of Adoni-Bezek, and the introduction of the Judahite, Othniel (cf. 3.9-11). Judah's success in the first part of the chapter is set in stark contrast with the ineffectiveness of the other Israelite tribes in the remainder of the chapter (vv. 21-36). The failure of the sons of Dan (vv. 34-35) concludes the report:

> [34] And the Amorites pressed the sons of Dan toward the hill country; and they did not allow them to descend to the plain. [35] And the Amorite persisted to dwell in Har-Heres, in Aijalon, and in Shaalbim; but the hand of the house of Joseph was heavy and they became as forced labor.

---

90. Noth identified the rest of these Dan texts as later additions. See the Overview in Anthony F. Campbell, 'Martin Noth and the Deuteronomistic History', in Steven L. McKenzie and M. Patrick Graham (eds.), *The History of Israel's Traditions: The Heritage of Martin Noth* (JSOTSup, 182; Sheffield: Sheffield Academic Press, 1994), pp. 31-62 (34).

[Notes on the MT:

Verse 34: For נתנו ('did not allow him'), one medieval manuscript of the Hebrew Old Testament, the LXX, the Syriac, the Targum, and Josh. 19.47a (according to the LXX) read נתנום ('did not allow *them*'). The MT is certainly the more difficult of the options, and perhaps originally recognized 'Dan' as the antecedent (it is easier to understand the plural form as a scribal correction to coordinate with the pronominal antecedent, 'the *sons of* Dan'). Alternatively, the consonantal text (נתנו) may be read as the qal perfect third common plural form of the verb, understanding 'the sons of Dan' as the definite direct object (its occurrence earlier in the verse serves a double-duty function).

Verse 35: For 'in Har-Heres', Josh. 19.41 reads 'Ir-Shemesh'. After the phrase '(and the hand of the house of Joseph) was heavy', the editor of the book of Judges in *BHS* (R. Meyer) suggests inserting 'upon them'; compare Josh. 19.48a and text-critical note c in Judg. 1.35. After 'the house of Joseph' in the MT, the LXX adds 'upon the Amorite'. Finally, after 'they became', the LXX adds 'to him', the LXX [Codex Vaticanus] and Josh. 19.48 (according to the LXX) adds 'to them'. Lacking any Hebrew manuscript support, and recognizing them as attempts to harmonize a difficult text along the lines of a similar passage (Josh. 19), none of the proposed emendations in v. 35 are adopted in the present translation.]

In several respects, these verses about Dan are unique within the context of Judges 1. First of all, here the tribe is referred to as 'the sons of Dan', rather than simply as 'Dan', as one would expect (cf. vv. 27, 29, 30, 31, 33). Second, the familiar refrain, 'N did not dispossess the inhabitants of X', is altogether absent. Rather than the Danites attempting unsuccessfully to dispossess the Amorites, the latter initiate the action (understood here as a challenge) and press the sons of Dan (back) into the hill country. Third, while all of the other Israelite tribes are mentioned in connection with specific places (cities and their daughter-villages; vv. 4, 8, 10, 11, 17, 18, 22, 27, 29, 30, 31, 33), the tribe of Dan's geographic location is described only in vague, general terms: there is a hill country and a plain. Fourth, it is in 1.34-36 alone that the indigenous population is designated 'the Amorites' rather than 'the Canaanites'. While this may seem to lend an air or authenticity or particularity to the passage, in fact it is no less a general designation than Canaanite.[91]

91. It is not clear why the editor of this passage used 'Amorites' in Judg. 1.34-35. Earlier scholars (see the discussion in Burney, *The Book of Judges*, pp. 30-31; George F. Moore, *A Critical and Exegetical Commentary on Judges* [ICC; New York: Charles Scribner's Sons, 1901], pp. 52-53) proposed that it was due to a different source (E rather than J). It has also been suggested (see Lindars, *Judges 1–5*, p. 68) that a later hand changed 'Canaanites' to 'Amorites' in vv. 34-35 under the influence of the textual confusion in v. 36 (where 'Amorites' is already a corruption from 'Edomites?'). In his

How does Judges 1 contribute to our understanding of Dan in the Hebrew Bible? Ironically, this text seems to relate more about the Amorites than the 'sons of Dan'. In both verses (cf. v. 36), the Amorites are the subject of the verbs: the Amorites oppressed the sons of Dan and prohibited them from expanding their territory into the plain; the Amorites also continued to dwell in certain cities (Har-Heres, Aijalon, and Shaalbim). In all of Judges 1, only Dan among the Israelite tribes occurs as the *object* of an action; every other tribe acts, rather than is acted upon.[92] While this text is often understood as a parallel to Josh. 19.40-48, there is here in Judges 1 no mention of the cities inhabited by the tribe of Dan, cities from which (according to the pattern in Judg. 1) the Danites attempted to dispossess the indigenous population. However, v. 35 lists the Amorite cities of Har-Heres, Aijalon, and Shaalbim, all of which are located in the Shephelah east of Gezer.[93] From this we may infer that Dan was located in the northern Judean hill country, while the Amorites either inhabited, or at least controlled access to the valley (of Aijalon).[94] Therefore, it is reasonable to conclude that Judg. 1.34-35 situates Dan in its southern inheritance (cf. Josh. 19.40-48). Nevertheless, the general way in which the editor describes the Danites's southern inheritance (completely lacking in specificity) suggests that the editor may not have been familiar with the details of the

study of the 'lists of pre-Israelite nations', Ishida concluded that the preferred use of 'Canaanite' or 'Amorite' to designate the people of Palestine generally follows a historical development, and that by the ninth or eighth century BCE, 'Amorite' was preferred (Tomoo Ishida, 'The Structure of the Lists of Pre-Israelite Nations', *Bib* 60 [1979], pp. 461-90 [477]).

92. The fact that the Amorites occur as the subject of the action in vv. 34-36 gives the impression that this section is really about the Amorites and not the Danites at all—who appear almost incidentally. While Ken Stone's study ('Gender and Homosexuality in Judges 19: Subject—Honor, Object—Shame?', *JSOT* 67 [1995], pp. 87-107), is primarily concerned with the issues of gender and homosexuality, and so is not readily applicable to this text, the subtitle is suggestive for reading Judg. 1.34 within the context of the categories of honor and shame (see esp. pp. 96-98). The inability to defend oneself successfully in an instance of challenge/riposte (as one may interpret the interaction between the Amorites and the Danites) results in the diminution of one's honor.

93. On the identification of Har-Heres with Beth-Shemesh/Ir-Shemesh, see Burney, *The Book of Judges*, p. 32; Aharoni, *The Land of the Bible*, p. 236. According to Josh. 19.41-43, these are cities within the Danite inheritance.

94. This is at odds with what is known about the Amorites, whom most scholars locate in the hill country, either to the east or to the west of the Jordan River.

Danite settlement in the south. That is, it looks as though this passage was written at a time when a Danite occupation in this region was remembered, although the details of Dan's habitation in the south had been forgotten. Significantly, this text is silent about the Danite migration northward and the conquest of Laish, although it is assumed that the editor was aware of this tradition. Its chief interest appears to be in the Danites's relationship with the Amorites.

An important question for understanding Dan in this text is: To what does the appellation 'Amorites' refer?[95] The term first occurs in Old Akkadian texts of the third millennium as a geographic reference to the region lying west of Mesopotamia. Schoville notes that while the term may refer primarily to Syria (since this is the region of greatest Mesopotamian interaction with the west), it may also connote the whole of Syria-Palestine.[96] It was only during the Amarna Period (MB) in the Levant that 'Amorite' designated a particular political entity. Liverani observes that 'at the end of the fifteenth century, [central or southern Syria] took on a definite political shape, with the beginning of the kingdom of Amurru under Abdi-Aširta and his descendants'.[97] By the end of the thirteenth century, however, Amurru ceased to exist as a separate state, and the term came to designate, once again, a larger geographical region. According to Mendenhall, 'during the LB Age, the Amorites had evidently become thoroughly assimilated into local populations both in the E and the W, as well as in the NE Syrian homeland, so that after that it is no longer possible to identify a specific Amorite cultural/linguistic group'.[98]

Thus, during the Iron Age, 'Amorite' was the usual way to refer generally to the population of Syria-Palestine. The Hebrew Bible contains numerous references to the Amorites. The Amorites are included, for example, in several lists of nations to be dispossessed by the settling

---

95. Contributions to the investigation of this question include: Kathleen M. Kenyon, *Amorites and Canaanites* (Schweich Lectures, 1963; London: Oxford University Press, 1966); M. Liverani, 'The Amorites', in D.J. Wiseman (ed.), *Peoples of Old Testament Times* (Oxford: Clarendon Press, 1973), pp. 100-33; George E. Mendenhall, 'Amorites', in *ABD*, I, pp. 199-202; Keith N. Schoville, 'Canaanites and Amorites', in Alfred J. Hoerth, Gerald L. Mattingly and Edwin M. Yamauchi (eds.), *Peoples of the Old Testament World* (Cambridge: Lutterworth; Grand Rapids: Baker Book House, 1994), pp. 157-82.

96. Schoville, 'Canaanites and Amorites', p. 160.

97. Liverani, 'The Amorites', p. 116.

98. Mendenhall, 'Amorites', p. 201.

Israelites (e.g. Deut. 7.1).[99] There are also many references to the Amorites which locate them east of the Jordan River, specifically in the Transjordanian hill country.[100] The two 'kings of the Amorites', Sihon and Og, against whom Israel fought en route to the land of Canaan, are both associated with cities east of the Jordan River: Heshbon, and Ashtaroth and Edrei, respectively (Num. 21.26; Deut. 1.4; 4.46-47). Nowhere else in the Hebrew Bible are the Amorites located precisely where they are in Judg. 1.34-35 (36).

The evidence argues against an understanding of the Amorites in the Hebrew Bible as a particular political entity, inhabiting a well-demarcated geographical area, and in favor of recognizing 'Amorite' as a general reference to the indigenous population of Syria-Palestine.[101] If this is the case, then the value of this text for the reconstruction of the history of the tribe of Dan is limited.[102] These verses are full of generalities, and short on specifics. The precise location of the confrontation described in v. 34 cannot be determined (there is only a vague reference to the hill country and the plain, and it is not certain that the cities mentioned in v. 35 mark the extent of Amorite control). In addition, it has just been shown that 'the Amorites' is best understood not as a reference to a specific nation, but to a portion of the indigenous population generally. While the editor responsible for this passage is aware of a Danite presence in the south at some time in history, he is no longer able to specify the geographical location.

99. Ishida ('Structure and Historical Implications', pp. 461-90) has studied the lists of pre-Israelite nations in the Hebrew Bible and has come to the conclusion (on the basis of the relative placement of Canaanite, Amorite, and Hittite in the lists) that some time after the rise of the monarchy in Israel, 'Amorite' replaced 'Canaanite' as the usual, general designation of the native population in Syria-Palestine. This corresponds with the evidence from Neo-Assyrian inscriptions of the ninth and eighth centuries, where Amurru is again used to refer to the entire area of Syria-Palestine (Liverani, 'The Amorites', p. 120).

100. See, e.g., Num. 21.13; 32.33; Deut. 3.8; Judg. 10.8; 11.22. Kenyon (*Amorites and Canaanites*, p. 3) understands the two terms, 'Amorites' and 'Canaanites', as designations for the major groups already in the land at the time of the Israelite settlement. According to Kenyon, 'Amorite' referred to inhabitants of the hill country on both sides of the Jordan, while 'Canaanite' referred to peoples who lived in the plains.

101. Liverani, 'The Amorites', p. 120.

102. Already in 1946, G. Ernest Wright ('The Literary and Historical Problem of Joshua 10 and Judges 1', *JNES* 5 [1946], pp. 105-14) challenged the 'dominant critical position' that Judg. 1 is of greater historical veracity than the book of Joshua. Of course, Wright was arguing in favor of the book of Joshua and the correlation of archaeology and the Israelite 'conquest' of Canaan, a position few critical scholars hold today.

According to Judg. 1.34, 'the Amorites pressed the sons of Dan toward the hill country'. The statement seems, at first pass, rather innocuous. Perhaps it was little more than two different groups of people competing for the same territory and, for whatever reason, the Amorites prevailed. However, closer attention to the vocabulary reveals something more. The predominant meaning of the verb (לחץ) here translated in its literal sense of 'press', is used elsewhere figuratively for 'put in a bind, rob of mobility, oppress, repress'. This more common, figurative usage, then, 'denotes repressive treatment of one social or political group by another'.[103] It most frequently refers to the treatment by one nation or its representative of another group of persons. This verb occurs, with this socially significant meaning, elsewhere in the book of Judges in 2.18; 4.3; 6.9; and 10.12.[104] Throughout the Former Prophets the verb is used of Israel's oppression at the hand of its enemies (cf. Exod. 22.21; 23.9, in which Israel is commanded not to oppress the 'resident alien'/client).

This dimension of the word suggests that a socially attentive reading of this text may contribute to a more meaningful understanding of Dan in Judg. 1.34-35. While there is, admittedly, insufficient evidence in these two verses to construct a full-scale honor/shame presentation, a few comments are in order. On the basis of this analysis, there is reason to interpret the 'sons of Dan' in this text not in a sympathetic, but in an unfavorable light. That is, the editor did not intend this passage to invoke sympathy in the reader at the unfortunate plight of the Danites. Instead, the Danites are to be seen as those who have diminished their own honor, and who have threatened the honor of all the tribes of Israel.

First of all, the fact that the 'sons of Dan' alone among the Israelite tribes in Judges 1 occur as the object of the action, has already been noted. Second, interpreting the action reported in v. 34 through the anthropological model of challenge–riposte, as recipients of a challenge (the Amorites pressed the sons of Dan toward the hill country) the Danites are expected to respond. Nothing of the sort, however, is narrated. Presuming that the Danites are capable of a riposte, this decision not to respond brings

---

103. J. Reindl, 'לחץ', in *TDOT*, VII, pp. 529-33 (532).

104. Other Hebrew Bible references for this root are: Exod. 3.9; 22.21; 23.9; Num. 22.25; Deut. 26.7; 1 Sam. 10.18; 1 Kgs 22.27//2 Chron. 18.26 ('bread and water of affliction' = reduced rations in prison); 2 Kgs 6.32; 13.4, 22; Job 36.15; Pss. 42.9; 43.2; 44.24; 56.1; 106.42; Isa. 19.20; 30.20; Jer. 30.20; Amos 6.14. In the vast majority of instances, the meaning is 'oppress' or 'oppression'. The literal meaning, 'press', occurs only in Num. 22.25 (of Balaam's donkey) and 2 Kgs 6.32 (with reference to the 'pressing' of a door against a messenger).

dishonor upon them.[105] A remark to the effect that 'the sons of Dan were *unable* to dispossess the Amorites' would at least suggest that the Danites made a response which was, ultimately, unsuccessful. In addition, the appearance of the 'house of Joseph' in v. 35 functions in the text not only as an *inclusio* around the second part of Judges 1 (cf. v. 22); it also points to still greater dishonor for the Danites. It may be supposed that the failure of the 'sons of Dan' to respond when challenged brought dishonor not only to their own members, but to the other Israelite tribes as well, having descended (ostensibly) from the same ancestor. The collective honor of the larger social group was endangered.[106] Thus, the response of the house of Joseph indicates that their honor was also challenged by the Amorite aggression. Since the house of Joseph is successful in reducing the Amorites to forced labor, their reputation is enhanced. The sons of Dan, however, having needed support from others in their cause, are further dishonored.[107]

Finally, the dishonor of the 'sons of Dan' is indicated by the overall structure of Judges 1, which reflects an obvious interest in Judah.[108] As it

105. Pierre Bourdieu, 'The Sentiment of Honour in Kabyle Society', in J.G. Peristiany (ed.), *Honour and Shame: The Values of Mediterranean Society* (Chicago: University of Chicago Press, 1966), pp. 191-241 (205). According to Julian Pitt-Rivers (*The Fate of Shechem, or The Politics of Sex: Essays in the Anthropology of the Mediterranean* [Cambridge Studies in Social Anthropology, 19; New York: Cambridge University Press, 1977], p. 5), 'to leave an affront unavenged is to leave one's honour in a state of desecration and this is therefore equivalent to cowardice'.

106. Pitt-Rivers (*The Fate of Shechem*, pp. 13-14) writes that 'social groups possess a collective honour in which their members participate; the dishonourable conduct of one reflects upon the honour of all... Honour pertains to social groups of any size, from the nuclear family...to the nation.'

107. Pitt-Rivers (*The Fate of Shechem*, pp. 7-8) notes: 'When a person reacts to a slight upon the honour of another, it can only be because his own is involved. Thus, according to ancient French law, a member of a slighted man's family or lineage could pick up the glove, or a man bound in liege to him, but no one else... The possibility of being represented by a champion in the judicial combat was restricted to those who were judged unable to defend their honour personally: women, the aged or infirm, or persons of a social status which prohibited them from responding to challenges, in particular, churchmen and, of course, royalty. It must otherwise always be an individual's own choice whether to maintain or abandon his claim to honour, whether to react to a slight and vindicate himself or to accept it and the dishonour which accompanies it. Thus a man is dishonoured if, when he is able to do so for himself, he allows another to pick up the glove for him.'

108. It is generally agreed that the DH (Joshua–2 Kings) is, in its present form, the exilic-era product of a movement based in Judah. As such, it is not surprising that it reflects a special interest in the affairs of the Southern Kingdom. In the last major

stands, Judges 1 falls into two distinct parts: the success of Judah and the
failures of 'Israel'. Judah's pre-eminence is matched by the subordinate
mention of Dan at the very end of the chapter. The resulting effect of this
structure is that Judah is glorified at the expense of all the other tribes,
especially those which later comprised the Northern Kingdom of Israel.
There can be little doubt that this is a clear reflection of the redactor's
Judean bias, a conclusion previously noted by several scholars.[109]

Judah is the first tribe mentioned in the chapter, and more than half the
chapter (vv. 2-20) is devoted to the activities of this tribe.[110] According to
the redactor, Yahweh chooses and names Judah as the tribe to go up first
against the Canaanites in the land (v. 2).[111] Yahweh's close connection

section of the work, in the books of Kings, while a few kings of Judah receive a
positive evaluation, none of the northern kings of Israel receive such a favorable summary judgment. All the kings of Israel are negatively appraised. A similar discrepancy
in evaluations of the southern and Northern Kingdoms is foreshadowed already near
the beginning of the DH, in Judg. 1, in its depiction of the relative honor status of the
tribes of Judah and Dan.

109. Lindars, *Judges 1–5*, p. 6; M. Weinfeld, 'The Period of the Conquest and of
the Judges as Seen by Earlier and Later Sources', *VT* 17 (1967), pp. 93-113; *idem*,
'Judges 1.1–2.5: The Conquest Under the Leadership of the House of Judah', in A.
Graeme Auld (ed.), *Understanding Poets and Prophets: Essays in Honour of George
Wishart Anderson* (JSOTSup, 152; Sheffield: JSOT Press, 1993), pp. 388-400; Marc
Brettler, 'The Book of Judges: Literature as Politics', *JBL* 108 (1989), pp. 395-418; E.
Theodore Mullen, 'Judges 1:1-36: The Deuteronomistic Reintroduction of the Book of
Judges', *HTR* 77 (1984), pp. 33-54; K. Lawson Younger, Jr, 'The Configuring of Judicial Preliminaries: Judges 1.1–2.5 and Its Dependence on the Book of Joshua', *JSOT*
68 (1995), pp. 75-92. Noteworthy is Mullen's observation that mention of Judah frames
the final form of the book of Judges (1.2-20; 20.18), while this eminent tribe remains
'silent through the account of the tumultuous period of the Judges' (Mullen, 'Judges
1:1-36', p. 53, cf. p. 44; see also Robert G. Boling, *Judges: Introduction, Translation,
and Commentary* [AB, 6A; Garden City, NY: Doubleday, 1975], p. 53). Mullen, however, overlooks the occurrence of Judah in 15.11—but if his observation is correct,
then this singular occurrence within the main section of the book of Judges may
suggest that the Samson narrative was added to the book after the Deuteronomistic
framework was already in place. This will be considered in my analysis of Judg. 13–16
below.

110. Brettler, 'The Book of Judges', p. 402; Younger, 'The Configuring of Judicial
Preliminaries', p. 92.

111. Such a favored position for Judah is significant because, according to the
biblical tradition, Judah was not the firstborn of the ancestors who lent their names to
the Israelite tribes (Gen. 29.31-35). However, the stories about the downfall and
disqualification of Judah's three older brothers, Reuben, Simeon, and Levi (Gen. 34;
35.22), justify the redactor's moving Judah to the top of the list.

with Judah is also an important part of the message of this chapter. Judah's victories in Canaan are the result of Yahweh's intervention (vv. 2, 4, 19), implying that Judah's success was because 'Yahweh was with Judah' and, by extension, that the other failures of the tribes were because Yahweh was not with them (but cf. 1.22 [house of Joseph]). Yahweh's expressed favor for Judah forms an *inclusio* around the first part of the chapter (vv. 2, 19).

For almost every other tribe the refrain is: 'N did not dispossess the inhabitants of X' (1.21, 27, 28, 29, 30, 31, 33). Judah, however, cannot fail. Verses 4-19a record success after success for Judah. In fact, Judah fares better in Judges 1 than in the book of Joshua. According to Josh. 15.63, Judah '*could not* dispossess the Jebusites, the inhabitants of Jerusalem'. Here in Judges 1, Judah's former inability becomes identified with Benjamin's willful disobedience: 'The Benjaminites *did not* dispossess the Jebusite inhabitants of Jerusalem' (v. 21).[112] The singular shortcoming of Judah in Judges 1, the tribe's inability 'to dispossess the inhabitants of the plain', is traced to no fault of the tribe. Rather, Judah was out-done by the superior technology of their enemy who had chariots of iron (v. 19).

It is not by chance, nor for simple reasons of geography that the tribe of Dan is the last Israelite tribe named in Judges 1.[113] Dan appears last, rather,

---

112. See Num. 33.50-56, part of a Deuteronomistic speech attributed to Moses, which outlines the method by which the Israelites are to enter and occupy the land of Canaan, and ends with a warning of the consequences to be faced if the people deviate from the divinely appointed plan (cf. Judg. 2.1-3). The bias of the redactor in Judges in adapting and modifying the Joshua material has been pointed out by several scholars. See, e.g., Mullen, 'Judges 1:1-36', p. 46; Weinfeld, 'The Period of the Conquest', p. 94; Brettler, 'The Book of Judges', p. 401; already Moore, *Judges*, pp. 38-39; Burney, *The Book of Judges*, pp. 1-2.

113. Boling (*Judges*, p. 63) suggests that the source materials used in Judg. 1 have been 'carefully arranged to report tribal activities roughly on a line from south to north, beginning with Judah eager for the offensive, and ending with Dan and native westerners at a stalemate'. If that were the case, then one would expect Ephraim to be mentioned before Manasseh. More importantly, Dan is clearly portrayed in vv. 34-35 in its southern inheritance (cf. Josh. 19.40-46; 21.23-34) and not in the north. While there is every reason to believe that the redactor knew of the story of the Danites's migration in Judg. 18, there is no hint of that event here. See also Younger ('The Configuring of Judicial Preliminaries', pp. 75-80), who begins with an identification of Judg. 1 as a 'deliberate geographically arranged narrative...(which) arbitrarily begins with Judah and ends with Dan', but goes on to point out a strand of moral decline that runs through the book of Judges. It is my contention that Dan appears where it does in Judg. 1 not for geographic or moral reasons, but as a result of the redactor's pro-Judah bias, in which Dan represents everything opposite of Judah.

because, in the opinion of the Judean redactor of the Deuteronomistic movement, Dan represents everything antithetical to Judah.[114] On the one hand, 'Judah' calls to mind the Southern Kingdom, the Davidic house and Yahweh's promise to it (2 Sam. 7), and the central sanctuary of Yahweh's choosing in Jerusalem. On the other hand, mention of 'Dan' evokes not only the eponymous ancestor, Dan (whose mother was a maidservant rather than a wife), and the tribe bearing his name. More importantly, 'Dan' recalls Jeroboam and the rebellious Northern Kingdom of Israel and the pair of apostate national shrines instituted by Jeroboam at Dan and Bethel (1 Kgs 12). It is ultimately this pro-Judah bias, grounded in Deuteronomistic theology, that necessitates locating Dan at the end of Judges 1.

Additional insight into the effect of the structure of Judges 1 on the interpretation of Dan is provided by the category of honor/shame drawn from the work of cultural anthropologists. Anthropologists frequently make use of the human body (with respect to which certain parts have greater and lesser honor values) in order to symbolize social relationships. On the map of the human body, the head (face) is the location of greatest honor.[115] Thus, just as the head of a person's physical body is the location of greatest honor, by extension the head of a family or organization, or the place at the head of a table at a meal, is a position of greater relative honor. Others are expected to assume their appropriate place in relation to the head, in declining order of status. In the case of Judges 1, the place of honor, at the head (metaphorically speaking) of the list of Israelite tribes, is occupied by the tribe of Judah. To the question, 'who shall go up for us...first?' (Judg. 1.1), Yahweh replies: 'Judah shall go up'.[116] Corresponding to Judah's position of pre-eminent honor at the head of the list—and of the chapter as a whole—is the location of the 'sons of Dan' at the end of the list and chapter, furthest from the place of honor.

This evaluation of the 'sons of Dan' occurs within a passage (Judg. 1) whose redaction history has perplexed critical scholars. In the early years

114. While the portrayal of Judah in Judg. 1 is better than its depiction in Josh. 15, Dan fares worse here when compared with Josh. 19. These are two sides of the same coin, which should be attributed to the *Tendenz* of the redactor.

115. Bruce J. Malina and Jerome H. Neyrey, 'Honor and Shame in Luke–Acts: Pivotal Values of the Mediterranean World,' in Jerome H. Neyrey (ed.), *The Social World of Luke–Acts: Models for Interpretation* (Peabody, MA: Hendrickson, 1991), pp. 25-65 (34); see also Pitt-Rivers, *The Fate of Shechem*, pp. 4-5.

116. What might be the social significance of the word here translated 'first', בתחלה, being derived from the same root as the verb meaning 'to pollute, defile, profane' (BDB, pp. 320-21)?

of this century, Moore and Burney published separate commentaries in which they suggested that an exilic editor (so Moore; Burney locates the editor in the postexilic period) prefaced ch. 1 to the book of Judges using literary material from the time of Solomon, namely, the work of J.[117] Both commentators observed that the J material was not simply adopted by the editor. Rather, the traditional material was altered in some way to accommodate the editor's point of view. Thus, Moore writes:

> The narrative has been considerably *abridged* by the editor who prefixed it to the pre-Deuteronomic Book of Judges, for the purpose…of showing how Israel sinned in making terms with the people of the land and leaving them to be a constant snare and peril; it has also suffered to some extent from *derangement and interpolation*, whether by the editor's own hand or that of scribes. Fortunately, the nature of the recension gives us confidence that he left intact those features of his original which are of chief interest and importance for us, proving that in the invasion the tribes acted singly, or as they were allied by older ties or common interest; and that Israelite supremacy in Canaan was not achieved by one irresistible wave of conquest, but only after an obstinate struggle lasting for generations.[118]

Moore and Burney wrote prior to Noth's 'Deuteronomistic History hypothesis'. In his 1943 study, Noth concluded that Judges 1 was an addition to the basic history since it 'shows no signs of Deuteronomistic editing'.[119] In Noth's proposal, the original work of Dtr proceeded from Joshua 23 directly to Judg. 2.6-19. According to Noth, the book of Judges reached its final form in the following way:

> Afterwards, in the style similar to that of Dtr., the Deuteronomistically edited passages Josh. 24.1-28 and Judg. 2.1-5 were added after the final chapter of the book of Joshua, chapter 23, and—later still—without any Deuteronomistic revision, the mass of old traditional fragments, which form the present Judges 1.[120]

Noth does not suggest a date for the additions of either Joshua 24 and Judg. 2.1-5, or for the final inclusion of Judges 1. What is more, he insists that the one responsible for the collection and addition of the fragmentary source material behind Judg. 1 (which Noth does not identify as J or E) was not influenced by the Deuteronomistic movement. While Noth was probably right to isolate ch. 1 as an addition to the basic work of Dtr, he

---

117. Moore, *Judges*, pp. xxxii-xxxv; Burney, *The Book of Judges*, p. 1.

118. Moore, *Judges*, pp. xxxii-xxxiii (emphasis added); cf. Burney, *The Book of Judges*, p. 2.

119. Noth, *Deuteronomistic History*, p. 23.

120. Noth, *Deuteronomistic History*, pp. 23-24.

was probably incorrect to dissociate this material from the realm of 'Deuteronomism'. It seems likely that the editor responsible for Judges 1, while not necessarily bound by Deuteronomistic vocabulary or phraseology, nevertheless shared the interests of Dtr. This correlates directly with Smend's proposal of multiple, exilic redactions of the DH.

In the wake of Noth's hypothesis, Smend focused on several passages in the books of Joshua and Judges (including Judg. 1), most of which were identified by Noth as additions to the DH.[121] Specifically, the texts studied by Smend are: Josh. 1.7-9; 13.1bβ-6; 23; Judg. 1.1–2.9; 2.17, 20-21, 23.[122] He concluded that these texts were concerned with either the relationship of the Israelite tribes with the peoples still in the land after the 'conquest', or obedience to the Law (a fundamental theme of the DH). Smend follows Noth in arguing that these are secondary additions by a later redactor to the original version of the Deuteronomistic History (DtrG). In light of the interest in the Law in many of these passages, Smend identified this redactor by the siglum DtrN (N for 'nomistic').[123] Smend moved scholarship beyond Noth by finding a particular design of this additional material.

While Noth and Smend recognized Judges 1 as an addition to the original edition of the sixth-century DH, Boling and Mullen see this chapter as the contribution of Dtr himself, although fashioned out of older material.[124] Boling uniquely traces the growth of the book of Judges

121. Rudolf Smend, 'Das Gesetz und die Völker: Ein Beitrag zur deuteronomistischen Redaktionsgeschichte', in Hans Walter Wolff (ed.), *Probleme biblischer Theologie: Gerhard von Rad zum 70. Geburtstag* (Munich: Chr. Kaiser Verlag, 1971), pp. 494-509.

122. With the exception of Josh. 23, in Noth's estimation these are all secondary additions to the basic DH. On Smend's study of Josh. 12–Judg. 2, see Mark A. O'Brien, *The Deuteronomistic History Hypothesis: A Reassessment* (OBO, 92; Göttingen: Vandenhoeck & Ruprecht, 1989), pp. 75-81.

123. While Smend did not date the work of DtrN, his student, Walter Dietrich, who expanded Smend's work by adding a DtrP (P for 'prophetic') redactional layer, presents the following chronology: DtrG, about 580 BCE; DtrP between 580 and 560 BCE; and DtrN, about 560 BCE. The work of Smend and his students (the 'Göttingen School') is helpfully summarized in Campbell, 'Martin Noth and the Deuteronomistic History'; S.L. McKenzie, 'Deuteronomistic History', p. 163; and Mark A. O'Brien, 'Judges and the Deuteronomistic History', in Steven L. McKenzie and M. Patrick Graham (eds.), *The History of Israel's Traditions: The Heritage of Martin Noth* (JSOTSup, 182; Sheffield: Sheffield Academic Press, 1994), pp. 235-59.

124. Boling and Mullen accept the 'double redaction' hypothesis revived and advanced by Frank Moore Cross (*Canaanite Myth and Hebrew Epic: Essays in the History of the Religion of Israel* [Cambridge, MA: Harvard University Press, 1973],

through four stages, and identifies Judg. 1 as part of the latest stage which he labels 'Deuteronomistic framework' (together with Judg. 19.1–21.25), and to which he assigns a date in the sixth century (after 587).[125] Nevertheless, Boling does not understand Judges 1 to be the original composition of Dtr. Following the path of Moore and Burney, he suggests, instead, that it has been carefully arranged and 'built up of preformed narrative units together with archival details and notices of various sorts... The bulk of the chapter is generally assigned by scholars to *J* (Eissfeldt to *L*), as stemming from a great tradition-gathering enterprise of the tenth to ninth centuries.'[126] Mullen also identifies Judges 1 as the work of the sixth-century Dtr. However, he differs from Boling in locating the chapter's source material not in largely hypothetical tenth- or ninth-century traditions (such as J), but in chs. 13–21 of the Deuteronomic (seventh-century) book of Joshua, from which he selected especially those notices that reported the Israelite tribes' incomplete control of the land.[127]

There is then, at the present time, no definitive answer to the question of the origin of Judges 1. The majority opinion among critical scholars, reflected in each of the studies reviewed here, is that this chapter was not part of the original edition of the DH (but cf. Cross). While Noth may be

pp. 274-89), although both differ from Cross in assigning Judg. 1 to the exilic edition of the DH (Cross's Dtr²). Cross implicitly accepts Judges 1 as part of the seventh century, Josianic edition of the history (Dtr¹) in his foundational article (although he does not deal specifically with the chapter). A sympathetic reading of Judg. 1 will detect each of the two main Dtr¹ themes traced by Cross through the book of Kings: (1) the sin of Jeroboam (the generally negative depiction of the northern tribes, and, perhaps, Dan in particular [1.22-36]), and (2) the promise to David (the primacy and generally favorable portrayal of Judah [1.2-20]).

125. Boling, *Judges*, pp. 29-38.

126. Boling, *Judges*, p. 63.

127. Mullen, 'Judges 1:1-36'. Part of the purpose of this 'Deuteronomistic re-introduction' is, according to Mullen, to 'reflect the eminence of Judah and the failure of Israel. The intent is to protect and project the significance of Judean primacy and to explain why Judah emerged in monarchical times as the dominant tribe' (p. 53). For his exilic audience, 'the deuteronomistic writer recreates the past to instruct the Israel of the present of the necessity to follow the lead of Judah, the leader chosen by Yahweh, and to follow the laws of Moses in the taking of the land allotted it by Joshua' (p. 54). An additional contribution of Mullen's article is his attention to the evidence of Joshua's less than complete success in conquering the land in Josh. 13–21, thereby calling into question the supposed irreconcilable distinction between the depictions of Israel's settlement of the land in the books of Joshua and Judges. On this question, see the earlier investigation of Wright ('The Literary and Historical').

correct in denying obvious Deuteronomistic editing in Judges 1, I am inclined to follow others in seeing in these verses a redactional level that may be traced to a member of the Deuteronomistic movement.[128] Thus, the portrayal of Dan in Judg. 1.34-35 is, in large part, dependent on the pro-Judah perspective of this literary agent at work, most likely, in the exilic or early postexilic period. The notion that there is material about Dan in this chapter on the basis of which one might reconstruct the early history of this Israelite tribe is ill-informed.[129]

b. *Judges 5*[130]
In his 1975 commentary Boling observed that 'a catalogue of full-dress studies of the Song of Deborah would read like a Who's Who in biblical research'.[131] The last 25 years have witnessed the appearance of additional studies of Judges 5, from full-length dissertations on the whole of the chapter, to short notes on specific words.[132] It is not only impossible to review all of this material in its entirety; it is also unnecessary. In what follows, I will concern myself with those issues that relate most directly to the goal of the present study, which is interpreting Dan in the biblical tradition.

128. Further, the suggestion that Josh. 13–21 (cf. Mullen, 'Judges 1:1-36', p. 42) served as the material source for the editor of Judg. 1 appears sound. The conclusion that the book of Joshua narrates a complete conquest and settlement of the land of Canaan is based on a reading of only Josh. 2–12. There are, in fact, numerous instances in Josh. 13–19 which suggest that the conquest and settlement was not so comprehensive (Josh. 13.2-3; 15.63; 16.10; 17.12; 19.47). These are the notices the redactor behind Judg. 1 has selected (and in some cases modified [Josh. 15.63]) in order to set the stage for the divine messenger's indictment of the Israelites in Judg. 2.1-3. See also Younger, 'The Configuring of Judicial Preliminaries', pp. 75-76.

129. Niemann, *Die Daniten*, pp. 9-35.

130. Noth (*Deuteronomistic History*, p. 47) accepts the Song of Deborah as part of an old tradition that has been incorporated (with glosses) into the DH.

131. Boling, *Judges*, p. 105.

132. E.g. Marvin L. Chaney, '*ḤDL*-II and the "Song of Deborah": Textual, Philological, and Sociological Studies in Judges 5, with Special Reference to the Verbal Occurrences of *ḤDL* in Biblical Hebrew' (unpublished PhD dissertation, Harvard University, 1976); Ulrike Bechmann, *Das Deboralied zwischen Geschichte und Fiktion: Eine Exegetische Untersuchung zu Richter 5* (Dissertation Theologische Reihe, 33; St Ottilien: EOS Verlag Erzabtei, 1989); Silvia Becker-Spörl, *Und sang Debora an jenem Tag: Untersuchung zu Sprache und Intention des Deboraliedes (Ri 5)* (Europäische Hochschulschriften Reihe, 23; Theologie, 620; Frankfort am Main: Peter Lang, 1998); Giovani Garbini, '**Parzon* "Iron" in the Song of Deborah?', *JSS* 23 (1978), pp. 23-24.

The antiquity of the Song of Deborah is generally acknowledged; Judges 5 is accepted by the majority of critical scholars as one of the oldest texts in the Hebrew Bible. The consensus is that it is to be dated to sometime in the twelfth or eleventh century BCE; that is, to a time roughly contemporaneous with the events described in the Song.[133] In form, the Song has been identified as a 'victory hymn', 'victory song', or 'triumphal ode', resembling other compositions of approximately the same period.[134] Nevertheless, care must be taken in using the poetic descriptions of the actual battle for a reconstruction of the earliest history of Israel in Canaan. Freedman's balanced remarks concerning the Song of Deborah and the Song of the Sea (Exod. 15) are well-noted:

> The assumption is that these are the oldest sources available for [a reconstruction of Israel's earliest national experience], are roughly contemporary with the events, and should therefore provide an accurate description of the central and most important occurrences in the saga of early Israel. At the same time, it must be borne in mind that we are dealing with poetry with its characteristic literary features and emphases, not a journalistic report of battle actions. That means that we cannot expect a simple, sober, sequential account, but must deal with an impressionistic reflection and refraction of the events as they impinged on the creative, emotive mind of the poet. By balancing the various factors, it should be possible to recover significant historical information, not only about the events, but the impact they had on

---

133. W.F. Albright, 'The Song of Deborah in the Light of Archaeology', *BASOR* 62 (1936), pp. 26-31; Cross and Freedman, *Studies in Ancient Yahwistic Poetry*, p. 5; David Noel Freedman, 'Early Israelite History in the Light of Early Israelite Poetry', in *idem* (ed.), *Pottery, Poetry, and Prophecy: Studies in Early Hebrew Poetry* (Winona Lake, IN: Eisenbrauns, 1980), pp. 131-66 (131, 149); H.-J. Zobel, *Stammesspruch und Geschichte. Die Angaben der Stammessprüche von Gen 49, Dtn 33 und Jdc 5 über die politischen und kultischen Zustände im damalgin 'Israel'* (BZAW, 95; Berlin: Alfred Töpelmann, 1965), p. 92; Moore, *Judges*, pp. xxviii, 132-33; Burney, *The Book of Judges*, pp. 78, 171-76; Boling, *Judges*, p. 117. Of course, there are exceptions. Lindars (*Judges 1–5*, p. 168) settles on a date in the early monarchic period, while Ahlström (*Who Were the Israelites?* [Winona Lake, IN: Eisenbrauns, 1986], p. 80), in light of the first two cola of Judg. 5.2, argues for a later date, far removed from the events narrated in the Song (cf. *idem*, 'Judges 5:20f. and History', *JNES* 36 [1977], pp. 287-88; Peter R. Ackroyd, 'The Composition of the Song of Deborah', *VT* 2 [1952], pp. 160-62).

134. See, e.g., Cross and Freedman, *Studies in Ancient Yahwistic Poetry*, p. 5. For a comparative analysis, see P.C. Craigie, 'The Song of Deborah and the Epic of Tukulti-Ninurta', *JBL* 88 (1969), pp. 253-65.

the people who participated in them, and how they perceived their importance and meaning.[135]

Lawrence Stager urges similar caution:

> There is less consensus, however, about the historicity of events portrayed in the poem. Whether or not the Hebrew poet accurately recounted historical events or created them for his story need not trouble us here. Regardless of their historicity, for the past events of the Song of Deborah to ring true, the poet must have passed the test of verisimilitude, having grounded his story in setting and circumstance that seemed plausible to his contemporary audience.[136]

Thus, due to the poetic form of the text, and either the great antiquity of the piece or the possibility that the composition may be less than contemporaneous with the events portrayed in it, it is prudent to be circumspect in making definitive historical judgments on the basis of the Song of Deborah. Rather, my primary interest, following the important studies of Stager and Schloen, is on the social world reality reflected in the poem, and on the social status of the tribe of Dan in particular.

Dan is mentioned within the catalog of tribes in Judg. 5.14-18, at the center of the Song of Deborah.[137] The so-called 'muster of the tribes' is divided between those six tribes situated in the northern and central hill country that responded to the call and participated in the battle against the Canaanites (Ephraim, Benjamin, Machir [= Manasseh], Zebulun, Issachar, and Naphtali; vv. 14-15a, 18), and the other four tribes (Reuben, Gilead [= Gad], Dan, and Asher; vv. 15b-17) that did not participate.[138] Of this latter collection, the two transjordanian tribes, Reuben and Gilead (= Gad),

---

135. D.N. Freedman, 'Early Israelite History', p. 132. See also J. Alberto Soggin, *Judges: A Commentary* (OTL; London: SCM Press, 1981), p. 68; Lindars, *Judges*, p. 164. For a more optimistic evaluation of the historical reliability of the tradition preserved in the Song of Deborah, see Moore, *Judges*, pp. 132-33.

136. Lawrence E. Stager, 'Archaeology, Ecology, and Social History', p. 224; see also Michael David Coogan, 'A Structural and Literary Analysis of the Song of Deborah', *CBQ* 40 (1978), pp. 143-66 (144).

137. D.N. Freedman, 'Early Israelite History', p. 152; Coogan, 'A Structural and Literary Analysis', p. 152.

138. Johannes C. de Moor's attempt to reconstruct a list of twelve tribes, on the basis of the LXX, seems forced and is, in my estimation, finally unsuccessful ('The Twelve Tribes in the Song of Deborah', *VT* 43 [1993], pp. 483-94). As Freedman has pointed out ('Early Israelite History', p. 157), there is no reason not to imagine that at the time of the action portrayed in the Song of Deborah only ten tribes comprised the 'people of Yahweh' (cf. Judg. 5.11).

are associated with specialized pastoralism, while the tribes of Dan and Asher are situated along the Mediterranean and are associated with maritime ventures.[139] As Stager has persuasively demonstrated, the reason why these four tribes were unable to participate in the battle against the Canaanites was their economic dependence on other, non-Israelite groups.[140] The work of Stager on the Song of Deborah will be the point of departure for the present investigation.

(1) *Judges 5.14-18*

[14] From Ephraim, their root is in Amalek,
   after you Benjamin among your kinsmen;
from Machir commanders descended,
   and from Zebulun, marchers with the scepter of the muster-officer.
[15] Now the captains of Issachar are with Deborah,
   and so Issachar, thus Baraq,
   into the valley he was sent off on foot;
among the divisions of Reuben, great were the resolves of heart.
[16] Why do you remain between the hearths—
   to listen to the pipings for the flocks?
In the divisions of Reuben, great were the questionings of heart.
[17] Gilead in the region across the Jordan encamped,
   and Dan—why did he serve as a client on ships?
Asher dwelt at the coast of the sea,
   and upon its harbors he encamped.
[18] Zebulun was a people who scorned his life to death—and Naphtali;
   upon the heights of the open field.

[Notes on the MT:
   Verse 14: The critical apparatus notes that the form שרשם is corrupt; the Versions have a verb (the editor proposes אשרו, 'they advanced'). It is better to interpret the action of the tribes in v. 14a in light of the verb ירד in v. 13 (note that the same verb

139. On the existence of an Asherite enclave in the southern part of the hill country of Ephraim, north of the territory of Benjamin, see now Diana Edelman, 'The Asherite Genealogy in 1 Chronicles 7:3-40', *BR* 33 (1988), pp. 13-23.

140. Stager, 'Archaeology, Ecology, and Social History'. In fact, Stager's thesis is not original; his work builds on the insights of earlier scholars. What Stager has done, however, by drawing not only on the archaeology of the highlands of Canaan but also on what is known about the social conditions of the agrarian world, is provide a clear social and economic backdrop before which to interpret the biblical text. Stager's student, J. David Schloen, has argued an equally persuasive hypothesis regarding exactly why the six tribes listed in the Song of Deborah *did* join together against the more powerful Canaanite inhabitants of the plains ('Caravans, Kenites, and *Casus belli*: Enmity and Alliance in the Song of Deborah', *CBQ* 55 [1993], pp. 18-38).

also occurs in v. 14b, thus forming an envelope construction around v. 14a). For בעמלק the LXX and Theodotion's Greek translation of the Old Testament read ἐν κοιλάδι; the editor (R. Meyer) suggests reading the Hebrew בעמק ('in the valley'). In support of the MT 'Amalek', see now Schloen, 'Caravans, Kenites, and *Casus belli*', p. 27. On 'kinsmen', see Gottwald, *The Tribes of Yahweh*, p. 284. The editor suggests reading the pronominal suffixes on the preposition 'after' and the noun 'kinsmen' as third masculine singular rather than the MT's second masculine singular (a proposal without support from either Hebrew manuscripts or the Versions; it may be conjectured, however, that the suffix on 'after' in the MT has been affected by the suffix on the last word in the line). For סמר, the editor suggests a possible revocalization, corresponding to the Akkadian *siparru* ('copper, bronze'). Finally, the editor suggests (unnecessarily) that v. 18 be transposed to follow v. 14 immediately (thus grouping together all the tribes that participated in the action against the Canaanites; but thereby eliminating the MT's *inclusio* of participating tribes around the non-participating tribes).

Verse 15: I read ושרי ביששכר as 'the captains of Issachar' (the construct chain [revocalizing the MT] with an intervening preposition; see Dahood, *Psalms*, III, p. 381; Boling, *Judges*, p. 112); cf. the first note in the critical apparatus, which lists support for this reading from the LXX, the Syriac version of the Old Testament, the Targum, and the Vulgate (see also v. 18, note b). The LXX omits 'and so Issachar, thus Baraq'. The editor proposes that the preposition ב be inserted between the conjunction and 'Issachar' (with כן following; BDB, p. 486). The MT is *lectio difficilior* and to be preferred. The editor suggests possibly transposing the soph passuq to immediately after 'on foot', thereby creating a clear break between participating and non-participating tribes. This is unnecessary. For חקקי, the editor suggests reading with a few medieval manuscripts of the Hebrew Old Testament and the Syriac version of the Old Testament חקרי, which is the form found in v. 16. The MT is to be preferred, recognizing the two different words as an occurrence of paronomasia in the text, and the possibility that the two words together form a regular pair of parallel words. On 'divisions (of Reuben)', see Gottwald, *The Tribes of Yahweh*, p. 284.

Verse 16: I translate המשפתים as 'hearths', following Boling (*Judges*, p. 112) and Stager ('Archaeology, Ecology, and Social History', p. 227); cf. BDB, p. 1046. Verse 16b is recognized by the editor as a doublet (compare v. 15b). However, as I have suggested (see my note on v. 15), the 'doublet' is less than perfect. A Hebrew manuscript from the Cairo Geniza and several medieval manuscripts of the Hebrew Old Testament read the preposition ב, rather than the ל of the MT before 'divisions' in v. 16b (compare v. 15b). Since both prepositions may express the same movement, the MT should be accepted.

Verse 17: The למה in the midst of the saying about Dan is absent from two medieval manuscripts of the Hebrew Old Testament, the Targum, and the Vulgate; the editor suggests that it be deleted (cf. Cross, *Canaanite Myth and Hebrew Epic*, p. 235 n. 74, who identifies this form as an 'emphatic *lamed* extended by –*mā*, known from Ugaritic'). Finally, the editor suggests that v. 23 be transposed to follow immediately v. 17 (assuming that the curse of Meroz more appropriately belongs with the list of the other tribes that failed to participate in the battle against the Canaanites). The editor fails to see the sharp contrast created between Meroz, on the one hand, and Jael (who is 'most blessed of women'), on the other hand, when the MT order of verses is left unaltered.]

As already noted, the setting of the battle portrayed in the Song of Deborah and circumstances leading up to it have been persuasively described in the articles by Stager and Schloen. *In nuce*, Schloen argues that the militarily weaker Israelite inhabitants of the highlands engaged in battle with the more powerful Canaanite population of the lowland city-states (Judg. 5.19) chiefly for economic reasons. In the introductory section of his article Schloen writes:

> The nature of the hill tribes' threatened interests is revealed in the Song of Deborah itself. There are indications in Judges 5 that the Israelite tribes were allied with Midianite (including Kenite and Amalekite) caravan opera-tors and that they profited from trade through the hills of Palestine and across the Jezreel Valley. Through extortion of exorbitant tolls, or even outright plunder, Sisera and his Canaanite allies had stifled caravan traffic through the plain of Jezreel, provoking the Israelite highlanders into a war to protect their economic interests.[141]

While certain members the tribes of Ephraim, Benjamin, Machir, Zebu-lun, Issachar, and Naphtali depended for their livelihood on the caravan traffic through their respective territories, the four tribes that failed to participate had other, more substantial economic alliances with other non-Israelite neighbors that prohibited their involvement.[142] While the highland agriculturalists were able to maintain an economically independent exis-tence in the hill country (with only limited need for trade with neighboring groups), Stager argues that the tribes of Reuben and Gilead in Transjordan (as specialized pastoralists), and Dan and Asher near the Mediterranean (as clients of maritime traders), were economically dependent on non-Israelites.[143]

---

141. Schloen, 'Caravans, Kenites, and *Casus belli*', p. 20.

142. Schloen does not suggest that the entire population of the highland tribes was engaged as caravan drivers and escorts. By far, the majority of highland villagers were involved in a mixed agricultural economy of subsistence farming combined with the raising of livestock (see also Hopkins, 'Life on the Land'). Those sons who were not in line to inherit the patrimony would have been likely candidates to attach themselves to caravaneers as clients (Schloen, 'Caravans, Kenites, and *Casus belli*', p. 36; see also Stager, 'Archaeology of the Family', pp. 24-28).

143. Stager, 'Archaeology, Ecology, and Social History', esp. pp. 222-24, 228-32.

I have followed Stager in translating the remark about Dan in Judg. 5.17 (ודן למה יגור אניות) as 'And Dan—why did he serve as a client on ships?'[144] Of course, while these four Hebrew words are insufficient for confidently making specific historical judgments about this Israelite tribe, but they do, nevertheless, illuminate the social reality of Dan at the time of the Song of Deborah.[145]

This rhetorical question about Dan in Judg. 5.17, associating this tribe of Israel with ships, has led commentators to speculate whether this remark refers to a time before or after the story of the Danite migration narrated in Judg. 18.[146] At which of the two Danite locations known from the traditions in the Hebrew Bible (in the south, Josh. 19.41-46; Judg. 13–16; or in the north, Judg. 18) would the tribe more likely be engaged with ships? On the one hand, perhaps because of the Phoenicians's well-founded and widely recognized reputation as outstanding maritime traders, many earlier scholars were inclined to date this reference to Dan in the Song of Deborah to a time after the events narrated in Judges 18. According to this view, the Danites had already migrated northward from their allotted territory in the south, conquered Laish, and renamed the city after their eponymous ancestor when this mild reproach was first spoken.[147] The

144. 'Ships' is the preferred reading, rather than 'at ease'. On the basis of the Ugaritic texts, Craigie endorses the translation: 'and Dan abode at ease' (P.C. Craigie, 'Three Ugaritic Notes on the Song of Deborah', *JSOT* 2 [1977], pp. 33-49 [38-41]). There is, however, sufficient reason to read 'ships'. First of all, this is the plain meaning of the MT, and all the versions agree with the MT. The supposed awkwardness arising from the (apparent) lack of an expected prefix preposition can be readily attributed to the peculiarities of Hebrew poetry. Second, the reading 'at ease' in the Ugaritic material requires an emendation of the Ugaritic text (which Craigie himself recognizes as a weakness). Finally, Dan and 'ships' is a better parallel with Asher and the sea/ harbors in the following line.

145. Chaney's observation ('*ḤDL*-II and the "Song of Deborah"', p. 209) is well noted and sets the discussion that follows clearly in the realm of speculation: 'Elaborate discussions of the Danite migration and its chronology relative to the Deborah war based upon this half line appear to this writer to build too much upon too little. Throughout the premonarchic period, Dan's existence was marginal, with little land to which he could press solid claim. Just such populations have been a major source of lower ranking seamen since ships have sailed the sea. His characterization here tells more about his socioeconomic than geographic location.'

146. The serious question of the historical accuracy of the migration narrative will be treated in the section on Judg. 17–18, below.

147. See Moore, *Judges*, p. 155; Burney, *The Book of Judges*, p. 143. More recently, the northern view is adopted by Niemann, *Die Daniten*, p. 59; see also John

mention of the Phoenician port-city of Sidon and its inhabitants elsewhere in the Danite tradition (Judg. 18.7, 28) would seem to support this northern view.[148]

On the other hand, Stager has pointed to the description of the Danite territory in Joshua 19 and the situation of the Danites described in Judg. 18.1 (without an inheritance) as evidence that the remark in Judg. 5.17 supposes that the Danites are still in the south.[149] According to Josh. 19.46, the territory allotted to the tribe of Dan extended to include the territory opposite, or in front of, Joppa (עִם־הַגְּבוּל מוּל יָפוֹ). While some scholars have understood this to mean that the Danite inheritance *included* Joppa and reached to the Mediterranean Sea (although it is universally admitted that Israelite control did not reach this far to the west until, perhaps, the time of the United Monarchy), it is possible (and better) to interpret Josh. 19.46 to mean that the Danite territory *bordered* the area around Joppa. That is, the Danite inheritance reached to the main north–south overland trade route near the Mediterranean coast, the *Via Maris*. Since, therefore, the region controlled by Joppa was contiguous with the Danite territory, it is reasonable to conclude that Judg. 5.17 refers to Danites serving aboard ships which sailed from this neighboring port-city.[150] As Stager notes, if this description of Dan dates from a time before the arrival of the Sea Peoples, then אֳנִיּוֹת refers to Canaanite ships; if this remark dates to a time after 1175 BCE, then the ships were more likely Philistine.[151]

Gray, 'Israel in the Song of Deborah', in Lyle Eslinger and Glen Taylor (eds.), *Ascribe to the Lord: Biblical and Other Essays in Memory of Peter C. Craigie* (JSOTSup, 67; Sheffield: JSOT Press, 1988), pp. 421-55 (448).

148. However, the note in Judg. 18.7, 28, suggests that there were no close ties between the Sidonians and the residents of Laish.

149. Stager, 'Archaeology, Ecology, and Social History', p. 232.

150. Joppa (= Jaffa) is well known as a port city along the southern coast of the eastern Mediterranean. According to the biblical traditions, the timbers from Lebanon destined for Solomon's Temple were shipped by sea as far as Joppa, where they were unloaded and transported overland to Jerusalem (2 Chron. 2.15). Later, it was in Joppa that the prophet Jonah sought a ship (אֳנִיָּה) to carry him to Tarshish (Jon. 1.3-5). Joppa's significance is further attested by its mention in several extra-biblical documents (see *ANET*, pp. 22-23, 242, 287, 478, 662).

151. Stager, 'Archaeology, Ecology, and Social History', p. 232; cf. Boling, *Judges*, p. 112. The tribe of Dan's possible relationship with the Philistines suggested in Judg. 5 may contribute to our understanding of the references to Dan in the Samson stories, Judg. 13–16, which depict the hero moving freely between Danite and Philistine (Timnah, Ashkelon, Gaza) territories.

However, it is possible that in the mid-twelfth century the site of Joppa played a 'surprisingly unimportant' role in the region.[152] If Joppa is not required by my interpretation of Josh. 19.46 (the Danite inheritance did not include the city of Joppa), and, since the archaeological record raises questions about the significance of the site at about the time of the battle portrayed in the Song of Deborah, what are the alternatives? The Philistine city of Ashdod, also located near the coast, together with its harbor town of Tell Mor, presents itself as a likely candidate.[153] Ashdod is included among other towns located along the southern portion of the Levantine coast in Late Bronze Age II economic texts from Ugarit. The evidence suggests not only that merchants from Ashdod carried out commercial relations with the residents of Ugarit, but also that a number of Ashdod merchants resided in Ugarit.[154] The archaeological record at Ashdod reveals a destruction layer at the level of the last distinct LB II remains (Stratum XIV). This was followed by a 'transitional' level (Stratum XIII), above which 'clear Philistine strata were found'.[155] Might this be evidence to support the often-proposed hypothesis that the arrival of the Sea Peoples in the first quarter of the twelfth century so disrupted the relationship of the Danites with the Canaanite sea-traders that at least some of the tribe of Dan were forced to migrate northward to the city of Laish? Such a proposal would fit with the usually accepted chronology of the battle portrayed in the Song of Deborah (twelfth century).

The Ugaritic texts show that several cities near the Mediterranean were engaged in maritime trading in the LB II period.[156] The Egyptian story of Wen-Amon reveals that such maritime activity in the region continued

152. Ahimai Mazar, *Archaeology of the Land of the Bible: 10,000–586 B.C.E.* (ABRL; New York: Doubleday, 1990), p. 311.

153. Ashdod is located some three to four miles inland from the coast (with its ever-changing sand dunes). While Tell Mor was also not on the coast, the town was situated on the Lachish River, thus allowing trading ships safe harbor. On the relationship between Ashdod and Tell Mor, see Moshe Dothan, 'The Foundations of Tel Mor and Tel Ashdod', *IEJ* 23 (1973), pp. 1-17.

154. See Aharoni, *The Land of the Bible*, p. 17 n. 21, and the literature cited there; Moshe Dothan, 'Ashdod', in *ABD*, I, pp. 477-82 (477).

155. Moshe Dothan, *Ashdod II-III: The Second and Third Seasons of Excavations 1963, 1965* (ed. A. Biran, Inna Pommerantz and J.L. Swauger; 'Atiqot English Series, 9-10; Jerusalem: Israel Exploration Society, 1971), pp. 19, 26. Mazar (*Archaeology of the Land of the Bible*, p. 308) reports settlement and expansion of Ashdod throughout the twelfth and eleventh centuries.

156. See n. 154, above.

even after the arrival of the Sea Peoples.[157] It is unlikely that individual producers or local merchants owned and operated their own ships.[158] Rather, it is assumed that a special group of people were responsible for the actual transport of materials by sea throughout the Mediterranean. Sasson notes that, according to texts from Ugarit, maritime trade was the domain of the king:

> to conduct such operations, the king had a large number of prominent business men…working under his aegis… In addition to being his personal ambassadors at foreign courts, the merchants were responsible for purchasing, selling and shipping commodities to and from Ugarit. With special treaties contracted among the various powers protecting their lives and rights, Canaanite traders were widely dispersed throughout the Mediterranean world.[159]

Trading ships moved chiefly under sail power; ancient warships depended not only on sail power, but on a crew of rowers comprised of either lower class citizens or foreigners.[160] The Ugaritic evidence indicates that of the

157. *ANET*, pp. 25-29. The story itself mentions the city of Dor. It is fair to assume, however, that other (near-)coastal cities also continued to engage in sea trade.

158. See Jack M. Sasson, 'Canaanite Maritime Involvement in the Second Millennium B.C.', *JAOS* 86 (1966), pp. 126-38 (136). Cf. Acts 27.11, which mentions the ship's owner and pilot.

159. Sasson, 'Canaanite Maritime Involvement', p. 134. While dealing primarily with Mesopotamian trade overland, see A.L. Oppenheim, 'Trade in the Ancient Near East', in Hermann Van der Wee, Vladimir A. Vinogradov and Grigorii G. Kotovsky (eds.), *Fifth International Congress of Economic History, Leningrad 1970* (8 vols.; Leningrad: Mockba, 1976), V, pp. 125-49. In particular he writes that 'private persons as such could hardly participate in any form of overland trade without enjoying what we would call today diplomatic status. They had to be recognized as emissaries by their own king and by those of the regions crossed. Moreover, the capital needed to support large scale trade ventures or even to share in them could hardly have been amassed except under the protection of the palace organization, in fact, only by members of the latter. The king clearly acts as protector of overland merchants…' (p. 135)

160. Lionel Casson (*The Ancient Mariners: Seafarers and Sea Fighters of the Mediterranean in Ancient Times* [New York: Macmillan, 1959], p. 62) notes that rowing a galley 'was a complicated technique that demanded training and coordination'. Thus, it required a certain level of skill to serve on board a ship. According to Casson, these men were drawn largely either from the lowest class of citizens or from the pool of foreigners. Casson writes thus about working aboard Greek warships: 'To man a bench of a trireme was almost as difficult and as expensive as to build one. The Athenian contingent of two hundred ships at Salamis, for example, required no less than 34,000 men. Such a number was too much to be met by the populace alone, which among other things had to fill the ranks of the land forces at the same time. Moreover,

three terms used for ships, *'any* (the root corresponding to that occuring in Judg. 5.17) was the most common. It was used for both warships and cargo vessels.[161] It is reasonable to assume that even trading ships, with relatively small crews, were manned by foreign workers.

On the basis of the Ugaritic evidence, we may suppose that the shipping trade out of Ashdod was also under the control of the ruler of the city. It is also likely that he (or his shipping staff) employed a number of foreign workers, among them members of the tribe of Dan.[162]

Earlier commentators translated the verb in Judg. 5.17b, גור, as 'remain', 'abide', 'linger', or 'tarry'. Some even seem to have been aware of the notion of clientelism which Stager, however, makes explicit.[163] Moore

the army, not the navy, was the senior service. Anyone who could afford a soldier's armor and weapons understandably preferred to fight in the field rather than to sweat on a bench in a hot and foul ship's hold; he only submitted to it in emergencies when his city had no other recourse. Slaves in great enough numbers were hard to come by and even when enough were available, being untrustworthy and very expensive (they had to be supported forever instead of just for a given campaign), they were not often used; Athens turned to them only when she had run out of all other sources of man-power, and offered them their freedom as a reward at that. *The core of the rowing crews was the lowest class of citizens, those who couldn't afford to equip themselves as soldiers. The rest simply had to be hired, and the chief source of supply was the Aegean islands and the coastal towns of Asia Minor where people then as today lived off the sea. Since the service was both arduous and dangerous, it commanded attractive salaries...'* (pp. 95-96 [emphasis added]) Cf. R.D. Barnett ('Early Shipping in the Near East', *Antiquity* 32 [1958], pp. 220-30 [223]), who proposes that the Egyptians, more at home on the Nile than the more dangerous Mediterranean, employed foreigners on their sea-going ships.

161. Sasson, 'Canaanite Maritime Involvement', p. 132.

162. On the use of foreigners from the inland region 'in the king's service', see Amarna Letter 294. This is a letter from an officer of uncertain name to the pharaoh, whose contents may be summarized thus: 'A certain Bîya the son of Gulati had taken prisoners the troops which the writer had sent to Joppa to protect the king's interests. In obedience to the king's orders to follow the instructions of his commander, he has delivered the city and expelled the rebel Bîya. If the king chooses to visit it by day or by night, he will find it prepared to meet him' (C. Bezold and E.A. Wallis Budge, *The Tell El-Amarna Tablets in the British Museum with Autotype Facsimiles* [London: Harrison & Sons, 1892], p. lxxxii; a more recent translation of the text is in William L. Moran, *The Amarna Letters* [Baltimore: The Johns Hopkins University Press, 1992], pp. 336-37).

163. See already W.F. Albright, 'Some Additional Notes on the Song of Deborah', *JPOS* 2 (1922), pp. 284-85 (285), among others (cited by Stager, 'Archaeology, Ecology, and Social History', p. 229).

prefers to translate the remark about Dan thus: 'And Dan, why does he live as neighbor to the ships?' Assuming a northern location for the tribe of Dan (after their migration and conquest of Laish—Judg. 18), he imagines the Danites in a dependent relationship with the Phoenicians, protected by the Phoenician ships (against invaders from the Mediterranean?), but by no means in the employ of the Phoenician maritime merchants.[164] Burney, while similarly locating the tribe of Dan in the north, does, however, recognize the Danites in their client role:

> It is reasonable, however, to suppose that the Danites, living on friendly terms with the Phoenicians, may shortly after their settlement have entered into close relationship with them, and *taken service* on board their ships. It was probably the *protection extended by the Phoenicians* to the tribes of Asher and Dan (*in return, we may assume, for service rendered*) which made these tribes unconcerned to throw in their lot with the central Israelite tribes, and respond to the summons to battle.[165]

Stager has taken these comments about the tribe of Dan's life as a 'dependent', and their service on board ships, as his starting point. But using the results of archaeological surveys and excavations of highland villages, and the social and economic relationships inherent in agrarian society, he provides a compelling framework within which to understand more fully this note about Dan.[166]

Where the noun גר occurs in the Hebrew Bible, it is often translated as 'sojourner, newcomer, temporary dweller, stranger, or resident alien'. Stager points out, however, that in Phoenician and Punic the same word has the meaning of 'client'.[167] A study surveying the term 'sojourner' traces the same root also to Egyptian, Ugaritic, Old South Arabic, and

164. Moore (*Judges*, p. 155) writes: 'The words would be quite inexplicable if we had to translate "*why did he remain in the ships*" (RV)'. Moore assumes that his translation reflects the plain and clear meaning of the Hebrew text, and understands it to mean: 'Why does he live as a dependent, under the protection of the Phoenician seafarers?' In a related footnote he makes it clear that he does not understand the Danites to have been clients: 'it is not necessary to suppose that Danites served on Phoenician ships'.

165. Burney, *The Book of Judges*, p. 143 (emphasis added).

166. Stager, as already noted, differs from Moore and Burney in locating Dan in its southern territory, prior to their migration north and conquest of Laish. Thus Stager proposes not Phoenicians, but either Canaanites or Philistines as the Danites's patrons ('Archaeology, Ecology, and Social History', pp. 228-32).

167. Stager, 'Archaeology, Ecology, and Social History', p. 229. Unfortunately, he neglects to provide any textual references.

Aramaic. Socially and legally, 'sojourners'/'clients' did not enjoy full rights within the community where they resided, but were instead dependent on a patron for protection.[168] Throughout the Hebrew Bible, *gērîm* are frequently grouped with other socially vulnerable persons, such as widows, orphans, and even the Levites.[169] Control of one's own landed property was something a רֵג did not enjoy. According to Stager,

> the *gēr* was not a fully enfranchised citizen when residing outside his own descent group; the latter, which in ancient Israel was traced along the patrilineal line, oversaw rights of inheritance and succession of its members in matters related to landholding... When outside the protection of lineage and clan, it was important for the *gēr*, or client, to seek a patron for physical protection for himself, his family, or his kin group and aid such as employment or economic assistance. Of course, out of this relationship of inequality developed indebtedness and obligations on the part of the client toward his patron.[170]

The patron–client relationship in antiquity was thus a relationship of dependence. As a client dependent on a non-Israelite patron, the tribe of Dan was unable to respond to the summons and participate in the Israelite battle against the leaders of the Canaanite city-states.

A remaining question is whether the reference to Dan serving as client may be applied to the tribe as a whole. Stager suggests that 'we might speculate that at least enough of the Danites had been hired or pressed into duty by the ship-owners or shipping companies on the coast in the Jaffa region to inspire this saying about them'.[171] While the patron–client relationship is ordinarily defined as a relationship 'between *individuals* based on a strong element of inequality and difference in power', in which the 'patron has social, economic, and political resources that are needed by a client', it is not unknown to have the role of client assumed by a collective.[172] In fact, there are examples of such variations in the patron–client relationship where either the role of client or that of patron is occupied collectively. Eisenstadt and Roniger note that the

---

168. John R. Spencer, 'Sojourner', in *ABD*, VI, pp. 103-104. See also D. Kellermann, 'רוּג', in *TDOT*, II, pp. 439-49 (434).

169. See, e.g., Deut. 10.18; 14.29; 16.11, 14; 24.17, 19; 26.11-13; 27.19; Jer. 7.6; Zech. 7.10; Mal. 3.5; Ps. 146.9; cf. pp. 105-107, above.

170. Stager, 'Archaeology, Ecology, and Social History', p. 230.

171. Stager, 'Archaeology, Ecology, and Social History', p. 232.

172. The definition is from Moxness, 'Patron-Client Relations', p. 241 (emphasis added).

collective occupation of the role of client is found in Middle Eastern areas…where it arises within or involving supralocal groups of unilineal descent and including extended kinship ties, or in tribal areas, where the coopting of sheikhs by authorities and politicians sometimes leads to the emergence of clientelistic relations involving a whole tribal group.[173]

I interpret these 'supralocal groups' to mean, essentially, foreigners whom Eisenstadt and Roniger elsewhere label 'ethnically alien groups'—that is, people who are '"external" to the central structural core of society'.[174] In this case, the local, core society was the Canaanite or Philistine maritime traders located along the Mediterranean coast; the 'supralocals' were, of course, the landless Danites. It is reasonable to theorize that the Danites who, for whatever reason, were unable to possess and control the land allotted to them (Judg. 18.1; cf. Josh. 19.41-46), sought, as a collective, to enter into a clientelistic relationship with the coastal maritime traders. When people lack access to the resources essential for survival (in an agrarian society this means access to land), they may initiate the patron–client relationship simply by means of a request for aid (which, in the honor/shame culture, is interpreted as a positive challenge to which one is obligated to respond).[175]

In the final analysis, it must be admitted that, much like Judges 1, Judges 5—with just four words about the tribe of Dan—raises more questions about the Danites than it answers. For this reason, one is able to draw few, if any, definite historical conclusions. For example, since the text does not indicate whether Dan is in its southern or northern location, whether the note about the Danites antedates or post-dates their migration northward to Laish is not clear (this begins to explain the amount of ink spilled on pursuing the associated questions of date and location). Even so, on the basis of the available evidence, I conclude at this time that the better case can be made for a southern location of the Danites.

Also, while Judg. 5.17 situates at least a portion of the tribe of Dan aboard ships, the ship owners/operators are unnamed and the harbor is

---

173.   S.N. Eisenstadt and L. Roniger, *Patrons, Clients, and Friends: Interpersonal Relations and the Structure of Trust in Society* (New York: Cambridge University Press, 1984), p. 245.

174.   Eisenstadt and Roniger, *Patrons, Clients, and Friends*, p. 209.

175.   See Malina, *New Testament World*, p. 101. According to Eisenstadt and Roniger, 'sometimes it is also the potential clients that promote the emergence of such clientelistic ties among collective social units and organisations around powerful figures, in order to gain security and even as a locus of identity in a clientelistic setting' (*Patrons, Clients, and Friends*, p. 246).

unspecified. Neither, for that matter, does the text make clear that the ships were trading vessels. What is the likelihood that they had been warships? It is reasonable to suppose that foreign workers ('clients') served aboard both types of ship on the Mediterranean.

Finally, while 'serve as client' is the meaning of the verb גור, Judges 5 does not suggest anything about how the Danites became 'clients' of their more powerful, seacoast neighbors. The circumstances that contributed to the Danites's assumption of this precarious social status are simply unknown. One may only speculate that the arrival of the Sea Peoples contributed in some way (direct or indirect) to the Danites's landless condition.

Nevertheless, the following elements can be drawn from the present investigation of the Danites in Judges 5. First, the Song of Deborah is likely to preserve one of the earliest mentions of the tribe of Dan in the Hebrew Bible. While the tribe was, from the earliest, unquestionably included within some kind of Israelite association, it also had extra-Israelite economic relationships that prevented its members from participation in the battle portrayed in the Song of Deborah. Second, one consequence of this depiction of the tribe of Dan is the suggestion that its hold on its allotted territory was weak, and that the degree of probability that a significant proportion of the tribe was landless (not in control of its own land) is relatively high.

c. *Judges 13–16*
The marginal character of Dan in the Song of Deborah recurs in the stories of Samson in Judges 13–16. In these chapters the main character, Samson, is introduced as coming from the 'clan (משפחה) of Dan' (13.2), a social unit smaller and weaker than the tribe. In addition, according to the story, the Israelites (Danites, Judahites [15.11]) are subject to the ruling Philistines. Finally, the protagonist is portrayed according to the folklore motifs of a hero/trickster/underdog/bandit—figures whom folklorists have determined are often associated with marginal, oppressed groups.

In the following analysis, I will demonstrate that the stories of Samson in the Hebrew Bible have been *edited* so as to command a negative evaluation of the main character and, by extension, perhaps even of the Danites, with whom he is identified (Judg. 13.2). I will first show, however, that originally the stories told of a Danite hero who successfully and honorably wreaked havoc on the oppressive, neighboring Philistines. This story can still be reconstructed from the present Hebrew text. However, the work of the redactor, probably during the time of the exile, redirected the earlier, positive, Danite folktale in a wholly negative direction. The editor's hand can most clearly be seen in the portrayal of Samson as a (wholly unfaithful) Nazirite, as a judge in Israel (who is cast as the opposite of the first judge, Othniel, and most of the other judges), and in locating the Samson stories where they are in the book of Judges, at the end of the judge stories. Thus, the redacted version of the Samson cycle and, indeed, of the whole complex of 'judge' stories, suggests a disintegration of leadership in Israel leading up to the monarchy. While there seems to be no getting around the final form of the text with its negative appraisal of the Danite hero, Samson, and his legendary exploits, the results of folklore analysis and social science study well support the contention that originally the Samson stories were told among the Danites as hero tales to inspire and encourage a marginal and oppressed minority group in Israel.

Victor Matthews and Don Benjamin remind us that the modern, Western, industrial world is very different from the Eastern, agrarian world of the Bible. They note that, among other dissimilarities, while 'our genre of choice is history, theirs was story'.[176] This is most clearly the case in the present investigation of Dan in the stories of Samson in Judges 13–16. That we are not dealing with history (understood in a nineteenth-century, positivistic sense) in these stories should be obvious from even a casual reading of the text. Such extraordinary, heroic feats as killing a lion with empty hands, slaying Philistines with the jawbone of an ass, bearing the city gates and gateposts upon one's shoulders from Gaza to Hebron, and pulling down a temple, all point more in the direction of legend, myth, or folktale. In addition, the existence of stories parallel to those about Samson in the Hebrew Bible in other cultures calls into question any rigorous, (objective) historical interpretation of the details contained in these chapters.[177] For these reasons, no critical commentator has argued

176. Victor H. Matthews and Don C. Benjamin, 'Social Sciences and Biblical Studies', *Semeia* 68 (1994), pp. 7-21 (10).

177. Similar motifs have been noticed, in particular, in the stories of the Greek hero Heracles (= Hercules), the Phoenician Melqart, and in the Mesopotamian epic of Gilgamesh (especially Enkidu)—see the respective articles in *DDD*; see also Crenhaw, *Samson: A Secret Betrayed*, pp. 15-21. According to Susan Niditch (*Underdogs and Tricksters: A Prelude to Biblical Folklore* [New Voices in Biblical Studies; San Francisco: Harper & Row, 1987], pp. 2-3), 'if a biblical tale fits one of [Stith] Thompson's [motif-]types, the names, places, and settings being Israelite, we should be extremely cautious in drawing historical fact from the tale. The cross-cultural comparison made possible by the indices allows one to appropriate what is unique about the

for the essential historical veracity of either the individual, Samson, or Samson's numerous exploits, as preserved in the biblical text; all tend to recognize the mythological or heroic character of the narrative while, perhaps, nevertheless still holding out the possibility that the extraordinary protagonist and his stories are loosely based on a historic person.[178] In addition, the mythological elements (solar, nature [natural man]) in the Samson stories have not escaped the notice of interpreters over the years.[179]

Dissatisfied with these mythological and heroic categories, however, Crenshaw has interpreted the stories in terms of a saga, in which 'minimal historical events and personages' are treated in an 'elevated fashion'. According to Crenshaw, 'saga abounds in exaggerated feats; it tends toward hyperbole, and treats the fantastic as if it were ordinary'.[180] However, the 'minimal historical events' are not the focus of Crenshaw's study. Rather, his emphasis is on '[the saga's] beauty and art' as a 'literary piece'.[181] In his chapter on 'Literary and Stylistic Traditions', Crenshaw discusses six folklore motifs present in the Samson stories, and provides

biblical tale and its culture and to recognize what is not unique. Overhistoricization remains an unhealthy scholarly preoccupation in biblical scholarship. Folklorists too have long had an interest in distinguishing between history and folktale. Bible scholars do not draw the distinction often enough, sometimes failing to take account of the kind of literature with which they are dealing and to note that certain motifs may be included in a tale because such tales traditionally just go a certain way.'

178. See, e.g., Boling's favorable citation of Gaster's conclusion (originally from Frazer) about the portrayal of Samson (*Judges*, pp. 223-24). Cf. Moore, *Judges*, pp. 313-15, 365; Burney, *The Book of Judges*, pp. 338-40; Soggin, *Judges: A Commentary*, pp. 231-32.

179. The most detailed exposition available in English of Samson as solar myth is Steinthal, 'The Legend of Samson'. On Samson as 'natural man', see Burney's proracted discussion of the Gilgamesh epic (*The Book of Judges*, pp. 395-408); David E. Bynum, 'Samson as a Biblical φὴρ ὀρεσκῷος', in Susan Niditch (ed.), *Text and Tradition: The Hebrew Bible and Folklore* (Atlanta: Scholars Press, 1990), pp. 57-73; Gregory Mobley, 'The Wild Man in the Bible and the Ancient Near East', *JBL* 116 (1997), pp. 217-33.

180. Crenshaw, *Samson: A Secret Betrayed*, p. 19.

181. Crenshaw, *Samson: A Secret Betrayed*, p. 21. He describes his own method as 'aesthetic criticism', which he defines as 'an appreciation for the craft of a story or poem, as well as aesthetic enjoyment of the beauty inherent in words "fitly spoken"'. In short, aesthetic criticism studies a story or poem as a work of art' (p. 155). One might fairly characterize Crenshaw's work as the product the newer literary criticism, with attention to such matters as character, plot, and the like.

evidence of their occurrence elsewhere in the biblical material. These are: (1) the barren wife; (2) the hero helpless before a woman's wiles; (3) the quest for a deity's name; (4) the death wish of a hero; (5) the loss of charisma; and (6) the terror over theophany.[182] Of course, it is possible to extend this list to include folklore motifs that appear in Judg. 13–16 but which are not necessarily present in other parts of the biblical corpus.[183]

There seems to be sufficient evidence to conclude that the stories of Samson can profitably be interpreted by making careful use of folklore analysis. The propriety of folklore study to the task of biblical interpretation is no new discovery. In his ground-breaking, comparative work early in the twentieth century, Hermann Gunkel wrote that 'an ancient people without folktales seems hardly conceivable to us'.[184] While some folktales may have been prompted by everyday life experiences, others originated in the 'creative imagination' of particular individuals, stimulated either by dreams or visions. Still other stories, however, had their source in a

---

182. Crenshaw, *Samson: A Secret Betrayed*, pp. 41-50.

183. While not intended to be a complete list, the following folklore motifs present themselves as worthy of further study in conjunction with the Samson stories (the list is drawn from Stith Thompson, *Motif-Index of Folk-Literature: A Classification of Narrative Elements in Folktales, Ballads, Myths, Fables, Mediaeval Romances, Exempla, Fabliaux, Jest-Books and Local Legends* (6 vols.; Bloomington: Indiana University Press, rev. and enlarged edn, 1989): magic strength resides in hair, D1831; faithless wife ties sleeping husband's hair to bed, allowing lover to kill him, K713.1.7; fox produces fire by striking tail to ground, D1258.1.1; strong man carries off door-frame, F631.2.1; culture hero as trickster, A521; trickster outwits adulteress and paramour, K1570 (related motifs); clever wife, J1112; clever wife gets money from those who attempt to seduce her, K443.2; giant lion overcome by hero, B16.2.3; strong man kills lion with own hands, F628.1.1; betrayal of husband's secret by his wife, K2213.4; fatal secret revealed, C420.1; nagging wife, T253; younger child may not marry before elder, T131.2; mistreatment of prisoners, R51; blindness as punishment for murder, Q451.7.4; water gushes where strong man digs, F639.1.2; supplying water in land where it is lacking, H1138; well (spring) as refuge, R317; escape by deception, K500-699. See also the sections on Eating and Drinking Tabu (C200-299); Riddles (H530-899); Clever Verbal Retorts (J1250-1499); and Triumph of the Weak (L300-399).

184. Hermann Gunkel, *The Folktale in the Old Testament* (Historic Texts and Interpreters in Biblical Scholarship; trans. Michael D. Rutter; Sheffield: JSOT Press, 1987 [German original 1917]), p. 33. He went on to note that 'the proof that some Old Testament material belongs in the world of the folktale can be demonstrated in two ways: either parallels from undoubtedly folktale stock can be cited in other literature, or its folktale quality is patently manifested from the nature of the material itself' (p. 35). Both proofs, I suggest, are evident in the material in Judg. 13–16.

people's wish or hope borne of a difficult situation in life. Such 'boulo-matic folktales', Gunkel suggests, 'depict as reality what in hard life could, of course, only remain an unattainable desire'.[185] This, I shall demonstrate, was probably the case in the Danite stories of Samson. During a time of domination by extra-Israelite people, the Israelites (Danites) told the legends of Samson, a socially marginal figure who took on and wreaked havoc among the stronger, more powerful, greater Philistines.[186]

This social aspect of the Samson folktale is presented in a convincing way by Susan Niditch who argues that Samson is best understood as a culture hero/trickster/bandit.[187] By way of introduction she writes:

> ...in the framing hero pattern and in the more specific adventures of the hero as trickster and bandit, tales of Samson emphasize certain thematic pairs or contrasts that are at the heart of the Samson narrative as a whole: nature vs. culture; 'us' vs. 'them'; marginal status vs. centrality; Israelite vs. Philistine. These thematic contrasts all might be placed under the larger headings, the confrontation with authority and the issue of empowerment. Like the Book of Judges as a whole and very possibly the historical period and sociological setting which gave rise to its narratives, the Samson tale deals with the desire to obtain and hold autonomy, both personal and political.[188]

185. Gunkel, *The Folktale*, p. 30.

186. It remains to be determined whether the Philistines are to be understood as the actual oppressors of the Danites (which would situate the origin of the Samson stories in the Iron Age I), or whether they function as a symbol for another group at a later time.

187. Susan Niditch, 'Samson as Culture Hero, Trickster, and Bandit: The Em-powerment of the Weak', *CBQ* 52 (1990), pp. 608-24. In the opening pages of her study she provides some helpful definitions of these folklore motifs: 'At the heart of the trickster morphology, found in a large cross-section of traditional literatures, are questions of status, the hero's use of deception to increase his status at the expense of others, and others' often successful challenges to his status... The bandit is a variety of hero and trickster whose tale involves a challenge to the power of the establishment by weaker or oppressed elements in society. His adventures, like those of the trickster, involve deception and issues of status. His death is by betrayal and often features a trait of false invulnerability' (p. 609). See also her *Underdogs and Tricksters*, where she introduces the underdog and has additional remarks about the trickster (p. xi). See also the six elements characteristic of the successful clever hero outlined in Orrin E. Klapp, 'The Clever Hero', *Journal of American Folklore* 67 (1954), pp. 21-34. Most of these characterizations are immediately relevant for the present investigation of the stories of Samson, and of Samson as a Danite.

188. Niditch, 'Samson as Culture Hero', pp. 609-10. In her earlier *Underdogs and Tricksters*, Niditch concluded that tales about such heroes 'ultimately deal with funda-

Most important in her study for the present investigation is the matter of
'status' (= social standing, honor) as a prize of sorts in Samson's dealings
with the Philistines, who oppress (Judg. 15.9-13) and threaten the Israelites. Throughout the stories, Samson is seen attempting to wrest honor
from the Philistines, while the Philistines, for their part, strive to maintain
their standing in the face of Samson's challenges.[189]

Niditch's analysis may be at odds with most traditional interpretations
of the stories, according to which Samson—and perhaps, by extension, the
Danites—is negatively evaluated. If Samson is a hero at all, he is, as
Crenshaw identifies him, an 'anti-hero'.[190] Nevertheless, the results of
Niditch's folklore analysis are corroborated by the insights gained through
a social-science reading of the text. While the individual, extraordinary
episodes in the stories of Samson in Judges 13–16 are fundamentally
fiction, the overall story and portrayal of the protagonist do reveal something about the community in Israel within which these stories may have
originally circulated. That is, these folktales are more than just well-
crafted stories. They relate something about their sociological and historical setting. As Niditch has remarked, 'in contrast to some modern literary
critics, folklorists are not content to consider texts as texts in and of
themselves but view them as integral parts of particular value systems
grounded in time and place'.[191] Relating the contribution folklore study
may make to history and the task of biblical interpretation, she writes:

> Concern with the historical setting of the created composition rather than
> with historicity leads to biblical scholarship that is, in fact, very interested
> in 'history.' Such an approach treats biblical literature as coming from real
> people who had tastes, aesthetics, and talents, and who lived in settings—
> economic, political, ecological, cultural, and religious—that helped to shape
> who they were. It encourages us to search for these real people and their

mental aspects of individual and group identity, such as authority and empowerment,
stasis and change' (p. 152). See also Klapp ('The Clever Hero', p. 30), who describes
the social function of the clever hero in this way: 'Evidently he does something more
than provide the pleasure of comedy, which could be true of any fool… He is distinctly
the fool-*maker*, and his service lies in doing this to certain persons on certain occasions.
Whenever he "gets the best of it," someone else gets the worst of it. His opponents are
characteristically the great, the strong, the proud, and the cruel; he is essentially a
champion of the little man, a righter of wrongs, a protagonist of democracy, an agent
of comic justice.'

189. Niditch, 'Samson as Culture Hero', pp. 620-21.
190. Crenshaw, *Samson: A Secret Betrayed*, p. 130.
191. Niditch, *Underdogs and Tricksters*, p. 16.

worlds rather than to check the accuracy of their information, interesting though their past (and ours) may be. It is, however, also an approach that refuses to explore the text solely in terms of its meaning to readers or that suggests that the text can be interpreted without attention to its author's intentions, conscious or subconscious. It is, then, an approach that steers a course between biblical scholarship as a means of historical reconstruction and biblical scholarship as a wholly reader-responsed variety of literary criticism.[192]

In this way, folklore analysis corresponds to the objectives of some recent study of the biblical text utilizing interpretive models from the social sciences. While neither folklore study nor social-science analysis is preoccupied with the historical veracity of every datum in a given text—that is, they do not test the historical accuracy of related events—both interpretive methodologies are attentive to the conditions and events of everyday life of the communities in which the stories originated and circulated. While there is minimal data in the Samson stories upon which to base an elaborate reconstruction of the history of the Israelite tribe of Dan, this folktale complex does preserve for the reader something about the early Danites, for whom the protagonist, Samson, figures as a hero. In particular, I will demonstrate how the application of certain models of interaction or behavior subsumed under the more general categories of honor and shame contribute to a more complete understanding of Samson's typically antagonistic, even hostile, relationship with the ruling Philistines, and to a more positive evaluation of the hero and his actions.

It is helpful at this point to review a brief definition of honor and shame—what Bruce Malina has referred to as 'pivotal values' of the Mediterranean world.[193] Honor is well-defined by Malina as 'the value of a person in his or her own eyes (that is, one's claim to worth) *plus* that person's value in the eyes of his or her social group. Honor is the claim to worth along with the social acknowledgment of worth.'[194] According to Malina and Neyrey, honor 'serves as a register of social rating which entitles a person to interact in specific ways with equals, superiors, and subordinates, according to prescribed cultural cues of the society... Honor indicates a person's social standing and rightful place in society.'[195] Related to this notion is that of shame, which Joseph Plevnik calls

192. Susan Niditch, *Folklore and the Hebrew Bible* (GBS; Minneapolis: Fortress Press, 1993), p. 25.

193. Malina, *New Testament World*, p. 28.

194. Malina, *New Testament World*, p. 31.

195. Malina and Neyrey, 'Honor and Shame in Luke–Acts', p. 26.

the opposite of honor…a claim to worth that is publicly denied or repudi-
ated. To 'be shamed' is always negative; it means to be denied or to be
diminished in honor. On the other hand, to 'have shame' is always positive;
it means to be concerned about one's honor. All human beings seek to have
shame, no human being cares to be shamed.[196]

Honor may be either ascribed or acquired. Like inherited wealth, ascribed
honor is granted to a person by virtue of birth, family connections, or a
grant from a notable person such as a king or deity. Quaintly put, '*ascribed
honor*…is honor that you get simply for being you, not because of anything you do to acquire it'.[197] Acquired honor is that honor which a person
wins by achieving a victory over another who is, correspondingly, diminished in honor (honor was recognized in antiquity as a 'limited good').[198]
The chief manner by which honor is acquired is the social interaction
called 'challenge and riposte/response'.[199] There are two fundamental
criteria that must be met for a person's honor to be committed in challenge–riposte: (1) the challenge must always be issued in public; and (2)
the interaction over honor can only take place between social equals.[200]

  Just as certain folklore motifs reflect the particular social context or
historical setting of the community in which they originated or circulated,
so also does a close reading of the biblical text, informed by insights
drawn from cultural anthropology, shed light on the cultural setting/social
world of, in this case, the Danites, among whom the Samson stories were
first told. In addition, just as folklore motifs in part determine the course of

196. Plevnik, 'Honor/Shame', p. 96.
197. Malina, *New Testament World*, p. 33. Nevertheless, ascribed honor is not
inviolable. J.G. Peristiany ('Introduction', in *idem* [ed.], *Honour and Shame: The Values of Mediterranean Society* [Chicago: University of Chicago Press, 1966], pp. 9-18
[11]) has observed that 'even when honor is inherited with the family name it has to be
asserted and vindicated'.
198. On honor as limited good, see Malina and Neyrey, 'Honor and Shame in
Luke–Acts', p. 31. In preindustrial society, with neither the technology to mass pro-
duce goods, nor the notion of boundless opportunities or resources, everything
(tangible and intangible alike) was understood as limited.
199. For a detailed discussion of this social interaction, see Bourdieu, 'The Sentiment of Honour in Kabyle Society'.
200. Malina and Neyrey ('Honor and Shame in Luke–Acts', pp. 29-32) outline
three phases which together comprise the social event of challenge–response. These
are: (1) challenge in terms of some action (word, deed, or both) on the part of the
challenger; (2) perception of the message by both the individual to whom it is directed
and the public at large; and (3) reaction of the receiving individual and the evaluation
of the reaction on the part of the public.

the action in a story, so also do certain rules of social interaction in part govern the way in which a story unfolds to convey a particular message.

The following two texts will be studied: Judg. 14.10-19, Samson's Riddle; and Judg. 16.4-21, Samson, Delilah, and the Philistines.[201] In both stories, it is Samson as trickster who successfully defends his honor against the more powerful Philistines.

(1) *Judges 14.10-19*

[10] Then his father went down to the woman; and Samson prepared there a feast, for thus the young men did. [11] And it happened that as they saw him; that they took 30 companions, and they were with him. [12] Then Samson said to them, 'Let me propound for you a riddle; if you indeed make it known to me during the seven days of the feast and you guess (it), then I shall give to you 30 outer garments and 30 changes of clothing. [13] But if you are not able to make (it) known to me, then *you* shall give to me 30 outer garments and 30 changes of clothing.' And they said to him, 'Propound your riddle, and we shall listen to it'. [14] So he said to them,
'From the eater went out food,
        and from the strong/mighty went out sweetness'.
But they were not able to make known the riddle for three days. [15] Now it happened, on the seventh day, that they said to the wife of Samson, 'Persuade [entice/seduce/deceive] your husband, that he might make known to us the riddle, lest we burn you and your father's house with fire; have you invited us here for the purpose of impoverishing us?' [16] And the wife of Samson wept over him, and she said, 'Surely you hate me and you do not love me, the riddle you have "riddled" for the sons of my people, but to me you have not made it known'. And he said to her, 'Look! To my father and my mother I have not made it known, but to you I shall (or shall I) make it known.(?)' [17] And she wept over him the seven days which made up the feast; and it happened that on the seventh day he made (it) known to her, because she pressed upon him/brought him into straights, then she made known the riddle to the sons of her people. [18] And the men of the city said to him, on the seventh day before the sun set,
'What is sweeter than honey,
        and what is stronger than a lion?'

201. To these texts might be added Judg. 15, which contains several episodes that could be interpreted in terms of honor/shame (the giving of Samson's wife to another; Samson's response [setting fire to the Philistines' standing grain and vineyards]; the Philistines' revenge; and Samson's deception of the Philistines and Judahites alike, by which he bursts his bonds and slays 1000 Philistines). Judg. 14 and 16 have been selected for more extended analysis in the present study because the social interaction contained in them lends itself more readily to such explication.

And he said to them,
> 'Unless you had plowed with my heifer,
> > you would not have guessed the riddle'.

[19] And the spirit of Yahweh rushed upon him, and he went down to Ashkelon, and he slew from them 30 men, and he took their clothing and he gave the changes (of clothing) to the ones who made known the riddle; and his anger was kindled, and he went up (to) the house of his father.

[Notes on the MT:

Verse 10: The two notes in the critical apparatus attempt to smooth out what may look like a difficult text (different subjects for each verb). For 'his father', the editor of the book of Judges in *BHS* (R. Meyer) suggests that one read 'Samson'. In the second half of the verse, it is suggested that 'Samson' be deleted. However, there is no manuscript evidence to support either of these emendations. In addition, reading 'his father (went down)' in v. 10 forms a nice *inclusio* with 'he went up to the house of his father' in v. 19. For these reasons, the MT is to be preferred.

Verse 11: For 'as/when they saw (him)', the LXX (Alexandrinus) reads ἐν τῷ φοβεῖσθει αὐτοῦς (= 'because they feared [him]'; Vaticanus better represents the MT), on the basis of which the editor reconstructs בְּיִרְאָתָם. Of course, ראה and ירא may be easily confused. On the other hand, the notice in the LXX (Alexandrinus) may be understood as an interpretation of the original Hebrew ראה in an effort to explain the young men's action (the appointment of 30 companions). The arrival of a stranger in one's community would naturally evoke suspicion and distrust, but not necessarily fear. The MT is the preferred reading.

Verse 12: 'And you guess' is absent from the LXX and the Old Latin; the editor suggests that perhaps the word has been added to the MT (it does not appear, however, in vv. 13 and 14, where 'make known' [with which 'guess' is linked in v. 12] does occur; cf. v. 18). The idea of 'guessing' in v. 12 forms a nice *inclusio* with v. 18, and so is to be retained in v. 12.

Verse 14: For 'three (days)', one medieval manuscript of the Hebrew Old Testament reads 'seven' (but cf. v. 15, text-critical note b).

Verse 15: The introductory phrase, 'Now it happened, on the seventh day', is absent from one medieval manuscript of the Hebrew Old Testament. For the MT's 'seventh' in this opening phrase, the LXX (Syriac) reads τῇ τετάρτῃ ('on the fourth [day]'); thus the editor suggests reading הרביעי. The similar morphology of the Hebrew words in question (רביעי, שביעי) may well account for this corruption. However, the chronological markers throughout this text are not necessarily perfect. It is better to recognize the LXX as either a misreading of the Hebrew *Vorlage*, or as a later attempt to smooth out the chronology. In addition, since this entire episode is part of a folktale, it may not be required that the temporal/chronological notices fit perfectly (a preoccupation of a later age of interpreters?). Rather, what seems to be more important is the repetition of 'seven'/'seventh' in the story (vv. 12, 15, 17 [twice], 18). For 'for the purpose of impoverishing us' (qal infinitive construct) one medieval manuscript of the Hebrew Old Testament reads הליור' (piel?). The LXX reads πτωχεῦσαι ἐκαλέσατε ἡμᾶς ('Did you call/invite in order to make beggars of us?'); thus the editor proposes emending the MT to הלהורישנו (hiphil infinitive construct; see GKC, 69m). The form הֲלֹא is an unusual construction which would be translated 'or not' (in the sense of 'is this not true'); the expected form introducing the disjunctive question, however, is לֹא אִם (GKC, 150m). The editor suggests that the text be read with a few medieval manuscripts of the Hebrew Old Testament, Soraeis [K(ethib)] Nehardeaeis [Q(ere)] (Eastern massoretic traditions from schools at Sura and Nehardea, respectively), and the Targum, which have הֲלֹם ('hither'). This is a plausible emendation, and one that is reflected in my translation.

Verse 18: For 'the sun' (החרסה), the editor proposes החדרה ('the [bridal] chamber'); cf. 15.1. However, the MT is to be preferred. The primary interaction in this text is between Samson and the young men; Samson's wife does not participate in the face-to-face meetings between Samson and the young men of Timnah. The MT, which reads 'before the sun set (literally, "went in")', also builds suspense as the story nears its climactic scene. The MT raises the question, 'Will the young men make known the riddle to Samson within the agreed upon time, before the time is up?' The MT, more fully, reads 'on the seventh day, (just) before the sun set'; that is, just before the start of the next/eighth day, which began at sunset.]

Much ink has already been spilled on the story of Samson's riddle in Judges 14.[202] The purpose of the present analysis is to focus on the social dimension of the interaction between the Danite hero, Samson, and the Philistine young men (הבחורים). How do the interpretive categories of honor and shame and, in particular, the social interaction known as challenge–riposte, provide a fuller understanding of the events portrayed in this text?

Judges 14.10-11 set the scene for the subsequent interaction, and provide evidence in support of the two essential criteria that must be met. First, the occasion is a feast which, while perhaps taking place in a private residence, is nevertheless a *public* event. While the challenge–riposte involves Samson and the young men of Timnah, others assume the role of witness: Samson's father, the wife of Samson, and the 30 companions designated by the young men to be with Samson.[203] In addition, as this is a

202. Most recently, Jeremy Schipper ('Narrative Obscurity of Samson's חידה in Judges 14.15 and 18', *JSOT* 27.3 [2003], pp. 339-53) has examined again the complex relationship between the riddle and its solution and the narrative context in which the exchange occurs.

203. It is not clear whether these 30 companions are in addition to the unspecified number of young men. If they are in fact to be distinguished from the young men, then these 30 companions do indeed comprise a part of the 'court of public opinion' before whom the social interaction of challenge and response plays out. On the involvement of 'escorts' during marriage festivities, see Bourdieu, 'The Sentiment of Honour in Kabyle Society', p. 203. See also Pitt-Rivers's remarks about how 'local lads' react

folktale, told and retold within a community over time, the hearers or readers may also be counted as part of the audience before whom the action takes place. The audience's verdict at the end of the story is, therefore, crucial. Second, the young men and/or the 30 companions appear in the text as Samson's *peers*: all are of comparable maturity and are of marriageable age.[204] In short, they are social equals.

The challenge is given in vv. 12-13. A challenge may be a word or action by which the challenger seeks to 'enter the social space of another'.[205] A challenge may be either positive (such as a word of praise, gift, or genuine request for help) or negative (a threat or insulting word, or physical affront), but each demands a response if one is to defend one's honor. Samson is cast in the role of the challenger, and his challenge takes the form of a riddle: 'Let me propound for you a riddle; if you indeed make it known to me during the seven days of the feast and you guess (it), then I shall give to you 30 outer garments and 30 changes of clothing'.[206] On the idea of a riddle as challenge, Crenshaw's observation is important: 'Inasmuch as the language in riddles communicates on two levels simultaneously, we can say that it intentionally deceives. Essential to riddles is the setting of a trap... Riddles establish worth or identity rather than native intelligence.'[207] If Samson's intention is purposefully to deceive, contrary to what we may suppose, he is not automatically diminished in honor. While lying and deception strike the modern interpreter as always morally objectionable, they are dishonorable actions in the (ancient) Mediterranean culture only among one's kin group. It is acceptable, however, to lie for the purpose of deceiving an outsider who, it is held, has no right to the truth.[208] According to the stated terms of this challenge, there shall be

when a stranger comes into their community in search of a wife (*The Fate of Shechem*, pp. 33, 106).

204. BDB, p. 104 ('young man [choice, in the prime of manhood']).

205. Malina and Neyrey, 'Honor and Shame in Luke–Acts', p. 30.

206. Riddling is not unusual in the context of wedding festivities; see Thomas A. Burns ('Riddling: Occasion to Act', *Journal of American Folklore* 89 [1976], pp. 139-65 [143]), who notes that riddling as part of courtship often includes considerable sexual *double-entendre*, a point well developed by Crenshaw (*Samson: A Secret Betrayed*, pp. 102, 111-20). See also Moore, *Judges*, p. 334; Bourdieu, 'The Sentiment of Honour in Kabyle Society', p. 203.

207. Crenshaw, *Samson: A Secret Betrayed*, p. 100; see also his note about 'contest literature' (p. 110).

208. Malina and Neyrey, 'Honor and Shame in Luke–Acts', p. 37. See also Bourdieu, 'The Sentiment of Honour in Kabyle Society', pp. 228-29.

winners and losers; in some way the garments are, perhaps, symbolic of the gain or loss in honor (vv. 12-13).

It is not immediately clear that the young men perceive the riddle as a challenge. While Samson speaks of making known (נגד) the riddle, and guessing it (מצא), the young men only agree to listen (שמע) to the riddle. However, their inability to 'make known' the riddle on their own (vv. 14-15) creates great anxiety for them, insofar as it threatens to diminish their honor, and is good evidence that the riddle is perceived by them as a challenge to which they must respond.[209]

Between challenge (vv. 12-14) and riposte (when the young men of Timnah make known the riddle to Samson, v. 18), the seven days of the feast run their course (vv. 14-15, 18). On one level of reading, this passage of time without response heightens the tension in the story; there is a dramatic effect created by the delay in the young men's riposte. A social reading interprets this passage of time as the apparent approaching of impending dishonor. Bourdieu notes that 'dishonor remains virtual as long as the possibility of riposte remains; but it becomes more and more real the longer vengeance is delayed. Thus honour requires that the time lapse between the offence and its reparation should be as short as possible.'[210] The dishonor of the young men thus becomes a more imminent reality as the conclusion of the feast draws near. Then, suddenly, (literally) just before the sun goes down at the end of the seventh day, they make known the riddle. Their last-minute response answers the challenge and salvages their honor. Again, Bourdieu observes that 'revenge taken after a long delay is only praised in retrospect: before taken, it is all the more doubtful and uncertain; once it is taken, it is all the more meritorious'.[211]

Significantly, however, the story does not end here, with the hero, Samson, dishonored. The original Danite storyteller, for whom Samson fulfills the role of culture-hero, cannot leave off at this point. To end the social interaction at the point of the young men's riposte would leave Samson's honor diminished in at least two ways: (1) by his opponents' victory in the challenge issued by him; and (2) by their victory having been achieved by unfair means known to the public (= the audience) but apparently

---

209. The young men's acceptance of the challenge further confirms the assumption that they and Samson are social equals, since to accept the challenge of a person of inferior status is already to bring dishonor upon oneself (see Bourdieu, 'The Sentiment of Honour in Kabyle Society', p. 200).

210. Bourdieu, 'The Sentiment of Honour in Kabyle Society', p. 214.

211. Bourdieu, 'The Sentiment of Honour in Kabyle Society', p. 214.

unknown to Samson himself. But what the audience knows is somehow perceived by Samson (another folklore motif?), namely, that the young men of Timnah have not arrived at the correct answer to the riddle according to the 'rules of the game'.[212] In this way, the Timnites's riposte is to be interpreted as a counter-challenge to which Samson, if he is to maintain his honor, must respond. There are two elements to Samson's immediate retort: (1) the saying in v. 18b; and (2) the violent outburst against the men of Ashkelon.

First, Samson's saying brings to light what the audience already knows: the young men of Timnah have acted dishonorably by approaching the wife of Samson privately. Pitt-Rivers notes that for a stranger 'to enter [the women's quarters] other than as a supplicant (claiming protection) would be the gravest offence and a desecration of female purity'.[213] The young men's violation of the sexual purity of Samson's wife is implied in Samson's saying, in the metaphors of 'heifer' and 'plowing'. Samson charges that, as Crenshaw points out, his 'garden has been cultivated by strangers'.[214] The threat to Samson's honor as a result of the young men's action is further indicated by their encouraging Samson's wife to 'persuade [seduce/entice/deceive]' her husband so that he will 'make known the riddle' (v. 15). The verb in question is פתה. In the piel conjugation, the word means to 'persuade, seduce, entice, deceive'.[215] The persuasion implied, then, is essentially negative in character. (The same verb, in the piel, also occurs in Jer. 20.7, where the prophet laments: 'You have seduced me, Yahweh, and I was seduced; You have overpowered me, and you have prevailed'. Robert Carroll notes that some interpreters have understood this passage as the prophet's accusing Yahweh of rape.[216]) According to the story, the young men blackmail Samson's wife into shameful activity so that they might obtain the secret of the riddle.

Samson's wife yields to the deceitful ploy of the young men, which renders her shameless. In her collusion with the 'sons of [her] people' against her husband, she brings shame to herself and dishonor to her

212. Moore (*Judges*, p. 338), e.g., recognized 'plowed with my heifer' as indicating the use of 'illegitimate means'.

213. Pitt-Rivers, *The Fate of Shechem*, p. 116.

214. Crenshaw, *Samson: A Secret Betrayed*, p. 119.

215. BDB, p. 834. In the Samson stories, the same form (imperative) occurs again at 16.5, also on the lips of Philistines.

216. Robert P. Carroll, *Jeremiah: A Commentary* (OTL; Philadelphia: Westminster Press, 1986), p. 398; see also Abraham J. Heschel, *The Prophets* (New York: Harper & Row, 1962), pp. 113-14.

husband. She acts inappropriately, and so violates her loyalty to her new family. Citing a traditional maxim, Bourdieu underlines the woman's primary responsibility to her family (at marriage her loyalty is transferred from her father to her husband):

> 'The woman owes faithfulness to her husband; her household must be well kept; she must watch over the good education of her children. But above all she must preserve the secrecy of the family's intimate life; she must never belittle her husband or shame him (even if she has every reason to do so, and all the necessary evidence), either in her intimate life or before strangers; for such action would force him to repudiate her... She must not interfere in the discussions between men. She must have confidence in her husband, must not disbelieve him, or seek to prove anything against him' (*El Kalaa*). In short, since she is always 'the daughter of so and so' or 'the wife of so and so', her honour, the woman's 'glory' are none other than the honour of the group of agnates to which she belongs. She must therefore be on her guard against acting in any way that might prejudice the prestige and reputation of the group.[217]

Samson's wife in no way follows this model of such exemplary and honorable behavior.

His honor challenged by both the young men of Timnah and his new wife, Samson must respond. In addition to the saying (v. 18), Samson, propelled by the Spirit of Yahweh, 'went down to Ashkelon, and he slew from them 30 men, and he took their clothing and he gave the changes (of clothing) to the ones who made known the riddle' (v. 19). Samson's violence is not entirely unexpected. In part, Samson's outburst against Ashkelon may be attributed to his role as hero/trickster/bandit.[218] The scene at Ashkelon, then, is part of the expected development of the story. Additionally, there is social significance to Samson's action. McVann writes that 'attacks on family honor are serious matters and likely to result in acts of vengeance (e.g. Gen 34; Deut 22.13–33.1) or strong censure (Gen 9.20-27; 2 Sam 12.1-12)'.[219]

This episode concludes with the note that, in (justified) anger, Samson retreats to his father's house in the vicinity of Zorah and Eshtaol (cf. 13.2, 25). He leaves, however, having made satisfaction and restored his honor.[220] His effort at restoring his impugned honor is successful, and the

217. Bourdieu, 'The Sentiment of Honour in Kabyle Society', p. 223.
218. Niditch, 'Samson as Culture Hero', pp. 621-24.
219. McVann, 'Family Centeredness', p. 71.
220. See Malina and Neyrey, 'Honor and Shame in Luke–Acts', p. 38. Flight is not necessarily about cowardice, weakness, or sulking, but may be understood as part of

remark that he 'took their clothing and he gave the changes (of clothing) to the ones who made known the riddle' shows Samson to be, to the end, an (ironically) honorable man, who honors his word and abides by his promises (vv. 13, 19).

There can be little doubt that this Samson story, together with the rest of Judges 13–16, was told from the perspective of the Danites. There is no basis for a negative evaluation of Samson in this story. In the opinion of the original storyteller, and in the opinion of the audience, at the end of the story Samson escapes with his honor not only intact, but enhanced at the expense of the young men of Timnah (and Ashkelon). By the way the story ends, one can only conclude that the storyteller intended to demonstrate that Samson is an honorable person, a hero/trickster acting on behalf of the weak or marginalized Danites. A similar conclusion is drawn from the story of Samson, Delilah, and the Philistines in ch. 16.

(2) *Judges 16.4-30*

> [4] Now it happened afterwards that he (Samson) loved a woman in Nahal Soreq; and her name was Delilah. [5] And the lords of the Philistines went up to her and they said to her, 'Persuade [seduce/entice/deceive] him and learn about in what is his great strength, and in what way we might prevail against him, and (in what way) we might bind/imprison him in order to humble/humiliate him; then we ourselves shall give to you—each of us—1100 pieces of silver.'
>
> [6] So Delilah said unto Samson, 'Make known to me in what is your great strength; and in what way shall you be bound in order to humble/humiliate you'. [7] And Samson said to her, 'If they will bind me with seven fresh bowstrings which have not been dried, then I shall become weak and I shall be like an ordinary human being'. [8] So the lords of the Philistines brought up to her seven fresh bowstrings which had not been dried, and she bound him with them. [9] Now the ambush was waiting in her bedroom, and she said to him, 'The Philistines are upon you, Samson!' But he snapped the bowstrings just as the thread of tow is snapped when it smells fire; so his strength was not made known. [10] Then Delilah said to Samson, 'Behold, you have deceived/mocked me, and you have spoken to me lies/deceptive things; now make known to me in what way shall you be bound'.

the 'clever hero' motif from folklore. Fleeing means being able to 'return to fight another day' (cf. Judg. 15–16). Klapp ('The Clever Hero', p. 29) has noted that 'the fugitive gains prestige by his immunity just as those who chase him, by failure, become fools. Further, there is no dishonor in the retreat of a small from a greater force; on the contrary, it places all the risk of disgrace on the larger antagonist.'

[11] So he said to her, 'If they will surely bind me with new twisted cords with which work has not been done, then I shall become weak and I shall be like an ordinary human being'. [12] So Delilah took new twisted cords and she bound him with them, and she said to him, 'The Philistines are upon you, Samson!' Now the ambush was waiting in the bedroom; then he snapped them from upon his shoulders like (the) thread. [13] Then Delilah said to Samson, 'Until now you have deceived me, and you have spoken to me lies/deceptive things. Make known to me in what way you shall be bound'. So he said to her, 'If you will weave seven plaits of hair of my head with the web, and you shall thrust (it) with the peg into the wall, then I shall become weak and I shall be like an ordinary human being'. So she put him to sleep, and she wove the seven plaits of hair of his head with the web, [14] and she thrust the peg into the wall and she said to him, 'The Philistines are upon you, Samson!' But he awoke from his sleep, and he pulled out the peg of the loom and the web. [15] Then she said to him, 'How is it that you say to me, "I love you", but your heart is not with me? This is three times you have deceived me, and you have not made known to me in what is your great strength.'

[16] So it happened that she pressed upon him with her words all the days (day after day) and urged him, and his spirit was impatient to death. [17] Then he made known to her his whole heart, and he said to her, 'A razor has not gone up upon my head, for a Nazirite of God I have been from the womb of my mother. If I am shaven, then my strength shall depart from me, and I shall become weak and I shall be like every ordinary human being. [18] Then Delilah saw that he had made known to her his whole heart. So she sent and called for the lords of the Philistines, saying, 'Come up now, for he has made known to me his whole heart'. And the lords of the Philistines came up to her, and they brought up the silver in their hand. [19] Then she made him sleep upon her knees. And she called to the man, and she shaved seven plaits of hair of his head. So she began to humble/humiliate him, and his strength departed from upon him. [20] Then she said, 'The Philistines are upon you, Samson!' And he awoke from his sleep and he said, 'I shall go out as usual; and I shall shake myself free'. But he did not know that Yahweh had departed from upon him. [21] So the Philistines took hold of him and they bore out his eyes; and they brought him down toward Gaza. And they imprisoned him in two fetters of bronze. So he was a grinder in the house of the prisoners.

[22] But the hair of his head began to grow abundantly just as when it was shaven. [23] And the lords of the Philistines assembled themselves to slaughter a great sacrifice to Dagon their god and to be joyous. And they said, 'Our god has given into our hand Samson our enemy'. [24] And the people saw him, and they praised their god, for they said, 'Our god has given into our hand our enemy, and the desolator of our land, indeed, who has multiplied our slain'. [25] Then it happened that their heart was merry, and they said, 'Call to Samson and let him make sport for us'. So they

called to Samson from the house of the prisoners and he made sport before them. Then they caused him to stand between the pillars. [26] And Samson said to the young man who was giving support with his hand, 'place me and let me touch/so that I may touch the pillars upon which the temple is fixed, and let me lean against them'. [27] And the temple was full of men and women, and there all the lords of the Philistines were and upon the roof were about 3000 men and women watching Samson's sport. [28] Then Samson called unto Yahweh and he said, 'O Lord Yahweh! Remember me and strengthen me only this time, O God! And let me avenge myself—an act of vengeance of one of my two eyes—from the Philistines.' [29] So Samson grasped and twisted the two middle pillars upon which the temple was fixed, and he braced himself against them, one with his right and one with his left. [30] And Samson said, 'Let my life die with the Philistines!' And he stretched out mightily, and he brought down/caused to fall the temple upon the lords and upon all the people who were in it. And the dying ones whom he killed in his death were more than those he killed in his lifetime.

[Notes on the MT:

Verse 9: After 'he snapped (the bowstrings)', a few medieval manuscripts of the Hebrew Old Testament include a conjunctive accent (*mûnaḥ*), which the editor of the book of Judges in *BHS* (R. Meyer) recommends reading.

Verse 13: After the imperative, 'make known', several medieval manuscripts of the Hebrew Old Testament add the particle of entreaty, as in vv. 6 and 10. However, this particle, which tends to have the effect of softening the imperative, may have been intentionally omitted in v. 13 as a way to demonstrate Delilah's rising frustration at Samson's deception. This is, after all, the third time that Delilah has requested that Samson make known to her the source of his strength or how he might be bound. For literary reasons, I prefer the MT (without the particle נָא). The end of v. 13 and the beginning of v. 14 are textually difficult. At the end of this verse, it is suggested that several words have fallen out of the MT; the LXX adds καὶ ἐγκρούσῃς ἐν τῷ πασσάλῳ εἰς τὸν τοῖχον καὶ ἔσομαι ἀσθενὴς ὡς εἷς τῶν ἀνθρώπων, which is retroverted as וְתָקַעַתְּ בְּיָתֵד אֶל־הַקִּיר וְחָלִיתִי וְהָיִיתִי כְּאַחַד הָאָדָם ('and you shall thrust [it] with the peg into the wall, then I shall become weak and I shall be like an ordinary human being'). It is understandable that these words were omitted from the MT due to a kind of haplography involving הַמַּסָּכֶת at the end of both vv. 13 and 14. My translation reflects the witness of the LXX.

Verse 14: Before 'and she thrust', it is suggested that several words have dropped out of the MT. Before this, the LXX puts καὶ ἐκοίμισεν αὐτὸν Δαλιλα καὶ ἐδιάσατο τοὺς ἑπτὰ βοστρύχους τῆς κεφαλῆς αὐτοῦ μετὰ τῆς ἐκτάσεως, which may be retroverted as וַתִּישָׁנֵהוּ וַתַּאֲרִיג אֶת־שֶׁבַע מַחְלְפוֹת רֹאשׁוֹ עִם־הַמַּסָּכֶת ('and she put him to sleep and she wove the seven plaits of hair of his head with the web'). As is the case in the previous note, my translation reflects the LXX; it is reasonable to conclude that the LXX preserves a Hebrew text which has been lost due to haplography (the same haplography that accounts for the previous note). After 'the peg', the LXX adds εἰς τὸν τοῖχον, which would be אֶל־הַקִּיר in Hebrew ('into the wall'). This may be part of a

Hebrew text which has been accidently omitted from the MT. It is suggested that 'the peg of the loom' is a corrupt Hebrew text, for which 'the peg' is a proposed substitution. At the end of v. 14 (MT), the LXX adds 'and his strength was not made known', probably in an effort to harmonize this verse with a previous one; compare the last part of v. 9.

Verse 17: For 'like every (ordinary human being)', a few medieval manuscripts of the Hebrew Old Testament read 'like one of', as occurs in vv. 7 and 11. This is a scribal effort to harmonize this particular verse with earlier verses in the chapter. However, since v. 17 comes at the end of the conversation between Samson and Delilah, this divergent text may underline its emphatic intent. Read the MT.

Verse 18: For לֹה ('to me'), many medieval manuscripts of the Hebrew Old Testament read the *qere* לִי. It is possible that the *kethib* can be accounted for as being influenced by the last occurrence of the verb 'to make known', followed by the same preposition (v. 17). For וַעֲלִי, it is suggested that the text be read with many medieval manuscripts of the Hebrew Old Testament וְיַעֲלוּ, compare the LXX (which has an aorist form: καὶ ἀνέβησαν. Since yods and waws are at issue, and since the previous word ends in a waw, it is possible that a letter (yod) has dropped out accidently. The variant reading represents the expected form, which is reflected in my translation. It has been proposed that 'the silver' at the end of v. 18 be read 'and the silver', with the conjunction. There is no manuscript evidence to support this emendation, which may be unnecessary (see my translation, which interprets 'the silver' as a direct object).

Verse 19: For 'upon (her knees)', the LXX reads ἀνὰ μέσον; perhaps the text should be read בֵּין ('between [her knees]'). See, however, Gen. 30.3, where there occurs the same preposition with 'knees' as here in the MT. Read the MT. For 'and she shaved', it is suggested that the text be read instead 'and he shaved' with one medieval manuscript of the Hebrew Old Testament; compare the LXX which is not gender specific. With the introduction of 'the man' immediately preceding the verb in dispute, the MT (which makes sense) is the more difficult text and to be preferred. For 'so she began to humble/humiliate him', the LXX reads καὶ ἔρξατο ταπεινοῦσθαι ('so he began to be humbled/humiliated'), which may be retroverted as וַיָּחֶל לְעַנּוֹת. Following the previous note, the MT is to be preferred.

Verse 21: For the defectively written (*kethib*) MT, הָאֲסִירִים, many medieval manuscripts of the Hebrew Old Testament read with the *qere*, the definite plural passive participle of אָסַר (BDB, p. 63). However, the *kethib* form (without the dagesh in the yod) is an acceptable form, and should be maintained; thus my translation.

Verse 24: The editor of the book of Judges (R. Meyer) suggests that v. 24 be transposed after v. 25, thus ascribing the 'merry heart' and the invitation to Samson to make sport to the 'lords of the Philistines' rather than to the people, which is suggested by the MT. There is no manuscript evidence to support rearranging the text in this way. Read the MT. '(For) they said' is perhaps to be deleted; compare the LXX ^{Vaticanus}. The LXX more closely resembles the MT, which is to be preferred. At 'our enemy', one medieval manuscript of the Hebrew Old Testament substitutes 'Samson' ('Our god has given into our hand *Samson*'); another medieval manuscript of the Hebrew Old Testament adds 'Samson' to the MT ('Our god has given into our hand our enemy, Samson')—a conflate text which, while occurring at the end of v. 23, should not be read.

(The editor's suggestion that 'Samson' is to be inserted should be rejected.) The form of the word 'our enemy' is that which occurs in the Leningrad Codex ^{first hand}. However, many medieval manuscripts of the Hebrew Old Testament read the plural אויבינו. Read the MT.

Verse 25: 'That their heart was merry' reflects the Leningrad Codex. Many medieval manuscripts of the Hebrew Old Testament and the Editions read כיטוב (unusual qal infinitive construct [יטב] with the preposition): 'as their heart was glad'. The *kethib* is read by many medieval manuscripts of the Hebrew Old Testament: כי־טוב, which corresponds with my translation. The *qere* is read by several medieval manuscripts of the Hebrew Old Testament as כטוב (infinitive construct with the preposition): 'at the time that their heart was merry'. On the form of 'the prisoners', compare v. 21, note b (see above). For 'and he made sport before them', the LXX reads καὶ ἐνέπαιζον αὐτῷ, 'and they ridiculed/made a fool of him'. Read the MT. Note d (compare v. 24, note a) suggests again that v. 24 be moved immediately after v. 25. This is an unnecessary and unsupported rearrangement of the text.

Verse 26: For 'let me touch/so that I may touch', many medieval manuscripts of the Hebrew Old Testament read with the *qere* (והמשני, from the root מוש ['to feel', BDB, p. 559]); the *kethib* is read by a few medieval manuscripts of the Hebrew Old Testament: והימ(י)שני (from the root ימש, 'to touch' [BDB, p. 413]). In addition, a few medieval manuscripts of the Hebrew Old Testament read והשמני. It has been proposed that the text be read והמשני (hiphil imperative with first person singular pronominal suffix—'and cause me to feel'—from root משש, 'feel, grope' [BDB, p. 606]). While the textual tradition is confused, the sense of the text is clear. For 'and let me lean against them', the LXX adds ὁ δὲ παῖς ἐποίησεν οὕτως, which may be retroverted as ויעש הנער כן ('and thus the young man did'). This appears to be an expansion of the MT and should not be adopted. Read the MT.

Verse 27: It is suggested that the phrase 'and there all the lords of the Philistines were and upon the roof were about 3000 men and women' has been added. However, there is no manuscript evidence cited by the editor of the book of Judges in support of this literary-critical emendation based on the difference in number for men and women the second time around. Since the phrase in question does occur in the LXX, I prefer to read the MT.

Verse 28: It has been proposed that Yahweh be read for זה ('this'), which does not agree in gender with the noun it modifies. Lacking any textual support for omitting the word, it be preferable to read the MT. האלהים is absent from the LXX and the Old Latin; the editor suggests that this vocative is probably to be deleted. Read the MT, which has the support of the Hebrew manuscript tradition.]

Judges 16 is even more explicitly a story about deception than ch. 14. In the earlier story, Samson's riddle has a deceptive quality about it, as Crenshaw has noted. This is Samson's challenge. In addition, the young men of Timnah approach Samson's wife with the request that she 'persuade [seduce/entice/deceive]' her husband to make known the riddle (14.15), which functions as a counter-challenge to Samson's honor. As in ch. 14, the deception in Judges 16 runs both ways. Once again, the Philistines approach a woman connected with Samson with the command that she 'persuade [seduce/entice/deceive]' (פתה) him, in order to humble/humili-ate (ענה) him. At the same time, on three occasions Samson lies to Delilah about the source of his great strength or how he might be bound, although the storyteller does not use special vocabulary to indicate the deceptive character of his speech (only the hearer/reader who knows the source of Samson's great strength [cf. Judg. 13] is aware of the hero's less than truthful disclosure). Further, three times Delilah accuses Samson of deceiving/mocking (תלל) her, and speaking lies/deceptive things (כזב) to her.

Characterizing Judges 16 as a story about deception may be troubling for late twentieth-century, Western readers of the story. Truth—and the telling of the absolute truth under all circumstances—is highly prized and expected under threat of legal penalty in our culture. The moral obligation always to tell the truth is coupled with the presumption that everyone is entitled to the truth. In contrast, the ancient Mediterranean culture accepted that one was obligated to disclose the truth only to certain people. On the one hand, people were obliged to tell the truth to one's kin-group: to one's immediate household, extended family, and friends. On the other hand, outsiders or strangers were not entitled to the truth, and it was even considered honorable to lie to or deceive them.[221] In Judges 16, the Philistines are intent on deceiving (פתה) Samson, and Samson, for his part, freely lies to the Philistines (through Delilah) about the source of his strength. There is no dishonor in the way the Philistines and Samson interact with one another, but, as Malina and Neyrey point out, 'lying and deception…are inherently challenging, for to deceive or lie is to deprive another of respect, to refuse to show honor, and to humiliate'.[222] In this way, the social interaction between the Philistines and Samson may be interpreted in terms of honor/shame and challenge–riposte.

The category of insider/stranger provides the larger framework for interpreting the action in Judges 16. This is the fundamental question that drives the action in the narrative. It is Samson's apparent failure to maintain the important distinction between insiders and strangers that leads directly to his downfall. Telling the truth to someone who is not, according

221. Malina and Neyrey, 'Honor and Shame in Luke–Acts', p. 37.
222. Malina and Neyrey, 'Honor and Shame in Luke–Acts', p. 37. See also Klapp's discussion about the 'clever hero's' use of fraud and deception ('The Clever Hero', pp. 25-26).

to the culture, entitled to it, results in Samson's captivity, blindness, and ultimately to his death. However, this failure has been recast into a 'greater triumph' in the last part of ch. 16, where Samson kills more Philistines in his death than in his life.

The social interaction between the Philistines and Samson in Judges 16 is of a mediated nature. The Philistines work through Delilah who is, significantly, nowhere identified as Samson's wife (cf. the woman in Judg. 14.2-3, 15-16, 20; 15.1, 6). While popularly she may be assumed to be Samson's wife, Delilah is, in fact, portrayed throughout the story as an outsider to Samson, and thus as someone not to be trusted with the truth and only one more stranger to be deceived.[223] Thus, Samson's downfall is not due to her unfaithfulness or shameless behavior (cf. ch. 14), but only to his telling the truth to someone who is not entitled to it. Three times he lied to Delilah about the source of his strength (or how he might be bound) while she deceived him, and each time he escaped. Finally, however, when he reveals to her 'his whole heart', Samson is undone. As Niditch concludes: 'The message is clear—the only way to relate to "them" is through deception; truth and honesty bring defeat'.[224]

It is readily apparent, however, that the story narrated in Judges 16 does not unambiguously meet the two fundamental criteria by which a person's honor is committed in challenge–riposte: (1) the initial challenge is not publicly issued (16.5-6); and (2) the exchange does not take place between social equals. First, the text implies that the lords of the Philistines visit Delilah privately in order to persuade her to deceive Samson. Delilah's request of Samson (v. 6) also is well-interpreted as a private conversation (significantly, the only location/setting that is specified is '[her] bedroom' [vv. 9, 12], where the ambush, unidentified but presumably comprised of the lords of the Philistines, gathers to wait for Samson to be bound). Nevertheless, the Philistines' request of Delilah and their plot against Samson does not escape the latter's notice. The reader is not informed how Samson knows of their intention, but he does. According to v. 6, 'Delilah said unto Samson, "Make known to *me* in what is your great strength; and in what way shall you be bound in order to humble/humiliate you"'. Then in v. 7, Samson said to her, 'If *they* will bind me with seven fresh bow-strings which have not been dried...' Thus even private conversations

---

223. Note that while the text indicates that Samson loved Delilah (v. 4), nowhere is the reader told that she loved him.

224. Niditch, 'Samson as Culture Hero', p. 621.

appear to be public domain.[225] However, the latter challenge to Samson (a physical affront), involving his shaven head, bored-out eyes, and his being set to the mill-stone, together with his 'making sport' before those attending the festivities, is all publicly witnessed—there are the lords of the Philistines, and there are the people. In addition, as in ch. 14, the hearer/ reader of the story continues to fulfill the role of public witness to what transpires in the narrative as well. As for the second point, while in principle the challenge is to take place between social equals, it is not unheard of that a person of superior social standing challenges a person of inferior status. Bourdieu considers the occasion where

> the offender is clearly superior to the offended person. The code of honour, and public opinion charged with the duty of seeing that it is conformed to, demand nothing from the offended person except that he agrees to play the game. To draw back from the challenge is the only blamable attitude. At the same time, the offended person need not triumph over the offender in order to be rehabilitated in the eyes of public opinion. A defeated person who has done his duty is not blamed; indeed, although he is defeated according to the laws of combat, he is the victor according to the laws of honour. To have taken up the challenge at all is already to have won a victory.[226]

This scenario applies well to the case of Judges 16, where the social inequality favors Samson, the social inferior. The 'lords of the Philistines' (סרני פלשתים) are assumed to be the heads of the cities of the Philistine Pentapolis (Ashdod, Ashkelon, Ekron, Gath, and Gaza; although there is no other indication that they acted in concert as depicted in the book of Judges). They appear as part of the ruling political (military?) elite. Samson, on the other hand, if the category of hero/bandit is accurate, is probably to be located among the peasant class.[227] Samson, however, does not retreat from the Philistine threat (= challenge), but enters into the game. He is, therefore, blameless according to the rules of honor/shame, regardless of whether or not he is victorious. As the social inferior in the interaction, it is not necessary that he triumph in the game of challenge–

225. While this construction may be interpreted as the Semitic passive, it is also possible that this is a folklore motif about an omniscient hero who knows the intentions of his opponents and what lies before him.

226. See, e.g., Bourdieu, 'The Sentiment of Honour in Kabayle Society', p. 206.

227. Niditch, 'Samson as Culture Hero', pp. 621-22; cf. Lenski, *Power and Privilege*, pp. 271-74. The identification of Samson as a 'judge' in Israel (Judg. 15.20; 16.31; cf. 13.5; 14.4) is part of the later redaction of the story and not integral to the original folktale.

riposte; it is enough that he merely agrees to play. Samson takes up the challenge, and so demonstrates that he is honorable before the eyes of the observing public.

What Bourdieu writes about in terms of inferior and superior and honor/ shame, Klapp includes in his analysis of the clever hero under the sub-heading of 'the small hero as underdog'. He observes that:

> Since the chasm between the great and the small, the oppressor and oppressed, extends through all cultures, it is a strategic situation which everyone understands; and more are likely to be in the role of the underdog than the oppressor; hence there is a universal sympathy for anyone who overthrows a persecutor. The clever hero is likely to have the majority on his side, for the sake of morality as well as prudence... Because the power-ful opponent is expected to win, he gains little credit for victory. If he loses, on the other hand, he is disgraced... All in all, the clever hero is valued as a popular symbol because he teaches that the weak can defeat the great and provides an important lesson in practical life, a formula for success.[228]

A chief difference between the stories of Samson's riddle and Samson, Delilah, and the Philistines, however, is that while ch. 14 was only about a verbal affront as challenge, ch. 16 is concerned also with a challenge that is presented by means of a physical affront. That is, the Philistines want to know how Samson might *physically be bound*; and finally Samson is dishonored by having his head shaved, his eyes bored out (blinded), and being put to work as a grinder (טחן; grinding being ordinarily women's work [BDB, p. 377], and thus a confusion of gender and a source of dishonor).

According to Malina and Neyrey, 'a physical affront is a challenge to one's honor; unanswered it becomes a dishonor in the judgment of the people who witness the affront'.[229] In the case of Judges 16, the physical affront is witnessed not only by the crowd in the story that assembles for the festivities in the latter part of the chapter, but also by the hearer/reader of the story. Malina and Neyrey provide a model by which to interpret the treatment of Samson in this story:

> Honor is frequently symbolized by certain bodily features and the treatment given one's physical person. A person's body is normally a symbolized replication of the social values of honor. The head and front of the head

228. Klapp, 'The Clever Hero', p. 28.
229. Malina and Neyrey, 'Honor and Shame in Luke–Acts', p. 35. They go on to stress that 'physical affronts are always symbolic affronts that require a riposte', and that 'failure to respond means dishonor and disgrace' (p. 36).

> (face) play prominent roles… Honor is displayed when the head is crowned,
> anointed, touched, or covered. Dishonor, however, is symbolized when the
> head is uncovered or *made bare by shaving* and when it is cut off, struck, or
> slapped.[230]

Thus, Samson's being shaved, bound, imprisoned at the mill-stone, and
blinded is about more than simply torture or defeat at the hand of one's
enemies. By these actions the Philistines would strip Samson of his honor.

As Bourdieu has pointed out, a person of inferior social standing, whose
honor is challenged by a social superior, need not be victorious in his
riposte. It is enough that the one challenged make an effort to respond.
Indeed, it is not expected that he will triumph. It is the opinion of the narrator, however, at the end of the story, that Samson is triumphant over
those who have challenged him. In the final scene, Samson is out of prison,
his hair has begun to grow back 'abundantly' (symbolizing not only the
return of his strength [according to the folklore motif], but also the reha-
bilitation of his honor), and he prays to Yahweh that his blindness might
be avenged. Of greater significance is the narrator's summary remark in
v. 30: 'And the dying ones whom he killed in his death were more than
those he killed in his lifetime'. For the original Danite storyteller, the hero,
Samson, was ultimately victorious in death, while the ruling Philistines
and their god die in dishonor.

There are two approaches to the evaluation of Samson in the history of
interpretation, interpretations based on the final form of the Samson stories.
On the one hand, Samson is understood as a religious hero who suffers,
nevertheless, from certain weaknesses. Samson is included among the list
of heroes of faith in Hebrews 11, and was even viewed in the twelfth
century as a 'type' of Christ. On the other hand, Samson has also been
seen as a tragic hero, one of whose chief faults is sexual license. Samson is
thus an example of what one should not be or do, the opposite of a true
judge or faithful hero in Israel.[231] He is thus criticized for not playing fair
(by setting an impossible riddle), for violent outbursts against innocent
people (by slaughtering Ashkelon), for his weakness before women (by
associating himself with Delilah), and for his failure to aspire to anything
more than his personal grudges with the Philistines. As a judge in Israel
(15.20; 16.31; cf. 13.5), he is unimpressive to most interpreters.

230. Malina and Neyrey, 'Honor and Shame in Luke–Acts', p. 35 (emphasis
added).
231. See especially Crenshaw, *Samson: A Secret Betrayed*, pp. 130-48; Soggin,
Judges: A Commentary, pp. 258-59.

Samson has also been negatively evaluated because of his supposed betrayal of the Nazirite vow. That is, it is argued that Samson willfully and repeatedly violated his vow to live as a Nazirite. However, as I shall demonstrate, the Nazirite vow does not play a central role in the narrative. What is more, the entire question of the Nazirite is fraught with difficulty.

As a Nazirite, Samson is ordinarily evaluated on the basis of the law of the Nazirite in Numbers 6, a text either attributed to a sixth-century Priestly Writer or recognized as a later addition to P.[232] However, the argument for the antiquity of the Nazirite in Israel is based chiefly on the lives of Samson and Samuel, both of which present certain problems for the Nazirite question.

A Nazirite is a person who separates himself or herself, for a time, for dedicated service to God (although the specific nature of this service is uncertain). According to the law in Numbers 6, three restrictions characterize the Nazirite: (1) the prohibition against the consumption of wine or any other intoxicant (vv. 3-4); (2) the prohibition against shaving the hair of one's head (v. 5); and (3) avoidance of contact with a corpse (vv. 6-7; regardless of relation).[233] Numbers 6 also envisions a 'term' ('days') of the Nazirite vow; that is, it is recognized as a temporary condition.[234]

It is usually argued, however, that the Nazirite was a lifelong calling in Israel's earlier history, and the examples of Samson and Samuel are marshaled as evidence. Nevertheless, while in the case of Samuel, Hannah promises to dedicate her hoped-for child to Yahweh 'all the days of his life', and adds that 'a razor shall not go up upon his head', the boy is never identified as a Nazirite (1 Sam. 1.11).[235] This leaves us only with Samson

232. Davies, *Numbers*, p. 60.
233. As has been frequently pointed out, Samson hardly conforms to the requirements of this law: his consumption of wine is implied in Judg. 14.10; and he comes into contact with a dead body in 14.8; cf. 14.19; 15.8. Critics have seized on these 'failures' of Samson as a Nazirite in order to discredit him as a hero or judge in Israel.
234. Milgrom, *Numbers*, p. 43; Levine, *Numbers 1–20*, p. 229; Davies, *Numbers*, p. 58. Men and women could make the Nazirite vow (Num. 6.2). Significantly, according to Milgrom (*Numbers*, p. 358), the Nazirite vow was extremely popular in the Second Temple Period (see also Davies, *Numbers*, pp. 58-59).
235. See, however, McCarter's reconstruction of the 'defective' MT on the basis of the LXX and 4QSam[a], by which he is able to include explicit identification of Samuel as a Nazirite (P. Kyle McCarter, Jr, *I Samuel: A New Translation with Introduction, Notes & Commentary* [AB, 8; Garden City, NY: Doubleday, 1980], pp. 53-56; cf. Ralph W. Klein, *1 Samuel* [WBC, 10; Waco, TX: Word Books, 1983], p. 3, who suggests that the reading of the LXX and Qumran may be an accurate, although later, interpretation of

as depicted in Judges 13–16, who is hardly a Nazirite according to the law in Numbers 6. In fact, the list of Nazirite requirements in Numbers 6 does not appear as *Nazirite* requirements in Judges 13–16. First, nowhere in Judges 13–16 does Samson make a 'vow' to live as a Nazirite. Second, in the annunciation story in Judges 13, the only Nazirite characteristic that is applied to Samson is the prohibition against cutting his hair (13.5). A careful reading of Judges 13 reveals that the prohibition against the consumption of wine and unclean food is enjoined on Samson's mother, *not Samson* (13.4, 7, 14). Nothing is mentioned in Judges 13 about avoiding corpses. If Samson's feasting and contact with the lion's corpse were violations of his Naziriteship, and if this were the goal of the Samson stories, one might imagine that the final redactor would not have left the drawing of the conclusion up to the reader. This editor, intent on presenting a negative image of Samson, would have remarked how unfaithful the hero was to his vocation. This is not, however, the case. It is unsatisfactory (and most likely anachronistic) to apply the standards of Numbers 6 to the earlier narrative in Judges 13–16. This is not the perspective of the original storyteller behind Judges 13–16. Therefore, in the stories of Judges 13–16, Samson is only guilty of violating the prohibition against cutting his hair (although it should be noted that Samson does not himself cut his hair). Indeed, it is plausible that the note about Samson as a Nazirite is a secondary addition to the earlier folktale about a Danite hero whose magic strength resided in his hair. It is possible to remove the phrases involving 'Nazirite' from the text of Judges 13 and 16 and still leave the storyline intact. It is imaginable that the Nazirite note was added to the Samson stories at a later date (sixth century?), influenced by the folklore motif of 'magic strength residing in one's hair'. The hero's strength and later his downfall in the more original story are best attributed not to his Nazirite vow (which is never related), but to his long and, later, shorn, hair. It is reasonable to imagine that the idea of unshaven hair was known in later years from both folklore and the Nazirite law. The two came together in Judges 13–16. That is, the Nazirite vow was added in Judges 13 to an earlier story built on the foundation of a popular folklore motif ('strength resides in the hair'). This is a view arrived at recently also by Levine. He writes:

the MT). But McCarter also notes that the story of Samuel's birth and dedication as a Nazirite has possibly been transferred from stories about Saul (p. 65).

> Peculiarly, abstinence from wine (and from impure foodstuffs) is a condition imposed on Samson's expectant mother, not on Samson himself. It seems inescapable, nevertheless, that abstinence from wine was perceived by the story's author as material to the status of a *nāzîr*. Quite possibly, existing narratives about a hero named Samson were modulated by the specific classification of Samson as a *nāzîr*, a status not original to the story. All that the hero Samson knew was that his strength was in his hair. As Samson is depicted as a carousing adventurer, reveling in wine, women, and song, it would have strained the credibility of the stories about him to have defined him as an ascetic, or holy warrior, abstaining from wine! So the independent author of the annunciation narrative displaced the ban on drinking wine from the hero himself and imposed it on his expectant mother, along with a ritual admonition against eating anything unclean.[236]

The conclusion to be drawn from this is that there is no good evidence for reconstructing the life of a Nazirite in the period before the monarchy. The note about Samson as a Nazirite is better understood as a later addition to the Judges narrative. Whether Samuel was a Nazirite also remains unclear. While the eighth-century prophet Amos refers to Nazirites together with prophets (2.11-12), he sheds no real light on the question. In addition, as Milgrom has pointed out, the popularity of the Nazirite vow in the postexilic period suggests that one search for the origins of this vocation in the time of the Babylonian Exile, not the so-called period of the Judges.[237]

If Samson is only secondarily made a Nazirite, the same may also be true for his being numbered among the judges. There seems to be no reason to doubt that the references to the hero/trickster Samson as judge (15.20; 16.31; cf. 13.5; 14.4) are among the later, editorial additions to the original folktale about the Danite hero, Samson.[238] Noth regarded the whole of Judges 13–16 as a later addition to the sixth-century work of Dtr. Among other reasons he cites, these chapters do not fit the Deuteronomistic pattern of oppression, cry to Yahweh, deliverance, and rest.[239] In addition, according to Noth, the Samson stories

236. Levine, *Numbers 1–20*, p. 230.
237. Milgrom, *Numbers*, p. 358.
238. See, e.g., Crenshaw, *Samson: A Secret Betrayed*, pp. 40-41; Boling, *Judges*, p. 252.
239. Noth, *Deuteronomistic History*, pp. 84-85. There is, of course, also the chronological problem which is exacerbated by the inclusion of the Samson stories in the 480 years from the time of Moses to Solomon. See also J. Cheryl Exum, 'The Centre Cannot Hold: Thematic and Textual Instabilities in Judges', *CBQ* 52 (1990), pp. 410-31 (423).

show no sign of having been worked on by Dtr. and since Samson's name is conspicuous by its absence in 1 Sam. 12.11, a passage which clearly aims to be comprehensive (vv. 9-11), we must consider the possibility that the Samson stories were not added to Dtr.'s account until later. Then Dtr. could have followed Judg.13.1 directly with 1 Sam. 1.1.[240]

The appearance in Judg. 15.11 of the 3000 men of Judah, who are content to accept the *status quo* of Philistine domination, may also be evidence in support of the hypothesis that the Samson stories are late additions to the book of Judges. It was earlier observed that the tribe of Judah appears in the first chapter of the book of Judges (where it occupies pride of place), and then not again until it takes a leadership role against the Benjaminites in the final episode (20.18). Mullen's observation was duly and approvingly noted—namely, that mention of Judah frames the exilic edition of the book of Judges (1.2-20; 20.18), while this eminent tribe remains 'silent through the account of the tumultuous period of the Judges'.[241] At that time I suggested that Mullen, however, overlooks the occurrence of Judah in 15.11. Nevertheless, his observation is still correct if it is recognized that the Samson narrative was added to the book after the Deuteronomistic framework was already in place. This would mean dating the incorporation of Judges 13–16 to the postexilic period.[242]

Literarily, I follow Noth in understanding the Samson stories as secondary additions to the book of Judges. Indeed, they may well constitute the last section added to the book. Before the stories of Samson were added, however, Judges 17–21 were interpolated.[243] That is, Judg. 12.15 would have been originally followed immediately by 1 Samuel 1. It is noteworthy that Judges 12 ends with mention of the 'land of Ephraim, in the hill country of the Amalekites' (cf. 1 Sam. 1.1), and that Judg. 17.1 begins

240. Noth, *Deuteronomistic History*, p. 85. In fact, Samson occurs nowhere else in the Hebrew Bible (although a textual variant of 1 Sam. 12.11 [a verse recognized by text critics as very problematic] reads 'Samson' in place of 'Samuel'). He is mentioned, however, in Heb. 11.

241. Mullen, 'Judges 1:1-36', p. 53; see also n. 109, above.

242. The prayer of Samson in Judg. 16.28, that Yahweh 'remember' him, is reminiscent of the postexilic leader Nehemiah's repeated plea (5.19; 13.14, 22, 31; cf. 6.14; 13.29) to be remembered favorably by God. A final piece of evidence to support the absence of Judg. 13–16 from the original edition of the book of Judges is that without these chapters there are precisely twelve judge-figures in the book of Judges. There is an element of completion implied in this number.

243. Mullen, 'Judges 1:1-36', p. 50.

with a reference to the 'hill country of Ephraim', where the following story of Micah takes place. After Samson had been categorized as a judge in Israel, chs. 13–16 were placed after ch. 12 in order to locate Samson among the rest of the judges.

While the Samson stories in their final form are likely to be late additions to the book of Judges, it does not necessarily follow that the complex is of a late date in origin. The folklore motifs are difficult to date; they may be very old.[244] Judges 13 associates the Samson stories with the clan of Dan located in the vicinity of the cities of Zorah and Eshtaol—that is, while the Danites were (still) in the south. There seems little reason to doubt that the stories of the hero Samson circulated originally among the Danites. The geographical proximity to the Philistines fits, as does the association with the neighboring Judahites.

There seems to be no escaping the larger conclusion that the Samson stories originally depicted the hero in a positive way. This is based on folklore analysis, social-scientific criticism, and redaction criticism. The negative evaluation of the hero (especially according to the Nazirite law) arises only from the canonical placement of the stories—following Num. 6, and at the conclusion of the other judges stories.[245]

In what way are the Samson stories 'Danite' texts? That is, what do these stories, or what does Samson tell us about Dan? First of all, Dan is explicitly referred to only in Judg. 13.2—'Now there was a certain man from Zorah, from the clan of the Danites, and his name was Manoah...'— and again in v. 25—'And the spirit of Yahweh began to impel/disturb (Samson) in the camp of Dan, between Zorah and Eshtaol'. In addition, Samson's father and the district of Zorah and Eshtaol are referred to again at the end of the narrative, in 16.31 ('Then his kinsmen and all his father's house went down and took him away and brought [him] up, and they buried him between Zorah and Eshtaol in the grave of Manoah his father...'). While it is possible to dismiss these references as editorial

244. Daniel L. Smith (*The Religion of the Landless: The Social Context of the Babylonian Exile* [Bloomington, IN: Meyer-Stone, 1989], p. 171), however, observes that 'prison' may be a literary symbol of exile. Regarding Samson, he writes: 'In the commentaries...there is very little comment on the significance of (*bēt Ha'ăšyrîm* [prison]) in Judg. 16... Judg. 16 is usually considered a later addition to the Samson saga, dated to the Deuteronomic Historian at the latest. The presence of this term, however, should raise questions about the date of this material.'

245. See most recently Dennis T. Olson, 'The Book of Judges: Introduction, Commentary, and Reflections', in Leander E. Keck *et al.* (eds.), *The New Interpreter's Bible* (Nashville: Abingdon Press, 1998), II, pp. 721-888 (840-42).

additions, it is better to interpret them as orignal parts of the story by which the popular folktale was adapted to its local setting. The Samson stories were originally Danite stories, later added to the Deuteronomistic book of Judges. While the main character, Samson, is the son of a Danite from Zorah, the tribe of Dan plays no role in the stories. In fact, the only Israelite collective in the story is the 3000 men of Judah who capture and extradite Samson to the Philistines at Lehi. In many ways, this is a story about Samson, who should probably not be interpreted as representative of the Danites.[246] However, as folklore, the heroic figure of Samson and his stories project the aspirations of their community of origin, the clan of Dan.

It remains to ask what the Samson stories tell us about Dan, and in what way this traditional complex reflects the social reality of the Danites. As previously noted, one of the few occurrences of 'Dan' in Judges 13–16 is in 13.2, where it designates the social group to which Samson's father, Manoah, traces his ancestry. Manoah is introduced by the storyteller as ויהי איש אחד מצרעה ממשפחת הדני ('now there was a certain man from Zorah, from the clan of the Danites'). Significantly, the word משפחה, rather than שבט (or מטה), is used to designate the primary subdivision of Israel. The classic biblical text for understanding the social structure of early Israel is Joshua 7. According to this text (7.14), the search for the party guilty of bringing disaster on the Israelites of the siege of Ai (Achan) proceeds from the greater to the lesser social subdivisions: 'tribe' (שבט), 'clan' (משפחה), 'ancestral house' (בית), and 'man' (גבר). In Joshua 7, the tribe of Judah was indicated; then, from among the clans which made up the tribe of Judah, the clan of Zerah was indicated; next, from the clan of Zerah, the ancestral house of Zabdi was indicated; finally, the man Achan, the son of Zerah son of Zabdi, of the tribe of Judah, was indicated. By analogy, one expects the term 'tribe' (שבט) to occur in Judg. 13.2 to char- acterize Dan. Instead, 'clan' (משפחה) occurs.[247] While this word has been

---

246. Indeed, these chapters are not so much about the tribe of Dan as about the individual hero, Samson. Thus, we should not wonder about why a final Deuterono- mistic redactor, whose primary interest is in the southern, Judean traditions, should give so much space to a story about a member of the Danites. For the redactor, 'Dan' is really quite incidental to the story; it is simply the way the folktale came to him, and he was not in a position to alter his *Vorlage*. We should not be surprised, then, that these four chapters devoted to the exploits of a Danite have been preserved by a Southern redactor.

247. This is not the place for a detailed discussion of the suitability of the word 'clan' as a translation of משפחה. The reader is directed to Gottwald, *The Tribes of Yahweh*, pp. 249-51, 257-70; Niels Peter Lemche, *Early Israel: Anthropological and*

translated as 'tribe' (cf. NRSV, NJPS), the usual word for this primary social unit of the whole people is שֵׁבֶט.[248] The point is that מִשְׁפָּחָה ordinarily designates a secondary subdivision in Israel's social structure—a social group relatively smaller and weaker than the 'tribe'.[249] According to Gottwald,

> in the great majority of cases...*mishpāḥāh* is either directly referred to in context as social unit smaller than a *shēvet*, often clearly included within a *shēvet*, or is so described as to indicate that it is conceived as a social unit smaller than a *shēvet*.[250]

From this, it appears as though while Dan, in Judg. 13.2, is formally a 'tribe', it is, practically, a 'clan', with respect to size and strength. Again, Gottwald speculates on the 'declining historical fortunes of the *shēvet* [of Dan]':

> First the Canaanite and then the Philistine military pressure on Dan reduced the *shēvet*'s population and its internal cohesion. The migration of Dan to the far north probably further disrupted its internal organization and may actually have led to the reorganization of the survivors from the remnants of the originally separate *mishpāḥōth* into one *mishpāḥāh* which was virtually coterminus with the *shēvet*. The Danite warriors who move to the north are six hundred in number, and from all that we can judge of the account they are pictured as the total number of surviving arms-bearing Danites.[251]

Gottwald further argues that the reason why Samson was unable to muster a military force around himself against the Philistines was that there were, after the Danite migration narrated in Judges 18, so few Danites left in the south. Gottwald seems to assume that Samson as portrayed in Judges 13–16 was a historical personage, and so misses the folkloristic character of the Samson stories. It is, rather, part of the hero/trickster motif to act autonomously, just as Samson does in the biblical text.

Historical Studies on the Israelite Society Before the Monarchy (VTSup, 37; Leiden: E.J. Brill, 1985), pp. 260-74; McNutt, *Reconstructing the Society of Ancient Israel*, pp. 88-94.

248. Gottwald, *The Tribes of Yahweh*, p. 245.

249. Bendor (*The Social Structure of Ancient Israel*, p. 87) notes that 'in the biblical text just as the *beit 'ab* is considered part of the *mišpaḥa*, so the *mišpaḥa* is considered part of the tribe'.

250. Gottwald, *The Tribes of Yahweh*, p. 257.

251. Gottwald, *The Tribes of Yahweh*, p. 250. He states his conclusion thus (p. 251): 'Dan was technically and formally a *shēvet*, one of the major autonomous groups involved in the early formation of Israel, but it was reduced in its social substance to little more than a sub-section of a usual *shēvet*, i.e., to a *mishpāḥāh*'.

Gottwald's conclusion goes beyond what the Samson story indicates. The text itself does not account for the Danites's status as a מִשְׁפָּחָה. Reasonable possibilities include: Philistine aggression (assuming the stories of Samson come from the time of Philistine domination in Iron Age I); the migration of a significant portion of the tribe of Dan northward to Laish (Judg. 18.1; but cf. 18.11); or the deportation at the time of the Babylonian exile (thus interpreting the Philistines as a symbol of a later oppressor). All of this is in the realm of speculation. In response to Gottwald, however, it must be stated that there is no other indication in the text that the cycle of Samson stories is in any way related to the migration story in ch. 18. We simply do not know for certain whether the Samson stories are to be situated before or after the story of the migration of Danites northward. This is little more than the result of the redaction of the book of Judges, by which chs. 13–16 were placed before chs. 17–18. Regardless, Judg. 13.2 portrays a precarious existence for Dan either as an independent group within Israel, or as a Danite enclave within the territory of Judah (at some point in time, the district encompassing the cities of Zorah and Eshtaol came under the control of Judah [Josh. 15.33]). The point is that Dan is depicted as a marginal, relatively weak, even oppressed group (Judg. 14.4; 15.11). There is nothing here, or in the foregoing social-science analysis of the Samson stories, that contradicts this conclusion. In addition, this is precisely the type of social group that produces such heroic folktales as we find preserved in the biblical text. With this, we return to where the present study of the Samson stories began, with a note about Samson as a heroic figure of an oppressed and marginalized group.

In her study of the underdog and trickster in the Hebrew Bible, Niditch observes that

> the underdog is the poor relative, the youngest son, the exile, the ex-prince, the soldier of a defeated army—the person, in short, who is least likely to succeed and yet does… Underdogs make their way through native wisdom or physical prowess, often with the help of an agent, human or divine… The trickster is a subtype of the underdog… They never gain full control of the situation around them and often escape difficulties in a less than noble way. Their tale does not end with unequivocal success, but they survive to trick again—and, indeed, are survivors par excellence. Trickster narratives help us to cope with the insurmountable and uncontrollable forces in our own lives, personifying and in a sense containing the chaos that always threatens.[252]

252. Niditch, *Underdogs and Tricksters*, p. xi.

The appropriateness of the application of this character motif to the Samson stories is clear. First, in his interactions with the Philistines, in which he is tricked and betrayed by a superior opponent, Samson's likelihood of success seems slim. In addition, Samson's success stems from both wisdom or insight and physical strength (slaying a lion with empty hands, killing 30 men of Ashkelon, massacring 1000 Philistines with the jawbone of an ass, pulling down the temple of Dagon in Gaza), and he is aided by Yahweh who blesses, inspires, hears his prayers, and provides for his sustenance. Second, the use of the flight-motif, which makes the hero look as though he has run away in defeat, in fact, permits the hero to engage his opponent again another day. Finally, Samson's death with the 3000 Philistines corresponds with Niditch's observation that the underdog/trickster tale 'does not end with unequivocal success'. While the Samson stories conclude with the note that even in death (as a martyr?) the Danite hero wreaks havoc on his enemies, he nevertheless loses his life.

Niditch goes on to suggest that the telling and retelling of underdog/trickster tales serve an important social function within those communities who imagine themselves to be underdogs in the world. She proposes that

> claiming rights to a land miles from its roots in Mesopotamia, having as its major historical leitmotifs themes of enslavement and escape, exile and restoration, conscious of its origins as a mixed multitude, and self-conscious about its affinities with Canaanite culture, Israel produced narratives that ultimately served to shore up group identity and self-esteem, that emphasized independence from and superiority over hostile enemies, and that proclaimed Israelite uniqueness. The stories of Israelite heroes not only reflect the community that is Israel but, indeed, helped to form it.[253]

As a marginal, weak social group, characterized as a מִשְׁפָּחָה rather than as a שֵׁבֶט, the Danites certainly appear as a community within which a hero/underdog/trickster tale would originate.[254] In addition, if it is accepted that Samson functions as a hero, then the fact that the Danites told and retold such stories points to the Danites's self-perception as a marginal,

---

253. Niditch, *Underdogs and Tricksters*, p. xii. Regarding the social function of the hero, Klapp's comments ('The Clever Hero', p. 28) deserve note. He observes that 'All in all, the clever hero is valued as a popular symbol because he teaches that the weak can defeat the great and provides an important lesson in practical life, a formula for success: that the ruse is often more effective than the *tour de force*...'

254. See Klapp's ('The Clever Hero', pp. 27-28) remarks about 'The Small Hero as Underdog', in which he notes the 'chasm between the great and the small, the oppressor and oppressed'.

weak, and oppressed group in need of a heroic figure. According to Niditch, certain types of hero/trickster tales 'challenge...the power of the establishment by weaker or oppressed elements in society'.[255] In the conclusion to her study of Samson, Niditch writes that

> the overriding theme and concern of these topoi, whether Samson be viewed a culture hero, trickster, or bandit, is the marginal's confrontation with oppressive authority, more specifically Israel's dealings with its Philistine enemies. Scenes having to do with the birth of the hero, his adventures with women and assailants, and finally his death all emphasize the victory of the weak over seemingly implacable forces.[256]

The biblical text supports such an evaluation of the Danites: they are not only oppressed by the Philistines (14.4; 15.11), they are even subject to the Judahites (15.11-13).

In summary, it should be clear that there is little detail in the Samson stories upon which to reconstruct the history of the hero or the Danites in the period before the monarchy in Israel. I am not persuaded that there is anything particularly historical about either the character, Samson, or his celebrated feats (perhaps the only certain historical data are the references to the Philistine rulers as סרני פלשתים, and Philistine rule over Israel [15.9-11]). What is preserved in Judges 13–16 is a cycle of powerful stories reflecting the aspirations of a minority, oppressed Danite community, situated in a handful of cities in the southern part of the land, and living in tension with the Philistines. Thus, looking beyond the redactional layer of the exilic period, two of the more helpful and illuminating exegetical tools, by which to interpret the Samson stories in Judges 13–16, prove to be folklore analysis and social science study.

d. *Judges 17–18*[257]
The story narrated in Judges 17–18, about how an Israelite cult center was established at the city of Dan, is perhaps the central Danite tradition in the Hebrew Bible. According to the final form of the biblical text, this story of a Danite migration functions to bridge the disparate traditions which

255. Niditch, 'Samson as Culture Hero', p. 609. Later she writes about the Israelite hero acts on behalf of his people who are 'under subjugation, who are marginal in status' (p. 620).
256. Niditch, 'Samson as Culture Hero', p. 624.
257. Noth (*Deuteronomistic History*, p. 77) agrees with most interpreters in recognizing the whole of Judg. 17–21 as an appendix to Dtr's work. See, however, Veijola's study of these chapters in *Das Königtum* for a different conclusion.

appear to locate the territory of the tribe of Dan either in the south or in the north. In this story, the Danites originate in the south and, for reasons about which one can only speculate since the text is silent (Philistine aggression, lack or loss of allotted territory for habitation are only two possibilities), migrate northward through the hill country of Ephraim— where they collect a Levite and idol—eventually to conquer the Canaanite city of Laish, resettle and rebuild it, change its name to Dan, and establish a tribal sanctuary complete with a molten image and a priesthood descended from Moses (for this reading, see the critical notes on the MT below). There can be little doubt that the present text (final form) evaluates the content of the narrative negatively. That is, Micah's idol, the conquering Danites, the tribal sanctuary at the city of Dan and, perhaps most especially, the disloyal Levite, are all cast in a disapproving light.

(1) *Judges 17*

[1] Now there was a man from the hill country of Ephraim, and his name was Micayahu. [2] And he said to his mother, '1100 of the silver which was stolen from you, and you—you uttered a curse and even you said in my hearing—behold, the silver is with me, I—I took it.' And his mother said, 'Blessed is my son by Yahweh'. [3] And he returned the 1100 of the silver to his mother. And his mother said, 'I have indeed set apart the silver for Yahweh, from my hand to my son, to make an idol and a molten image, and now let me bring it back to you'. [4] So he returned the silver to his mother. Then his mother took 200 pieces of silver and she gave it to the smelter/goldsmith, and he made (of) it an idol and a molten image. And it was in the house/temple of Micayahu. [5] And to the man Micah belonged a house of god; and he made an ephod and teraphim and he filled the hand of one of his sons, and he became to him as a priest.
[6] In those days there was not a king in Israel; a man did whatever was right/pleasing in his own eyes.
[7] Now there was a young man from Bethlehem of Judah, from the clan of Judah; and he was a Levite and was serving as a client there. [8] And the man went from the city, from Bethlehem of Judah, in order to serve as a client wherever he could find a place. And he came to the hill country of Ephraim, as far as the house of Micah, as he made his way. [9] And Micah said to him, 'From where have you come?' And he said to him, 'I am a Levite from Bethlehem of Judah, and I am traveling to serve as a client wherever I might find a place'. [10] Then Micah said to him, 'Reside with me and be to me as a father and as a priest, and I shall give to you ten silver coins for the term and a suit of clothes and your sustenance'. So the Levite went. [11] And the Levite was pleased to reside with the man; now the young man was to him like one of his own sons. [12] And Micah filled the

hand of the Levite and the young man became to him as a priest. Now he was in the house of Micah. [13] And Micah said, 'Now I know that Yahweh shall deal well with me, since the Levite is to me as a priest'.

[Notes on the MT:

Verse 2: For וְאֹתִי, many medieval manuscripts of the Hebrew Old Testament read as the *qere*, וְאַתְּ, which is the more usual form of the second person feminine singular personal pronoun. The *kethib* וְאַתִּי, which is an earlier form of the pronoun (as in Syriac, Arabic, and Ethiopic; cf. Jer. 4.30 [GKC, 32h]). Read the *kethib*. After 'in my hearing', the editor of the book of Judges in *BHS* (R. Meyer) supposes that one or a few words have dropped out. Lacking any textual support for emending the MT (the LXX corroborates the reading of the MT), the MT, while admittedly difficult, is to be preferred. After 'I took it', the editor suggests transposing 'and now let me bring it back to you' from v. 3. There is no manuscript support for the proposed emendation. While the MT is difficult, apparently vv. 2-3 are to be read as though Micah, who had taken the silver, returns all of it to his mother (v. 3a). Then, after having designated 200 pieces of silver for the manufacture of the idol and the molten image, his mother returns the balance to Micah (v. 3b).

Verse 3: See the preceding note.

Verse 7: 'From the clan of Judah' is absent from one medieval manuscript of the Hebrew Old Testament (original hand, or so it is conjectured—the siglum in *BHS* is ambiguous), and the Syriac. The editor of the book of Judges in *BHS* (R. Meyer) supposes that its appearance in the MT is a gloss. Since the variant in the singular medieval manuscript may be due to haplography (cf. v. 8), the MT is to be preferred.

Verse 8: For 'from the city, from Bethlehem', the LXX Vaticanus, Catena read ἀπὸ βηθλεεμ τῆς πολέως (inverted word order).

Verse 10: After 'and your sustenance', the LXX Lucianic recension adds καὶ εὐδόκησεν ὁ Λευίτης, the Old Latin adds *et coegit eum*, on the basis of which the editor of the book of Judges in *BHS* reconstructs the following Hebrew text: וַיָּאֶץ בַּלֵּוִי, which would seem to be translated 'and he pressed the Levite' (which does not appear to correspond to the variant texts cited). 'So the Levite went' is considered to be a case of dittography, of confusion with the opening words of the following verse; the editor suggests that this phrase be deleted from v. 10. Lacking manuscript support for this deletion, and since the MT makes sense as it stands, the MT is the preferred reading.]

(2) *Judges 18*

[1] In those days there was not a king in Israel; and in those days the tribe of the Danites was seeking for itself an inheritance to inhabit, since it did not fall to it until that day in the midst of the tribes of Israel (as) an inheritance.

[2] And the sons of Dan sent out from their clan five men from the whole of them—men—sons of valor, from Zorah and from Eshtaol in order to go about and explore the land to search it, and they said to them, 'Go, search out the land'. And they entered the hill country of Ephraim as far as the house of Micah, and they lodged there. [3] They were close by the house of

Micah, and they recognized the voice of the young man, the Levite. So they turned aside there and they said to him, 'Who brought you here, and what are you doing in this place, and how are you doing here?' [4] And he said to them, 'Like this and so Micah did to me. He has hired me, and I have become to him as a priest.' [5] Then they said to him, 'Inquire of God, and let us know—shall our way, upon which we are going, be successful?' [6] And the priest said to them, 'Go in peace; your way upon which you are going is before Yahweh'.

[7] So the five men went, and they came toward Laish; and they saw the people who were in its midst, dwelling securely according to the manner of the Sidonians, undisturbed and confident, and there was none putting to shame anything in the land, possessing restraint, and they were distant from the Sidonians, and they had no dealings with anyone. [8] When they came to their kinsmen at Zorah and Eshtaol they said to them, 'What are you...?' [9] And they said, 'Arise, and let us go up against them, for we have seen the land, and behold—very good. But you are inactive! Do not be sluggish to go to enter in order to take possession of the land. [10] As you enter, you will come to a people confident and the land is broad of/as two hands. For God has given it into your hand—a place where there is no poverty of anything that is in the land.'

[11] So they set out from there, from the clan of the Danites, from Zorah and from Eshtaol, 600 men girded with instruments of war. [12] And they went up and they encamped in Qiryath Yearim in Judah; therefore, they call that place 'the camp of Dan' until this day, behold it is behind [west of] Qiryath-Yearim. [13] And they crossed over from there into the hill country of Ephraim, and they entered as far as the house of Micah. [14] Then five of the men, the ones who went to explore the land of Laish, answered and they said to their kinsmen, 'Did you know that there is in these houses an ephod and teraphim and an idol and a molten image? And now, consider what you shall do.' [15] So they turned aside toward there and they came to the house of the young man, the Levite, (to) the house of Micah, and they inquired of him, 'Is it well with you?' [16] Now 600 men girded with instruments of war were stationed at the door of the gate, who were from the sons of Dan. [17] And five of the men, the ones who went to explore the land, went up, they came toward there, they took the idol and the ephod and the terpahim and the molten image. The priest stationed himself at the door of the gate, and 600 men who were girded with instruments of war. [18] And these entered the house of Micah and they took the idol, the ephod, and the teraphim and the molten image. Then the priest said to them, 'What are you doing?' [19] And they said to him, 'Be silent, put your hand upon your mouth and come with us, and become to us as a father and as a priest. Which is better—your being a priest to the house of one man, or your being a priest to a tribe and to a clan in Israel?' [20] Now the heart of the priest was glad, and he took the ephod and the teraphim and the idol, and he entered into the midst of the people.

[21] Then they turned and went, and they set the children and the cattle and the riches before them. [22] They had gone far from the house of Micah, when Micah and the men who were in the houses which were with the house of Micah assembled and overtook the sons of Dan. [23] And they called to the sons of Dan, so they (the sons of Dan) turned their faces and they said to Micah, 'What are you doing, that you are assembling?' [24] And he said, 'My gods whom I have made for myself you have taken, and the priest, and you have left! Then what is left to me? And what is this, that you say to me, "What are you doing?"' [25] And the sons of Dan said to him, 'Do not cause your voice to he heard among us, lest men fierce of temper meet up with you so that you lose your life and the life of your household'. [26] So the sons of Dan went on their way; and Micah saw that they were stronger than he, so he turned around and returned to his house.

[27] And they took that which Micah had made and the priest which belonged to him and they came against Laish, against a people undisturbed and confident, and they slew them with the edge of the sword, and the city they burned with fire. [28] And there was no deliverer, since it was distant from Sidon and they had no dealings with anyone, and it was in the valley of Beth-Rehob. Then they rebuilt the city and they settled in it. [29] And they called the name of the city, Dan, according to/like the name of Dan their ancestor, who was born to Israel; although formerly Laish was the name of the city. [30] Then the sons of Dan set up for themselves the idol; and Jonathan, the son of Gershom, the son of Moses—he and his sons were priests to the tribe of the Danites until the day of the exiling of the land. [31] And they set up for themselves the idol of Micah, which he made, all the days that the house of God was in Shiloh.

[Notes on the MT:

Verse 1: For '(as) an inheritance', a few medieval manuscripts of the Hebrew Old Testament, the LXX, and the Syriac read the noun without the prefix preposition. According to *lectio difficilior*, the MT is to be preferred.

Verse 2: For 'from their clan', the LXX and the Targum read plural: 'from their clans', presuming that the 'tribe of the Danites' (18.1) was comprised of multiple clans. On a singular clan for the Danites, see Judg. 13.2. The parallel phrase, 'from the whole of them—men', is absent from the LXX and the Syriac. For 'and they said', a reading from the Cairo Geniza has the singular, 'and he said'. Read the MT. For 'and they lodged (there)', the LXX ^{Alexandrinus, Veronensis, and Origen's Hexaplaric recension} (the Vulgate and the Old Latin) read καὶ κατέπαυσαν ('and they stopped, rested').

Verse 4: For '(Like this) and so', Meyer proposes וְכָזֶה (compare 2 Sam. 11.25, וְכָזֶה כָזֹה—which Meyer/*BHS* prints at Judg. 18.4 as כָּזֹאת וְכָזֹאת). The MT is replicated in both 2 Sam. 11.25 and 1 Kgs 14.5.

Verse 5: For 'shall you bring to success our way, upon which we are going' in the MT, the editor suggests reading the verb with the Cairo Geniza and many medieval manuscripts of the Hebrew Old Testament as a qal third feminine singular rather than as the MT's hiphil second masculine singular form; compare the LXX, the Syriac, and the Vulgate. (The MT may intimate that the priest is to be understood as the subject of the verb, and thus himself capable of bringing to success the Danites's venture.) With 'our way' ('way' can be feminine) as the subject, the qal is a smoother reading. The present translation reflects this variant reading.

Verse 7: Meyer proposes that one insert 'dwelling securely according to the manner of the Sidonians' from later in the verse to immediately after 'toward Laish'. This emendation is without textual support, unnecessary, and not to be accepted (cf. v. 27). For the difficult 'and there was none putting to shame anything (in the land)', Meyer proposes (without manuscript support) וְאֵין־מֹלֵךְ מַדְבַּר ('and there was not a king leading/subduing'). Read the MT. For 'possessing restraint', the editor of the book of Judges in *BHS* proposes reading נוגש ועצר ('drawing near and restraining'), for which cf. the LXX ^{Vaticanus} and the Syriac. For 'with anyone', the LXX and Symmachus's Greek translation of the Old Testament read Συρίας, the equivalent of אֲרָם, which Meyer suggests perhaps should be read. The MT, nevertheless, makes sense, and is to be preferred.

Verse 8: For 'What are you…?', compare Ruth 3.16 מִי־אַתְּ ('who are you?'). The MT of Judg. 18.8 expresses interrupted speech, and is clear.

Verse 9: For the imperative singular with volative h, the editor suggests reading a plural form with the *qere* ^{eastern Masoretes}, several medieval manuscripts of the Hebrew Old Testament, and the Versions. The variant tradition clearly reflects a better Hebrew text and, although the MT's singular may be interpreted distributively, is to be preferred. It is suggested that 'against them' is corrupted from 'toward Laish'. There is no manuscript support for this reading, and the MT is both clear and understandable. Read the MT. After 'for (we have seen the land)', the LXX adds εἰσήλθαμεν καὶ ἐνεπεριεπατή-σαμεν ἐν τῇ γῇ ἕως σιγῆσαι (the LXX ^{K minuscule} Λαισά) καί. This seems to be a gloss; read the MT.

Verse 10: For 'As you enter', several medieval manuscripts of the Hebrew Old Testament read a different (better) prefix preposition (= 'when'); cf. the Syriac (this may be an instance of beth and kaph confusion). The MT as it stands is understandable, and the variant seems to be an expected improvement of what was perceived to be an unclear text. The MT is the preferred reading. In place of 'God' in the phrase 'For God has given it into your hand', one medieval manuscript of the Hebrew Old Testament and the Vulgate read the Tetragrammaton. The support for this variant, which may be interpreted as a minority effort to bring this verse into conformity with the rest of the biblical tradition about the 'giving of the land', is not compelling.

Verse 14: 'Laish' is absent from the LXX and is supposed by Meyer to be a gloss. While the proper noun does not occur in a similar passage (v. 2), the MT here is clear and should be preferred.

Verse 15: Meyer concludes, without evidence, that 'the house of Micah' is a gloss. In my translation, I assume that the preposition אֶל does double duty; it may also be possible to understand 'Levite' as a construct form, thus: 'to the house of the young man, the Levite of the house of Micah'.

Verse 16: For '(600) men girded (with instruments of war)', Meyer prefers to read הָאִישׁ הַזֶּ, compare the LXX ^{Vaticanus and the Lucianic recension} and v. 17. If the two passages were originally written as v. 17, it may be that the present state of v. 16 is due to haplography (note the letters immediately preceding and following the words in question). On the other hand, since definiteness is the question, it may be that at their first mention the 600 men are 'indefinite', while in later references to them they are 'definite' (this conforms to the MT). Read the MT. On the basis of the Syrohexaplaric text, the editor of the book of Judges suggests transposing 'who were from the sons of Dan' to follow immediately after 'instruments of war'. The MT, where the phrase almost appears as an afterthought, is likely to preserve a more original reading, and is to be preferred.

Verse 17: For 'and (they) went up', Meyer proposes reading 'and they were pleased/ resolved'. Lacking manuscript support for this proposal, the MT is to be preferred. For 'they took' (qal perfect; LXX reads an aorist), Meyer proposes reading the qal infinitive construct with preposition. Read the MT. Meyer supposes that the final phrase of this verse, 'and 600 men who were girded with instruments of war', has probably been added. Without textual support, it is better to read the MT.

Verse 18: Probably because the opening phrase of this verse nearly duplicates a portion of the preceding verse, Meyer supposes that it has been added. For 'the idol, the ephod', the LXX reads τὸ γλυπτὸν καὶ τὸ εφουδ ('the carved image and the ephod'), which may be retroverted as אֶת־הַפֶּסֶל וְאֶת־הָאֵפוֹד (sign of the definite accusative and definite article for each noun). This appears to be an improvement of an original text thought to be defective by the LXX scribes. Read the MT.

Verse 22: Put 'when Micah' before 'and the men'; compare the LXX. It is possible that 'when Micah' was omitted due to haplography (see the immediately preceding word). Verse 23 assumes that Micah is with the men. Read with the LXX.

Verse 24: After 'my gods whom I have made', the LXX (the Vulgate) adds ἐμαυτῷ ('for myself'). The editor of the book of Judges supposes that לִי is probably to be inserted (having been omitted due to haplography [see the following word]). The present translation follows the LXX (Vulgate).

Verse 27: After the sign of the definite accusative, two medieval manuscripts of the Hebrew Old Testament add הפסל ('the idol'). Meyer prefers to insert 'the gods' after the sign of the definite accusative (= 'the gods which Micah had made'); compare v. 24. In context, one would imagine that if any addition is to be made, 'the idol and the ephod' would be added. Leaving 'what Micah had made' unspecified in this verse is acceptable. The MT is to be preferred. For 'against (Laish)', Meyer notes that perhaps it is to be read with many medieval manuscripts of the Hebrew Old Testament, the LXX עַד (= 'as far as'); a few medieval manuscripts of the Hebrew Old Testament, the Syriac, and the Vulgate read אֶל (= 'unto'). Since elsewhere the preposition of the MT is used to denote the Danites's movement against Laish, the MT is the preferable reading. For '(and they slew) them', one medieval manuscript of the Hebrew Old Testament, Sebir, read אוֹתָהּ ('it'), the antecedent of which is probably to be understood as (the city) Laish. With Meyer, read the MT.

Verse 28: For 'with anyone', compare Judg. 18.7, note e.

Verse 29: For בְּשֵׁם, read with many medieval manuscripts of the Hebrew Old Testament and the LXX, כְּשֵׁם ('according to/like the name of'); the present translation follows this textual variant. The form in the MT, with the meaning required by the context, occurs nowhere else in the Hebrew Bible. On the other hand, the variant form occurs in Gen. 4.17; Josh. 19.47; 2 Sam. 7.9; Dan. 4.8; and 1 Chron. 17.8. It is also true that ב and כ are easily confused.

Verse 30: מְנַשֶּׁה—So reads the Leningrad Codex of the Hebrew Old Testament, B19ᴬ. Many medieval manuscripts of the Hebrew Old Testament read with the nun suspended; many other medieval manuscripts of the Hebrew Old Testament and the Editions read with the nun not suspended. Read with a few medieval manuscripts of the Hebrew Old Testament, the LXX, and the Vulgate מֹשֶׁה ('Moses'); compare the Syrohexaplaric text. Other occurrences of the suspended letters in the Hebrew Bible are Ps. 80.14; Job 38.13, 15 (all ע). The better text is read without the nun (that is, 'Moses', rather than 'Manasseh').

Verse 31: For 'in Shiloh', Meyer suggests reading either בליׁשה ('in Laishah'—site unknown; it has been conjectured to be 'Isawiye, a village two miles northeast of Jerusalem [BDB, p. 539]) or בשלוה ('at ease, in a time of security'). The present translation follows the MT, which, with its unexpected mention of Shiloh, may be *lectio difficilior*. For conflicting conclusions about the destruction of the Shiloh sanctuary, see Donald G. Schley, *Shiloh: A Biblical City in Tradition and History* (JSOTSup, 63; Sheffield: JSOT Press, 1989), pp. 127-31, and Israel Finkelstein (ed.), *Shiloh: The Archaeology of a Biblical Site* (Tel Aviv: Institute of Archaeology, 1993), pp. 388-89.]

While some other biblical stories relate concerns and characteristics of the tribe of Dan, other accounts deal with the city of Dan (Laish) in the north of the land. Still other stories mention the eponymous ancestor of the tribe, Dan the son of Jacob, or are interested in the affairs of individual members of the tribe (e.g. Lev. 24; Judg. 13–16). Judges 17–18 is unique in that it is the only story in the biblical corpus in which Dan as tribe, city, and ancestor occur together (see Judg. 18.27-29).

The story of the migration of 600 Danites (18.11; in addition to women, children, and property [18.21]) northward from their allotted tribal territory in the south, through the hill country of Ephraim, to the city of Laish, has been used by scholars to interpret other biblical events. For example, the story of the Danite migration has been used to situate the Israelite battle against Sisera and the Canaanite kings (Judg. 4–5; are the Danites still in the south, or are they already in the north?), and the Danite hero Samson, in Israel's history.[258] Indeed, many commentators assume the historical reliability of the story of the Danite migration. Moore, for example, gives high praise to the account: 'The historical value of these chapters is hardly inferior to that of any in the book. The picture of the social and religious

---

258. Typically, Samson is dated to a time after the Danite migration, his story assumed to have originated and circulated among a clan of Danites who remained in the region of Zorah and Eshtaol (Judg. 13.2). See Gottwald, *The Tribes of Yahweh*, pp. 250-51; Niemann, *Die Daniten*, p. 193, cf. p. 145.

state of the times which they contain is full of life, and bears every mark of truthfulness.'[259]

In my judgment, however, the use of Judges 17–18 in the reconstruction of the history of the tribe of Dan is questionable. I propose that there is credible evidence to conclude that the tribe of Dan possibly may not ever have migrated northward, and that the underlying story contained within Judges 17–18 may be better interpreted as an etiology explaining only how the city of Dan (Laish), at the northern border of Israel, got its name (18.29).[260]

Several reasons call into question the presumed historical reliability of this migration story and the resettlement of the tribe of Dan at Laish.[261] First, Judges 18 is the only biblical text to locate unambiguously the Danites in the north, at the city of Dan (see the discussions regarding Deut. 33, Josh. 19, and Judg. 5, above; as well as 2 Chron. 2, below). Beyond the present text, there is no other unequivocal mention of the *tribe* of Dan in the north. The only other biblical reference to the Danite migration is in Josh. 19.47, which I have shown to be among the latest additions to the book of Joshua and most likely dependent on this narrative in Judges 18. Second, the repeated associations of Danites and Judahites (see Gen. 29.35–30.5; Exod. 1.1-6; Josh. 15.33; 19.41; Judg. 13.2; 15.11; note also that the tribes of Judah and Dan are the largest according to the census numbers in Numbers 1 and 26, and Dan and Judah [together with Reuben and Ephraim] are adjacent to the Tent of Meeting while the tribes are en-

---

259. Moore, *Judges*, p. 370; see also Burney, *The Book of Judges*, p. 416.

260. This is a rather fresh approach to Judg. 17–18, since most interpreters consider the sanctuary established in 18.30-31 to be the goal of the narrative. The main argument in the present study is, however, hinted at by Nadav Na'aman ('The "Conquest of Canaan" in the Book of Joshua and History', in Israel Finkelstein and Nadav Na'aman [eds.], *From Nomadism to Monarchy: Archaeological and Historical Aspects of Early Israel* [Washington, DC: Biblical Archaeology Society of America, 1994], pp. 218-81 [271]).

261. Further issues are raised if one proposes that the account of the conquest of Laish, the change of the city's name to Dan, *and* the founding of a tribal sanctuary are all historically accurate. It is wholly unique in Israelite history and tradition that the city of Dan bears the name of one the tribes of Israel. In addition, this would be the only record of a 'tribal' sanctuary, in the sense that the sanctuary at Dan was intended for the limited needs of the Danites (Judg. 18.30). Elsewhere in Israelite tradition pertaining to the pre-monarchic period, sanctuaries such as Shechem (Judg. 24) and Shiloh (Josh. 18.1; 19.51) served 'all Israel', held together in some type of tribal alliance.

camped in the Sinai wilderness [Num. 2]) is more readily understood if the tribe of Dan persisted in the south, where it existed as Judah's neighbor. Third, Malamat's study has highlighted the literary similarities between Judges 17–18 and the Israelite conquest tradition (Exodus–Joshua).[262] Malamat does not treat the historical question at length, concluding only that while both the 'conquest' and 'migration' stories include elements which 'are undoubtedly founded in historical substance', the Judges story is 'generally of a more realistic stamp'.[263] His thorough analysis of the literary character (pattern), however, should caution against making definitive historical judgments based only on the biblical text. In addition, if the idea of an all-Israelite 'conquest' is correctly understood as a literary and theological construction of the monarchic period, then might not the account of the Danite migration likewise be better interpreted as a literary creation from the same era and not necessarily grounded in Israel's early history? Fourth, the assumption that the number of Danites (600) who migrated north to conquer and resettle Laish (18.11) represents a historically accurate count of a portion of the tribe, and that the remainder stayed in the south (among whom, some argue, the Samson stories originated and circulated), overlooks the possibility that the amount of 600 may be a literary figure for a standard number of people in a group. Elsewhere in the Hebrew Bible the figure of 600 is used of the survivors of the Benjaminite slaughter (Judg. 20.47), of Saul's troops (1 Sam. 13.15; 14.2), and of David's men (1 Sam. 23.13; 25.13; 27.2; 30.9-10). It is interesting to note that the total number of Hebrew men who fled Egypt at the Exodus (in addition to women and children, Exod. 12.37; cf. Judg. 18.21) is given as 600,000.[264] Fifth, to date, there has been no incontrovertible archaeological evidence for the Danite migration uncovered by the excavations at Tell Dan, although Biran interprets some of the finds in precisely this way.[265]

---

262. Abraham Malamat, 'The Danite Migration and the Pan-Israelite Exodus-Conquest: A Biblical Narrative Pattern', *Bib* 51 (1970), pp. 1-16. He does not suggest that one account is dependent on the other; rather, both are derived from the same 'pattern', of which the story of the Danite migration is 'a sort of diminutive model'.

263. Malamat, 'The Danite Migration', p. 16.

264. It is further reported that Pharaoh sent 600 picked chariots in pursuit of the fleeing Hebrews (Exod. 14.7).

265. See Biran, *Biblical Dan*, pp. 125-46 (Chapter 8). This is not the place for a comprehensive critique of Biran's conclusions concerning the supposed migration of the tribe of Dan based on his excavations at Tell Dan. Nevertheless, a few remarks are in order. Biran attributes the twelfth-century destruction layer at Tell Dan to the conquering Danites, which brought to an end the Late Bronze Age urban culture at the

Destruction layers and changes in material culture and settlement patterns
do not necessarily indicate the arrival of the supposed nomadic or semi-

site. Among the finds he associates with the new, Israelite population group (Stratum
VI) are: large storage pits (some lined), collared-rim jars, and a radically different
lifestyle 'more suitable to a nomadic or seminomadic society' (p. 128). First of all,
there is no clear biblical evidence that the early Israelites were, as a group, nomads or
seminomads. This was certainly not the case for the Danites, as one of the earliest texts
about the tribe of Dan (Judg. 5) associates the Danites not with herding but with
maritime trade. In general, the traditional notion that the Israelite ancestors were
nomads who eventually settled down in urban centers has been undermined by recent
anthropological and archaeological studies. In addition, the rapid return to an urban
culture at Tell Dan (from Stratum VI to Stratum V) may be evidence against Biran's
interpretation of the Danites's original lifestyle, and even against his identification of a
new population group. It seems more likely that the temporary change in settlement
pattern was due either to the arrival of a new population group which was not (semi-)
nomadic, or, better, to a lifestyle change by the inhabitants of Laish due to the thirteenth–twelfth century destruction of their city. After a relatively short period of
rebuilding they were able to restore their urban culture. Second, while the collared-rim
jars seem to debut at Tell Dan in the twelfth century, this does not automatically point
to the advent of an Israelite group (the Danites). It is no longer widely held that this
type of vessel indicates Israelite provenance. Unfortunately, Biran only remarks in
passing that the identification of the collared-rim jars with the Israelites is today a
matter of much debate (p. 132). What is more, this type of vessel is not the only type
uncovered in this Stratum at Tell Dan. The presence of pottery from other locations
may point to continuing trade relations between the residents of Laish and neighboring
peoples (the location of Laish/Dan on a main crossroads made it a significant commercial center throughout most of its history [pp. 27, 40, 135]). On the pottery from Strata
VI and V, see Joseph Yellin and Jan Gunneweg, 'Instrumental Neutron Activation
Analysis and the Origin of Iron Age I Collared-Rim Jars and Pithoi from Tel Dan', in
Seymour Gitin and William G. Dever (eds.), *Recent Excavations in Israel: Studies in
Iron Age Archaeology* (AASOR, 49; Winona Lake, IN: Eisenbrauns, 1989), pp. 133-41.
Biran suggests that the presence of such large storage vessels 'indicate[s] a population
whose economic and social organization required ways of storing large amounts of
food, both solid and liquid' (*Biblical Dan*, p. 129). Again, this does not require a new,
mobile (nomadic) population group. It is reasonable that the inhabitants of Laish, who
had recently suffered the destruction of their city (and the loss of their food storage
facilities), adopted temporarily an alternate way of storing their provisions. Third,
(lined) storage pits cannot any longer be traced to the early Israelites since excavations
at Late Bronze Age Hazor and Taanach have uncovered evidence of this technology
(see Yigael Yadin *et al.*, *Hazor I: An Account of the First Season of Excavations, 1955*
[Jerusalem: Magnes Press, 1958], pp. 118, 127, 140; Paul W. Lapp, 'The 1968 Excavations at Tell Ta'annek', *BASOR* 195 [1969], pp. 2-49 [33]). A major catastrophe suffered by the city would have required its survivors to utilize alternative storage methods.

nomadic Danites. Generally, archaeologists are less inclined to attribute a phenomenon such as this automatically to a new population group. In addition, and perhaps most significantly, Biran himself reports that so far his excavations have not revealed any structures of a cultic character that antedate the tenth century BCE.[266]

In the present study, I develop a pair of hypotheses and finally conclude that since each hypothesis has its merits and disadvantages, there is presently no way to choose between them. According to the first hypothesis, which follows a more traditional approach to the biblical text and Israelite history, the story in Judges 17–18 originally told of the migration of at least a portion of the Danites to Laish, which they conquered and renamed Dan, and where they founded a tribal sanctuary with a sacred image and a priesthood descended from Moses (the fundamental story seems to be contained within Judges 18, while ch. 17 provides details about the cult-image and priest). This tradition was known to Jeroboam I in the last quarter of the tenth century, and on account of the sanctuary tradition already connected with the city of Dan he located one of his royal shrines there (cf. 1 Kgs 12.25-33). The second hypothesis, while admittedly more speculative, is intended to take seriously some of the important historical and literary questions raised by the text, and one which I hope may stimulate further investigation into this biblical tradition concerning Dan. In this latter proposition, I attempt to isolate three layers in the text: an original etiological narrative about how the city of Dan got its name; a first, northern redaction from about the time of Jeroboam I defending and undergirding his religious activity; and a second redaction from the southern (Judean) perspective, criticizing Jeroboam and his cultic undertaking, in particular the priesthood at Dan.

(a) *Hypothesis One*. The fundamental premise of the first hypothesis is that the narrative in Judges 17–18 reflects an old Danite tradition (itself probably a combination of similar parallel accounts of the same story) about the migration of the tribe of Dan to Laish, their conquest and renaming of the city, and their founding of a sanctuary at the site complete with a cult image and priesthood. This tradition was known to Jeroboam I in the last quarter of the tenth century.[267] At the beginning of this century, Burney

266. Biran, *Biblical Dan*, p. 165.

267. Contrary to Noth ('The Background of Judges 17–18', in Bernhard W. Anderson and Walter Harrelson [eds.], *Israel's Prophetic Heritage: Essays in Honor of James Muilenburg* [New York: Harper & Brothers, 1962], pp. 68-85 [79]), who is

and Moore credited a late pre-exilic or exilic redactor (R^{JE}) with the combination of two older, similar narratives (J and E).[268] While Moore, probably rightly, found no indication of Deuteronomic editing in Judges 17–18, Toews traces the present form of this narrative to the Judean author of the first (pre-exilic) edition of the DH.[269] Unfortunately, his enumeration of particularities in the narrative which, he argues, presuppose the 'Deuteronomistic perspective' (namely, the reference to 'Mahaneh-dan to this day', 18.12; the contrast between the illicit shrine at Dan with the true sanctuary at Shiloh, 18.31; and the formulae in 17.6 and 18.1a, in which he perceives a concern for centralization and with which he connects Deut. 12.8) is not wholly persuasive. Of note, however, is his concession that

> in writing the polemical composition the author of Judges 17–18 made use of much older traditions that had their original setting at the sanctuary at Dan... [The] stories must have related with pride certain facts about how God had given the city of Laish into the hands of the Danites and about how cultic objects and a levitical priest were brought from Ephraim to establish this sanctuary at Dan.[270]

Whether literary or pre-literary, Jeroboam appealed to this older, Danite sanctuary tradition and acted in continuity with it when he founded a *royal* sanctuary at Dan after the dissolution of the United Kingdom of David and Solomon.[271] There are three items in particular in this older Danite tradition that were of apologetic significance for Jeroboam and his selection of

followed now by Toews (*Monarchy and Religious Institution in Israel*, pp. 117-18), I attribute the evaluative formulae in 17.6 and 18.1a to the polemical attitude of a later editor. Apart from these notices, Judg. 17–18 reads as a neutral reflection of life in general, and of domestic religion in particular, in the period before the monarchy in Israel. The phrase 'until the exiling of the land' in 18.30 (reflecting the fall of Israel in 722 BCE) is also a secondary addition to the basic narrative.

268. Burney, *The Book of Judges*, pp. 410-11, 416; Moore, *Judges*, pp. xxix-xxx, xxxiv.

269. Toews, *Monarchy and Religious Institution in Israel*, p. 120; cf. Moore, *Judges*, p. xxx; Noth, *Deuteronomistic History*, p. 77.

270. Toews, *Monarchy and Religious Institution in Israel*, p. 121. Later, he suggests that these 'much older traditions' probably had the form of a 'pre-literary, positive cult-aetiology' (p. 122).

271. In contrast, Noth ('Background', pp. 78-82) understands Judg. 17–18 as a polemic against the tribal sanctuary of the Danites, composed (that is, there was not an earlier tribal tradition) by adherents of the newly established royal sanctuary at Dan. His point is that, in every way, Jeroboam's royal chapel was not only discontinuous with, but superior to, the earlier tribal sanctuary.

Dan as the site of one of his royal chapels. First, the tradition of a tribal sanctuary at Dan marked the site as Israelite.[272] That is, it was not an unknown site that Jeroboam elevated to the status of royal cult center. With this decision Jeroboam may have intended his own selection to contrast with David's choice of the Canaanite (= Jebusite) stronghold, Jerusalem, as the religious center of the United Kingdom, and the Southern Kingdom's continued maintenance of this site. While it is not indicated in the Hebrew Bible that Jerusalem was originally chosen by God to be the site of the sanctuary (according to 2 Sam. 5.9, David unilaterally seems to have decided on the selection of Jerusalem, to which he gave the name 'city of David'), the Danite tradition in Judg. 18.5-6, 10, indicates explicitly that Laish was delivered into the Danites's hands by God.

Second, although the precise shape of the cult image is unspecified in the text of Judges 17–18, there is sufficient evidence to conclude that the 'idol and molten image' of Micah that ended up at Dan was taurine in form. This, at least, seems to be the usual meaning of מסכה in the Hebrew Bible.[273] Thus, with the manufacture of the calves of gold which were set up at Bethel and Dan, Jeroboam sought to maintain his royal cult in continuity with Israel's earlier religious traditions and practices.[274] If the Danite (tribal) sanctuary persisted at Dan alongside Jeroboam's royal sanctuary, the fact that Jeroboam's calf image was made of gold may be understood as a mild indication of superiority over the other local image made of silver.[275]

Third, there is reason to conclude that Jeroboam drew at least part (if not all) of his priesthood at Dan from the ranks of the levitical priests descended from Moses (Judg. 18.30) who served the tribal sanctuary in the city since its founding; it is far more difficult to imagine that Jeroboam would have been so innovative as to have consecrated *exclusively* non-

---

272. Just as Dan had a tribal tradition connected with it (the Danites), Bethel, the site of Jeroboam's royal sanctuary on Israel's southern border, had the Jacob tradition associated with it (Gen. 28.10-22; 35.1-15).

273. Note especially Hos. 13.2, which describes the bull of Samaria as having been fashioned by craftsmen from silver (cf. Judg. 17.3-4). It is possible that the reason the shape of the image is not described is that it was well known to the original audience and did not need to be defined. See Baruch Halpern, 'Levitic Participation in the Reform Cult of Jeroboam I', *JBL* 95 (1976), pp. 31-42 (36).

274. On the bull-calf iconography and early Israelite religion, see Toews, *Monarchy and Religious Institution in Israel*, pp. 41-69.

275. Noth, 'Background', pp. 81-82.

levitical priests to serve his royal shrines.[276] Once more, Jeroboam's levitical (Mushite) priesthood at Dan demonstrates his continuity with the earlier tribal cultic tradition at the site.

The original tradition in Judges 17–18 was neutral concerning its contents. This position must be compared with that advocated by Noth and accepted by, for example, Toews. Noth argued that the evaluative comments in 17.6 and 18.1a were an integral part of the original composition of Judges 17–18. Thus, according to Noth, the original form of the narrative was polemical.[277] In the present hypothesis, it is only as a result of the editorial notes in 17.6 and 18.1a, added by a later redactor, that the actions narrated in the tradition come under negative criticism. This point of view has been favored by both Burney and Moore who, while allowing for the possibility that the formulae criticize the verses that follow, regard the irregularities narrated in the preceding verses to be the object of criticism.[278]

I agree with Noth that chs. 17–21 were not originally part of the DH.[279] It is reasonable to conclude that the old traditions in Judges 17–18 were omitted because they depicted an (uncensured) religious attitude at odds with that of the Deuteronomists in the sixth century.[280] It is my conclusion

276. The remark in 1 Kgs 12.31 that Jeroboam appointed priests from among the ranks of the whole people who were not of levitical descent should not be accepted at face value, but must be recognized as a Deuteronomistic attempt to denigrate the northern cult of Jeroboam. Noth ('Background', p. 78), surprisingly, accepted the text of 12.31 as a reliable account of the northern priesthoods. See the discussion of 1 Kgs 12.25-33, below.

277. Noth, 'Background', p. 79. According to Noth, while the formulae in Judg. 19.1 and 21.25 occur at the very beginning and very end of a narrative (where, supposedly, one is to expect editorial comments), in 17.6 and 18.1a they mark 'junctures between the beginning of the chief theme and the first subsidiary theme, and between the introductions of the secondary themes'. (See also, Toews, *Monarchy and Religious Institution in Israel*, p. 118.) However, it should be recognized that 17.1-5 (concerning Micah's household shrine, cult image, and priest) and 17.7-13 (concerning the Levite) are discrete narrative units. Using Noth's criterion, one might expect editorial additions in the middle and at the conclusion of ch. 17. It is my position that an earlier, non-polemical tradition was polemicized by means of the addition of these comments at a later time.

278. Burney, *The Book of Judges*, pp. 410, 422, 424; Moore, *Judges*, pp. 369, 382, 387.

279. Noth, *Deuteronomistic History*, p. 77.

280. If 17.6 and 18.1a belonged to the original composition of Judg. 17–18, it is more difficult to explain why these chapters were not included in the DH.

that Judg. 17.6 and 18.1a come from the latest editor who integrated chs. 17–21 into the book of Judges and into the DH. It is most natural to interpret these formulae as evaluations of the preceding verses. If this view is accepted, then it will be noticed that, in each case, a cultic practice is criticized: Judg. 17.6 polemicizes against both the use of images in the Yahweh-cult, and the appointment of non-levitical priests; 18.1a seems to criticize Micah's exploitation of the Levite for personal gain.[281] Further, the appearance of the formula in Judg. 19.1 is probably intended to critique the Danites for their setting up of Micah's image at their newly founded tribal sanctuary (18.30-31). Thus, on the basis of their location within Judg. 17.1–19.1, I conclude that this later editor was probably Priestly in character, and at work in the exilic period. Therefore, the final form of Judges 17–18 (which was originally pro-Dan[ite]) reads as a strong polemic against the cultic practices reported in these chapters.[282]

(b) *Hypothesis Two*. That the MT is comprised of more than one source has been recognized by critical scholars for many years (see, e.g., the parallels in 17.7-13//18.30-31). The larger question has been whether there were originally two fundamentally parallel sources (a documentary hypothesis), or whether a single account underwent significant interpolation (a supplementary hypothesis).[283] While some interpreters regard both sources as equally neutral in regard to the contents of the narrative, leaving the negative judgments to the hand of a later redactor,[284] others seem to divide

281. The supposition that 18.1a is intended to condemn what follows (the Danite migration) may be due to the present division of the book of Judges into chapters. It is better to understand 18.1a as the concluding comment to what precedes (17.7-13).

282. It is uncertain whether this late polemic was directed against the tribal sanctuary at Dan, Jeroboam's royal shrine at the same site, or both.

283. Moore, *Judges*, pp. 366-70; Burney, *The Book of Judges*, pp. 408-16; Boling, *Judges*, pp. 258, 266. The influence of the source-critical approach to the Pentateuch is evident here. Burney (*The Book of Judges*, p. 409) makes an astute observation: 'It is not, however, always easy to disentangle the strands with any certainty, probably because the two versions of the story were originally closely similar in detail' (cf. Moore, *Judges*, p. 367: 'In nearly all the places where the text is redundant and confused it is possible to disengage two strands of narrative; but to which of the two sources they should be attributed, there are in many instances no criteria to determine; every attempt at a reconstruction in detail must at best be one of several possibilities'). While the present investigation differs from most past studies, I agree that there are places in Judg. 17–18 where the separation into redactional layers is an inconclusive endeavor.

284. Burney, *The Book of Judges*, p. 416.

the text into sources depending on its perspective with regard to the cultic image and priest.[285]

In my second hypothesis, I attempt to isolate three layers in Judges 17–18: an original etiological narrative concerned only with how the city of Dan got its name; a first, northern redaction from about the time of Jeroboam I defending his religious activity in Dan; and a second redaction from the southern (Judean) perspective, criticizing Jeroboam and his cultic undertakings. While this proposal of three levels in these chapters is riskier than the analysis in my first hypothesis, a plausible argument can be made in its defense. My premise is that, at its most fundamental level, the narrative in Judges 17–18 is not about a tribal or royal sanctuary at Laish/ Dan. Rather, the original story underlying Judges 17–18 is an etiology explaining how the city of Dan got its name. (At the present time, and on the basis of the available evidence, I am inclined to be skeptical about the historical veracity of the narrative.[286])

In the final form of the text (what appears in the MT), Judges 17 and 18 are linked together by references to the Ephraimite Micah, his cult image(s), and the Levite. Significant, especially for the present study, however, is the fact that the tribe of Dan occurs only in ch. 18, the story of the tribe's

---

285. Moore (*Judges*, pp. 369-70), e.g., concludes that the first version of the story was essentially neutral, while the motive of the second version was to cast aspersion on the sanctuary at Dan.

286. In his monograph (*The Problem of Etiological Narrative in the Old Testament* [BZAW, 108; Berlin: Alfred Töpelmann, 1968], pp. 1-2), Burke O. Long refers to a debate between John Bright and the 'Alt–Noth School' regarding the value of etiological traditions in the reconstruction of history. While Alt argued for a negative evaluation of the historical worth of etiological narratives, Bright argued that the etiological element was often secondary to a historical tradition, rather than the primary impetus for the tradition (although he concedes that 'the etiological factor...may have given rise to many details in the tradition'). According to Friedemann W. Golka ('The Aetiologies in the Old Testament: Part 1', *VT* 26 [1976], pp. 410-28 [410]), 'traditio-historical research has shown that the presence of an aetiological factor in a narrative can neither positively nor negatively determine the historicity of the event described'. Following Noth, Long (*The Problem of Etiological Narrative*, p. 2) allows for the possibility that 'genuine historical recollections might take an etiological form. But they might not. One has to reckon, therefore, with a whole range of probabilities. This necessitates a careful analysis of individual cases to see whether the link between the events narrated and the phenomenon explained is genuinely historical or secondary.' At the very least, the relationship between the biblical, etiological narrative and genuine history may need to remain an open question at least until the completion of the excavations at Tell Dan.

migration northward and conquest of Laish. It is my thesis that at the basis of Judges 17–18 is an etiological narrative, limited to portions of ch. 18 only, whose purpose is to explain the origin of the name of the city of Dan in the north of the land.[287] That is, this fundamental etiology is not concerned first of all with the religious history either of Laish/Dan or of the Israelite tribe of Dan, but with the tribe of Dan itself, the city of Laish, and the new name given to that city.

(a) *Level 1: The original story—the migration of Dan and the renaming of Laish.* I propose that the following portion of Judges 18 comprises the original etiological narrative:

> [1] Now in those days the tribe of the Danites was seeking for itself an inheritance to inhabit. [2] And the sons of Dan sent out from their clan five men from the whole of them—men—sons of valor, from Zorah and from Eshtaol in order to go about and explore the land to search it, and they said to them, 'Go, search out the land'. [7] So the five men went, and they came toward Laish; and they saw the people who were in its midst, dwelling securely according to the manner of the Sidonians, undisturbed and confident, and there was none putting to shame anything in the land, possessing restraint, and they were distant from the Sidonians, and they had no dealings with anyone. [8] When they came to their kinsmen at Zorah and Eshtaol they said to them, 'What are you...?' [9] And they said, 'Arise, and let us go up against them, for we have seen the land, and behold—very great. But you are inactive! Do not be sluggish to go to enter in order to take possession of the land. [10] As you enter, you will come unto a people confident and the land is broad as two hands. For God has given it into your hand—a place where there is no poverty of anything that is in the land.'
> [11] So they set out from there, from the clan of the Danites, from Zorah and from Eshtaol. [12] And they went up and they encamped in Qiryath Yearim in Judah; therefore, they call that place 'the camp of Dan' until this day, behold (it is) behind (= west of) Qiryath-Yearim. [21] Then they turned and

287. Long provides this definition of etiology: 'A type of story or report set in primordial or historical times, involving god(s) and/or human beings, and designed to explain the origins of certain elements of knowledge, experience, practice, custom, and the like shared by a cultural group. Developed etiology (story) is rare in the Old Testament, but brief reports and etiological motifs imbedded in larger narrative traditions are common. A common type, etymological etiology, explains a name by associating some event with that name by means of wordplay or folk etymology...' (*1 Kings, with an Introduction to Historical Literature* [FOTL, 9; Grand Rapids: Eerdmans, 1984], pp. 248-49). Also helpful is the concise definition by Golka: 'An investigation of the aetiologies in the Old Testament has to concern itself with all those texts which explain the origin of existing facts from an action which took place in the past' ('The Aetiologies in the Old Testament', p. 410)

went, and they set the children and the cattle and the riches before them.
[26] So the sons of Dan went on their way; [27] and they came against Laish,
against a people undisturbed and confident, and they slew them with the
mouth of the sword, and the city they burned with fire. [28] And there was
no deliverer, since it was distant from Sidon and they had no dealings with
anyone, and it was in the valley of Beth-Rehob. Then they rebuilt the city
and they settled in it. [29] And they called the name of the city, Dan, according to the name of Dan their ancestor, who was born to Israel; although
formerly Laish was the name of the city.

It is rather surprising that the recognition of this passage as an etiological
narrative has escaped the notice of most interpreters. It is possible that this
is due, at least in part, to biblical scholarship's traditional preoccupation
with the *religious* history of early Israel as portrayed in Judges 17–18
(elements of which I consider to be secondary additions to an earlier text).

The etiological notice in Judg. 18.29 bears some similarity to J. Fichtner's 'Form I', which consists of (1) an act of name giving, and (2) an
explanation.[288] The full Form occurs only rarely in the Old Testament, and
Exod. 2.22 is given as the best example ('And he called his name Gershom,
for he said, "a client/sojourner I have been in a foreign land"'). Many
minor variations of the Form are evident. The regular elements in the
Form are as follows:

> (a) The *act* of naming is *narrated* in the historical tense by the use of waw
> conversive prefix form of the verb *qr'* with a specific subject.
> (b) The etymological explanation (γ element), with the affix verb form
> follows the name giving itself…
> (c) The γ element always contains a key word which is assonant with the
> name given…[289]

The relevant part of Judg. 18.29 may be analyzed as follows:

ויקראו שם־העיר דן

בשם דן אביהם אשר יולד לישראל

The first part of the etiological note corresponds exactly to Fichtner's
Form I. That is, the verb קרא occurs in the narrative past (historical tense),

---

288. I refer to Fichtner's study ('Die etymologische Ätiologie in der Namengebung
der geschichtlichen Bücher des Alten Testaments', *VT* 6 [1965], pp. 372-96) as it is
related in Long's *The Problem of Etiological Narrative*, pp. 5-8, 27-37. The Form
looks like this: 'And he (she) named the (his, her, or its) name (of the or that) place so
and so / For he (she, they) said: (now follows the etymological explanation for the
name).'

289. Long, *The Problem of Etiological Narrative*, pp. 5-6.

the imperfect with waw conversive; the subject is not impersonal but is specified in v. 26 (the sons of Dan). While the second part of the note (the explanation of the name) does not directly correspond with Fichtner's schema (introduced by כִּי אָמַר), it must be remembered that the complete Form occurs only occasionally, and that variant forms are more common.[290] Nevertheless, it is clear that the purpose of Judg. 18.29aβ is to explain why the name was given: the city was named not after the conquering tribe, but after the tribes' eponymous ancestor.

That this is more than a case of an etiological note appended to or inserted into an earlier narrative finds support in Golka's study of Old Testament etiologies. In his article he builds on the earlier work of Claus Westermann and distinguishes between three groups of etiologies: etiological narratives, etiological motifs in narratives, and etiological notes.[291] The first is of greatest significance for the present investigation of the primary narrative in Judges 18. Following Westermann, Golka characterizes an etiological narrative as a narrative 'in which the question provided and the answer given by the aetiology are identical with the arc of tension, which leads from this tension to its solution'.[292] In the case of Judges 18 as here delimited (once vv. 30-31, regarding the cultic installation and priesthood, are removed from the original edition), the issue is raised in the opening verse: 'Now in those days the tribe of Dan was seeking for itself an inheritance to inhabit'. The question which creates tension in the narrative is: Will the Danites find a place to live? And if so, where shall it be? The migration motif moves the action from this problem to its ultimate resolution in vv. 27-29:

290. A variant may be accounted for here due to the fact that this is a place name etiology, for which Fichtner's analysis prefers his Form II (see Long, *The Problem of Etiological Narrative*, pp. 6-7). Recall, too, that many medieval manuscripts of the Hebrew Old Testament and the LXX read כְּשֵׁם. Is it possible that this kaph (here the prefix preposition) is actually a remnant from an earlier כִּי (the demonstrative conjunction)? In this case, the text would be translated 'And they called the name of the city, Dan, because of the name of Dan their ancestor'. Without manuscript evidence such a reading can only be speculated.

291. Golka, 'The Aetiologies in the Old Testament', pp. 410-11; cf. Claus Westermann, 'Arten der Erzählung in der Genesis', in *idem*, *Forschung am Alten Testament: Gesammelte Studien* (TBü, 24; Munich: Chr. Kaiser Verlag, 1964), pp. 9-91.

292. Golka, 'The Aetiologies in the Old Testament', p. 411. Contrast Long (*The Problem of Etiological Narrative*, p. 87), who concludes that a Form I etiology shows 'no functional connections with narrative material surrounding it'.

> And they came against Laish, against a people undisturbed and confident, and they slew them with the mouth of the sword, and the city they burned with fire. And there was no deliverer, since it was distant from Sidon and they had no dealings with anyone, and it was in the valley of Beth-Rehob. Then they rebuilt the city and they settled in it. And they called the name of the city, Dan, according to/like the name of Dan their ancestor, who was born to Israel; although formerly Laish was the name of the city.[293]

The vast majority of biblical references, early and late, seem to know of some manner of residence of the tribe of Dan in the south (Josh. 19.40-48; Judg. 5.17). In addition, at some point in time (perhaps during the reign of Saul, but more likely during that of David) Israel encountered a city at the northern boundary of the nascent kingdom (in the region of Galilee) having the same name.[294] According to my proposal, this etiological narrative was formulated as the city of Laish/Dan first came under Israelite control, probably during the years of the United Monarchy under David. When Israel came upon the city of Dan in the north, the etiology explaining the origin of the city's new name was created.[295] Thus the etiology in Judges

293. Golka ('The Aetiologies in the Old Testament', p. 417) includes the cities of Bokim and Gilgal as places for which there is an etiological narrative about their name. In the final form of the MT, the etiological note in v. 29 is not the end of the story. There are, however, other instances where subsequent additions have been added after the naming episode (Gen. 28.20-22; see Golka, 'The Aetiologies in the Old Testament', p. 412). In addition, neither is it unheard of for interpolations of a theological interest to be inserted into the etiological narrative (the details about Micah, his image[s], and the Levite; see Golka, 'The Aetiologies in the Old Testament', p. 412).

294. At issue is whether the region around the city of Laish/Dan was controlled by Saul. As Miller and Hayes (*A History of Ancient Israel and Judah*, p. 141) have indicated, 'no texts associate Saul in any way with Galilee'. Aharoni (*The Land of the Bible*, p. 289), however, interprets the note about the extent of the kingdom of Saul's son, Ish-bosheth, in 2 Sam. 2.8-9, as an indication of the earlier kingdom of Saul. The extent of David's kingdom is clearer. The account of David's census (2 Sam. 24), the list of levitical cities (Josh. 21), and the list of unconquered cities (Judg. 1.27-33) have all been identified as pointers to the reach of David's jurisdiction (Miller and Hayes, *A History of Ancient Israel and Judah*, p. 180). In addition, it is likely that the expression 'from Dan as far as Beersheba' originated in the period of the United Monarchy and reflected its geographical limits (see below).

295. The original name of the city, Laish, occurs in the following extra-biblical sources: the early second millennium Execration Texts from Egypt (in which the king of Laish is identified as Horon-Ab [*ANET*, pp. 328-29]), the Mari Texts (also from the first quarter of the second millennium; see G. Dossin, 'La route de l'étain en Méso-potamie au temps de Zimri-Lim', *Revue d'Assyriologie* 64 [1970], pp. 97-106; see also A. Malamat, 'Syro-Palestinian Destinations in Mari Tin Inventory', *IEJ* 21 [1971],

18, including the migration/conquest motif, originally served to link these two Dans in the land.

(b) *Level 2: In defense of Jeroboam's royal sanctuary at Dan.* Recognizing that in certain places the assignment of a given verse (or part of a verse) to one or the other of the two later redactional layers is imprecise, the presence of parallel statements suggest that multiple versions have been edited together. I conclude provisionally that the following version of Judges 17–18 comes from a group of supporters of Jeroboam's religious initiatives in the Northern Kingdom (the italicized verses were added to the original etiological narrative by this partisan group some time near the reign of Jeroboam I in the last quarter of the tenth century). Thus, Jeroboam's supporters are responsible for making the city-name etiology into an etiology explaining the origin of an early Israelite sanctuary at Dan.

Judges 17:

[1] *Now there was a man from the hill country of Ephraim.* [5] *And the man Micah, to him was a house of God; and he made an ephod and teraphim and he filled the hand of one of his sons, and he became to him as a priest.*

Judges 18:

[1] Now in those days the tribe of the Danites was seeking for itself an inheritance to inhabit. [2] And the sons of Dan sent out from their clan five men from the whole of them—men—sons of valor, from Zorah and from Eshtaol in order to go about and explore the land to search it, and they said to them, 'Go, search out the land'. *And they entered the hill country of Ephraim as far as the house of Micah, and they lodged there.* [5] *Then they said to him, 'Inquire of God, and let us know—shall you bring to success*

---

pp. 31-38 [35-36 (note that the Akkadian spelling of this city name includes mimation; cf. Leshem, Josh. 19.47)]), and in the fifteenth-century list of cities conquered by the Egyptian Pharaoh Thutmosis III (*ANET*, p. 242). Much later, a bilingual (Greek and Aramaic) dedicatory inscription, uncovered in the course of the excavations at Tell Dan, refers to the 'God who is in Dan' (Biran, *Biblical Dan*, pp. 221-24). There is no earlier, extra-biblical reference to the city as Dan. Apart from the biblical etiology, one may only speculate about other reasons for the change in the city's name. John Gray (*Joshua, Judges, Ruth*, p. 344) suggests that a local river, one of the sources of the Jordan, lent its name to the city. This, however, only begs the question, transferring the issue from the city to the river (how did the river get this name?). Another possibility is that the survivors of the city's destruction at the end of the Late Bronze Age interpreted the event as a divine judgment against the city (cf. the semitic root דין). Thus, in memory of that event, the name of the city was changed. This is, of course, pure speculation, and it is, in the final analysis, best to admit that we simply cannot be certain how the city got its new name.

our way, upon which we are going?' [6] *And the priest said to them, 'Go in peace; your way upon which you are going is before Yahweh'.* [7] So the five men went, and they came toward Laish; and they saw the people who were in its midst, dwelling securely according to the manner of the Sidonians, undisturbed and confident, and there was none putting to shame anything in the land, possessing restraint, and they were distant from the Sidonians, and they had no dealings with anyone. [8] When they came to their kinsmen at Zorah and Eshtaol they said to them, 'What are you...?' [9] And they said, 'Arise, and let us go up against them, for we have seen the land, and behold—very good. But you are inactive! Do not be sluggish to go to enter in order to take possession of the land. [10] As you enter, you will come unto a people confident and the land is (as) broad as two hands. For God has given it into your hand—a place where there is no poverty of anything that is in the land. [11] So they set out from there, from the clan of the Danites, from Zorah and from Eshtaol. [12] And they went up and they encamped in Qiryath-Yearim in Judah; therefore, they call that place 'the camp of Dan' until this day, behold (it is) behind (= west of) Qiryath-Yearim. [13] *And they crossed over from there (into) the hill country of Ephraim, and they entered as far as the house of Micah.* [14] *Then five of the men, the ones who went to explore the land of Laish, answered and they said to their kinsmen, 'Did you know that there is in these houses an ephod and teraphim?'* [18] *And these entered the house of Micah and they took the ephod and the teraphim. Then the priest said to them, 'What are you doing?* [19] *And they said to him, 'Which is better—your being a priest to the house of one man, or your being a priest to a tribe and to a clan in Israel?'* [20] *Now the heart of the priest was glad, and he took the ephod and the teraphim, and he entered into the midst of the people.* [21] Then they turned and went, and they set the children and the cattle and the riches before them. [26] So the sons of Dan went on their way; [27] and they came against Laish, against a people undisturbed and confident, and they slew them with the mouth of the sword, and the city they burned with fire. [28] And there was no deliverer, since it was distant from Sidon and they had no dealings with anyone, and it was in the valley of Beth-Rehob. Then they rebuilt the city and they settled in it. [29] And they called the name of the city, Dan, according to/like the name of Dan their ancestor, who was born to Israel; although formerly Laish was the name of the city. [30] *Then the sons of Dan set up for themselves (the ephod); and Jonathan, the son of Gershom, the son of Moses—and his sons were priests to the tribe of the Danites.*

It is frequently supposed that Jeroboam I chose the city of Dan as the site of one of his two royal sanctuaries (the other city being Bethel) because of the city's important history (going back to the premonarchic period) as an Israelite religious center. Interpreted as a historical source, Judges 17–18 is thought to document the founding of a tribal sanctuary by the migrating and conquering Danites. Thus, Jeroboam I is seen to be either acting in continuity with this tribal tradition (carrying the cultic significance of the city into the monarchic period), or reacting against the tribal sanctuary of the Danites.[296]

Unfortunately, the excavations at Tell Dan have so far failed to uncover any remains of a cultic installation that antedates the tenth or ninth century. According to Biran, 'the earliest evidence of a cultic character found in the course of the excavations goes back only to the 10th century B.C.E., to the time of King Jeroboam I, the son of Nebat'. While Biran supposes that Jeroboam set up the golden calf '*in* the original Danite sanctuary', the fact is that there is no evidence of this earlier, tribal sanctuary at Tell Dan.[297] Therefore, the idea of Jeroboam appealing to a long (Israelite) religious tradition at the site in order to validate his own cultic initiatives is questionable. Nevertheless, in the absence of evidence of an earlier tribal shrine, there are other possible reasons for Jeroboam's selection of Dan as the site of one of his royal sanctuaries.

Although there is no evidence of a Danite (tribal) sanctuary at Laish/ Dan, Biran's excavations have uncovered other premonarchic evidence of possibly cultic significance at the site.[298] For example, in the Early Bronze Age III level (Stratum XIV), there were discovered a number of small figurines of animals, clay models of beds/couches, and 22 cylinder impressions—all of which Biran considers to be of religious significance.[299] Late Bronze Age finds include a structure and a female pottery mask, both associated by Biran with cultic activities.[300] Two more items, of Egyptian provenance, were uncovered in the 'Sacred Precinct' in the area of the Dan springs, on the north side of the site, but out of their original context. The first of these is a described as 'a statuette of red granite depicting a person sitting cross-legged and wearing a long dress, and with the position of the hands suggestive of prayer'. Found in the remains of a ninth-century

296. The former is preferred by, among others, Biran (*Biblical Dan*, p. 165). The latter possibility is that preferred by Noth in his important study, 'The Background of Judges 17–18'. In short, Noth argues that Judg. 17–18 is a pro-Jeroboam text intended to demonstrate the superiority of the royal sanctuary relative to the competing sanctuary which traced its history to the tribe of Dan.

297. Biran, *Biblical Dan*, p. 165 (emphasis added).

298. I suggest, however, that perhaps Biran is a little overzealous in attributing cultic significance to some of the finds.

299. Biran, *Biblical Dan*, pp. 40-44. Is it possible that the clay model beds/couches, which Biran connects with fertility rites, might instead be small incense altars?

300. Biran, *Biblical Dan*, p. 105.

Israelite wall, the statuette has been dated to the Late Bronze Age II.[301] The second statuette, in the form known as a 'block statue', has been dated to the first quarter of the second millennium.[302] Additional finds from the time before Jeroboam I include an Astarte figurine and a four-horned altar.[303]

The city of Dan was also significant as a border town on the northern frontier of the kingdom of Israel. The phrase, 'from Dan as far as Beersheba', used by Dtr to designate the whole of the land (cf. the similar phrase, 'from Beersheba as far as Dan', in 1 and 2 Chronicles), is probably from a source much older than the exilic period (see below). Situated near the juncture of major trade routes, Dan was of economic and strategic significance (recall that the Mari texts record tin being delivered to Laish).[304] It is possible that following the destruction of the city in the middle of the eleventh century, the site was rebuilt and refortified by David and Solomon.[305] It is not surprising that a location of such strategic and political importance should be associated with a religious center, and that Jeroboam would want to undergird the integrity of the site in whatever way possible. The reference in 1 Kgs 15.20 to the attack on the city by the Syrian king Ben-hadad in the ninth century is evidence of its continuing importance.[306] (Indeed, it is conceivable that during its history, control of the city changed hands several times.)

It is my hypothesis that the earlier etiological narrative about how the city of Dan got its name was expanded by a group sympathetic to Jeroboam I and his cultic practices, in order to bolster the Northern Kingdom's religious status. I am proposing, then, that the tradition of a Danite tribal

301. Biran, *Biblical Dan*, p. 161.

302. Biran, *Biblical Dan*, p. 161.

303. Biran, *Biblical Dan*, p. 165.

304. See n. 295, above. See also the remarks about the location of the city in the entry on Dan in LeMoine F. DeVries, *Cities of the Biblical World: An Introduction to the Archaeology, Geography, and History of Biblical Sites* (Peabody, MA: Hendrickson, 1997), p. 164.

305. Biran, *Biblical Dan*, p. 247.

306. The discovery at Tell Dan in 1993–94 of fragments of an Aramaic inscription dated by the excavator (Biran) and epigrapher (Naveh) to the ninth century has generated a storm of controversy. The preliminary translation by Biran and Naveh includes reference to the 'house of David' which, if correct, is the only known extra-biblical reference to the David (see Avraham Biran and Joseph Naveh, 'An Aramaic Stele Fragment from Tel Dan', *IEJ* 43 [1993], pp. 81-98; *idem*, 'The Tel Dan Inscription: A New Fragment', *IEJ* 45 [1995], pp. 1-18).

sanctuary at Laish/Dan was created by Jeroboam (or perhaps by his priest-hood) near the end of the tenth century, in order to establish Dan as a sig-nificant Israelite sanctuary with which Jeroboam's cultic innovations were in continuity. Building on both the religious history of the site and the etiological story of the Danite migration available to him, and by adding the tale of the Danite founding of a sanctuary at Laish/Dan in the pre-monarchic period, Jeroboam sought to ground his religious center in old *Israelite* tradition.

Several elements in Judges 17–18 support this position, namely, that one of the redactional levels was undertaken in order to undergird Jero-boam's religious initiatives in the north after the division of the Kingdom of David and Solomon. First, that this redactional layer begins with mention of the hill country of Ephraim is probably not accidental (Judg. 17.1). Ephraim, it will be recalled, is one of the names by which the Northern Kingdom is referred to in the Hebrew Bible (Isa. 7.2; 17.3; Jer. 7.15). What is more, according to 1 Kgs 11.26, Jeroboam the son of Nebat was an Ephraimite from Zeredah. And not only was Ephraim the tribe of Jeroboam, the first king of the north after the dissolution of the United Monarchy in Israel, Jeroboam also fortified the city of Shechem in the Ephraimite hill country and established it as his capital (1 Kgs 12.25). There are, thus, in this tradition, significant ties between the Ephraimite origin of the cultic equipment and leadership introduced in Judges 17–18— which are later transferred to Dan—and Jeroboam I.

Second, according to the present redactional analysis of Judges 17–18, among the cult paraphernalia belonging to Micah were an ephod and teraphim (17.5; 18.14, 20). Of special interest is not the intriguing question of the identity or character of the teraphim (see the commentaries on their use in divination), but the occurrence of this term exclusively in northern Israelite traditions.[307] According to Moore, '*teraphīm*, which are not often mentioned in the O.T....are found in the Hexateuch only in E'.[308] This would seem to situate this redactional level of Judges 17–18 in the north. In Judges 17–18, the teraphim are associated with an ephod. While the Hebrew Bible does not present a simple picture of this item, there is

307. The teraphim are explained in Moore, *Judges*, pp. 378-80; Burney, *The Book of Judges*, pp. 420-21; Boling, *Judges*, p. 256.

308. Moore, *Judges*, p. 368. Among pentateuchal source critics, E is traditionally traced to the Northern Kingdom (see, e.g., Robert H. Pfeiffer, *Introduction to the Old Testament* [New York: Harper & Brothers, 1941], pp. 168-77; more recently, Fried-man, *Who Wrote the Bible?*, p. 87).

sufficient reason to conclude that it, too, had a role in divination rites (see, e.g., Judg. 8.27; 1 Sam. 15.23; 23.6-13; 30.7-8; Hos. 3.4). The resultant picture of the cult instituted by Jeroboam is one in which divination, by means of the ephod and teraphim, played a central role. For this reason I am inclined to conclude that in the pro-Jeroboam redaction, 'ephod' (or 'ephod and teraphim') stood in the place of 'idol' in Judg. 18.30.[309] In the third level of the tradition, 'idol' was substituted in an effort to disparage further the northern sanctuary as apostate. However, Jeroboam's initiative in this regard may also be recognized as part of his 'archaizing' tendency. According to de Vaux, 'after the reign of David, there is no evidence that the ephod, with the Urim and Thummim, was ever used for oracles'.[310] However, the eighth-century Israelite prophet Hosea indicates that ephod and teraphim were in use in the Northern Kingdom until its fall in 722 BCE (Hos. 3.4). The substitution of 'idol' (פסל) in Judg. 18.30 by the later hand functions to show Jeroboam and the northern sanctuary to be idolatrous and in violation of one of the central tenets of the Law (Deut. 5.8-10).[311]

Third, the prominence given to the figure of Moses further grounds this redactional layer in the north, where he was recognized as a hero.[312] According to Judg. 18.30, 'Jonathan, the son of Gershom, the son of Moses' and his sons served as priests at the Danite sanctuary since its inception. (Of course, since there is no evidence of a tribal sanctuary at Tell Dan antedating the time of Jeroboam, this entire passage must be recognized as a literary creation from the late tenth century at the earliest. It may be the case that this redactional layer of Judges 17–18 was prepared as a northern counterpart to 1 Kgs 12.25-33, a text which bears the distinct bias of a southern, Judean scribe.) If the unnamed Levite in the earlier parts of Judges 17–18 is to be properly identified with this Jonathan (who is, in 18.30, not introduced as a/the Levite), then in this pro-Jeroboam tradition, it is to be understood that a levitical priesthood at Dan, descended from

309. See already Moore, *Judges*, p. 400.

310. Roland de Vaux, *Ancient Israel*. II. *Religious Institutions* (2 vols.; New York: McGraw–Hill, 1961), pp. 352-53.

311. In time the 'idol' became identified with the golden calf images which Jeroboam made and installed at Bethel and at Dan—according to Dtr (1 Kgs 12.28-32; cf. 15.30, 34; 16.2, 7, 19, 26; 2 Kgs 3.3; 10.29, 31; 13.2, 6, 11; 14.24; 15.9, 18, 24, 28; 17.21; 23.15).

312. Friedman (*Who Wrote the Bible?*, pp. 71-74) traces this to the E source of the Pentateuch. It should be noted, however, that the very existence of this Pentateuchal source (in particular) is much debated.

Moses no less, was founded long before the ascendency of Judah and Jerusalem in the south.[313]

An additional way in which the figure of Moses is directly connected with Jeroboam is the compilation of parallels in the portrayal of the two individuals's lives. Jeroboam and Moses share the following characteristics: both are from a royal circle; both show solidarity with their oppressed people; both stand up to and rebel against their overseer; both flee to escape punishment from the hand of a king.[314] Archaeological evidence from Tell Dan further underlines the significance of Moses for Jeroboam and the northern sanctuary. According to Biran, in the stratum of the Sacred Precinct (Area T) corresponding to the time of Jeroboam there were uncovered three complete pithoi decorated with an encircling snake relief.[315] The association of the snake motif with Moses is clear from Num. 21.9, where Moses is reported to have fashioned a copper serpent and affixed it to a standard for the well-being of the people in the wilderness. According to 2 Kgs 18.4, Hezekiah is depicted destroying Nehushtan, the bronze serpent made by Moses, which had been venerated in the Jerusalem Temple. Could this note in 2 Kings have been intended as a polemic against the Moses tradition in the north?

I concur with those scholars who argue that Jeroboam's cultic purpose was to 'out-archaize' the religious innovations ushered in by David and Solomon.[316] While the Jerusalem temple had a high priest of uncertain background (Zadok), a single, central sanctuary identified with the royal house, and new ideologies (Zion theology, Davidic covenant); in the north Jeroboam I boasted these traditional interests: a levitical priesthood descended directly from Moses, multiple sanctuaries distinct from the capital city and, perhaps, a cult image in continuity with the wilderness period (although the form of the image is not specified in Judges 17–18; if 'idol' is original in 18.30, it is conceivable that the image was of a calf [cf. Exod. 32; 1 Kgs 12]). Finally, partisans of Jeroboam's religious initiatives in the north sought to establish Jeroboam's practices with one additional

313. This suggestion fits nicely with Cross's theory of priestly families in Israel: a Mushite priesthood at Dan, and an Aaronid priesthood at Bethel (see *Canaanite Myth and Hebrew Epic*, p. 199).

314. See Rainer Albertz, *A History of Israelite Religion in the Old Testament Period*. I. *From the Beginnings to the End of the Monarchy* (OTL; 2 vols.; Louisville, KY: Westminster/John Knox Press, 1994), pp. 141-42.

315. Biran, *Biblical Dan*, pp. 165, 168, 177.

316. See, e.g., Cross, *Canaanite Myth and Hebrew Epic*, p. 199; Miller and Hayes, *A History of Ancient Israel and Judah*, p. 242.

archaizing move: they sought to project the foundation for Jeroboam's cultic activity into the past, back into the premonarchic period. That is, far from being innovative and apostate in the wholly conservative realm of the cult, Jeroboam was, rather, depicted in direct continuity with Israel's earlier religious history.[317]

Because I prefer to date this redactional layer to a time near the reign of Jeroboam I, I have excluded 18.30b ('until the day of the exiling of the land'). This note may have been added either by a scribe of the Northern Kingdom after the deportation of the inhabitants of northern Galilee by Tiglath-pileser in 734 BCE, but before the fall of Samaria in 722 BCE, or by a southern editor sometime after the events of 722.[318]

(c) *Level 3: A Judean polemic against Israel's sanctuary at Dan.* The third redactional level of Judges 17–18, according to the present analysis, creates essentially the final form of the text as represented by the MT (see my translation and textual analysis above). I am inclined, however, to regard the formulaic phrases beginning 'In those days there was no king in Israel...' (17.6; 18.1; cf. 19.1; 21.25) as still later editorial additions whose purpose was to fit chs. 17–21 into the book of Judges.[319] I agree with the vast majority of scholars in interpreting this edition as a strong polemical attack on the northern sanctuary at Dan. Toews's recent comment is representative of this point of view:

317. One complication of this analysis is that, contrary to the remark in 1 Kgs 12.31, Jeroboam probably did not have an exclusively non-levitical priesthood at Dan. While some Levites, who persisted in their loyalty to the house of David, needed to be dismissed and/or replaced, it does not necessarily follow that all Levites were expelled or fled from the Northern Kingdom (cf. 2 Chron. 11.13-15; 13.9).

318. Burney's suggestion that 'land' (ארץ) be read 'ark' (ארון), thus creating an even closer parallel between v. 30 and v. 31, is not persuasive (*The Book of Judges*, pp. 415, 435).

319. Robert G. Boling ('"In Those Days There Was No King in Israel"', in Howard N. Brean, Ralph D. Helm and Carey A. Moore [eds.], *A Light unto My Path: Old Testament Studies in Honor of Jacob M. Myers* [Gettysburg Theological Studies, 4; Philadelphia: Temple University Press, 1974], pp. 33-48) traces this phrase to the hand of the seventh-century Deuteronomic redactor (Dtr[1]), while W.J. Dumbrell ('"In Those Days There Was No King in Israel; Every Man Did What Was Right in his Own Eyes": The Purpose of the Book of Judges Reconsidered', *JSOT* 25 [1983], pp. 23-33) prefers the hand of an exilic redactor (sixth century). I also attribute the last, grammatically difficult part of Judg. 18.1 to a later hand; cf. Moore, *Judges*, p. 387. This phrase seems to presuppose a time prior to the allotment of tribal territories in Josh. 13–19, and may represent a late, variant tradition (well after the story of the migration) which omitted reference to a Danite territory in the south.

> As the narrative in Judges 17–18 now stands there can be no doubt about its
> intent to ridicule or to criticize the religious ventures of which it tells…
> Since the whole story moves toward the moment of the establishment of the
> Danite sanctuary, one must conclude that the primary intention of the
> narrative is to point out the illegitimacy of the sanctuary at Dan.[320]

In particular, this editor is responsible for the longer form of the Ephraimite's name, Micayahu (17.1, 4; meaning 'Who is like Yahweh?'), in
order more explicitly to ridicule the religious practices described in the
succeeding narrative. This third layer also introduces the sacred image as
the 'idol (פֶּסֶל) and the molten image (מַסֵּכָה)' (17.3-4; 18.14, 17, 18, 20,
30-31).[321] Indeed, 17.2-4 sets the tone for the rest of the story that follows,
and is a strong indicator of the source of this layer (to aniconic Yahwism,
the presence of such a graven figure in an Israelite sanctuary was heretical).
This image that ultimately is erected in the sanctuary at Dan is also ridiculed for having been stolen twice, thus robbing it of any integrity: first,
the silver from which it was manufactured was stolen from Micah's mother
(following which a curse was uttered); second, the image was stolen by the
migrating Danites and taken to Laish. It is also possible that the Levite
who is most likely not introduced until this layer is portrayed negatively in
the final form of the narrative. He is pictured as being disloyal to his
patron, Micah, preferring instead the (in)tangible benefits offered by the
Danites.[322] The net result of this is that the legitimacy of the northern
sanctuary and its priesthood at Dan is wholly undermined.

320. Toews, *Monarchy and Religious Institution in Israel*, pp. 115-16. See also
John L. McKenzie, *The World of the Judges* (Backgrounds in the Bible Series; Engle-
wood Cliffs, NJ: Prentice–Hall, 1966), p. 163; Soggin, *Judges: A Commentary*, p. 268;
Moore, *Judges*, p. 370; John Gray, *Joshua, Judges, Ruth*, pp. 223-24.

321. See pp. 195-96, above. Soggin (*Judges: A Commentary*, p. 268) writes: 'it is
enough to recall that the term *pesel* stands for the idolatrous image *par excellence*
mentioned in the Decalogue, Ex. 20.4-6//Deut. 5.8-10, and Deutero-Isaiah, cf. Isa.
40.18-20; 44.14-20'.

322. According to Wolf (*Peasants*, p. 87), a client 'must offer not merely protesta-
tions of loyalty. He must also demonstrate that loyalty when the chips are down. In
times of political crisis, he must rally to the patron to whom he is bound by the
informal contract and from whom he has received favors. At the same time, crises also
constitute a challenge to establish contracts… *A patron who has less to offer may be
deserted for a patron who offers more; a patron whose star is in the decline will lose
his clients to a man whose star is in the ascendancy. Thus patrons compete with each
other, purchasing support through the granting of favors in many such dyadic coalitions*' (emphasis added). On the voluntary character of the patron–client relationship,
see also Moxness, 'Patron–Client Relations', p. 248.

There is no agreement on the date of the final form of Judges 17–18, a narrative inclusive of the original etiology and two later redactional layers. Proposals range from the time of the United Monarchy to the Deuteronomistic movement in the late pre-exilic period.[323] I venture a new possibility—namely, that this third redactional layer may have come from a (proto-Deuteronomistic) scribe living in Judah sometime late in the tenth or early in the ninth century, soon after the ascendency of Jeroboam in the Northern Kingdom and the establishment of royal sanctuaries at Bethel and Dan, which were intended to compete with the central temple in Jerusalem associated with the Davidic monarchy.[324] It is possible to imagine that the source of this redactional level was among those Levites who were loyal to the house of David and who did, in fact, leave the Northern Kingdom with the rise of Jeroboam. This would, among other things, account for the negative portrayal of the Levite (whose ultimate origin was, interestingly, in Judah [17.7]) and priesthood in Judges 17–18. The polemic was specifically against fellow Levites who had abandoned the Jerusalem cultic establishment, centered around the Ark, for the iconic cult of the rebellious north. The chief criterion against which the northern sanctuary was measured was the administration and ideology of the central sanctuary in Jerusalem.

Usually, the mention of Shiloh in 18.31 has prompted scholars to seek the date of this reference in the archaeological record of that site in the Ephraimite hills north of Bethel.[325] More importantly, however, this refer-

323. See the review given in Toews, *Monarchy and Religious Institution in Israel*, pp. 119-21. Noth uniquely situates this complete text in the priestly circle connected with the royal court of Jeroboam I. According to Noth, the polemic is directed against the earlier, tribal sanctuary at Dan with its small, silver (rather than large, gold) image and priesthood made up of 'vagabond' Levites rather than royally appointed priests ('The Background of Judges 17–18', pp. 81-82). Cf. Toews (*Monarchy and Religious Institution in Israel*, p. 120), who dates the present composition of Judg. 17–18 to the time of Cross's Dtr[1], that is, in the latter part of the seventh century (see also Boling, *Judges*, pp. 30, 267; Soggin, *Judges: A Commentary*, p. 269).

324. While a late pre-exilic date is attractive, especially when it is allied with the Deuteronomistic group, the central item of critique in Judg. 17–18 is the Levite, not the graven image or religious site (subjects which play a more crucial role in Deuteronomistic thought). Hence the present conclusion.

325. The evidence of the destruction of Shiloh is not unambiguous, and has been variously interpreted. Some scholars (e.g. Finkelstein) identify a destruction layer in the mid-eleventh century, while others (e.g. Schley) date the destruction of the site to the eighth century. Even if an eleventh-century date is correct, it is not the case that the site was abandoned. Rather, settlement at the site persisted into the exilic period (see

ence to the 'house of God...in Shiloh' is further evidence that this redactional layer has its origin within the religious circle associated with the Davidic–Solomonic temple in Jerusalem, and is intended to discredit both sanctuaries at Shiloh and at Dan (also Bethel?). According to the biblical tradition, Shiloh was the site of one of the central sanctuaries of the Israelite tribes during the pre-nation period (see Josh. 18–21; 1 Sam. 1–4). It was the site of the Tent of Meeting (Josh. 18.1; 19.51), the House of Yahweh (1 Sam. 1.24), and the Ark of God (1 Sam. 3.3). Miller and Hayes suggest that the sanctuary ascended in importance during the reign of Saul, with whom the house of Eli at Shiloh aligned itself.[326] However, just as David replaced Saul as king of Israel, Jerusalem eclipsed Shiloh with David's transfer of the Ark to his new royal sanctuary (2 Sam. 6). I propose that the significance of the remark about Shiloh in Judg. 18.31 is that just as Jerusalem supercedes Shiloh in importance, so, too, does its Solomonic sanctuary surpass the one at Dan. The implication is that, according to this editor, when the house of God was removed from Shiloh at the ascendency of David, at the same time the sanctuary at Dan (according to tradition), practically speaking, also ceased to exist.[327]

There is, then, reason to accept and question each of the proposed hypotheses. On the one hand, Hypothesis One has the advantage of taking the biblical text essentially as it is. It also follows a traditional interpretation of the history of the tribe of Dan and its migration northward. On the other hand, it leaves the historical and literary questions raised in the present study unanswered. Hypothesis Two deserves consideration and provisional assent first and foremost because it takes seriously these issues. At the same time, its three redactional layers may attempt to draw more from the text than its final form will permit. Of greater importance for the

Baruch Halpern, 'Shiloh', in *ABD*, V, pp. 1213-15 [1214]). It is possible that the reference to '*the* house of God...in Shiloh' is intended to contrast this legitimate sanctuary with '*a* house of God' which belonged to Micah (17.5). However, I suggest that the Shiloh sanctuary in the territory of Ephraim (home of Jeroboam and location of the Bethel sanctuary) is here polemicized against from the perspective of the Jerusalem establishment.

326. Miller and Hayes, *A History of Ancient Israel and Judah*, p. 133.

327. It is possible that in light of the catastrophe of 587 BCE, 'Moses' was changed to 'Manasseh' (18.30) by a Deuteronomistic editor who was offended by the Mushite priesthood at Dan. The addition of the supralinear nun may also have been intended to call to mind King Manasseh, on whom Dtr placed the blame for the Babylonian Exile (the editor did not intend the reader to understand that the priests were actually descended from this Manasseh).

present study of Dan in the biblical traditions is my recognition that the original form of Judges 17–18 was fundamentally neutral concerning Dan and the Danites. It is only as a result of later editorial additions that the tradition reflects negatively on the religious history of the tribe and city of Dan.

3. *The Books of Samuel*

Apart from its occurrence in the formula 'from Dan to Beersheba' (1 Sam. 3.10; 17.11; 24.2; cf. Judg. 20.1), Dan does not occur in the Hebrew text of the books of Samuel. The reference to Dan in 2 Samuel 20 (LXX) is not, strictly speaking, part of the Danite tradition in the *Hebrew Bible*, since it is not included in the MT. A variant tradition is preserved, however, in the LXX. The Hebrew text of 2 Sam. 20.16-19 is translated as follows:

> [16] Now a wise woman called out from the city: 'Listen! Listen! Say to Joab, "Draw near hither", and let me speak to you'. [17] So he drew near to her and the woman said, 'Are you Joab?' And he said, 'I am'. And she said to him, 'Hear the words of your maidservant'. And he said, 'I am listening'. [18] And she said, saying, 'They indeed spoke formerly, saying, "Let them indeed inquire in Abel, and thus they finish (it)". [19] I am (one of the) covenanters of peace of the faithful ones of Israel. You are seeking to put to death a city and a mother (or, a mother city) in Israel; why are you destroying the inheritance of Yahweh?'

According to the critical apparatus, in v. 18, in place of the MT's 'and thus they finish (it)', the LXX has: καὶ ἐν Δαν εἰ ἐξέλιπον ἃ ἔθεντο οἱ πιστοὶ τοῦ Ισραελ in addition to many words from a duplicate version; the Old Latin [91.93.94] reads *et in Dan dicentes*; the Targum has (*lmš'l…*) *'m mšlmjn*. The LXX of 2 Sam. 20.16-19 is translated thus:

> [16] And a wise woman called from the wall and (she) said, 'Listen! Listen! Say now to Joab, "Draw near to this place", and I will speak to him'. [17] And he drew near to her, and the woman said, 'Are you Joab?' And he said, "I am". Then she said to him, 'Hear the words of your servant'. And Joab said, 'I am listening'. [18] And she said, saying, 'A word they spoke as of first importance saying, "Surely it was asked in Abel and in Dan whether what the faithful of Israel have set up has been eclipsed/come to an end; they will indeed inquire in Abel, and thus whether they have been eclipsed/come to an end". [19] I am a peaceable one of the strong ones of Israel; but you are seeking to destroy a city, even a mother city at that, in Israel—why have you chosen to drown the inheritance of the Lord?'

There is a tendency among critical scholars to adopt the LXX (and its Hebrew *Vorlage*) over the supposedly problematic MT as the preferred text.[328] In particular, at issue are the last two words of v. 18 and the first two words of v. 19. Specifically, the MT may be compared to a divergent Hebrew text, reconstructed on the basis of the LXX, in this way:

MT	שלמי אמוני ישראל	וכן הימו
Reconstruction[329]	אשר שמו אמוני ישראל	ובדן התמו

Thus, the LXX presupposed a Hebrew text according to which one was instructed to inquire at Abel and at Dan, if one desired to find a place at which old Israelite tradition and institutions were most faithfully kept. McCarter writes that 'the woman defends Abel as a model city. Here and in Dan, she says, one could expect to find the intentions of the founding fathers of Israel cherished and faithfully performed. Why, then, would Joab harm Abel?'[330] The difficulty with this reading is that it is hard to imagine that such a favorable tradition regarding the city of Dan would have been originally part of a document coming from Dtr. It seems preferable to follow the MT which is, in fact, intelligible, as Gordon has argued.[331] The LXX reading is not required to make sense of the text. According to the MT, the wise woman cites a well-known proverb about the wisdom of the inhabitants of Abel. Perhaps later editors were no longer familiar with the proverbial saying and, unsure of what to do with a text they no longer understood, emended it. This altered Hebrew text would have later served as the *Vorlage* for the LXX translators.[332] At the same

328. Samuel Rolles Driver, *Notes on the Hebrew Text of the Books of Samuel* (Oxford: Clarendon Press, 1890), pp. 265-66; Henry Preserved Smith, *A Critical and Exegetical Commentary on the Books of Samuel* (ICC; Edinburgh: T. & T. Clark, 1899), pp. 371-72; P. Kyle McCarter, Jr, *II Samuel: A New Translation with Introduction and Commentary* (AB, 9; Garden City, NY: Doubleday, 1984), pp. 428-30.

329. The most significant variation is שלמי in the MT and שמו in the reconstruction. McCarter writes that 'the variation of *śmw* and *šlmy* (< **šlmw*)…is to be explained by reference to the other examples of the interchange of *śym* and *šlm* cited by Talmon (1975.347)' (*II Samuel*, p. 429, citing Shermaryahu Talmon, 'The Textual Study of the Bible—New Outlook', in Frank Moore Cross and Shemaryahu Talmon [eds.], *Qumran and the History of the Biblical Text* [Cambridge, MA: Harvard University Press, 1975], pp. 321-400 [347]).

330. McCarter, *II Samuel*, p. 430.

331. Robert P. Gordon, 'The Variable Wisdom of Abel: The MT and Versions at 2 Samuel XX 18-19', *VT* 43 (1993), pp. 215-26.

332. There is as yet no manuscript evidence from Qumran to support the Hebrew text reconstructed on the basis of the LXX.

time, however, allowance should be made for the (albeit remote) possibility that the Hebrew text behind the LXX is not later, but earlier, than that included in the DH. That is, one ought to consider the possibility that the Hebrew text reconstructed on the basis of the LXX preserves an early Israelite (= northern) tradition about the cities of Dan and Abel as seats of ancient, genuine Israelite institutions and tradition. As an early, northern tradition, it is characteristically pro-Israelite vis-à-vis Judah/Jerusalem/ Davidic innovations, and thus one would not expect it to have been used as a source by the Judean Dtr.

4. *The Books of Kings*

As a reference to the city in the north, Dan occurs in three passages in the books of Kings. 1 Kings 12 and 2 Kings 10 refer to the golden calves (the 'sins of Jeroboam', 2 Kgs 10.29) manufactured by Jeroboam I and erected at royal sanctuaries in the cities of Bethel and Dan; 1 Kings 15 mentions Dan among other cities in the northern part of the old territory of Naphtali that were conquered by the Syrian King, Ben-hadad, early in the ninth century. While these texts may contain a variety of older sources (reports, story fragments, etc.), their final form, shaped by the polemical Jerusalemite perspective, bears the unmistakable theological imprint of Dtr.

a. *1 Kings 12*
Although not as extensive, 1 Kings 12 is, with Judges 17–18, among the most significant parts of the Danite tradition in the Hebrew Bible. 1 Kings 12 begins with the acclamation of Rehoboam as king of 'all Israel'; this is soon followed, however, by the secession of the northern tribes (according to the Shilonite prophet, Ahijah; cf. 1 Kgs 11.11, 29-32) and their investiture of Jeroboam, the son of Nebat, as king over their portion of 'all Israel' in revolt against the 'House of David' (12.19-20). The chapter concludes in vv. 25-33 with an outline of the political and religious initiatives undertaken by Jeroboam I, including: (1) the setting up of a capital at Shechem and the fortification of Penuel in Transjordan; (2) the manufacture of two golden calves; (3) the establishment of Bethel and Dan as cult centers; (4) the founding of additional sanctuaries and the appointment of non-levitical priests; and (5) the further elevation of Bethel (and also Dan?) as the site of an annual festival to rival the New Year festival in Jerusalem. The significance of this text lies chiefly in its polemical stance against the politically motivated religious initiatives undertaken by Jeroboam in the frontier

cities of Dan and Bethel. The negative depiction of Dan in 1 Kgs 12.25-33 (v. 30 explicitly associates the city of Dan with the 'sin [of Jeroboam]') has overshadowed much of the remaining biblical and extra-biblical Danite tradition. 'Dan' (it seems) is always interpreted through the darkened lense traced to the supposed apostasy of Jeroboam at the city of that name depicted by Dtr. The text is translated as follows:

[25] Now Jeroboam fortified Shechem in the hill country of Ephraim and he resided in it; then he went out from there and he fortified Penuel. [26] Then Jeroboam said to himself: 'Now the kingdom shall return to the house of David. [27] If this people will go up to offer sacrifices in the house of Yahweh in Jerusalem, then the heart of this people will return to their lord, to Rehoboam the king of Judah; and they will kill me, and they will return to Rehoboam the king of Judah.' [28] So the king took counsel, and he made two calves of gold; and he said to them, 'It is enough of your going up to Jerusalem. Here is/are your god(s), O Israel, who brought you up from the land of Egypt.' [29] And he set up the one in Bethel; and the (other) one he put in Dan. [30] Now this matter became as a sin; the people went before the one as far as Dan. [31] And he made the houses of the high places; and he made priests from the whole of the people, who were not among the sons of Levi. [32] And Jeroboam made a festival in the eighth month, on the fifteenth day of the month, like the festival which is in Judah. And he went up upon the altar; thus he did in Bethel, in order to sacrifice to the calves which he had made. And he appointed in Bethel the priests of the high places which he had made. [33] And he went up upon the altar which he had made in Bethel on the fifteenth day of the eighth month, in the month which he devised on his own. So he made a festival for the sons of Israel, and he went up upon the altar to make sacrifices smoke.

[Notes on the MT:

Verse 27: The second occurrence of the demonstrative adjective 'this' ('then the heart of *this* people will return to their lord') is absent from the LXX. Since the MT of this text is well-balanced by the prior occurrence of the demonstrative in this verse, the MT is to be preferred. 'And they will kill me' is absent from a few medieval manuscripts of the Hebrew Old Testament and the Lucianic recension of the LXX. However, as this phrase is enveloped by comparable expressions concerning the anticipated action of the people, attention is drawn to it. The witness of the rest of the LXX tradition, together with Josephus (*Ant.* 8.225) and the (apparent) corroboration of Qumran, leads me to read the MT. 'And they will return to Rehoboam the king of Judah' at the end of this verse is absent from a few medieval manuscripts of the Hebrew Old Testament and the LXX; A. Jepsen (the editor of the books of Kings in *BHS*) considers this phrase to be an addition. While conceding the merits of this emendation, this phrase may serve a resumptive function following the central phrase 'and they will kill me', and for this reason the present translation reflects the MT.

Verse 28: For 'so (the king) took counsel', the LXX ^{Alexandrinus} reads καὶ ἐπορεύθη ('and he went'), but compare the remaining LXX tradition (LXX ^{Vaticanus} preserves a longer reading: καὶ ἐβουλεύσατο ὁ βασιλεὺς καὶ ἐπορεύθη, 'and the king deliberated and he went'). Jepsen suggests reading וילך ('and he went'). There is no Hebrew manuscript evidence to support this simple emendation, and the LXX tradition reinforces the inclusion of 'and he took counsel/deliberated'. Read the MT. For 'and he said *to them*', it is suggested that one read 'to the people'; compare the LXX. The referent in the MT is ambiguous (*lectio difficilior*); either the people or the golden calves (the immediate antecedent) may be intended. The LXX obviously clarifies a vague (and possibly humorous) Hebrew *Vorlage*. Read the earlier MT.

Verse 30: After 'as a sin', the Lucianic recension of the LXX adds τῷ Ισραελ (according to Jepsen, perhaps rightly). This may be understood as an effort to make explicit the guilty; that is, to situate the sin squarely within the Northern Kingdom, thus absolving the kingdom of Judah of any guilt tied to Jeroboam's golden calves. The shorter MT, which also has the support of the rest of the LXX tradition, is to be preferred. After 'before the one', Jepsen suggests the insertion of בת־אל ולפני האחד, so that the text would read: 'and the people went before the one (of) Bethel and before the one as far as Dan'. The MT, while not impossible, is difficult, since one expects mention of Bethel together with Dan. The Lucianic recension of the LXX adds καὶ πρὸ προσώπου τῆς ἄλλης εἰς Βαιθήλ *after* Dan, which may be an attempt to restore text that had been lost (Jepsen proposes that this was the result of homoioteleuton). The attractiveness of the Lucianic text is that it creates a fine chiasm with v. 29 (Bethel–Dan// Dan–Bethel). The MT (reflected in my translation) may be better understood as having suffered not from homoioteleuton (*BHS*), but from homoioarchton involving לפני האחד עד (see Gary N. Knoppers, *Two Nations Under God: The Deuteronomistic History of Solomon and the Dual Monarchies*. II. *The Reign of Jeroboam, the Fall of Israel, and the Reign of Josiah* [HSM, 53; 2 vols.; Atlanta: Scholars Press, 1994], p. 7).

Verse 31: For (literally) 'house (of high places)', the LXX and the Vulgate read the plural ('houses'; in the Hebrew it is a matter of shifting the yod from medial to final position) with 1 Kgs 13.32. However, since the MT may also be understood as a plural, the MT may be accepted (see Knoppers' note [*Two Nations Under God*, II, p. 27] about the 'composite plural' [GKC, 124r]).

Verse 32: 'And he went up upon the altar; thus he did in Bethel' reflects (although not exactly) the first part of v. 33. For this reason, Jepsen suggests that it be deleted from v. 32. Lacking manuscript support for this change, the MT (although it appears expansionistic) is to be preferred. For 'thus (he did in Bethel)', one medieval manuscript of the Hebrew Old Testament and the LXX reads the relative particle ('which') with v. 33. This may be an attempt to harmonize similar texts. Read the MT, which is a sensible text.

Verse 33: 'And he went up upon the altar which he had made' is absent from the Syriac ^{Walton's London Polyglot}; a variant reading to bβ (the last portion of v. 33) to be deleted (so Jepsen)? The MT is supported by the LXX and other Versions, and is the preferred reading. 'In Bethel' is absent from the LXX. For 'in the month (which he devised on his own)', the LXX reads ἐν τῇ ἑορτῇ (= בחג), 'for the festival'. Apparently the LXX misunderstood the MT's focus on the date of the festival, preferring

instead to criticize the festival itself. Read the MT. For מלבד, several medieval manuscripts of the Hebrew Old Testament read with the *qere* (with the pronominal suffix),
מִלְּבֹו (compare the Versions); thus the text is to be read (so Jepsen). The vocalized
form of the MT occurs nowhere else. Since resh and waw are graphically confused (P.
Kyle McCarter, *Textual Criticism: Recovering the Text of the Hebrew Bible* [GBS;
Philadelphia: Fortress Press, 1986], p. 47), it is reasonable to suppose that dalet and
waw may be similarly confused. Thus the *qere* is readily accounted for, and is reflected
in the present translation.]

Knoppers has observed that the present passage is pivotal in the depiction
of Jeroboam I in the Hebrew Bible. While the preceding references to
Jeroboam son of Nebat are positive (in 1 Kgs 11.26 he is first introduced
as a capable and responsible servant of Solomon), those that follow 1 Kgs
12.25-33 are entirely negative.[333] Jeroboam appears in 1 Kings 11 as one
who raised his hand against 'the king'.[334] If Solomon is identified as the
king in question, then Jeroboam's rebellious action is justified, however, in
the opinion of the narrator, since at this point in the story of Solomon, the
king has 'loved many foreign women...and his heart was not true to
Yahweh his God' (1 Kgs 11.1, 4), and Yahweh has decided to tear the
kingdom away from Solomon. Ahijah the prophet from Shiloh (cf. Judg.
18.31) subsequently reveals to Jeroboam that he (Jeroboam) has been
divinely chosen to rule over ten of the tribes of Israel. Throughout 1 Kgs
12.1-20, Jeroboam plays a largely silent, passive role, and it is Rehoboam
who is cast in the more negative light. Beyond the present passage, however, Jeroboam is portrayed in a wholly negative way. References to the
'sins of Jeroboam' (the phrase is grounded in 1 Kgs 12.30) run like a constant refrain throughout the history of the Northern Kingdom (1 Kgs
13.33-34; 14.16; 15.26, 30, 34; 16.2, 7, 19, 25, 31; 22.51; 2 Kgs 3.3;
10.29; 13.2, 6, 11; 14.24; 15.9, 18, 24, 28; 17.21-22). It is apparent that, in
the final analysis, while 1 Kgs 12.25-33 may be interpreted as a neutral
account of Jeroboam's political and religious initiatives necessitated by the
circumstances of the time, when read in the full light of the Deuteronomistic narrative that follows there can be little question that the portrait of
Jeroboam in the present passage is intended to be disparaging.[335]

333. Knoppers, *Two Nations Under God*, II, p. 7.
334. Presumably the king is Solomon, but the text is ambiguous. Might Rehoboam
be intended? That is, does this text (in light of 1 Kgs 12) remember Jeroboam as one
who rebelled against Solomon's successor?
335. Clear indications of the Deuteronomistic perspective in this text include:
Jeroboam's (ironic) concession that the 'House of Yahweh' is in Jerusalem (rather than

One is able to identify in 1 Kgs 12.25-33 the probable historical reality of Jeroboam's political and cultic initiatives. That is, by 'reading between the lines', one may be able to reconstruct the actual, historical character of Jeroboam's tenth-century cult.

While there is good reason to conclude that Jeroboam did indeed do those things Dtr accuses him in this text of doing, it is reasonable to suppose that his intention was never to engage in heterodox religious practices. It was probably not the case that Jeroboam promoted foreign religious ideas, or instituted radically new religious practices, since his purpose was to secure control of the nascent kingdom in the north, not alienate his constituency. Politically speaking, it would have been counter-productive (even disastrous) for Jeroboam to have tried to establish an alternative religion when the new nation was in such turmoil. Certainly the introduction of new religious initiatives, that would have been interpreted by the Israelite populace as other than Yahwistic, would have been unnecessarily risky to Jeroboam's political objectives. It is more likely that Jeroboam intended to maintain, even demonstrate more clearly, continuity with the old Israelite religious traditions antecedent to the perceived novelties in Jerusalem ushered in under David and Solomon. Thus, Toews has recently offered a persuasive argument for the archaic character of each of Jeroboam's initiatives: the golden calves, the multiplication of religious sites, the royal appointment of priests, and the institution of a harvest festival in the Fall. All of these, it is maintained, have antecedents in the earlier history and ancient traditions of Israel; by these, it is argued, Jeroboam sought to 'out-archaize' David.[336] Toews concludes that his investigation demonstrates that, far from being apostate innovations which incurred the wrath of his prophetic contemporaries,

> Jeroboam officially sponsored a cult that followed in line with Israel's ancient traditions. According to all indications he encouraged the traditional Israelite devotion to El=Yahweh... [T]his conclusion has been argued both positively and negatively. It has been argued positively beginning with the evidence of the cultic cry *hinnēh 'ĕlōhêkā yiśrā'ēl 'ăšer he'ĕlûkā mē'eres*

in Bethel or Dan); Jeroboam's equally ironic identification of Rehoboam as the northern population's 'lord'; the implication that multiple calves mean multiple gods; and (if v. 30a belongs to the Deuteronomistic edition of the text) the evaluation of Jeroboam's construction of the calves and their placement in Bethel and Dan as a 'sin'.

336. Toews, *Monarchy and Religious Institution in Israel*, pp. 41-107. On 'out-archaizing' David, see Wellhausen, *Prolegomena*, p. 283; Cross, *Canaanite Myth and Hebrew Epic*, pp. 73-74, 199.

misrāyim on the grounds that in the Hebrew Bible formulae concerning the Exodus only attribute that act of deliverance either to Yahweh or to El. It has been argued negatively on the grounds that evidence of opposition to Jeroboam's policies by his contemporaries is completely lacking. If Jeroboam had abandoned the ancient traditions of Israel one would expect opposition to have arisen, and if Jeroboam in his initiatives with the calf iconography had sponsored an innovatively 'Baalized' cult one would expect evidence of opposition on that account from persons such as Ahijah, Elijah, Jehu, or DtrH.[337]

He further proposes that only under the influence of a developing icono-clasm (the beginning of which he traces to the prophet Hosea) and the centralization interest of the Deuteronomistic movement in Judah did Jeroboam's initiatives become interpreted as apostate and idolatrous inno-vations, and as the sin that led to the eventual fall of the Northern Kingdom (2 Kgs 17.7-23; although only v. 16 explicitly links the fall of Israel to Jeroboam's activity).[338]

In the present text, Dtr has characterized Jeroboam as the leader of a faction, who sought to imprint a particular ideology on his movement in order to distinguish it from the legitimate Yahweh-cult in Jerusalem.[339] According to the anthropological literature, a fundamental characteristic of a faction is a focus on the leader around whom others are gathered for a particular purpose.[340] This is precisely what Dtr has done in the case of Jeroboam. At the unmistakable center of 1 Kgs 12.25-33 is the figure of Jeroboam; the narrator goes to great length to depict Jeroboam as the source of Israel's troubles: *Jeroboam* fortified; *Jeroboam* said to himself, and then took counsel; *Jeroboam* made two calves of gold and set them up in Bethel and in Dan; *Jeroboam* made the houses of the high places; *Jeroboam* made non-Levites priests; *Jeroboam* made a rival festival

---

337. Toews, *Monarchy and Religious Institution in Israel*, p. 145 (cf. the similar summary statement on p. 147); see also Wellhausen, *Prolegomena*, p. 283. Neither, it should be noted, does the prophet Amos rail against any questionable (calf) icono-graphy at Bethel, although he did prophesy at the royal sanctuary there (Amos 7.10-13).

338. Toews, *Monarchy and Religious Institution in Israel*, pp. 151-72.

339. According to Jeremy Boissevain (*Friends of Friends: Networks, Manipulators and Coalitions* [New York: St Martin's Press, 1974], pp. 192-205), fundamental to the existence of a faction (defined as a temporary alliance constructed around a particular individual to achieve limited purposes) is the phenomenon of rivalry. That is, a faction must be opposed to something or someone, or some other faction ('a faction supports a person engaged in a hostile competition for honour and resources' [p. 194]).

340. Boissevain, *Friends of Friends*, p. 192.

according to his own design. The Deuteronomistic reference to the 'sins of Jeroboam' throughout the books of Kings likewise corresponds to this characterization. In this way, the demise of the breakaway Northern Kingdom is laid squarely at the feet of Jeroboam I. It remains unknown whether Jeroboam himself (or the Northern Kingdom) ever perceived the formation of the Northern Kingdom of Israel as a faction; it is as likely that the northern population understood itself as the heirs of Israel's ancestral traditions, and the ideological legacy of David and Solomon as a division from the premonarchic identity of Israel. The biblical material about Jeroboam and the Northern Kingdom of Israel has come to us through the interpretive framework of Dtr. Nevertheless, what Dtr sought to characterize (caricature?) as new, anti-Yahweh, polytheistic, and iconic in Jeroboam's kingdom was, in reality, probably a return to an older form of Yahweh religion that Israel knew from its ancestral traditions, before the time of David and Solomon and the royal theology associated with Jerusalem and its Temple.

While Jeroboam's actions with respect to Bethel and Dan are usually interpreted theologically as religious apostasy (already in the biblical tradition—see the references to the 'sins of Jeroboam', *passim*; Amos 5.4-5; Hos. 10.5; 13.2), this is partly due to the issue having been cast largely in religious terms in 1 Kings 12. However, the reality is that in the ancient world politics and religion were never completely dissociated from each other; rather, religion was embedded in either politics or kinship system.[341] A careful reading of 1 Kgs 12.25-33 reveals the political interests of Jeroboam (as interpreted by Dtr) that motivated his initiatives. First, v. 25, which reports the fortification of Shechem as the royal residence as well as Penuel in Transjordan, is concerned with clear political actions. This verse sets the scene for what follows in vv. 26-33: in all of this, Jeroboam was primarily interested in establishing himself as king over the ten tribes that together comprised the Northern Kingdom of Israel. Second, in vv. 26-27,

---

341. Malina and Rohrbaugh, *Social-Science Commentary on the Synoptic Gospels*, pp. 256-57: 'There could be domestic religion run by "family" personnel and/or political religion run by "political" personnel, but no religion in a separate, abstract sense run by purely "religious" personnel. Thus the Temple was never a religious institution somehow separate from political institutions' (p. 257). On the association of politics and religion in this text, see also Knoppers, *Two Nations Under God*, II, p. 37; Long, *1 Kings*, p. 141. See also Boissevain (*Friends of Friends*, p. 194), who comments that the competition between factions for honor and resources makes the rivalry political.

the narrator permits the reader a glimpse into the private thoughts of Jeroboam. (Of course, since this comes from the narrator, whom the reader must imagine did not himself know Jeroboam's thoughts, its reliable use is subject to question. This is the *narrator's* explanation for Jeroboam's actions, not Jeroboam's own testimony for why he did what he did.) What the reader learns is that Jeroboam feared the return of the Israelite population to the 'house of David…to their lord, to Rehoboam the king of Judah'. It was in order to maintain his hold over the people in the north that Jeroboam arrived at the decision to construct the two calves of gold—intended, in some way, to represent the power and the presence of the God (= Yahweh) who brought Israel out of Egypt—which he set up at Bethel and Dan; to found additional sanctuaries, presumably throughout the land; to invest non-Levites as priests; and to initiate a festival to rival the one in Jerusalem. Jeroboam's initiatives are better understood, then, as religious means to achieve a political goal.[342]

Since Jeroboam's actions need not necessarily be interpreted negatively, the conclusion to be drawn is that it is the final editor's Judean bias that contributes to the overall negative tenor of the passage, according to which Jeroboam is guilty of introducing an idolatrous iconography and heretical cult. There can be little doubt that the text of 1 Kgs 12.25-33, from the hand of Dtr, is intended to provide an explicit denunciation of the cult instituted by Jeroboam I. A disinterested (or Israelite) writer of history (even of a religious history) would probably tell a very different story. By reading the text as it is, in the context of the DH, one experiences the full force of the southern, Jerusalemite polemic against the Northern Kingdom and its first king. It is further the case that this second level of reading, with its literary-rhetorical force, has more greatly influenced the interpretation of Dan elsewhere in the biblical and post-biblical traditions.

The result is that Jeroboam is guilty by anachronism. The biblical material critical of Jeroboam and his religious initiatives derives from a much later period, and may have been intended to explain the fall of the Northern Kingdom in 722 BCE. According to this Deuteronomistic interpretation of history, Israel fell because the nation and its kings followed its first king, Jeroboam, who instituted an illegitimate cult, went after other gods (of his own making, 1 Kgs 12.28; cf. Judg. 17.3-4; 18.24, 31), and

---

342. Choon-Leong Seow, 'The First and Second Books of Kings: Introduction, Commentary, and Reflections', in Leander E. Keck *et al.* (eds.), *The New Interpreter's Bible* (12 vols.; Nashville: Abingdon Press, 1999), III, pp. 1-295 (104). See also Cross, *Canaanite Myth and Hebrew Epic*, p. 279.

abandoned Yahweh.[343] Nevertheless, since there is lacking any (near) contemporary criticism of Jeroboam's religious initiatives, it must be concluded that his activities were not perceived to be heterodox at the time (cf. Amos 7.10-13, where the Judean prophet goes to Bethel but says nothing about/against a calf-image). Thus, 1 Kgs 12.25-33 cannot be held up as a reliable source for understanding the reaction to Jeroboam and his cultic actions in the tenth century. This text is a judgment of Jeroboam by Dtr, who applied criteria anachronistically in order to achieve his objective.

For the present analysis, which is interested in interpreting Dan in the biblical traditions, this text reveals that Jeroboam established a royal sanctuary at the city of Dan, in which he erected a golden calf (1 Kgs 12.29). Of significance is the hypothesis of Eduard Nielsen, who has called into question the historical reliability of the Danite sanctuary in 1 Kgs 12.29-30. Simply put, he doubts that reference to Dan belonged to the original form of the text.[344] According to his reconstruction of the tradition (which requires radical surgery on the biblical text and is not compelling), the text was originally concerned only with a single golden calf (cf. Exod. 32) at Bethel. Nielsen reconstructs an original reading of 1 Kgs 12.29-30 as follows: 'And he placed the calf (העגל) at Bethel and the people went in procession before it even unto Dan'.[345] That is, Israelites from as far away as Dan—the northernmost city of the Israelite kingdom—went in ritual procession before the single golden calf set up by Jeroboam in the sanctuary at Bethel. According to Nielsen,

> the reference to *two* calves and to the installation of one of them at Dan is more probably due to a misinterpretation of the words of v. 30b: 'So the people went before the one even unto Dan'... For later traditionists to make Jeroboam construct *two* calves, and install the other in Dan, was quite a natural mistake, partly in view of v. 30b, and partly because Bethel, as the sanctuary on the southern border, formed the counterpart to Dan.[346]

343. Judah, for its part, also most likely had a long history of multiple sanctuaries. See most recently Beth Alpert Nakhai, 'The Meaning of Religious Centralization for the Israelite Monarchy', an unpublished paper presented at the 'Archaeological Excavations and Discoveries: Illuminating the Biblical World Section', Annual Meeting of the Society of Biblical Literature, Boston, MA (22 November 1999).

344. Eduard Nielsen, *Shechem: A Traditio-Historical Investigation* (Copenhagen: G.E.C. Gad, 1959), pp. 195-96.

345. Nielsen, *Shechem*, p. 196. The presupposed Hebrew text is: וישם את־העגל בבית־אל / וילכו העם לפני האחד עד־דן.

346. Nielsen, *Shechem*, p. 196.

There is sufficient reason to challenge Nielsen's reconstruction of both the text and the tradition of a single calf/single sanctuary. First, there is, on the one hand, absolutely no manuscript evidence to support his text. While v. 30 *may* have suffered in its transmission (cf. the Lucianic recension of the LXX), Nielsen's reading is wholly unique. On the other hand, the MT is unambiguous about Jeroboam having constructed two calves of gold (v. 28), and having set them up—one each—in Bethel and in Dan (v. 29).[347] Second, driving Nielsen's reconstruction of the tradition seems to be an assumption that since the Jerusalem temple posed such an imminent challenge to Jeroboam's nascent kingdom, Jeroboam required only a single rival, royal sanctuary in close proximity to Jerusalem. Bethel, on Israel's southern border, fulfilled this need. Nielsen does not consider how a sanctuary at Dan, on the northern border and far removed from Jerusalem, could have prevented Israelites from leaving for Jerusalem. It must be noted, however, that relative proximity to Jerusalem is nowhere stated to have been Jeroboam's sole or even primary criterion in the selection of his cultic sites. The sanctuary in Dan would certainly have held tremendous appeal for the Israelite population in the vicinity of the region of Galilee, for whom it would have been a local shrine. What is more, a multiplicity of sanctuaries (Bethel, Dan, and 'the houses of the high places', v. 31; cf. the ancestral traditions) would be interpreted by Jeroboam's population as

347. The multiplication of royal shrines and cultic images has been interpreted by some scholars as part of Dtr's polemic against Jeroboam. According to this view, Jeroboam was responsible for propagating a form of polytheism (polytheistic Yahwism?) in the Northern Kingdom (see James A. Montgomery, *A Critical and Exegetical Commentary on the Books of Kings* [ICC; New York: Charles Scribner's Sons, 1951], p. 255; Harald Motzki, 'Ein Beitrag zum Problem des Stierkultes in der Religionsgeschichte Israels', *VT* 25 [1975], pp. 475-76; Ernst Würthwein, *Das Erste Buch der Könige, Kapital 1–16* [ATD, 11.1; Göttingen: Vandenhoeck & Ruprecht, 1977], p. 164.) The Hebrew text of Jeroboam's declaration before the calf images is ambiguous. Is it 'Here are your gods, O Israel, who brought you up from the land of Egypt', or 'Here is your God, O Israel, who brought you up from the land of Egypt?' While the noun in question is plural in form (אלהיך), the same noun is used elsewhere in reference to Israel's single deity. Neither does the verb provide an unambiguous answer to the dilemma: does the plural form of the verb (העלוך) imply multiple deities, or does its form simply correspond to the *form* of the noun, which nevertheless denotes a singular deity (see Gen. 20.13; 35.7; 2 Sam. 7.23; 2 Chron. 32.15; cf. GKC, 145h Rem.; Exod. 32.4, 8, raise another problem, since the plural demonstrative [אלה] is used with a single image)? Of course, the Deuteronomistic Historian may certainly have intended this noun and verb to be understood as plurals, thus charging that Jeroboam's cult was polytheistic.

a challenge to the developing policy of cultic centralization in Judah that resulted from the founding of the royal/national shrine in the capital city. Third, Biran's excavations at Tell Dan have recovered evidence of a large sacred precinct (measuring 60 × 45 m, in Area T) and a number of religious artifacts attributable (on the basis of ceramic evidence) to the time of Jeroboam.[348]

It is likely that this tradition in 1 Kings 12 has influenced the interpretation of much of the rest of the Danite tradition in and beyond the Hebrew Bible. In Jeremiah, Dan is the place through which the enemy from the north passes en route to Jerusalem (if the enemy is not imagined as actually originating from Dan). Hippolytus takes up the antagonism between Israel and Judah, Dan/Bethel and Jerusalem, and traces the descent of Antichrist to the tribe of Dan, just as Christ was descended from the tribe of Judah. The association of 'sin' and the idols of Jeroboam with the tribe of Dan in the north reappears in the Jewish Legends, once more indicating the way in which city and tribe (and ancestor?) are tied together. While it may, of course, preserve historical recollection, the possibility exists that the blasphemer in Leviticus 24 is identified as a Danite under the influence of this passage. Due to the prominence of the work of Dtr in the Hebrew Bible, it seems as though every reference to Dan—the ancestor, the tribe, the city—or an individual Danite falls under the shadow of 1 Kgs 12.25-33.

b. *1 Kings 15*

According to 1 Kgs 15.20, Ben-hadad of Damascus conquered the city of Dan, together with a number of other cities in the 'land of Naphtali'. According to the report, a border conflict between Israel and Judah precipitated the Syrian attack.[349] King Baasha of Israel invaded the kingdom of Judah and began to fortify the city of Ramah along the strategically significant main route to Jerusalem from the north. As such, the undertaking posed a threat to Judah and Jerusalem (15.17). Evidently unable to halt Baasha's building program on his own, King Asa of Judah sent money from the temple and royal treasuries to King Ben-hadad in Damascus in

---

348. Biran, *Biblical Dan*, pp. 165-83.

349. The consensus among critical scholars is that the border war narrated in 1 Kgs 15.16-21 comes from a source (form-critically designated a 'report'; perhaps an archival source from Judah) available to the Deuteronomistic redactor, who reproduced it without interpolation or editorial comment (see G.H. Jones, *1 and 2 Kings*, I, pp. 282-85; Long, *1 Kings*, p. 168; John Gray, *I & II Kings, A Commentary* [OTL; London: SCM Press, 1964], p. 319).

order to enlist the latter's help. After reminding Ben-hadad of the treaty that existed between Judah and Syria, Asa commanded Ben-hadad to break the latter's treaty with Baasha of Israel. The expectation was that an unallied Baasha would be compelled to leave off his fortification of Ramah. Ben-hadad acceded to the king of Judah's request and sent troops against the cities of Israel: 'So they (MT reads "he") attacked Ijon, Dan, Abel-beth-maacah, and all the Kinneroth; against the entire land of Naphtali' (15.20).[350] The Syrian attack had its desired result: Baasha, threatened on his northern border, left off the fortification of Ramah in the south and retreated to Tirzah, the capital city of the Northern Kingdom.

There is some evidence of the attack of Ben-hadad in the archaeological record at Dan. According to Biran's excavations, Stratum IV (second half of tenth–beginning of ninth centuries) shows some signs of a conflagration in the area of the temple complex: stones bear evidence of fire, and a layer of ash was found in the store rooms.[351] There is not, however, evidence of the complete destruction of the site.[352] It does not appear that this reference to Dan in a historical report has influenced other biblical or extra-biblical Danite traditions.

c. *2 Kings 10*

At the end of the reign of the Israelite king, Jehu, it is stated that 'he exterminated the Baal from Israel' (2 Kgs 10.28). There follows immediately after this rather positive statement, however, a caveat: 'Only the sins of Jeroboam the son of Nebat, by which he caused Israel to sin, Jehu did not turn away from (going) after them—the calves of gold which were in Bethel and in Dan' (2 Kgs 10.29). This specification of the 'sins of Jeroboam' as the golden calves at Bethel and at Dan is otherwise unattested in the Hebrew Bible. While it is certain that Dtr had these objects in mind whenever he wrote about the 'sins of Jeroboam', only here are the calves of gold mentioned.

---

350. On the *possible* relationship between this campaign against Israel in the early ninth century and the recently discovered 'Tel Dan Inscription' see Biran and Naveh, 'An Aramaic Stele Fragment from Tel Dan', pp. 95-98 (cf. the alternative scenarios which date the inscription in the latter part of the ninth century in *idem*, 'The Tel Dan Inscription: A New Fragment', pp. 17-18; Baruch Halpern, 'The Stela from Dan: Epigraphic and Historical Considerations', *BASOR* 296 [1994], pp. 63-80 [69-74]).

351. Biran, *Biblical Dan*, pp. 181-83.

352. Biran (*Biblical Dan*, p. 183) correlates this with the choice of wording in 1 Kgs 15.20: Ben-hadad 'smote' the cities when he invaded Israel.

The reason for this cannot be known for certain. It has been suggested (*BHK* [3rd edn], *BHS*) that the latter portion of this verse was added to the text some time later (the LXX agrees with the MT). This is no more than speculation. I prefer to see this specification as having been necessitated by the fact that the source for the reign of Jehu available to Dtr had little that was negative. According to 2 Kings 9–10, Jehu showed himself to be a wholly faithful Yahwist, so zealous for Yahweh (10.16) in fact that he slaughtered every worshiper of Baal in the Northern Kingdom and destroyed the temple of Baal in the capital city of Samaria (10.21-27).[353] Obviously, this presented a challenge to Dtr, for whom no king of Israel could escape a negative theological appraisal. For this reason, the Deuteronomistic redactor needed to make clear Jehu's failures—all other evidence to the contrary not withstanding. Thus, in his summary evaluation, Dtr (whose sources did *not* indicate that Jehu *also* destroyed the idols and the sanctuaries at Bethel and Dan) criticizes Jehu for following in the 'sins of Jeroboam'—that is, 'the calves of gold which were in Bethel and in Dan'. In this way, together with 1 Kings 12 (to which 2 Kgs 10.29 refers), this text casts a dark shadow of sin/apostasy over the Danite tradition in and beyond the Hebrew Bible.

5. *'From Dan as far as Beersheba'*

On seven occasions in the Former Prophets there occurs the expression 'from Dan as far as Beersheba' (מדן ועד־באר שבע): Judg. 20.1; 1 Sam. 3.20; 2 Sam. 3.10; 17.11; 24.2, 15; 1 Kgs 5.5 (ET 4.25). In each case, the reference to Dan is to the city in the north, at the northern border of Israel (its southern counterpart is Beersheba).[354] The historical context for each occurrence of the expression is (ostensibly) in the period before the division of David and Solomon's Kingdom into the kingdoms of Israel in the north and Judah in the south. In every occurrence but one (2 Sam. 24.15), the phrase appears in conjunction with some other descriptor of the

353. Although it is an argument from silence, the story of Jehu may also be enlisted as evidence in support of the hypothesis that the calf images in Bethel and in Dan were not perceived as incompatible with legitimate Yahwism at this time. Nowhere in 2 Kgs 9–10 (apart from Dtr's evaluative remarks at the end of ch. 10) do the calves of gold present a threat to the authentic worship of Yahweh.

354. It is probably the case that Dan and Beersheba represent important points in the northern and southern parts of the land, respectively, and do not, themselves, represent the exact boundary points (so Kallai, *Historical Geography of the Bible*, p. 309).

entirety of Israel ('all the sons of Israel'; 'all Israel'; 'all the tribes of Israel'; 'Israel and Judah/Judah and Israel'). For this reason the scholarly consensus is that this phrase was used as 'a conventional way of describing the full extent of the United Kingdom of Israel'.[355]

While the precise antiquity of the phrase cannot be known for certain, it is at least possible that it comes from the time of David.[356] 2 Samuel 24 narrates David's census, a story that culminates with the purchase of the threshing floor of Araunah, upon which was ultimately constructed Solomon's temple. In addition to the occurrence of the phrase 'from Dan as far as Beersheba', twice in this chapter (24.2, 15) the cities of Dan and Beersheba are mentioned individually in the description of the census itself (24.5-8). This at least suggests that the phrase may have had its origin in the Davidic census of the land.[357] It is significant to observe that there appear no negative connotations with this phrase in the DH. This is somewhat surprising in light of the otherwise disparaging evaluation of Dan elsewhere in this corpus. Therefore, like the mention of the city of Dan in 1 Kings 15, the phrase 'from Dan as far as Beersheba' most likely was not coined by the Deuteronomistic redactor, but was so well integrated into his source material that he could neither alter nor omit it.[358]

6. *Summary: Dan in the Former Prophets*

The results of the preceding study of the occurrences of Dan in the books of Joshua–2 Kings may be summarized as follows. While the date of the material in Joshua 13–19 and in Joshua 21 remains uncertain, there is good reason to locate the former in the tenth century, and to recognize the list in the latter as dependent on the details in Joshua 13–19. Whether the final form of the list of levitical cities in Joshua 21 is best dated to the tenth or eighth or sixth century remains an open question. There is no question,

355. McCarter, *II Samuel*, p. 114; R.W. Klein, *1 Samuel*, p. 34; G.H. Jones, *1 and 2 Kings*, I, p. 147.

356. In the preceding discussion of Judg. 17–18, it was noted that Israel probably did not gain control over the area around the city of Dan until the time of David.

357. While some interpolations may have been made subsequently to the original story in 2 Sam. 24, McCarter identifies the original story as a 'public document' from the time of David; cf. Na'aman, *Borders and Districts*, p. 45.

358. Since the phrase begins with Dan in the north, and ends with Beersheba in the south, one may speculate that the source used by Dtr originated in the northern part of the land. Alternatively, the prominence of the place given Dan in the expression may reflect David's effort to strengthen his ties to the north as he consolidated his kingdom.

however, about the location of the levitical cities assigned from the terri-tory of the tribe of Dan: they are in the south. If this particular list origi-nated in the exilic period, then it is evidence of the persistence of the tradition (if not the actual settlement) of Danite territory in this southern territory. According to these texts, the tribe of Dan occupied a territory in the hill country to the west of the territory of Benjamin, north/northwest of the city of Jerusalem. That the tribe of Dan continued to dwell in this terri-tory during the tenth century cannot be demonstrated from these texts alone. Nevertheless, at the very least, such a memory persisted into this period, to which the compiler of the book of Joshua was faithful. It is the conclusion of this study that the earlier form of Joshua 19 did not include mention of the Danite migration northward and the conquest of Leshem. Josh. 19.47 in the MT is best understood as an interpolation by a later hand; the LXX is altogether silent at this point about any action on the part of the tribe of Dan.

The social world reflected in these texts is that of a simple agrarian society in which the preindustrial city and its surrounding villages existed interdependently in a single system. Key evidence from the biblical tradi-tions includes not only the repeated mention of 'these cities and their villages' throughout Joshua 13–19, but also the identification of the Levites as administrative officials supported by a portion of the peasant farmers' tribute to the king.

In the book of Judges, Dan occurs most often in reference to the tribe. In Judges 1, Dan is the last of the Israelite tribes mentioned in a report of their settlement of Canaan. The inability of the Danites to settle their in-heritance is contrasted with Judah's litany of successes in the first half of the chapter. The negative portrayal of Dan in Judges 1 is probably to be traced to the perspective of the (exilic) Deuteronomistic redactor who inserted Judges 1 into the original edition of the DH. For this reason, it is difficult to reconstruct the early history of this Israelite tribe on the basis of the portrayal of Dan in this text. While lacking in detail, the mention of Dan in the Song of Deborah (Judg. 5) is likely to preserve some of the earliest information about this tribe. According to this text, the Danites were, in addition to being members of some form of Israelite association, dependent on other, neighboring groups for economic support. Specifi-cally, a significant portion of the tribe of Dan became clients of their sea-coast neighbors (either Canaanites or Philistines). While Dan, along with Reuben, Gilead, and Asher, comes in for a rather harsh censure in the catalog of tribes in Judg. 5.14-18, a social-science interpretation of these verses provides a new model for understanding the social reality in which the members of these tribes lived, and so an apologetic explanation for their absence from the Israelite battle against the Canaanites.

Other references in Judges are to an individual Danite (Samson) and to the city Laish, renamed Dan in the story of the Danite migration. I have argued in the present study that the stories of the Danite hero, Samson, and the Danite migration account in Judges 17–18 were, from the perspective of the tribe of Dan, originally positive narratives. The negative evaluation that appears in the final form of these texts is best traced to the hand of a later editor. Thus, on the basis of folklore analysis, social-scientific criticism, and redaction criticism, I have concluded that the Samson stories were originally favorable tales told among the Danites in order to inspire and encourage this marginalized and oppressed minority group in Israel. It is only at a later stage that the stories and the hero at their center suffer a negative judgment from an editor who situated these stories where they are in the Hebrew canon—after both the Nazirite Law in Numbers 6 and the other judges stories (Judg. 3–12). In each of the two hypotheses I developed for interpreting Judges 17–18, I suggested that the earlier form of the tradition in these chapters was in no way critical of the tribe of Dan or their religious practices. It is only from the perspective of a later editor (Hypothesis One: exilic; Hypothesis Two: ninth century, in Judah) that the cult image, priesthood, and establishment of a tribal sanctuary at the city of Laish/Dan fall under harsh criticism.

All occurrences of Dan in the books of Kings refer to the city in the north of the land. 1 Kings 12.25-33 describe the cultic actions taken by Jeroboam I in the border cities of Bethel and Dan. Following other scholars, I argued that Jeroboam's activity is better understood as anything but innovative. Important in the interpretation of these verses in 1 Kings, however, is the strong Deuteronomistic polemic against Jeroboam, according to which the cult images, the priesthood, the festival calendar, and location of the royal shrines in the Northern Kingdom are all negatively evaluated. Together with the final form of Judges 17–18, this text has functioned to cast a shadow over many of the biblical and extra-biblical traditions about Dan. Less influential is 1 Kgs 15.20, which simply mentions Dan among other cities conquered by Ben-hadad of Syria in the ninth century. Finally, 2 Kgs 10.29 specifies the 'sins of Jeroboam' as the calves of gold set up in Bethel and Dan. This part of Dtr's theological appraisal of the Israelite king, Jehu, was necessary since the account of Jehu's reign available to him was insufficiently negative. In addition to these occurrences, Dan appears seven times in Judges–1 Kings in the expression 'from Dan as far as Beersheba'. I have argued that this neutral expression, used in Dtr's source material, was so well received that it could not be altered—even in a composition which elsewhere consistently refers disparagingly to Dan.

Chapter 4

INTERPRETING DAN IN THE LATTER PROPHETS

1. *The Book of the Prophet Jeremiah*

Dan occurs in two passages in the book of Jeremiah: 4.15-17 and 8.14-17. Both of these references appear in oracles of impending judgment related to the coming of the 'foe from the north' against Judah (cf. 1.13-15; 6.1, 22; 10.22; 25.9; 46.24; 47.2-3). The early church father Irenaeus made much of the mention of Dan in Jer. 8.16, interpreting the coming enemy as Antichrist whose origin is in the *tribe* of Dan:

> And Jeremiah does not merely point out his sudden coming, but he even indicates the tribe from which he shall come, where he says, 'We shall hear the voice of his swift horses from Dan; the whole earth shall be moved by the voice of the neighing of his galloping horses: he shall also come and devour the earth, and the fulness thereof, the city also, and they that dwell therein'. This, too, is the reason that this tribe is not reckoned in the Apocalypse along with those which are saved.[1]

In this way, Irenaeus contributed to the largely negative portrayal of Dan in post-biblical literature. In fact, Irenaeus's interpretation tells us only about Irenaeus and the predominance of the Deuteronomistic theology in and beyond the Hebrew Bible, and has nothing to do with the context of Jeremiah. Dan in Jeremiah does not refer to the tribe of that name. The mention of Dan in these passages is benign and fundamentally about the geography of Palestine. In both Jer. 4.15-17 and 8.14-17, the reference is to the city of Dan at the northern boundary of Israel (cf. the expression 'from Dan as far as Beersheba'). The perspective is that of an inhabitant of Judah or Jerusalem.[2]

---

1. Irenaeus, *Against Heresies* 30.2.
2. That Judah would continue to acknowledge Dan as a national boundary point, even after the Fall of Samaria and the Northern Kingdom to the Assyrians in 722, may be due to the continued Israelite presence in the region (Jer. 3.12; cf. 1 Kgs 17.21-28;

a. *Jeremiah 4*

According to Jer. 4.15-17, Dan and the hill country of Ephraim (set in parallel; cf. Judg. 18) are specific locations from which proclamations are made concerning the coming of adversaries from a distant land. Since the order Dan, then Ephraim, represents movement toward Judah and Jerusalem, there is a sense of urgency created by this text—the enemy is approaching quickly, and the terrifying news of his advent travels fast:

[15] קול מגיד מדן
ומשמיע און מהר אפרים:
[16] הזכירו לגוים הנה השמיעו על־ירושלם
נצרים באים מארץ המרחק
ויתנו על־ערי יהודה קולם:
[17] כשמרי שדי היו עליה מסביב
כי־אתי מרתה נאם־יהוה:

[15] For a voice is announcing from Dan;
     and proclaiming trouble from the hill country of Ephraim.
[16] Mention to the nations—'Look!'
     Make proclamation concerning Jerusalem:
     'Watchers are coming from the distant land;
          And they shall raise their voice against the cities of Judah.
[17] Like watchers of fields they are upon her on every side;
     for against me she has rebelled'—oracle of Yahweh.

[Notes on the MT:
   Verse 16: For 'Mention to the nations—"Look!"', it has been proposed that the text be emended to הזהירו לבנימין ('give warning to Benjamin'; thus the approaching army draws closer still to Jerusalem [Dan–Ephraim–Benjamin]) or הגידו ביהודה ('tell [it] in Judah'). For 'watchers' (נצרים), the LXX reads συστροφαὶ ('bands'); thus Rudolph (the editor of the book of Jeremiah in *BHS*) suggests emending the text to צרים (from the root צרר). The parallel, however, with 'watchers of fields' in v. 18, favors the MT, perhaps with the sense of 'shouters, callers' (see William L. Holladay, *Jeremiah. I. A Commentary on the Book of the Prophet Jeremiah, Chapters 1–25* [Hermeneia; 2 vols.; Philadelphia: Fortress Press, 1986], p. 159).]

The enemy approaches from an unspecified location ('from the distant land') beyond the city of Dan. Elsewhere in the book of Jeremiah, it is reported that evil comes upon Judah and Jerusalem from 'the north'. Earlier in ch. 4, this northern foe is described as 'the lion' and 'the destroyer of nations' (vv. 6-7). It is this adversary's coming that is announced in 4.15-17. As Lundbom has recently pointed out,

2 Chron. 30.5-12). Clearly, the evidence tells against a complete exile of Israelites from the territory of the conquered Northern Kingdom.

the 'north' (*ṣāpôn*) in the Old Testament is generally understood as the place where 'powers of disaster are bred' (Berridge 1970: 70). Later, an enemy will come upon Babylon 'from a land of the north' (50.9), and Ezekiel's destructive agent 'Gog' will come from his place in 'the furthest north' (Ezek 38.15; 39.2)… The north also just happens to be the direction from which eastern armies invade Palestine. Direct travel to Palestine and Egypt from Assyria or Babylon is not possible across the desert. In Zeph 2.13 'the north' = Assyria.[3]

Since this enemy's origin is to the north of Israel, it follows that its route to Jerusalem passes first through that site which demarcates Israel's traditional northern boundary—namely, the city of Dan. Jeremiah 4 does not suggest that the enemy's origin is in Dan (*contra* Irenaeus), only that its coming against Judah and Jerusalem in divine judgment is announced first in the city of Dan, then throughout the hill country of Ephraim.

b. *Jeremiah 8*
Dan occurs next in the book of Jeremiah in ch. 8. Once again, the form of the passage is an oracle of impending judgment. There are clear similarities with the text from Jeremiah 4 just discussed: both concern the coming of the 'foe from the north', and in each text Dan refers to the city on the northern frontier of Israel. If there is any direct relationship between 4.15-17 and 8.14-17, then the enemy now seems closer, since, according to Jer. 8.16, its horses are heard 'from Dan':

עַל־מָה אֲנַחְנוּ יֹשְׁבִים הֵאָסְפוּ [14]
וְנָבוֹא אֶל־עָרֵי הַמִּבְצָר
וְנִדְּמָה־שָּׁם כִּי יְהוָה אֱלֹהֵינוּ הֲדִמָּנוּ
וַיַּשְׁקֵנוּ מֵי־רֹאשׁ כִּי חָטָאנוּ לַיהוָה:
קַוֵּה לְשָׁלוֹם וְאֵין טוֹב [15]
לְעֵת מַרְפֵּה וְהִנֵּה בְעָתָה:

---

3.   Jack R. Lundbom, *Jeremiah 1–20: A New Translation with Introduction and Commentary* (AB, 21A; New York: Doubleday, 1999), p. 242. The reference is to John Maclennan Berridge, *Prophet, People, and the Word of Yahweh: An Examination of Form and Content in the Proclamation of the Prophet Isaiah* (Basel Studies of Theology, 4; Zürich: EVZ-Verlag, 1970), p. 70. See also David J. Reimer ('The "Foe" and the "North" in Jeremiah', *ZAW* 101 [1989], pp. 223-32), who prefers צָפוֹן as the place of Yahweh's dwelling (cf. Baal in the Ugaritic texts); thus, the enemy—while historical—comes from the deity and is intimately related to the divine will for judgment, rather than necessarily from a particular point of the compass. Nevertheless, the perspective of the text of Jeremiah, looking from Judah/Jerusalem northward toward the Ephraimite hill country, the city of Dan, and beyond, better commends the reading of צָפוֹן as 'north'.

מדן נשמע נחרת סוסיו [16]
מקול מצהלות אביריו
רעשה כל־הארץ
ויבואו ויאכלו ארץ ומלואה עיר וישבי בה:
כי הנני משלח בכם [17]
נחשים צפענים
אשר אין־להם לחש
ונשכו אתכם נאם־יהוה:

[14] Why are we sitting? Assemble!
    And let us enter the fortified cities,
        and let us be silent there;
for Yahweh our God has silenced us
    and has given us to drink bitter/poisonous water—
        for we have sinned against Yahweh.
[15] Wait for peace, but there is no good;
    for a time of healing, but lo, terror/dismay.
[16] From Dan is heard the snorting of his horses,
    from the sound of the neighing of his mighty steeds
        the whole earth quakes.
They have entered and they have consumed the earth and its fulness,
    the city and the inhabitants in it.
[17] For I am about to send among you
    serpents, vipers
        for which there is nothing to charm them;
    they shall bite you—oracle of Yahweh.

[Notes on the MT:
    Verse 15: This verse is equivalent to Jer. 14.19b, and it is suggested that it be deleted from ch. 8. Since there is no sound reason why a phrase cannot be duplicated in a document, the MT is to be preferred. For מרפה, many medieval manuscripts of the Hebrew Old Testament and the Editions read an alternate form (BDB, p. 951) ending in ־פא.
    Verse 17: 'Oracle of Yahweh', at the end of the verse, is absent from the LXX; it is suggested that this phrase be deleted from the MT. Since the arguments for its possible addition to the MT (editorial gloss) are similar to those for its accidental omission from the LXX (neither has significant bearing on the interpretation of the text since with or without the phrase it is clear that the deity is speaking), the present translation reflects the MT.]

Verses 16 and 17 are most immediately pertinent to the present study. Jeremiah 8.16 begins, 'From Dan is heard...' The vantage point of the hearer is Jerusalem. The text is hyperbolic: a listener in Jerusalem hears the sound of the snorting of the enemy's cavalry horses emanating from the city of Dan, far to the north, where the foe has already arrived on his southward march. Most commentators seem to assume that the unnamed city (singular) referred to in the last phrase of 8.16 is Jerusalem.[4] Alternatively, the city of Dan may be intended. Dan is, after all, the city named in the first phrase of v. 16; reference to that city again at the end of the verse forms an *inclusio*. In addition, from the vantage point of the hearer, the threat remains at some distance. Jerusalem is, at least for the moment, untouched. The imperfect verb form with waw consecutive, however, suggests a past event. For these reasons, it is preferable to understand Dan as the city that has been entered, its inhabitants who have been consumed.

Unfortunately, the archaeological record is inconclusive on the question whether the invading Babylonians destroyed the city of Dan. Biran's excavations at the site have revealed several settlement phases in Stratum I (end of the eighth century BCE–fourth century CE). A destruction layer has been uncovered which dates to the end of the eighth century BCE and is attributed to the Assyrian conquest.[5] Biran goes on to note that a change occurred in the archaeological record and in the material culture at the end of the seventh century/beginning of the sixth century 'although there is no evidence of destruction'.[6] This seems to correlate with the time of Jeremiah, when the city was large, prosperous, and unfortified.[7] While Biran writes that 'the large city of Stratum I came to an end with the Babylonian conquest of the country', and that 'Dan suffered the destructive impact of the Babylonian army on its march southward to Jerusalem', the only documentation he offers is Jer. 4.15 and 8.16. He provides no archaeological evidence of this destruction early in the sixth century BCE.[8] Indeed, there appears to be a gap in the excavations (if not in the archaeological record) at the site between the Assyrian and Hellenistic periods. Biran must, at the present time, rely on the biblical text and other secondary evidence to reconstruct the history of the city of Dan in the Babylonian and Persian periods.

In v. 17, the 'snorting of horses' of the northern foe gives way to a threat of 'serpents, vipers'. Scholars do not agree whether real snakes are meant,

---

4. See, e.g., Carroll, *Jeremiah*, p. 234; most explicit in this identification is Lundbom, *Jeremiah 1–20*, p. 526.

5. Biran, *Biblical Dan*, pp. 260-61.

6. Biran, *Biblical Dan*, p. 270.

7. Avraham Biran, 'Tel Dan: Biblical Texts and Archaeological Data', in Michael D. Coogan, J. Cheryl Exum and Lawrence E. Stager (eds.), *Scripture and Other Artifacts: Essays on the Bible and Archaeology in Honor of Philip J. King* (Louisville, KY: Westminster John Knox Press, 1994), pp. 1-17 (16).

8. Biran, *Biblical Dan*, p. 270.

or whether the language is metaphorical.[9] The other images or metaphors used in the book of Jeremiah to characterize the enemy (i.e. steaming pot, 1.13; lion, 4.7; cf. 5.16) support the latter position. The shift from an image of raging horses to crawling snakes has not escaped the attention of previous commentators.[10] However, to my knowledge, no one has yet connected the 'serpents, vipers' with the mention of Dan in the previous verse.[11] In an earlier Israelite tradition—namely, the Blessing of Jacob in Genesis 49 (where the final form of the text allows reference to either the ancestors or the tribes; see the discussion of Gen. 49.16-17 in Chapter 2, above)—Dan is metaphorically called a 'serpent' (נחש) and a 'viper/ horned snake' (שפיפן). These words in the Hebrew text are either identical with, or phonetically similar to, those in Jer. 8.17. The word for 'serpent' is the same, and the word for 'viper' in Jeremiah 8 (צפענים) may have been substituted for the more unfamiliar, but similarly sounding, 'viper/ horned snake' (Gen. 49.17—a *hapax legomenon* in the Hebrew Bible). Is it possible that the mention of Dan in Jer. 8.16 called to mind the image of Dan in the earlier tradition? That is, is the use of these metaphors for the invading army from the north (a phenomenon in the Hebrew Bible unique to this text), due at least in part to the occurrence of Dan in this passage? Would this adequately account for the shift in metaphor in Jer. 8.16-17?[12] The full significance and meaning of this possible connection between these two texts cannot be determined at the present time.

2. *The Book of the Prophet Ezekiel*

a. *Ezekiel 48*
In the book of Ezekiel, Dan occurs only in the final chapter, in the description of the division of the land (48.1-2) and in the enumeration of the city gates of new Jerusalem (48.32). In terms of form, Ezekiel 48 is part of the

9.   See Holladay (*Jeremiah*, I, p. 292) for the 'scholarly divide'.

10.   Walter Brueggemann, *To Pluck Up, To Tear Down: A Commentary on the Book of Jeremiah 1–25* (International Theological Commentary; Grand Rapids: Eerdmans, 1988), pp. 86-87.

11.   Henning Graf Reventlow (*Liturgie und prophetisches Ich bei Jeremia* [Gütersloh: Gütersloher Verlagshauser (Gerd Mohn), 1963], p. 193 n. 318) has, however, suggested a wordplay in צפענים ('vipers') and צפון ('north', the direction from which the enemy comes).

12.   Since neither נחשים nor צפענים occurs elsewhere in the book of Jeremiah, in reference either to the invading army or to anything else, the proposal suggested in the present study calls for careful consideration.

prophet's vision of the restored temple in the restored land of Israel. It is a vision of the new fulfillment of Yahweh's ancient promise to the ancestors (47.14), in which the prophet anticipates Israel's re-entry into the land and the people's second opportunity to live in the land in justice and righteousness in response to Yahweh's mercy. In his popular study of this exilic prophet's life and message, Klein has summarized the principle issues pertaining to the division of the land among the tribes of Israel and the city gates in Ezek. 47.13–48.35. These are: the exclusion of Transjordan from the land to be allocated, the order of the tribes (especially relative to the central area [תרומה] reserved for the temple, the priests and Levites, the city, and the prince [נשיא]), and the assignment of one of twelve city gates to each of the tribes.[13]

The scholarly trend has been to ascribe the majority to Ezekiel 40–48, including 47.13–48.29, to the exilic prophet (of course there have been dissenting views as well). In his recent monograph, Steven Tuell has argued that 47.13-23 (the boundaries of the land) and 48.1-29 come, rather, from the hand of a postexilic redactor living in the restoration community.[14] His study is a response to Jon Levenson's characterization of the temple vision as a description of the eschatological kingdom of Israel, unrealized in history.[15] Tuell's fundamental thesis is that institutions and details in the prophetic vision are reflections of the actual situation of the Israelite community restored to Palestine in the Persian period. His main suggestion of interest for the present study is that the land within the boundaries delimited in Ezekiel 47 corresponds to the Persian province of Abar-Nahara. In addition, the north to south progression of the division of the land indicates, to Tuell, a Persian perspective (repatriated Israelites would have re-entered Palestine from the north and west).[16] Tuell's proposal is, finally, unpersuasive, and even he admits that the Persians' provincial borders were taken over largely intact from their Babylonian predecessors who, in turn, had adopted them from the Assyrians.[17] In

13. Ralph W. Klein, *Ezekiel: The Prophet and His Message* (Studies on Personalities in the Old Testament; Columbia: University of South Carolina Press, 1988), pp. 183-89. See also Steven Shawn Tuell, *The Law of the Temple in Ezekiel 40–48* (HSM, 49; Atlanta: Scholars Press, 1992), pp. 170-72.

14. Tuell, *The Law of the Temple in Ezekiel 40–48*, pp. 72, 75.

15. Tuell, *The Law of the Temple in Ezekiel 40–48*, p. 13. See Jon Douglas Levenson, *Theology of the Program of Restoration of Ezekiel 40–48* (HSM, 10; Missoula, MT: Scholars Press, 1976).

16. Tuell, *The Law of the Temple in Ezekiel 40–48*, pp. 153-70.

17. Tuell, *The Law of the Temple in Ezekiel 40–48*, p. 156 n. 7.

addition, the north to south orientation need not presuppose a postexilic date, since even exiles hoping for repatriation would probably envision the Palestinian landscape from this perspective (insofar as the Babylonian invasion came from, and the way into exile went toward the north). It continues to be better to assume that the majority of the text under consideration comes from the exilic prophet Ezekiel and not from a later editor.[18]

The first mention of Dan is in Ezek. 48.1-2. This section on the division of the land, as well as the names of the city gates after the traditional tribes of Israel, is irrefutable evidence that this material is part of Ezekiel's vision for the future and not a description of historical reality. The order of tribal allotments reflects no known time in Israel's history. At no time after the exile were Israelites resettled by tribes in the land; neither were tribal allegiances then a significant part of community life.[19] It is generally agreed that order of the tribal allotment is an ideal never realized in history. Even Tuell rightly observes that

> most scholars have seen in this scheme an unrealistic, utopian idea of the land, removed from its realities, grounded in archaic, premonarchic ideals. Clearly, the division portrayed here could not have been carried out. The tribes no longer existed, save as a literary ideal, and the precise, symmetrical divisions described make no allowance for the asymmetry and varying quality of the land itself.[20]

Nevertheless, Ezekiel has utilized the ancient epic traditions of Israel (J and E) to construct his vision of the restored land. While the locations of the individual tribes in the land do not correspond primarily to their earlier history, they do correlate with the interests contained within the birth narratives in Genesis 29–30 and 35. (In the earlier history, Zebulun and Issachar were located in the region of Galilee, and Gad was in Transjordan.

---

18. With Walther Zimmerli, *Ezekiel.* II. *A Commentary on the Book of the Prophet Ezekiel, Chapters 25–48* (Hermeneia; 2 vols.; Philadelphia: Fortress Press, 1983), p. 542. Interestingly, while most commentators (among them, G.A. Cooke, *A Critical and Exegetical Commentary on the Book of Ezekiel* [ICC; Edinburgh: T. & T. Clark, 1951], p. 536; Walther Eichrodt, *Ezekiel: A Commentary* [OTL; Philadelphia: Westminster Press, 1970], p. 593; Zimmerli, *Ezekiel*, II, pp. 545, 552-53; R.W. Klein, *Ezekiel*, pp. 187, 189; Leslie C. Allen, *Ezekiel 20–48* [WBC, 29; Dallas: Word Books, 1990], p. 277) recognize 48.30-35 to be an addition to Ezekiel's work, Tuell argues just the opposite: that these verses, not 47.13–48.29, are part of the prophet's original vision (*The Law of the Temple in Ezekiel 40–48*, p. 75).

19. The tribes of Israel play no role in the postexilic works of Ezra and Nehemiah.

20. Tuell, *The Law of the Temple in Ezekiel 40–48*, pp. 170-71; cf. Levenson, *Theology of the Program of Restoration*, p. 112.

In Ezekiel 48, all three are relocated to the south.) It is ordinarily noted (see the standard commentaries) that the arrangement of tribes relative to the central, consecrated area (48.8-22) depends on the status of the birth mothers. All things are envisioned in good order. In much the same way as the Priestly writer, Ezekiel orders the tribes hierarchically based on the status of the mothers. The tribes descended from Leah, the eldest sister and first wife of Jacob, take precedence over those of the younger sister, the second yet favorite wife of Jacob, Rachel. The tribes descended from the sons of Jacob's wives take precedence over those born to Jacob's wives' maidservants. This interest in hierarchical order and in degrees of purity reflects the Priestly concerns of the prophet Ezekiel, who is identi-fied as a priest in the opening vision (1.3), and suggests consideration of the notion of the symbolic universe.[21] According to this interpretive model, there are certain 'maps' (of persons, times, uncleanness, as well as of places) by which a culture orders and classifies its world. Maps of places order space in terms of zones, or progressive degrees, of holiness. In Ezek. 48.1-29, the central, consecrated area, in which the restored Temple is located, is the most holy region. Moving outward from this reserved area the degree of holiness decreases. Those tribes descended from the wives of Jacob, Leah, and Rachel, are closer in proximity to the reserved area, while those tribes descended from the maidservants (Zilpah and Bilhah) are situated at a greater distance from the center.[22] Thus, on the one hand, the tribes of Judah (pre-eminent tribe throughout the monarchic period) and Benjamin (descended from the first son born to Jacob's favorite wife, Rachel) occupy the bands of greatest holiness nearest the sacred reserve. On the other hand, in the case of the maidservant tribes, the firstborn of each—Bilhah = Dan//Zilpah = Gad—is are located farthest away, on the northern and southern boundaries, respectively, the space of least holi-ness.[23] Nevertheless, one cannot argue that there is anything negative or peculiarly anti-Dan in this text.

The only other occurrence of Dan in the book of Ezekiel is in 48.33. In 48.30-35, focus shifts from the land to the restored city. The new city has

---

21. See, e.g., Jerome H. Neyrey, 'The Symbolic Universe of Luke–Acts: "They Turn the World Upside Down"', in Neyrey (ed.), *The Social World of Luke–Acts*, pp. 271-304 (276-82).

22. See the map in Levenson, *Theology of the Program of Restoration*, p. 117.

23. According to this interpretation, Dan's distant location has nothing to do with the religious developments at the city of Dan under Jeroboam I, which drew harsh criticism from Dtr. Surprisingly, this does not come through in the Priestly traditions.

twelve exits or gates, each named after one of the tribes of Israel.[24] The list begins on the north side of the city (contrast the configuration of the tribes around the wilderness sanctuary [Num. 2] with which Ezek. 48.30-35 is often compared, which begins with the east side) with the Leah tribes of Reuben, Judah, and Levi. It is possible that these tribes and this direction (north) are mentioned first (rather than the east) since the allotted lands of the important tribes of Judah and Reuben are located directly north of the sacred reserve. Levi, the third important Leah tribe, joins them. The remaining Leah tribes (Simeon, Issachar, Zebulun) appear opposite these three, on the city's south side. Moving in a clockwise direction from the north, the eastern gates of the city are listed next: Joseph, Benjamin, and Dan. These are all related to Rachel: Joseph was her first-born, and Benjamin was born to Rachel at the time of her death; Dan, born of Rachel's maidservant, Bilhah, 'on [Rachel's] knees' (Gen. 30.3), and thus possessing special status among the maidservant tribes, is counted among the tribes descended from the sons actually born to Rachel. Finally, the remaining maidservant tribes (Gad, Asher, Naphtali) are set on the (apparently) least favored, west side of the city (cf. 8.16). Thus, the final occurrence of Dan in Ezekiel locates the tribe at one of the sites/gates at the most favored side of the restored city, the east side which opened toward the entrance of the restored Temple (47.1).

3. *The Book of the Prophet Amos*

While the occurrences of Dan in the books of Jeremiah and Ezekiel tend to be little more than geographical notices without significant interpretive value for the present study, the situation is different in the book of Amos where Dan is mentioned in ch. 8 in an oracle of judgment.

a. *Amos 8*

[13] In that day:
>   the beautiful virgins shall swoon away,
>   and the choice young men—from thirst.
[14] The ones who swear by the guilt of Samaria
>   and say, 'As your god lives, O Dan';
>   And 'As the way of Beersheba lives',
>   They shall fall and shall not rise again.

---

24. See the diagram in Levenson, *Theology of the Program of Restoration*, p. 120.

[Notes on the MT:

While most commentators agree that Amos 8.13-14 forms a discrete oracle, there is obvious instances of paronomasia which link v. 13 with previous unit (vv. 11-12): note 'thirst' (צמא), 'find' (מצא), and 'from north' (מצפון).

Verse 13: On the one hand, Elliger (the editor of the Minor Prophets in *BHS*) suggests that 'from thirst' has been added. On the other hand, he notes that others have proposed emending בצמא in the MT to האמצים, from the adjective אמיץ/אמץ (BDB, p. 55), with metathesis, thus corresponding with the feminine plural adjective in the previous colon. Such an emendation lacks support in the Versions, and is unwarranted.

Verse 14: It has been proposed to emend באשמת ('by the guilt of') in the MT to באשרת ('by the A/asherah of'). There is no support for such an emendation, and seems to betray the interests of the commentators who prefer this reading. For 'way of', the LXX reads ὁ θεός σου, as in the previous phrase regarding Dan. It has been suggested, however, that θεῖος ('uncle') should be read in place of θεός and that the intended meaning is 'your patron deity/tutelary god'; thus Elliger's דדך. See Shalom M. Paul, *Amos: A Commentary on the Book of Amos* (Hermeneia; Minneapolis: Fortress Press, 1991), p. 271. It is sometimes suggested that the final colon in v. 14 ('they shall fall and shall not rise again') is a secondary addition to the text (see Saul M. Olyan, 'The Oaths of Amos 8.14', in Gary A. Anderson and Saul M. Olyan [eds.], *Priesthood and Cult in Ancient Israel* [JSOTSup, 125; Sheffield: JSOT Press, 1991], pp. 121-49 [121-22]). While I am not persuaded by this proposition, it is nevertheless of interest to note the envelope structure that results from the occurrence of 'the ones who swear by' at the beginning of v. 14, and 'Beersheba' just before the final colon (in Hebrew, both words are formed, at least in part, from the root שבע).]

According to this text, those who utter oaths or swear (שבע) by Samaria, Dan, and Beersheba are destined for irrevocable destruction. A glance at the scholarly literature on this passage indicates that the main question is whether or not cults of foreign gods at the sites of Samaria, Dan, and Beersheba are attacked by Amos. That is, is the Northern Kingdom attacked for its patronage of deities other than Yahweh (cf. Hosea)? Or is it rather the case that Amos's critique is of syncretistic practices at Yahwistic cult centers, where Yahweh was worshiped either alongside other (Canaanite) deities, or worshiped exclusively but with rituals borrowed from Israel's Canaanite neighbors? If either of these scenarios were the case, then the sanctuary at Dan would be classified among those where Israel practiced apostasy, and the evaluation of Dan would clearly be negative. I prefer another possibility, which makes any condemnation of Dan incidental. I intend to argue that the prophetic attack on Dan (and Samaria and Beersheba) is more indirect and is not as a result of the particularities of an illicit cult practiced at these ritual sites, but is accounted for by two other notions that reflect the broader context of the book of Amos: (1) Dan

seems to be one of the religious centers at which the Israelites offer up
their worship to God but fail to live ethical lives of justice and righteousness in the land; and (2) these sanctuaries (Dan and Beersheba, in particular) are polemicized against because they are not Jerusalem and, from the
perspective of Amos, a Judahite prophet, Jerusalem is the only legitimate
sanctuary at which to worship Yahweh (cf. 1.2: 'Yahweh roars from Zion;
and from Jerusalem he utters his voice').[25]

In the following pages I undertake, first of all, an examination of Amos
8.14 in order to understand what the text says. After this, I will situate the
text within the broader context of the book of Amos.

Amos 8.14 is a difficult text, remarkable for its ambiguity. 'The ones
who swear by the guilt of Samaria' remains the most enigmatic portion of
the verse, and there is no agreement among interpreters as to what is intended by 'the guilt of Samaria'. Most recent critical commentaries include
a survey of proposed interpretations.[26] Among the suggestions are that this

25. It is not certain that Amos 1.2 is an authentic statement of the prophet, and
there is no agreement in the scholarly community. This verse has been traditionally
attributed to a Judean redactor from the time of Josiah (see, e.g., Hans Walter Wolff,
Joel and Amos: A Commentary on the Books of the Prophets Joel and Amos [Herme-
neia; Philadelphia: Fortress Press, 1977], pp. 121-22), although more recent commentators are less satisfied with this conclusion. Francis I. Andersen and David Noel
Freedman (*Amos: A New Translation with Introduction and Commentary* [AB, 24A;
New York: Doubleday, 1989], p. 197) who, it should be noted, are more interested in
the interpretation of the book of Amos in its final form, suggest that this is one of
Amos' last oracles rather than a secondary introduction to the following oracles. Paul
(*Amos*, pp. 36-42) is among the minority of scholars who understand this as an
authentic word of Amos.

26. Jörg Jeremias, *The Book of Amos: A Commentary* (OTL; Louisville, KY:
Westminster/John Knox Press, 1998), p. 152; Paul, *Amos*, pp. 269-70 (including the
footnotes); Andersen and Freedman, *Amos*, pp. 706-11, 828-29; J. Alberto Soggin,
The Prophet Amos: A Translation and Commentary (London: SCM Press, 1987),
pp. 140-41; Douglas Stuart, *Hosea–Jonah* (WBC, 31; Waco, TX: Word Books, 1987),
pp. 386-87; Wolff, *Joel and Amos*, pp. 331-32; Erling Hammerschaimb, *The Book
of Amos: A Commentary* (New York: Schocken Books, 1970), pp. 128-30; James
Luther Mays, *Amos: A Commentary* (OTL; Philadelphia: Westminster Press, 1969),
pp. 149-50; William Rainey Harper, *A Critical and Exegetical Commentary on Amos
and Hosea* (ICC; New York: Charles Scribner's Sons, 1905), pp. 184-86. See also
Olyan, 'The Oaths of Amos 8.14', pp. 148-49; Hans M. Barstad, *The Religious Polemics of Amos* (VTSup, 34; Leiden: E.J. Brill, 1984), pp. 157-58; Max E. Polley, *Amos
and the Davidic Empire: A Socio-Historical Approach* (New York: Oxford University
Press, 1989), p. 92.

is: (1) a reference to the goddess Ash(i)mah (cf. 2 Kgs 17.30; however, according to 2 Kgs 17, this foreign deity was not introduced to the territory of the Northern Kingdom until after the fall of Samaria and Israel in 722, more than a century after Amos's ministry); (2) a reference to the goddess Asherah (requiring an emendation of the MT); (3) a circumlocutory reference ('guilt of Samaria') to the calf supposedly worshiped at Bethel, the royal sanctuary (under the influence of Hos. 8.5-6; cf. Amos 7.10-13; 1 Kgs 12.28-33 ['sins of Jeroboam']); or (4) a pejorative reference to a Yahweh sanctuary in the city of Samaria otherwise unmentioned in the biblical tradition and not yet uncovered in the archaeological excavations at the site (cf. the Deuteronomistic Historian's evaluative summary of the reign of Ahab [1 Kgs 16.29-33], in which is mentioned an 'altar to Baal' and a 'temple of Baal' which Ahab established in Samaria). Although the evidence is silent, I am inclined to favor (in part) the fourth suggestion. It is important to recall that Amos was a Judean prophet, possibly with affinity for Jerusalem (1.2), and whose prophetic ministry may indicate that long before Josiah there was a sense of the cultic centrality of Jerusalem.[27] If a Yahwistic religious center in Samaria is meant here (and one should probably assume that such a cultic installation existed in the capital city, although the biblical text is silent about it; cf. 1 Kgs 16.29-33), it was probably a Yahwistic sanctuary *geographically out of place*. Since, from the Judean perspective, Jerusalem was understood to be the only legitimate sanctuary at which to worship Yahweh, then worship at any other site— particularly one in the Northern Kingdom (the 'sin of Jeroboam')—was false worship and deserving of prophetic attack.

Even so, there may be another possibility which has not yet, to my knowledge, been proposed. In this case, the 'guilt of Samaria' would be less narrowly concerned with cultic matters than with broader political and economic interests.[28] Is it possible that the 'guilt of Samaria' is somehow

27. Polley (*Amos and the Davidic Empire*, pp. 107-109) traces several attempts to reform cultic activity in the south antecedent to the reign of Josiah: Asa (913–873), 1 Kgs 15.9-14; 2 Chron. 14.1-5; 15.8-16; Jehoshaphat (873–849), 1 Kgs 22.43; 2 Chron. 17.3-6; Joash (837–800), 2 Kgs 12.4-16; 2 Chron. 24.4-14; Hezekiah (715–687), 2 Kgs 18–20; 2 Chron. 29–32. His point is 'to dispel the idea that Josiah was the only advocate in Judah for centralization of worship in Jerusalem...' (p. 109). Of course, one must consider the possibility that these notices of incomplete centralization originated with Dtr in order to highlight the more complete effort of this latter king. On the question of the authenticity of Amos 1.2, see n. 25, above.

28. It is important to recognize that, in the ancient world, politics and religion were never as separate as they are (or as some people might like them to be) in the

to be associated more directly with the establishment of a breakaway kingdom in the north and, in particular, with the monarchy in northern Israel? This polemic against the Northern Kingdom and its leadership is echoed elsewhere in Amos, where the northern monarchy and the capital city of Samaria are attacked for other than overtly religious reasons (see 3.9-15; 4.1; 6.1; 7.9-13). According to Amos, Samaria and the 'House of Jeroboam' are destined for destruction (3.15; 7.9). Interpreted within the broader context of the book of Amos, the prophet's pejorative reference here to the 'guilt' of the capital city, the seat of power, may have some-thing to do with the socio-economic policies permitted by the Israelite monarchy to thrive to the benefit of the wealthy minority which had, in Amos's opinion, led to all sorts of social injustices: oppression of the poor, exploitation of the needy, corruption in the courts, and a general moral malaise. In short, what I am suggesting is that 'those who swear by the guilt of Samaria' were those in Israel who had pledged allegiance not to some foreign god or goddess or idol, but to the 'House of Jeroboam' (Amos 7.9), and who were thus opposed to vowing loyalty to the Davidic king in Judah.[29]

The possibility that the first colon of Amos 8.14 targets the political institutions of the Northern Kingdom, together with their socio-economic abuses, as distinct from the following two cola concerning the religious abuses at the well-known cult centers at Dan and Beersheba, may be indi-cated by the different introductions. The attack on the 'guilt of Samaria' is more of a report in form and begins with the phrase 'the ones who swear by', while the attacks on Dan and Beersheba quote specific religious oaths or slogans, introduced by חי ('as...lives'). It must be conceded that this verse represents a wholly unique use of the term אשמה ('guilt') in the

modern, industrial West. Interpreters such as Barstad (*The Religious Polemics of Amos*, pp. 1-10), who prefer to focus exclusively on the religious polemics of Amos, often fail to appreciate the close association of political and religious institutions in ancient Israel.

29. It is likely that Amos 7.9, which refers to the '*house of* Jeroboam', is a redactor's correction of Amos who had said that *Jeroboam* would die by the sword (cf. 7.11; see Wolff, *Joel and Amos*, pp. 108-11, 295). Nothing is reported in 2 Kgs 14 about Jeroboam II dying a violent death. However, his son and successor, Zechariah, was the first in a long line of Israelite kings to be assassinated in the final century of the Northern Kingdom's existence (see 2 Kgs 15.10). Whether Jeroboam II or the dynasty of Jeroboam (which conceivably could be either Jeroboam I or Jeroboam II) is intended is not crucial for the present study. Regardless, the issue is devotion to the kings of the Northern Kingdom rather than to the dynasty of David in Judah.

Hebrew Bible; nevertheless, in light of the vast uncertainty about the interpretation of Amos 8.14, perhaps this suggestion has something to commend it and will stimulate further investigation.

The way the verse flows, the 'ones who swear by the guilt of Samaria' are probably to be identified with the those who say 'As your god lives, O Dan', and 'As the way of Beersheba lives' in the next cola. While it is clear that these latter phrases in Amos contain religious polemic, the identity of the unnamed deity invoked in each slogan is shrouded in uncertainty. A bilingual dedicatory inscription discovered at Tell Dan, interestingly enough, similarly leaves the name of the god at Dan unidentified, and even Biran, the excavator of the site, has not ventured an identification (although he suggests that it was probably not a Greek deity).[30] Barstad, however, assumes that the reference is to 'the local Ba'al, the city-god of Dan... In all likelihood this deity represented a local variety of the ancient Canaanite Ba'al type, a deity for whom the Old Testament gives ample evidence and who, for this reason, nevertheless can be said to represent a familiar figure.'[31] It must be acknowledged that nothing in the book of Amos suggests this identification, and nowhere else in Amos (cf. Hosea) does the prophet polemicize against Baal. Barstad's theory further assumes that Jeroboam's cultic reform in the tenth century was not Yahwistic in nature, a position that cannot be completely substantiated. More likely is the interpretation according to which it is Yahweh who is invoked at the Yahwistic cult established by Jeroboam I in the northern city of Dan. This is not to suggest that Amos was explicitly attacking the worship of the calf image at Dan (cf. 1 Kgs 12.28-30), although in such a polemical and emotionally charged text that is, of course, possible.[32] The god of Dan, in my opinion, is best understood to have been Yahweh. The prophetic judgment is spoken here, in part, against the worship of Yahweh *outside Jerusalem*.

30. Avraham Biran, '"To the God Who is in Dan"', in *idem* (ed.), *Temples and High Places in Ancient Israel* (Jerusalem: Nelson Glueck School of Biblical Archaeology of Hebrew Union College/Jewish Institute of Religion, 1981), pp. 145-47; *idem*, *Biblical Dan*, pp. 221-24.

31. Barstad, *The Religious Polemics of Amos*, p. 187. The recent identification of 'the god who is in Dan' as Hadad (based chiefly on the recently discovered and controversial 'House of David' inscription from Tell Dan) by K.L. Noll is intriguing but finally not compelling ('The God Who is Among the Danites', *JSOT* 80 [1998], pp. 3-23).

32. On the 'thoroughly Yahwistic and even conservative nature of Jeroboam's religious reform', see Olyan, 'The Oaths of Amos 8.14', pp. 139-41; Paul, *Amos*, pp. 270-71; and the analysis of 1 Kgs 12 in Chapter 3 above.

A similar situation holds for the reference to Beersheba. For the interpretation of 'And "As the way of Beersheba lives..."', a handful of suggestions have been offered. The Hebrew text is puzzling. It is agreed that as the text stands (חֵי דֶּרֶךְ בְּאֵר־שֶׁבַע), the usual translation (see above) is problematic. What does it mean to say 'And "As the way of Beersheba lives"'? To what does דֶּרֶךְ refer? Those who maintain the traditional translation of the MT (see above) tend to understand דֶּרֶךְ as a reference to the 'way' or pilgrimage route to Beersheba, thereby creating an oath formula otherwise unparalleled in the Hebrew Bible but possibly analogous to the Muslim practice of swearing by the pilgrimage way to Mecca.[33] Others interpret this word (דֶּרֶךְ) on the basis of Ugaritic *drkt*, meaning 'power' or 'dominion'.[34] According to this reading, in Amos 8.14 is an appellative for the deity of Beersheba. Another suggestion is to treat the kaph as a pronominal suffix (second masculine singular) appended to דֹּר ('generation')—thus, 'council', 'assembly' (BDB, pp. 189-90)—and so, by extension, '(your) pantheon, circle of deities'.[35] The most well-accepted alternative to the difficult MT involves a slight emendation of the consonantal text (resh to daleth) and revocalization: from דֶּרֶךְ to דֹּדְךָ (so Elliger, *BHS*). In this case, דֹּדְךָ is translated 'your kinsman', and is interpreted as a familial title for Yahweh.[36] The LXX, which has ὁ θεός σου, is often cited in support of this emendation, the assumption being that the LXX translators interpreted דֹּדְךָ as a divine title. It is also possible, however, that the LXX translators were as befuddled by the MT as modern commentators and simply duplicated ὁ θεός σου from the previous colon. The suggestion that θεός is a corruption of an original θεῖος ('uncle') is no more than speculation. While I find the arguments in favor of this last proposal persuasive, I do not find them compelling. The other reference to Beersheba in Amos ('and do not cross over to Beersheba', 5.5) includes a verb of motion, thus perhaps indicating that Beersheba was a popular pilgrimage destination in the south for Amos's northern targets.[37] Hence,

---

33. See Paul, *Amos*, p. 272; Polley, *Amos and the Davidic Empire*, p. 109; Harper, *Amos and Hosea*, p. 184.

34. Barstad, *The Religious Polemics of Amos*, pp. 193-98; see also Olyan, 'The Oaths of Amos 8.14', p. 123 n. 1. This is also the meaning preferred by Soggin, *Amos*, pp. 140-41.

35. Andersen and Freedman, *Amos*, pp. 709, 830-31.

36. See especially Olyan, 'The Oaths of Amos 8.14', pp. 122 n. 3, 123-35; Hammerschaimb, *The Book of Amos*, p. 129.

37. For evidence of the presence of northern Israelites at religious sites in the south, cf. the expression 'Yahweh of Samaria' in the well-known dedicatory inscription at

the traditional translation and interpretation, as uncertain as it may be, is accepted in the present study.

It must be conceded that this enigmatic verse permits at least three readings. First, along the lines of the traditional interpretation, foreign deities worshiped at Samaria, Dan, and Beersheba, are condemned. I am persuaded, however, that Amos 8.14 does not attack the Northern King-dom for worshiping foreign gods.[38] Foreign deities do not otherwise play a role in the book of Amos; the mention of Sikkuth and Kiyyun in 5.26 is sometimes recognized as occurring in a secondary (Deuteronomistic) addition to the text.[39] Rather, according to a second reading, Amos 8.14 probably refers to the worship of Yahweh at Dan in the far north and Beersheba in the far south by Israelites of the break-away Northern Kingdom. That is, at issue is Yahweh worship outside Jerusalem and its temple. However, it is not wholly accurate to say, as Barstad does, that 'Amos is the only prophet to condemn the cult of Dan'.[40] That is to say too much. In addition, a careful reading shows that neither Dan, nor Beer-sheba, nor Samaria—as either city or sanctuary—is explicitly condemned in Amos 8.14. This text does not say that Samaria, or Dan, or Beersheba shall fall. Judgment probably did not come against the worship of foreign gods. The exact identity of these deities or images referred to in this verse, or the rituals associated with them, is not most important; there is insuffi-cient evidence in both the text and archaeological record to offer definitive identifications. What is condemned is not so much the cult (what happens at the religious center) as the worshipers themselves. And so a third reading recognizes that the emphasis of this oracle of judgment is on 'the

Kuntillet 'Ajrud. While most scholarly and popular interest has centered on the ques-tion of the relationship between Yahweh and a certain A/asherah, not to be overlooked is the reference to Samaria in this inscription. The conclusion to be drawn is that the worshiper's god was known to him as a deity whose manifestation was localized at Samaria, quite possibly the worshiper's home town. Kuntillet 'Ajrud was probably a wayside sanctuary on a major caravan route well south of Beersheba in the northern Negev. The scholarly literature on this subject is extensive; see Ze'ev Meshel, 'Teman, Horvat', in *NEAEHL*, IV, pp. 1458-64; *idem*, 'Kuntillet 'Ajrud: An Israelite Religious Center in Northern Sinai', *Expedition* 20 (1978), pp. 50-54; Philip J. King, *Amos, Hosea, Micah—An Archaeological Commentary* (Philadelphia: Westminster Press, 1988), p. 104.

38. Contra Barstad, *The Religious Polemics of Amos*, pp. 143-201; Andersen and Freedman, *Amos*, pp. 706-10, 828-32.

39. Wolff, *Joel and Amos*, pp. 262-65; Polley, *Amos and the Davidic Empire*, p. 91.

40. Barstad, *The Religious Polemics of Amos*, p. 187.

ones who swear by...', rather than any deity. The people against whom Amos polemicizes had been doing all the correct 'Yahweh rituals' at all the right times and in all the right places, swearing all the right oaths, but without ethical living, that is, without pursuing justice and righteousness. Judgment is proclaimed against 'the ones who swear by...and say...', that is, the inhabitants of the Northern Kingdom who are, everywhere, polemicized against in the book of Amos. These are the ones who are destined to fall, never to rise again. The reason for their destruction is what may be termed, colloquially, 'empty religiosity'. It is my assertion that the proper interpretation of this verse is one that situates it within the broad context of the book of Amos.

It is generally agreed that the primary concern of the prophet Amos was social injustice in Israel.[41] Premier texts include 2.6-8; 4.1; 5.10-15; 6.4-6; 8.4-6. The years during which Amos prophesied, chiefly during the reign of Jeroboam II in the mid-eighth century BCE, were peaceful and prosperous for Israel. Shalom Paul characterizes this period as Israel's 'Silver Age', nearly comparable to the era of David and Solomon.[42] This was a time of geographical expansion for the Northern Kingdom (2 Kgs 14.25), and the accompanying increase in trade and commerce (Syria, Phoenicia, Egypt) resulted in tremendous material prosperity for a small, developing wealthy upper class. This affluence is widely reflected in the book of Amos (see, e.g., 3.15; 5.11; 6.4-6) and well-attested in the material culture of Samaria and other northern cities.[43] While the rich and powerful enjoyed life to its fullest, they victimized the disenfranchised by their legal exploitation and economic deceit. It was more than a case of the rich

---

41. See, e.g., Polley, *Amos and the Davidic Empire*, pp. 131-38. In response to this position, Barstad wrote *The Religion Polemics of Amos*, in which he focuses instead on what he deems a neglected component of Amos' message, arguing that the words of Amos were, in the first place, *religious* in character: 'The fight fought by the Yahwistic prophets was primarily of a religious/polemical if also of an ethical, character. Their main concern was to convince their fellow countrymen that Yahweh was the only god worth worshiping. He alone could help them in their daily life and with the provision of the fertility so vital to their existence' (p. 10). Generally, Barstad sees more in the text of Amos than is there, and some of his conclusions are insufficiently substantiated. It is also the case that, in the ancient world, the spheres of religion, politics, and economics, which Western cultures have endeavored to separate, were inextricably bound together. The economy was tied to the religious establishment and the political leadership; priesthood and monarchy were closely allied.

42. Paul, *Amos*, p. 1.

43. See King, *Amos, Hosea, Micah*, pp. 139-49.

simply overlooking the poor; the poor were oppressed and intentionally exploited, and the civil courts were corrupt (5.10). According to King, 'wealth had created a social imbalance, which resulted in two separate classes, the rich and the poor. Those at the top of the pyramid exploited the weak and oppressed the poor by alienation of land, forced labor, and heavy taxes.'[44] The book of Amos demonstrates how Israelite religion had become entangled in the socio-economic pursuits of the wealthy. The impression given is that the rich and powerful considered their wealth and security evidence of Yahweh's blessings and pleasure.[45] It gradually became the case, however, at least in the opinion of the prophet, that the people only engaged in the outward activities of the cult to the neglect of the ethical dimension of living lives of justice and righteousness in daily life. Paul has aptly stated that Amos's

> defiant words were aimed not only at braggarts and baccanalian behavior but also at all those who exchanged the upkeep of shrines, sanctuaries, and sacrifices for God's true desire of honesty, justice, and righteousness... Ritual can never be a surrogate for ethics... When the cult became a substitute for moral behavior, it was severely denounced and condemned... For the prophet, religion was identified with a person's everyday life style. Thus any ritual act performed by a worshiper whose moral character was blemished was categorically criticized.[46]

Similarly, King has written:

> Amos' severe judgment is a repudiation, not of the cult itself, but of the cult as it was practiced in the eighth century B.C.E.... To perform ritual worship without at the same time fulfilling the requirements of morality is meaningless. One's conduct in the marketplace must always conform to one's attitude in the holy place.[47]

I am persuaded that these two scholars have touched on the primary issue in the interpretation of Amos 8.14. In this verse Amos does not condemn the cult at Dan or Beersheba, but rather the attitude and actions of those who participate in the worship at these religious centers, those 'who swear by...and say...' Paul has even given the subtitle, 'Condemnation of Popular Oath Formulae', to his commentary on 8.13-14.[48] There are several passages in the book of Amos that raise the issue of the worshipers's

44. King, *Amos, Hosea, Micah*, p. 22.
45. Bruce E. Willoughby, 'Amos, Book of', in *ABD*, I, pp. 203-12 (206).
46. Paul, *Amos*, p. 2.
47. King, *Amos, Hosea, Micah*, p. 89.
48. Paul, *Amos*, p. 268.

attitude. In Amos 4.4-5, Yahweh, speaking through the prophet, says sarcastically:

> Come to Bethel and rebel,
>> to Gilgal and increase rebellion.
> Present your sacrifices in the morning,
>> your tithes on the third day.
> Offer up in smoke leavened bread as a thank offering,
>> and proclaim free-will offerings—make them heard.

The next colon, however, is key to interpreting this passage: 'For thus you love, O sons of Israel'. This may simply suggest that God perceives in the actions of the people a preoccupation with ritual activity, as if it were an end in itself. However, it may also be that case that in this line at the end of v. 5 we have Yahweh's observation that the Israelites do in the cult what *they* love, rather than what *God* loves and expects them to do.

A second text is Amos 8.4-6. These verses are addressed to 'those who trample the needy, destroying the humble of the land' (8.4) and who say:

> If only the new moon were over, so we could sell grain,
>> the sabbath, so we could offer wheat for sale.
> Using an ephah that is too small, and a shekel that is too big;
>> and tilting dishonest scales,
> We will buy the poor for silver, the needy for a pair of sandals;
>> and sell the refuse of grain as grain. (Amos 8.5-6)

Here it is evident that the sacred character of the festival calendar and the weekly sabbath had been profaned by the anticipation of unjust gain the day after. Apparently, the worship of Yahweh had become little more than external ritual and an unwelcome interruption of the working week.

A third text is Amos 5.21-24 where Yahweh speaks again; the language is harsh:

> [21] I hate, I reject your festival-gatherings;
>> I take no delight in your sacred assemblies.
> [22] For if you offer up whole burnt offerings to me
>> or your grain-offerings—I will not be pleased;
>> And the peace-offering of your fatlings I will not pay attention to.
> [23] Take away from me the sound of your songs;
>> and to the melody of your lutes I will not listen.
> [24] But like waters let justice roll along;
>> and righteousness like an everflowing wady.

In this passage, Yahweh's refusal of Israel's festivals and offerings is matched by his expectation of justice and righteousness among the people in the land. The unmistakable conclusion is that Israel's ritual activity is rejected not because it is undesired by God, but because Israel's cultic expressions of devotion to God are not a substitute for proper moral or ethical behavior outside the sanctuary.

These three passages in the book of Amos, in which Israel's cultic activity is condemned because it is 'empty', provide the context within which to interpret Amos 8.14. In this verse, the Northern Kingdom is criticized for its lip-service to Yahweh that is uncoordinated with the pursuit of justice and righteousness in the land. The prophet reminds Israel that there is no place for pious slogans disembodied from ethical living. In addition, the mention of Samaria in this verse may imply a condemnation of the division of the United Kingdom of David and Solomon in the days of Jeroboam I. As previously noted, in Amos 4.4-5, Yahweh says: 'Come to Bethel and rebel, to Gilgal and increase rebellion'. One cannot help but sense political overtones in the choice of the root פשע.[49] What is the likelihood that the Judean Amos had in mind the Northern Kingdom's rebellion against the House of David?

I have already pointed to the significance of Amos as a Judean prophet called to prophesy in the Northern Kingdom. Amos's pro-Judah/Jerusalem perspective would naturally translate into rejection of both the Northern Kingdom (Samaria) and its cultic establishments (such as the royally established sanctuary at Dan). According to Polley, 'for Amos, the only way true religion could be reestablished in Israel was for that nation to reunite with Judah, rejecting both northern cult and monarchy'.[50] I have sought to demonstrate that this is certainly a possible way of interpreting Amos 8.14. Nothing is reported in detail about the cult at either Dan or Beersheba. Thus, Dan is not condemned for anything necessarily associated with that religious center, but rather more simply because it was not Jerusalem, the place where Yahweh was properly worshiped, and because the cultic slogans rehearsed by the worshipers at the sanctuary were unconnected to the rest of the worshipers' conduct of life. On the several occasions in the book of Amos (3.14; 5.4-6; 7.9) where the prophet condemns what goes on at the northern sanctuaries, his polemic is probably best understood as being grounded in his pro-Judah position.

A final comment about the occurrence of Dan and Beersheba in Amos 8.14. It is likely that Dan was mentioned by the prophet because of its status as a significant royal chapel of the Northern Kingdom (cf. 1 Kgs 12).

---

49. The noun, פשע, occurs in Amos 5.12.
50. Polley, *Amos and the Davidic Empire*, p. 95.

Beersheba was an ancient cult site associated with the ancestors Abraham, Isaac, and Jacob.[51] On a more literary level, 'from Dan as far as Beersheba' occurs in the books of Judges, 1–2 Samuel, and 1 Kings as a conventional reference to the land encompassed by the United Kingdom of Israel, probably from the days of David and Solomon. The possibility exists that by naming both of these sites in this verse, Amos intended an allusion to this expression to show just how widespread the practices he condemned were throughout the whole land, including among the inhabitants of the territory of the kingdom of Judah (the Southern Kingdom is not exempt from the roll-call of nations against which Yahweh threatens judgment [2.4-5]).

---

51. Gen. 21.14, 32-33; 22.19; 26.23-25, 31-33; 28.10; 46.1, 5; 1 Kgs 19.3-4; 2 Kgs 23.8.

Chapter 5

INTERPRETING DAN IN THE BOOKS OF CHRONICLES

1. *1 Chronicles*

a. *1 Chronicles 1–9*

While Dan occurs only once within the genealogical material found in chs. 1–9 of 1 Chronicles, two texts within these nine chapters are examined here to determine the significance of Dan in the books of Chronicles. The texts under consideration are 1 Chron. 2.1-2 and 7.12.

(1) *1 Chronicles 2.1-2*

[1] These are the sons of Israel: Reuben, Simeon, Levi, and Judah, Issachar and Zebulun. [2] Dan, Joseph, and Benjamin, Naphtali, Gad, and Asher.

As it stands, this list of the sons of Israel (= Jacob) is unparalleled in the Hebrew Bible; nowhere else do these twelve sons appear in exactly this order. The consensus among critical scholars is that this list is based on Gen. 35.23-26.[1] The placement of Dan is what is exceptional about this register of names. In Genesis 35, the sons of Jacob are enumerated according to the criterion of matriarchal origin. Thus, Dan appears after the sons of Rachel (Joseph and Benjamin), and among the sons of the maidservants (in Gen. 35, the sons of Bilhah precede the sons of Zilpah). While other proposals have been proffered, most commentators agree that the placement of Dan in 1 Chron. 2.1, immediately preceding the sons of Rachel, is

---

1.   See, e.g., Edward Lewis Curtis and Albert Alonzo Madsen, *A Critical and Exegetical Commentary on the Books of Chronicles* (ICC; New York: Charles Scribner's Sons, 1910), p. 81; Wilhelm Rudolph, *Chronickbücher* (HAT, 21; Tübingen: J.C.B. Mohr [Paul Siebeck], 1955), p. 9; Jacob M. Myers, *I Chronicles: Introduction, Translation, and Notes* (AB, 12; Garden City, NY: Doubleday, 1965), p. 12; Williamson, *1 and 2 Chronicles*, p. 45; Japhet, *I and II Chronicles*, p. 65; Thomas Willi, *Chronik* (BKAT, 24.1; Neukirchen–Vluyn: Neukirchner Verlag, 1991), p. 46.

the result of a scribal error in the transmission of the text.[2] I concur. Rudolph is responsible for the critical apparatus to the books of Chronicles in *BHS*. In 1 Chron. 2.2, he suggests transposing Dan to a position after Benjamin, which is certainly the more expected location of Dan in the list of the sons of Israel (cf. Gen. 35.24-25, omitting the details). This emendation of the MT, admittedly only speculation (the Versions agree with the MT), would represent an easier, even better reading.[3] It is reasonable to suppose that Dan was moved to a position following Zebulun (end of v. 1) for reasons of homoeoteleuton (cf. the last consonant [= final nun] of Benjamin and Zebulun). Originally, the list of the sons of Israel in 1 Chron. 2.1-2 probably read: 'Reuben, Simeon, Levi, and Judah, Issachar and Zebulun; Joseph and Benjamin; Dan, Naphatli, Gad, and Asher'.[4] However, at some point in time, a scribe may have moved erroneously from Zebulun to Benjamin, and mistakenly wrote Dan after Zebulun. Of course, this cannot be assured, but may account for the unusual MT.

2.   Rudolph, *Chronickbücher*, p. 9; Myers, *I Chronicles*, p. 12; Williamson, *I and II Chronicles*, p. 45; Japhet, *I and II Chronicles*, p. 65; Martin Noth, *The Chronicler's History* (JSOTSup, 50; Sheffield: JSOT Press, 1987 [1943], p. 38 n. 23). See, however, the following for alternate suggestions regarding the placement of Dan in this list: C. F. Keil, *The Books of Chronicles* (Edinburgh: T. & T. Clark, 1878), pp. 57-58; Adrien-M. Brunet, 'Le Chroniste et ses Sources', *RB* 60 (1953), pp. 481-508 (490-91); Jack M. Sasson, 'A Genealogical "Convention" in Biblical Chronography?', *ZAW* 90 (1978), pp. 171-85. Keil and Brunet suggest that Dan's position, preceding the sons born to Rachel, is based on Gen. 30.1-6, and conclude that Dan was counted as Rachel's own, firstborn son. Sasson proposes that the seventh position in a genealogy (Dan's position in 1 Chron. 2.1-2) is a place of prominence, although he refers to 1 Chron. 2.1-2 only in passing and does not even speculate on why Dan occupies this position in this text. I am not persuaded that the seventh position in genealogies is necessarily the most prominent place in the biblical genealogies and list. Willi (*Chronik*, p. 46) follows Keil, Brunet, and Sasson, in affirming not only the significance of the seventh position in a genealogy, but also the view that Dan was considered the first-born of Rachel by her maidservant, Bilhah. Nowhere else in the Hebrew Bible is Dan counted as Rachel's son, and such an appraisal is not mandated by 1–2 Chronicles.

3.   In this case the text-critical rule *Lectio difficilior praeferenda est* does not apply. While the MT represents the more difficult reading, it is probably because it is a corrupt text.

4.   Note that a chiastic arrangement appears in this reconstruction of the original text: three names followed by one name preceded by the conjunction; one name followed by one name preceded by the conjunction//one name followed by one name preceded by the conjunction; three names followed by one name preceded by the conjunction.

(2) *1 Chronicles 7.12*

While the scope of the present study is the occurrences of Dan in the Hebrew Bible, it is necessary to look briefly at 1 Chron. 7.12 because even though the MT no longer preserves a mention of Dan in this verse, many scholars have detected here the remains of a Danite genealogy.[5] It is nearly universally agreed that an earlier form of this verse included a limited Danite genealogy similar to that preserved in Gen. 46.23 and Num. 26.42. The MT of 1 Chron. 7.12 is:

ושפם וחפם בני עיר חשם בני אחר:

[12] And Shuppim and Ḥuppim the sons of 'Ir, Ḥushim the sons of Aḥer.

[Notes on the MT:

For ושפם וחפם, it is suggested that one read instead וְשֻׁפָּם וְחֻפָּם (variant ending vowels), according to Num. 26.39. (It must be noted, however, that Num. 26.39 actually has שְׁפוּפָם and חוּפָם.) In addition, Rudolph (the editor of the books of Chronicles in *BHS*) assumes that before these names several words have dropped out of the text. For עיר, Rudolph proposes reading דן, compare Gen. 42.23; LXX [Vaticanus] has Ραωμ (corrupted from ιρ ασωμ = עיר חשום [transliterated in the LXX]). חֻשִׁם occurs in Gen. 42.24, but in Num. 26.48 the name is שֻׁחָם. For the second occurrence of בְּנֵי ('sons of'), we are encouraged to read בְנוֹ ('his son', singular) with the LXX. Finally, for אַחֵר ('Aḥer'; perhaps, 'another'), it is suggested that one read, instead, אַחַד ('one').]

While the text of the books of Chronicles is generally in good shape, those sections which include various list-materials tend to be more problematic.[6] The MT of 1 Chron. 7.12 raises several questions, as indicated by the notes to all but one word in this verse in the critical apparatus in *BHS*. 1 Chronicles 7.12 is almost certainly a fragment of an originally longer text.[7] While it is not unique for the Chronicler to have a proper name in the first

---

5.   Similarly, it is sometimes supposed that mention of Dan has been lost from the list of levitical cities in 1 Chron. 6.46, 54 (see *BHS*). It is likely that a verse based on Josh. 21.23 has been accidentally omitted (homoeoteleuton [מִגְרָשֶׁיהָ]) prior to 1 Chron. 6.54. The situation concerning v. 46 is more problematic because the text is not in good shape. Nevertheless, it is possible that mention of Dan has been lost in the course of the transmission of the text (the degree of difficulty with the MT leaves sufficient room for scribal error).

6.   Curtis and Madsen, *Chronicles*, p. 36; Japhet, *I and II Chronicles*, p. 29; Noth, *The Chronicler's History*, p. 37 ('…these verses [7.12-13] are apparently hopelessly corrupt and so have always remained unexplained').

7.   Noth, *The Chronicler's History*, p. 38; H.G.M. Williamson, 'A Note on 1 Chronicles VII 12', *VT* 23 (1973), pp. 375-79 (378).

position of a verse (cf. 1 Chron. 7.21), this is an unusual way for genealogical material to begin in 1 Chronicles 1–9. More typical is a verse
beginning 'the sons of...' Several commentators assume that these two
names, Shuppim and Huppim, are secondary glosses to the text, whose
purpose is to link the first part of v. 12 with the preceding Benjaminite
genealogy.[8] Given the likelihood that the MT is corrupt, it is just as reasonable to conclude that originally the genealogy of Benjamin continued into
v. 12. Thus, I recognize Shuppim and Huppim as authentic components of
the genealogy of Benjamin in 1 Chron. 7.6-12a, and not glosses. I also see
no reason in denying that these names are linked to 'Ir; they are listed as
the 'sons of 'Ir'.

   This decision, however, is contrary to most critical commentators, but I
assert that it can be defended. 'Ir is probably to be identified with 'Iri in
1 Chron. 7.7; the loss of the final yod should not be unexpected in a verse
that has suffered in transmission. Since Klostermann in the latter half of
the nineteenth century, however, the MT (עִיר בְּנֵי) is usually emended at
this point to read 'sons of Dan' (דָּן בְּנֵי).[9] This proposal is accepted by
Madsen and Curtis, Rudolph, Myers, and Japhet (see n. 1, above), but it is
not without difficulty. A primary criticism is the orthographic dissimilarity
between these two words, דָּן and עִיר, in Hebrew. It is hard to imagine
that either gave rise to the other. On the one hand, Rudolph recognizes this
problem, but accepts Klostermann's conjecture nonetheless.[10] On the other
hand, this is one of several reasons which has led Williamson to conclude
that דָּן has not been emended to עִיר but has dropped out completely from
the verse.[11] I am inclined to agree with Williamson. I suppose that originally the phrase, 'the sons of Dan', followed 'Ir in 1 Chron. 7.12, which
may have concluded the genealogy of Benjamin. There is sound evidence
in 1 Chronicles 7 that a Danite genealogy originally appeared at some
point in vv. 12-13. First, the name Hushim occurs as the name of a Danite
in Gen. 46.23 (the same person may be meant in Num. 26.42 where the MT
has שׁוּחָם [= חֻשָׁם, by metathesis?]). Williamson, who prefers to understand the whole of v. 12 as a continuation of the Benjaminite genealogy of

   8.   Curtis and Madsen, *Chronicles*, p. 150; Japhet, *I and II Chronicles*, p. 174.
   9.   A. Klostermann, 'Chronik, die Bücher der', in Johan Jacob Herzog (ed.),
Realencyklopädie für protestantische Theologie und Kirche (Leipzig: J.C. Hinrichs,
1898), pp. 84-98 (94).
   10.   Rudolph, *Chronickbücher*, p. 68.
   11.   Williamson, 'A Note on 1 Chronicles VII 12', p. 379; so also Myers, *I Chronicles*, p. 54.

1 Chron. 7.6-11, however, identifies this person with the Hushim in the genealogy of Benjamin in 1 Chron. 8.8-11.[12] The chief difficulty with this argument is the matter of gender (in 8.8-11 Hushim is a woman). Second, one probably expects a genealogy of Dan to follow the Benjaminite gene-alogy in 7.6-12a and precede the Naphtalite genealogy in 7.13. In what was likely the original form of 1 Chron. 2.1-2, Dan fell between Benjamin and Naphtali (see above on 1 Chron. 2.1-2). In addition, at the end of 1 Chron. 7.13 occurs the phrase 'the *sons* of Bilhah', which implies not only Naphtali (mentioned in 7.13a; cf. Gen. 30.7-8) but also the elder son of Bilhah, Dan (Gen. 30.1-6).

It is possible, though by no means irrefutable, that בני אחר at the end of 1 Chron. 7.12 also refers to a genealogy of Dan. It has been suggested that אחר (Aher) be emended to אחד ('one').[13] The orthographic confusion of dalet and resh is common in the Hebrew Bible, and should not be unexpected in this textually problematic verse.[14] If this last word in v. 12 does not refer to a Danite otherwise unknown from the biblical tradition, then it is possible that the emendation is correct: in both Genesis 46 and Numbers 26, only one descendant is listed for the 'sons of Dan'. Thus, the possibility exists that originally 1 Chron. 7.12b read: 'and the sons of Dan, Hushim his son (so LXX), one'. While this agrees with most commentators, I admit that the way in which I reconstruct it is somewhat unusual.

In all likelihood, 1 Chronicles 7 originally included a genealogy of Dan. Thus, it is not the case that in the postexilic period (the era of the Chron-icler) the tribe of Dan had been intentionally eliminated from considera-tion in Israel. Dan was remembered and included among the tribes of Israel (cf. 1 Chron. 2.1-2). This indicates that the Deuteronomistic program, according to which anything associated with Dan by virtue of the 'sins of Jeroboam' at the city of Dan in the north was negatively evaluated, did not reign exclusively in the years after the Babylonian exile (cf. the neutral-to-favorable occurrences of Dan in Ezek. 48). The 'disappearance of *Dan*' from the genealogical material in 1 Chronicles 1–9 is the result, not of the influence of the Deuteronomistic movement, nor of the theological inter-ests of the Chronicler, but of problems in the transmission of the text. Dan has disappeared from 1 Chron. 7.12 quite accidentally.[15]

---

12. Williamson, *1 and 2 Chronicles*, p. 78.

13. For other suggestions, see Japhet, *I and II Chronicles*, p. 174.

14. See the examples in McCarter, *Textual Criticism*, pp. 45-46.

15. Roddy Braun's hypothesis (*1 Chronicles* [WBC, 14; Waco, TX: Word Books, 1986], p. 107) that the omission of a mention of Dan in this text is not accidental but

b. *1 Chronicles 12*
1 Chronicles 12 divides into two parts of approximately equal length: vv. 1-23 and vv. 24-41 (MT—ET: vv. 1-22 and 23-40). Dan is mentioned as a reference to the tribe of the Danites in the second half of the chapter, in the list of the military units from the tribes which came to David's support in Hebron as the kingdom of Saul was turned over to David (12.36). The chapter begins, however, with a register of those valiant men who came to David at Ziklag and at the wilderness stronghold while Saul reigned as king (12.1-23). These warriors came from Benjamin, Gad, Judah, and Manasseh.

Perhaps the proper model by which to interpret this phenomenon is that of a faction. The definition of a faction provided by Malina and Rohrbaugh fits well the circumstances of this period of David's growing power while Saul was king. They write:

> A faction is a type of coalition [a type of impermanent groups gathered for specific purposes over a limited period of time] formed around a central person who recruits followers and maintains the loyalty of a core group. Factions share the common goal of the person recruiting the faction. Membership is based on a relationship with that central personage... Rivalry with other groups is basic; hence hostile competition for honor, truth (an ideological justification) and resources is always present.[16]

A very different scenario is depicted in part two of the chapter, 1 Chron. 12.24-41. Here, an assembly of all the constituent elements of Israel (14 tribes) gathered at Hebron for the purpose of conferring the kingship over 'all Israel' (12.39) upon David.[17] The tribes are listed geographically, in roughly a south to north arrangement (cf. the Chronicler's characteristic 'from Beersheba [south] as far as Dan [north]', 1 Chron. 21.2; 2 Chron.

---

represents an 'aversion to Dan' on the part of the Chronicler is tenuous. The evidence within the books of Chronicles does not support this claim (cf. Williamson, *1 and 2 Chronicles*, p. 75, who similarly disputes an anti-Dan bias on the part of the Chronicler).

16. Malina and Rohrbaugh, *Social-Science Commentary on the Synoptic Gospels*, p. 86; see also Boissevain, *Friends of Friends*, pp. 192-200; and Ralph W. Nicholas, 'Factions: A Comparative Analysis', in Steffen W. Schmidt *et al.* (eds.), *Friends, Followers, and Factions: A Reader in Political Clientalism* (Berkeley: University of California Press, 1977), pp. 55-73. It would be worthwhile to pursue this question of 'faction' as it relates more generally to the rise of monarchy in ancient Israel.

17. The number of tribes, 14, is unusual, and is attained by including not only Levi and the sons of Joseph (Ephraim and Manasseh) in the same list, but also by further dividing Manasseh into its Cisjordanian and Transjordanian sections (12.31, 38).

30.5), first of those in Cisjordan, next of those in Transjordan (1 Chron. 12.38). According to Japhet, in the books of Chronicles

> the complete people must include every element, and thus a number of different approaches to the identity of the 'twelve tribes' are synthesized. This creates a tension between the two goals: to portray Israel as a complete whole in keeping with the concept of 'twelve tribes' and, at the same time, to provide the broadest possible description of the people, incorporating all its components.[18]

Thus, according to this passage, the entire people (cf. 12.38) make David king over 'all Israel' at Hebron. Japhet raises questions about the historical accuracy of this episode, noting, among other things, the 'strikingly literary character' of 1 Chron. 12.24-41.[19] She notes that the entire scene depicted in these verses 'seems historically unlikely' in light of what is reported of the events in other biblical sources (2 Sam. 5). Nevertheless, the interest in the entirety of Israel affirming the kingship of David fits well into the ideology of the Chronicler:

> The absence of a grand enthronement festival is therefore a genuine reflection of the circumstances. For the Chronicler, however, the all-Israelite ingathering was not only feasible, but indispensable... In his opinion there was nothing that could justify the absence of a grand enthronement in the description of Samuel, and the ceremony, which for him was conspicuous by its absence, is fittingly supplemented.[20]

The significance for the present study is that in the postexilic era of the Chronicler, the tribe of Dan was portrayed as participating with the rest of the Israelite tribes in supporting David as he was made king at Hebron. This is, thus, further evidence against an exclusively anti-Dan perspective after the exile.

c. *1 Chronicles 27*

1 Chronicles 27.16-22 is a list of tribal chieftains set within an enumeration of political, religious, and military leaders from the time of David (23.1-2). In addition to these rulers of the tribes of Israel, chs. 23–27 include census figures (23.3) of Levites, priests, musicians, and other leaders. There is no

---

18. Sara Japhet, *The Ideology of the Book of Chronicles and Its Place in Biblical Thought* (Beiträge zur Erforschung des Alten Testaments und des Antiken Judentums, 9; New York: Peter Lang, 1989), p. 281; cf. p. 287. See also Braun, *1 Chronicles*, p. 171; Curtis and Madsen, *Chronicles*, p. 200.

19. Japhet, *I and II Chronicles*, p. 258.

20. Japhet, *I and II Chronicles*, p. 258.

consensus on the date of the material contained within these chapters: some scholars attribute it to the Chronicler himself, others recognize it as a secondary addition to 1 Chronicles.[21] More important than whether this is the free composition of the Chronicler or the contribution of a later redactor based on unknown sources (see, however, the reference in 1 Chron. 27.24 to the 'chronicles of King David') is the interest, in a document from the postexilic period, in Israel's ancient tribal structure. The tribes of Israel played no role in postexilic, Judahite society, yet their prominent role in Israel's earlier, monarchic history is remembered in the Chronicler's historical work.

It is agreed that the list of tribes listed in 1 Chron. 27.16-20 corresponds perfectly with no other tribal list in the Hebrew Bible; this list is unique. First of all, the tribes of Gad and Asher are omitted. It is sometimes assumed that their omission was by design, in order to keep the total number of tribes to twelve. Madsen and Curtis, for example, suggest that since Gad and Asher appear at the end of the lists in 1 Chron. 2.2 (cf. Gen. 35.24), they were the most likely ones to be left out.[22] As Japhet has proposed, however, the Chronicler may not have felt restricted to the number twelve in compiling his tribal lists. While twelve may signify completion, in fact 'all Israel' included as many as 14 or 15 tribes.[23] In this text, then, it may be unnecessary to postulate that the Chronicler needed to limit the number of tribes to twelve. Thus, it is possible that Gad and Asher have been lost for some other unknown reason, or more possibly as the result of textual corruption.[24] As the text stands, the arrangement of the tribes is

21. E.g. Noth (*The Chronicer's History*, p. 31) and Rudolph (*Chronickbücher*, p. 152) see 1 Chron. 23–27 as a great interpolation. Curtis and Madsen (*Chronicles*, p. 260) and Japhet (*I and II Chronicles*, pp. 406-10) are inclined to trace the origin of this material to the Chronicler. Williamson (*1 and 2 Chronicles*, pp. 157-59) represents a third position, attributing part of these chapters to the Chronicler and the rest to a redactor a generation later.

22. Curtis and Madsen, *Chronicles*, pp. 291-92. Of course, this argument fails to convince since the present list is unique. One cannot assume that Gad and Asher appeared in the final positions of the tribal list that the Chronicler had at hand. In addition to Gen. 35, 1 Chron. 27.16-22 is also frequently compared with Num. 1.5-15 or 1.20-42 (see Japhet, *I and II Chronicles*, pp. 471-72; Braun, *1 Chronicles*, pp. 260-61). However, Gad and Asher do not appear together in the final two positions in either of these lists.

23. Japhet, *Ideology of the Book of Chronicles*, pp. 280-81, 287-88.

24. Japhet, *I and II Chronicles*, p. 471. Japhet further notes that, even with the omission of Gad and Asher, the number tribal leaders is 13 (Zadok is listed as the chief of Aaron in v. 17, where Levi, like Manasseh later, seems to be divided into two units).

according to matriarchal origin rather than by geography (cf. 1 Chron. 12). First in order are the six Leah tribes. These are followed by Naphtali, the second son of Rachel's maidservant, Bilhah, who, together with Dan in last place, forms an envelope around the sons of Rachel: Ephraim and Manasseh (Joseph), and Benjamin. As just noted, the tribe and Dan and its chief, Azarel son of Jeroham, appears at the end of the list.

There is no agreement as to the origin of this list of the names of tribal leaders. Some of the names are known from elsewhere in the Hebrew Bible (especially the books of Chronicles), and many of them are common names. None of the names, however, occurs elsewhere as tribal chiefs. Myers hints at the possibility that the names are authentic from the time of David, although he admits that the list in its present form (including the unusual mention of Zadok as an Aaronite) is late.[25]

The significance of this list of tribal leaders for the present study of Dan in the biblical tradition would seem to be this: that 'all Israel', occasionally depicted in the books of Chronicles by the tribes of Israel, supported the monarchy of David until his demise (1 Chron. 29.28; cf. 23.1). The enumeration of the tribes and their leaders at this point in the text functions to confirm implicitly the continued support of 'all Israel' for David and his descendants at the time of the succession of Solomon and perhaps in the Chronicler's own age. The tribe of Dan was counted among the tribes of Israel, affirming their 'portion in David', their 'share in Jesse's son' (2 Chron. 10.16).

2. 2 Chronicles

a. *2 Chronicles 2*

According to 2 Chronicles 2, Huram King of Tyre sent, at Solomon's request, the skilled craftsman Huram-abi to Solomon in Jerusalem to oversee the manufacture of the assorted accoutrements required for the temple of Yahweh. A parallel to this passage is found in 1 Kings 5–7, especially 7.13-14. In the DH, the craftsman bears the name Hiram, and he is introduced as the 'son of a widow woman who was from the tribe of Naphtali, and his father was a man of Tyre, a worker in bronze' (בֶן־אִשָּׁה אַלְמָנָה הוּא מִמַּטֵּה נַפְתָּלִי וְאָבִיו אִישׁ־צֹרִי חֹרֵשׁ נְחֹשֶׁת). In the Chronicler's History,

---

It is interesting that Braun (*1 Chronicles*, p. 261; cf. p. 107), who supposes an anti-Dan bias in Chronicles, makes no comment on why Gad and Asher were omitted rather than Dan, other than that the Chronicler needed to limit the number of tribes to twelve.

25. Myers, *I Chronicles*, p. 184. Similarly, Japhet, *I and II Chronicles*, p. 4472.

while the craftsman's father remains a man of Tyre (although he is not described as a bronze worker), not only is the craftsman's name slightly different (Huram-abi, instead of Hiram), but his mother is no longer a widow, nor is she connected with the tribe of Naphtali. According to the Chronicler, she was a woman from among the 'daughters of Dan' (בֶּן־אִשָּׁה מִן־בְּנוֹת דָּן). 2 Chronicles 2.13 goes on to mention the skills this crafts- man brings to the task: he is skilled at 'working in gold and in silver, in bronze, in iron, in stone and in wood; in purple, in blue, and in crimson thread, and in fine Egyptian linen; and to do every kind of engraving and to design every kind of device that is required of him'. These details are absent from 1 Kings 7, which notes only the craftsman's ability to work in bronze, a skill apparently inherited from his father (1 Kgs 7.14).

It is usually supposed that the account of the construction of the temple and the manufacture of the various Temple accouterments in the DH served as the basis for the work of the Chronicler, and that the substitution of Dan for Naphtali is to be traced to the Chronicler himself.[26] It is some- times further argued that the description of the Danite craftsman associated with the wilderness tabernacle (Oholiab—Exod. 31.6; 35.34–36.2; 38.23) influenced the Chronicler, and that one of the Chronicler's objectives was to more closely associate the Solomonic temple of Yahweh with the wilderness tabernacle.[27] However, the present writer is unsatisfied that this particular line of argument has been adequately demonstrated. It is not altogether clear (or proven) that the mention of Dan in this text is the contribution of the Chronicler. As I suggested earlier in the analysis of Exodus 31–40, it is questionable whether a later writer would have substi- tuted Dan for Naphtali, given the influence of Dtr, had Naphtali actually stood in the tradition about the construction of Solomon's temple. As previously noted, it is, in the mind of the present writer, possible that Dan stood originally in the common tradition known to both Dtr and the Chronicler, and that the Chronicler has more faithfully represented this earlier tradition.[28] The texts of 1 Kgs 7.13-14 and 2 Chron. 2.12-13 are

26. E.g. Williamson, *1 and 2 Chronicles*, pp. 197-201; Japhet, *I and II Chronicles*, p. 545; Jacob M. Myers, *II Chronicles: Translation and Notes* (AB, 13; Garden City, NY: Doubleday, 1965), p. 12; Curtis and Madsen, *Chronicles*, p. 322; Dillard, *2 Chronicles*, pp. 18-21.

27. See the commentaries cited in the previous note.

28. The admittedly unproven assumption is that some record of the construction of the Temple was preserved in a temple archive, and that this formed the common tradition known to both Dtr and the Chronicler (see, e.g., G.H. Jones, *1 and 2 Kings*, I, pp. 57, 151-52).

sufficiently different (as are their respective contexts), making it possible that each writer worked over this antecedent, common tradition to accommodate his own purposes.[29] While it cannot be proven on the basis of the available evidence, it is possible that Dan occurred in both the wilderness and temple construction traditions with which the Chronicler was familiar.[30] Thus, the parallel between Oholiab from the wilderness period and Huram-abi from the Solomonic age was already part of the tradition before the Chronicler. The Chronicler was not responsible for the mention of Dan in 2 Chron. 2.13. Instead, it seems more reasonable to suppose, in light of the strong polemic against Dan in the DH, that Dtr changed Dan to Naphtali in order to dissociate the apostate tribe from the furnishing of Israel's central sanctuary of Yahweh in Jerusalem. Naphtali may have been deemed an appropriate substitute for Dan due to the relative proximity of that tribe's territory to the city-state of Tyre on the Mediterranean coast.[31] Remarkably, there is no polemic against Dan in the Chronicler's History; nowhere in the books of Chronicles is Dan evaluated in a negative way. In fact, a conclusion to be drawn on the basis of the present study is that Dtr is almost independent in his negative judgment of Dan in the Hebrew Bible. As I have demonstrated, the references to Dan in the prophetic corpus are neutral-to-positive; likewise, the majority of texts in

29. A glance at a synopsis of the books of Kings and Chronicles (see, e.g., Primus Vannutelli, *Libri Synoptici Veteris Testamenti seu Librorum Regum et Chronicorum Loci Paralleli* [2 vols.; Rome: Pontificio Instituto Biblico, 1931, 1934], I, pp. 212-22; James D. Newsome, Jr, *A Synoptic Harmony of Samuel, Kings, and Chronicles, With Related Passages from Psalms, Isaiah, Jeremiah, and Ezra* [Grand Rapids: Baker Book House, 1986], pp. 99-103) reveals that there is much material in these parallel texts that is found in only one tradition. This at least suggests that if the Chronicler knew the account in 1 Kgs 7, he did not feel bound to follow it closely but was, rather, free to adapt the tradition to suit his own interests.

30. The tabernacle tradition in the book of Exodus is usually considered part of the Priestly strand in the Pentateuch. A temple archive would most likely also have been kept by priests in Jerusalem. The priestly interests of the Chronicler are well known (see, e.g., Williamson, *1 and 2 Chronicles*, p. 17). It is probable, however, that the Chronicler updated some of the language in his sources for his audience (see Japhet, *I and II Chronicles*, p. 545; Williamson, *1 and 2 Chronicles*, p. 199).

31. It is the case that Dan and Naphtali may have been the only options available to the Chronicler, if Edelman is correct in situating the tribe of Asher in the southern hill country of Ephraim (Edelman, 'The Asherite Genealogy in 1 Chronicles 7:3-40'). Recall also that Dan and Naphtali are both descended from the sons of Rachel's maidservant, Bilhah (Gen. 30.1-6), and that the city of Dan is located within the territory ordinarily allotted to the tribe of Naphtali.

the Pentateuch. Even certain passages contained within the DH may have had an antecedent existence in which Dan was not negatively evaluated.

There is another matter of interest in this passage from 2 Chronicles—namely, whether the mention of Dan here refers to the tribe or the city of that name. Although commentators tend to assume that the tribe is meant, it must be admitted that the text is ambiguous. While 1 Kgs 7.14 explicitly mentions the '*tribe* (מטה) of Naphtali', the word 'tribe' nowhere occurs in 2 Chron. 2.12-13. The mother of the craftsman Huram-abi is referred to as 'a woman from among the daughters of Dan'. Indeed, nowhere else in the Hebrew Bible does the expression 'daughters of [tribe]' occur, although 'daughters of [city]' occurs in several texts scattered throughout the Hebrew Bible.[32] The absence of any word meaning 'tribe', together with the other occurrences of the phrase 'daughters of [city]' in the Hebrew Bible, makes it reasonable to conclude that, in the present form of the text, the *city* of Dan is intended.[33] This may well reflect the time of the Chronicler, when the territories of the tribes were no longer a reality but when the city of Dan continued to exist, albeit not as the major urban center it was decades earlier.[34] While the craftsman is sent by the king from the city of Tyre, it was remembered in the tradition that his mother was connected with Dan. Nevertheless, there is no polemic against Dan in this passage from 2 Chronicles.

b. *2 Chronicles 16*
The conquest of several of the leading cities in the northern part of Israel by Ben-hadad of Aram (Syria) reported in 2 Chron. 16.1-6 is parallel to 1 Kgs 15.16-20. While there are minor variances between the two accounts, they do not directly effect the mention of the city of Dan.[35] (See the discussion of this event in Chapter 3 of the present study.)

---

32. Shiloh: Judg. 21.21; Judah//Zion: Pss. 48.11; 97.8; Zion: Song 3.11; Isa. 3.16-17; 4.4; Jerusalem: Song 1.5; 2.7; 3.5, 10; 5.8, 16; 8.4; Rabbah: Jer. 49.3.

33. One cannot be certain whether the Chronicler's supposed archival source any more explicitly indicated tribe or city. It may have been just as ambiguous, and Dtr is responsible for the reference to 'tribe'. On the other hand, the omission of 'tribe' may have been part of the Chronicler's reworking of his source. Thus, this text from 2 Chronicles cannot be used to locate the tribe of Dan in the north.

34. Biran, *Biblical Dan*, pp. 270-71.

35. See Vannutelli, *Libri Synoptici Veteris Testamenti*, II, pp. 396-98; Japhet, *I and II Chronicles*, pp. 730-34.

3. *'From Beersheba as far as Dan'*[36]

On two occasions in the books of Chronicles, (all) Israel is defined as encompassing the land (and its inhabitants?) 'from Beersheba as far as Dan'.[37] 1 Chronicles 21.2 (the census during the reign of David) is parallel with 2 Sam. 24.2, while 2 Chron. 30.5 (in the Chronicler's unique account of Hezekiah's celebration of the Passover) is without parallel in the DH. Following the lead of the DH, each occurrence functions to give definition to what is meant by 'Israel' (1 Chron. 21.2) or 'all Israel' (2 Chron. 30.2). For this reason, it is the consensus among scholars that the phrase represents a traditional way of designating the full dimension of the kingdom of Israel. Of some interest is the fact that whereas all the occurrences of the related phrase, 'from Dan as far as Beersheba', in the DH appear in historical contexts ostensibly from the period before the division of David and Solomon's Kingdom into the kingdoms of Israel in the north and Judah in the south (hence, during the years of the *United* Monarchy), here in the books of Chronicles the second of two occurrences is situated, quite remarkably, soon after the collapse of the Northern Kingdom.[38] This appears to suggest that, in the Chronicler's scheme of things, during the 200-year existence of the Northern Kingdom, the north was not considered part of an 'all Israel' made up of both the Northern and Southern Kingdoms. While 'all Israel' is used during the time of the divided monarchy to designate each of the separate kingdoms, it does not seem to be used to denote the whole Israelite people.[39] Yet, early in the reign of Hezekiah, a proclamation is decreed throughout 'all Israel, from Beersheba as far as Dan', encouraging people in every part of the land to come to Jerusalem to keep the festival. The rhetorical effect of this text is important: under the reign of Hezekiah the land is imagined as having returned to its full extent under Solomon. Not even the Assyrian conquest of the Northern Kingdom can limit the extent of Hezekiah's reign. The closing remark to Hezekiah's Passover—namely, that nothing comparable had been celebrated in Israel since the days of David and Solomon (1 Chron. 30.26)—hearkens back to

36. See also the section 'From Dan as far as Beersheba' in Chapter 3 of the present study.

37. See Japhet, *I and II Chronicles*, pp. 46-47.

38. Of course, the Chronicler does not narrate the fall of the Northern Kingdom to Assyria (cf. 1 Kgs 17–18); see, however, the reference to this event in 2 Chron. 30.6-9; cf. 1 Chron. 5.26.

39. See Japhet, *Ideology of the Book of Chronicles*, pp. 257-78.

1 Chronicles 21–22, where David prepares for the succession of Solomon and the construction of the temple of Yahweh in Jerusalem.

There is a consensus that the inversion of the order of city names in the books of Chronicles (from Dan/Beersheba to Beersheba/Dan) is due to the Chronicler's focus on the Southern Kingdom.[40] I see no reason to suppose otherwise. Certainly at the time of the composition of the Chronicler's History, the perspective of the land was from the perspective of Judah. Besides this particular expression, the preference for the south to north orientation in the books of Chronicles has been noted by Curtis and Madsen, and Japhet.[41] Significantly, in the postexilic period the city of Dan was remembered as the northern boundary point of the land of Israel during Israel's 'golden years'.

4. *Summary: Dan in the Books of Chronicles*

In the books of Kings, every northern king is evaluated and found lacking due to the 'sins of Jeroboam', by which Dtr means the golden calves which Jeroboam I commissioned and erected at the ancient sanctuary cities of Bethel and Dan. Chiefly on account of Jeroboam's cultic adjustments, Dan and the Northern Kingdom are negatively critiqued in the DH. Interestingly enough, considering the near certainty that the Chronicler used the books of Samuel and Kings as one of his sources, there is no polemic against Dan in the books of Chronicles. Even in the Chronicler's report of the division of the Kingdom of David and Solomon during the reign of Rehoboam, Dan is unmentioned. Of course, the Chronicler's omission of most of the history of the Northern Kingdom begins to account for this reality. Since the Chronicler's interest was in the Davidic line traced through the kings of the Southern Kingdom of Judah, the Northern Kingdom and its kings appear only when their involvement with the kings of Judah serves the Chronicler's purpose. So, for example, there are references to the Northern Kingdom during the reigns of the Judean kings Jehoshaphat (2 Chron. 19.2; 20.35-37), Ahaziah (22.1-7), Amaziah (25.17-24), and Ahaz (28.1-16). On each occasion, the reference serves as a means of

---

40. E.g. Williamson, *1 and 2 Chronicles*, p. 144. Note, however, A. Hurvitz's linguistic-stylistic proposal ('"Diachronic Chiasm" in Biblical Hebrew', in Benjamin Uffenheimer [ed.], *Bible and Jewish History: Studies in Bible and Jewish History Dedicated to the Memory of Jacob Liver* [Tel Aviv: University of Tel Aviv Press, 1972]), cited in Japhet, *I and II Chronicles*, p. 376.

41. Curtis and Madsen, *Chronicles*, p. 247; Japhet, *I and II Chronicles*, p. 259.

judgment on the king of Judah (cf. 10.15, where the genesis of the Northern Kingdom of Israel is recognized as the fulfillment of God's promise [presupposing 1 Kgs 11.28-39, although this narrative of Jeroboam and Ahijah is not preserved in 2 Chronicles]); in 2 Chron. 28.5, it is Yahweh who gives Ahaz over to the king of Israel (Pekah) so that Israel functions as the instrument of God's punishment of Judah (cf. Israel as God's tool of judgment during the reign of Amaziah, 2 Chron. 25.20-24).

Even with a casual reading of the text, one notices that when allusion is made to Jeroboam's establishment of a cult in the north, there is *no* mention of Dan (2 Chron. 11.13-15; 13.8). In 2 Chron. 11.15, Jeroboam's manufacture of the calves and his reorganization of the priesthood are mentioned (cf. 1 Kgs 12.28-31); 2 Chron. 13.8 makes explicit mention of the golden calves which Jeroboam made 'as gods/God' (cf. 1 Kgs 12.28). Still, there is mention of neither Dan nor Bethel, the sanctuary sites at which the golden calves were placed. It is possible that the Chronicler felt no need to mention Dan, assuming knowledge of the places where Jeroboam set up the golden calves on the part of his readers. It may also be the case that in the Chronicler's opinion there is no sanctuary but that one in Jerusalem (the temple of Yahweh), and so he would not even want to suggest that there was another—even a rival sanctuary of Yahweh—at Dan.[42] Yet another way to account for the silence concerning Dan is simply to recognize that it was a northern sanctuary (and one that had long before the time of the Chronicler ceased to exist) and the Chronicler's interest was in the Southern Kingdom of Judah.

The silence concerning the northern sanctuary established by Jeroboam I at the city of Dan is significant. Equally significant are the references to Judean kings following in the ways of the 'kings of Israel' (2 Chron. 21.6, 13; 28.2), or in the practices of 'the house of Ahab' (21.6, 13; 22.3), and not to the 'sins of Jeroboam' (cf. the judgment formula of northern kings

---

42. See Japhet's comments regarding the cult of satyrs (*I and II Chronicles*, p. 668), by which the Chronicler may have intended to delegitimize the northern cult by distinguishing it from the legitimate cult practiced in the Jerusalem temple, the successor of the wilderness Tent of Meeting: 'the only reference added here is "satyrs", known to us as the object of some cult only in Lev. 17.7. This addition is carefully considered. Jeroboam's transgression in establishing his new cult is placed within the frame of reference determined by Lev. 17—the forbidding of sacrifices not offered with the proper blood-rites before "the tent of meeting". Such offerings are regarded as "sacrifices for satyrs". The full identification of the Temple in Jerusalem with the "tent of meeting" makes the entire sacrificial institution of the northern kingdom just such a "cult of satyrs".'

in 2 Kings). In fact, while the evaluation of the Northern Kingdom is wholly negative in the DH, the Chronicler's History is more ambiguous. That is, there are occasions where the attitude of the Chronicler toward the Northern Kingdom is more open and positive, while in other passages the evaluation is relatively negative. Japhet's summary statement on 'the Chronicler's attitude towards the northern kingdom' is instructive:

> Thus the Chronicler's attitude towards the northern kingdom is somewhat ambivalent: the kingdom is based on a sin, yet its establishment fulfills the word of Yahweh to Ahijah the Shilonite. The historical narrative does not focus on Israel, since only Judah is considered the true extension of David and Solomon's monarchy, yet all the connections between the two kingdoms are described systematically and even more fully than in the book of Kings. The Chronicler must make literary as well as theological adjustments to include these descriptions, even at the expense of the image of Judah's kings. His ambivalence can only be explained by the fact that the northern kingdom, for all its sins, is an integral part of the people of Israel.[43]

There are certainly negative critiques of Jeroboam I and the Northern Kingdom in the books of Chronicles. In the first place, the report of the division of the kingdom of Rehoboam concludes with the remark that 'Israel has been in rebellion against the house of David until this day' (2 Chron. 10.19). To revolt against the house of David is, according to the Chronicler (2 Chron. 13.8, unparalleled in 2 Kings), to rebel against the 'kingdom of Yahweh'. Yahweh's intimate association with the Southern Kingdom means that 'Yahweh is not with Israel' (2 Chron. 25.7).[44] Jeroboam's cultic reorganization also comes in for criticism; the admission of new priests led to an exodus of Levites from the Northern Kingdom to Judah (2 Chron. 11.14-15). Finally, in the Chronicler's story of Hezekiah's Passover, the inhabitants of Ephraim, Manasseh, and Zebulun, upon hearing the proclamation inviting them to the feast in Jerusalem, are reported to have laughed at and mocked the king's messengers (2 Chron. 30.10).

There are also, however, several passages in which the Northern Kingdom is portrayed in Chronicles in a more favorable light. For example, framing the period while the kingdom of Israel was in existence, there are references to faithful residents of the Northern Kingdom who came to Jerusalem. According to 2 Chron. 11.16-17,

---

43. Japhet, *Ideology of the Book of Chronicles*, p. 318.
44. Japhet (*Ideology of the Book of Chronicles*, p. 320) observes that this is the only example of a 'negative attitude towards the people of Israel'.

> after them [the Levites] from all the tribes of Israel, the ones who gave their
> heart to seek Yahweh the God of Israel came to Jerusalem to sacrifice to
> Yahweh the God of their fathers. They strengthened the kingdom of Judah,
> and they strengthened Rehoboam the son of Solomon for three years; for
> they walked in the way of David and Solomon for three years.

This notice is matched in 2 Chron. 30.11. Immediately after the remark
about those northerners who mocked Hezekiah's messengers inviting them
to the Passover celebration, the Chronicler reports: 'Yet, men from Asher
and from Manasseh and from Zebulun humbled themselves and came to
Jerusalem'. Other positive mentions of the Northern Kingdom include:
2 Chron. 11.4, which refers to the people of Israel as Judah's kinsmen;
2 Chron. 15.9, which notes people from Ephraim and Manasseh who came
(deserted?) to Judah during the reign of Asa; and 2 Chron. 31.1, which
reports the wholesale demolition of pillars, sacred posts, shrines, and altars
throughout not only Judah and Benjamin, but also the territories of
Ephraim and Manasseh after the celebration of Passover in the reign of
Hezekiah.

All of this demonstrates, quite remarkably, that there is no unrelenting
polemic against Dan or the Northern Kingdom in the books of Chronicles.
Since Jeroboam's sins are not explicitly associated with the city of Dan in
the north, this site does not have the same negative connotations as it does
in 2 Kings. In the early monarchic period, Dan appears among the rest of
the tribes of Israel in support of the kingship of David, and then of his son,
Solomon (1 Chron. 12; 27). After the division of the United Monarchy of
David and Solomon, the Northern Kingdom was always considered an
integral part of 'all Israel'. Even though the Northern Kingdom does not
play a prominent role in Chronicles, it has been neither written out nor
written off by the Chronicler. While the Northern Kingdom had strayed,
and was in a persistent state of rebellion against the 'house of David' and
the 'kingdom of Yahweh', its residents were nevertheless recognized as
Judah's relatives.

Chapter 6

CONCLUSIONS AND FINAL REMARKS

At the beginning of this study I proposed certain guiding questions. Here in conclusion, I suggest responses to those questions on the basis of the present investigation.

1. What does the Hebrew Bible, in fact, tell us about Dan—the ancestor, the tribe, and its territory, the city?

According to biblical tradition, Dan was the firstborn son of one of Jacob's secondary wives. His mother was Bilhah, Rachel's maidservant. While Dan's birth of a secondary, rather than of a primary, wife of Jacob in large measure determines the placement of Dan (the ancestor as well as the tribe) in various lists of the sons of Jacob (= tribes of Israel), among the sons of the maidservants Dan occupies a special place. Not only was he the first son to be born of a secondary wife of Jacob, his mother was also Rachel's maidservant, and Rachel was Jacob's favorite wife. These relationships, as presented in Genesis 29–30, are important in establishing the background for interpreting the relative status of the ancestors and tribes. In addition, in Gen. 30.1-6 Rachel makes a special claim on Dan, since he is born 'on [Rachel's] knees'. Also, Rachel exercises authority by naming the child who, according to Rachel, represents her vindication by God.

In the biblical tradition, the sons of Jacob become the eponymous ancestors of the tribes of Israel. I have suggested, however, that the actual development was likely to have been in the other direction. That is, the notion of the 'tribes of Israel' was antecedent to the system of the sons of Jacob. Regardless, there is a clear connection between the traditions about the ancestors and those about the tribes. In the numerous lists in the Hebrew Bible, the relative position of both ancestors and tribes are usually determined by the birth-mother of the sons of Jacob, with the sons of Jacob's wives taking precedence over the sons of their maidservants. In no place is Dan, as the son of Jacob, evaluated any more uncomplimentarily than the other sons of the maidservants of Jacob's wives.

I have indicated that one must be judicious in drawing conclusions about the nature of the tribe of Dan on the basis of the biblical narratives alone, since many of these are highly literary in character and/or have passed through the hands of multiple editors. In what is probably the earliest reference to the tribe of Dan (Judg. 5.17, the Song of Deborah), Dan is criticized for failing to participate in Israel's war against the Canaanite kings. Following the lead of certain other scholars, I conclude that at the time of this battle the tribe of Dan was not an independent social group in the hill country, but had, rather, a marginal existence and was probably landless and economically dependent on other, non-Israelite communities. These extra-Israelite ties prohibited members of the tribe of Dan from participating in the battle. The marginal character of Dan appears again in the hero-stories of Samson which, I have argued, are based on folk stories of an oppressed group, articulating its members's unrealized hopes. In addition, the issue of the Danites's precarious control over their own land resurfaces in the story of the tribe's migration in Judges 18. According to Judges 18, (a portion of) the tribe of Dan migrated northward to conquer Laish, resettled the site, and renamed it Dan. Unfortunately, there is no extra-biblical evidence (prior to the the bilingual inscription from the Hellenistic period) either to corroborate this event or to confirm that the city was called Dan already in the Iron Age. For these reasons, in addition to what I have identified as the etiological character of Judges 18, I have raised doubts about the historical veracity of this migration story and of the tribe of Dan's habitation of the city of the same name. (Such a depiction of the Danites' as one discovers in Judg. 18 [as a significant military power] is at odds with other portrayals of the strength of the tribe [Judg. 5; 13–16].)

It is also observed that Dan appears frequently in some degree of relation to the tribe of Judah. In some cases the relationship is without prejudice, while in other instances, I have argued, a Judean perspective denigrates the tribe of Dan (e.g. Judg. 1). Geographically, these two tribes' respective territories are contiguous (in Josh. 15.19 certain cities are listed as being within the possession of both tribes). Dan and Judah are the only tribes named in the Samson stories, and it is from these two tribes that the two named craftsmen in Exodus 31–40 come. Also, Dan and Judah are each referred to as a 'lion's whelp' (Gen. 49.9; Deut. 33.22). In the census of tribes leaving Egypt at the time of the Exodus, Judah and Dan are the largest. In both Judges 1 and Ezekiel 48, Judah and Dan envelope the other named tribes.

The prominence given to the tribe of Dan in certain traditions may be understood in connection with the political realities of the early monarchic period in Israel. It is worthwhile noting that biblical texts about Dan traditionally traced to the time of the United Monarchy portray Dan in a favorable light. The present study generally supports the following scheme about Dan: pre-monarchic texts (e.g. Judg. 5), as well as late- and post-monarchic texts (the DH and Priestly material) are negative, while texts from the period of the United Monarchy tend to be positive (e.g. Gen. 30; 49). It is conceivable that the positive appraisal of Dan in the texts traced to the time of the United Monarchy is related to David's effort to unite an earlier tribal league into a kingdom with a central authority. Indeed, per- haps it is not the case that Dan is important because Rachel is Jacob's favorite wife; rather, Rachel is Jacob's favorite wife because of the impor- tance of Dan in the early years of David's monarchy. David, a Bethlehem- ite from Judah, needed to make a play for the northern tribes in order to consolidate his kingdom. It is possibly for this reason that Dan is given such a prominent place, for example, in the birth stories in Genesis 29–30.[1] (In an effort to bring along the followers of Saul after that kingdom's demise, the tribe of Benjamin is similarly given a significant place in the traditions from the time of the United Monarchy.)

While there are certain things that can be asserted about this tribe, the reconstruction of a 'history of the tribe of Dan', based on a careful reading of the available evidence, is tenuous. In the final analysis, it is simply too facile to take the historical claims of the biblical literature regarding Dan at face value. The interpreter must deal seriously with the question of the literary character of these compositions, as well as with the cultural con- text and theological intentions of their authors and subsequent redactors.

The territory of the tribe of Dan was situated in the hill country in the southern part of the land, adjacent to the territories occupied by Ephraim, Benjamin, and Judah. All of the traditions in the Hebrew Bible locate the territory of Dan in this area (Judg. 5 is frequently a subject of debate on this question, but I concur with those scholars who defend the southern location of Dan). In the course of this investigation, I have raised the question about how broadly the biblical traditions attest to the presence of a Danite territory in the north. I conclude that there is no such unequivocal

---

1.   Theodore Hiebert, private communication.

tradition. Apart from the etiological narrative in Judges 18, the only biblical tradition that seems to situate the tribe in the north is Deuteronomy 33 (cf., however, the *visionary* description of the tribal territories in the restored land in Ezek. 48, a vision never fully realized). Yet, even in the case of Deut. 33.22, I have suggested that the content of the saying about Dan is not unquestionably about the *tribe* of Dan, but that the character and status of the *city* of Dan from a later period may be reflected in this portrayal of the tribe.

In the Hebrew Bible, the city of Dan appears as the leading city on the northern boundary of the land traditionally given to Israel. According to Judges 18, the city was formerly a Canaanite (Phoenician?) outpost called Laish (Leshem in Josh. 19.47). The name occurs anachronistically in Genesis 14 (it is anachronistic with respect to content since, according to biblical tradition [Judg. 18], in the time of Abram the city was not yet named Dan). In the DH and in the books of Chronicles, Dan is paired with Beersheba in the south in the expression 'from Dan as far as Beersheba' (DH, the order of cities is reversed in 1–2 Chronicles), marking the ideal boundary of the Israelite territory. Dan's significance as a border city appears also in Jeremiah; Dan is the leading city at the northern border over which the invading enemy from Mesopotamia or Syria crossed to enter Palestine. In Amos 8, while the reference is explicitly to the city of Dan, the criticism is less of the city and more narrowly of those citizens of the Northern Kingdom generally who repeat a certain religious slogan ('...and say, "As your god lives, O Dan..."') and worship Yahweh outside Jerusalem, but whose lives do not reflect an ethic (concerned with justice and righteousness) appropriate to worshipers of Yahweh. I have also offered the suggestion that the city of Dan may be intended in 2 Chronicles 2, where the mother of the craftsman, Huram-abi, is introduced as a woman from among the 'daughters of Dan', a positive reference to the city of Dan.

Due to the dominance of the DH and its theology in both Jewish and Christian communities, it is difficult to encounter 'Dan' anywhere in the Hebrew Bible and not recall the polemic against the city of Dan that comes through this block of material. At the center of Dtr's critique of the city of Dan is 1 Kings 12, which cannot be construed as anything less than a partisan statement originating in the kingdom of Judah. Although I have indicated that what Jeroboam I may in fact have done in establishing sanctuaries at Dan and Bethel was reasonable and not intended as heterodoxy, as described by Dtr in 1 Kings 12 Jeroboam's activity is anti-Yahwistic, polytheistic, iconic, and idolatrous. This, I contend, is the enduring image the reader, ancient and modern, finally has of the city of Dan: it is a site of straying from Yahweh's chosen House of David, of apostasy, and of continuing sin. My conclusion, then, is that this passage has over-shadowed mention of Dan elsewhere in the biblical traditions.

2.   How have the (Deuteronomistic) criticisms of Jeroboam's cult center at the city of Dan affected the portrayal of the ancestor or tribe? What can be said about the effect of the relationship between the city, the tribe (and its territory), and the ancestor as preserved in the Hebrew Bible?[2]

I believe that the response to this question is among the most significant contributions of the present study. First, it is noteworthy that there is no polemic against Dan in the Latter Prophets or in 1–2 Chronicles. As these documents have been transmitted through the years, they seem to have escaped any significant editing, with respect to Dan, by a deuteronomisti-cally inspired editor.[3] I have also proposed that the character of the tribe of Dan in Deut. 33.22 is dependent on that of the city of Dan from the time of Jeroboam I. Thus, here is an example of a 'city tradition' exercising a positive influence over a 'tribal tradition'.

Nevertheless, in certain texts, especially in the DH, the evaluation of the city has negatively influenced the depiction of the tribe. For example, I have argued that the very structure of the Deuteronomistic composition in Judges 1 plainly honors the kingdom and tribe of Judah, while at the same time disparaging the constituent tribes of the Northern Kingdom and the tribe of Dan in particular. I have also indicated that the present shape of the stories about the Danite protagonist, Samson, serves to transform origi-nally encouraging and hopeful stories about the hero of a marginal tribe into stories about a faithless Nazirite and self-serving judge whose conduct contributes to the downward spiral of life in Israel prior to the emergence of the Israelite monarchy.

Most significantly, I have proposed that the final form of Judges 17–18 (the third redactional level in my Hypothesis Two) comes from the hand of Dtr, and is a strong polemical attack on the northern sanctuary at Dan.

2.   There is some confluence of ancestral and tribal traditions already in the Hebrew Bible, as indicated by later editors who were not always clear about which expression of Dan (or other ancestors/tribes) was intended in the material available to them. So, e.g., Gen. 49 makes reference in the framework to both sons of Jacob and tribes of Israel.

3.   This is not, of course, to deny *any* Deuteronomistic editing in the Latter Prophets.

In this narrative, the tribal sanctuary established by the Danites at the city of Dan is ridiculed numerous times and criticized as illegitimate on account of its idol and molten image, and priesthood descended from a disloyal, opportunistic Levite. It is my conclusion that the impetus for this reshaping of the earlier tradition was the cultic activity of Jeroboam at the city of Dan. While scribes in the time of Jeroboam may have sought to enhance the legitimacy of Jeroboam's work by an appeal to more ancient tradition, Dtr, by also creating an ancient story, sought to undermine the cultic center's legitimacy and in so doing cast a long shadow over not only the city, but also the tribe of Dan and its eponymous ancestor.

Finally, I have also attempted to show that an editor (possibly Priestly) late in the postexilic period, perhaps influenced by the legacy of the Deuteronomistic caricature of Jeroboam's religious activity with respect to the golden calves at the cities of Bethel and Dan, added the ancestry of the anonymous blasphemer's mother (Lev. 24). In the present (final) form of the text, his mother is descended from the tribe of Dan.

    3.   How do the narratives about individual members of the tribe of Dan contribute to one's appraisal of the tribe generally?

Narratives about three individuals associated with the tribe of Dan appear in the Hebrew Bible: Oholiab (Exod. 31–40), an anonymous blasphemer (Lev. 24), and Samson (Judg. 13–16). First, Oholiab is one of only two craftsmen whose names are preserved in the account of the construction of the wilderness tabernacle and its appurtences, the other being Bezalel from the tribe of Judah. Not surprisingly, Oholiab occupies a role secondary to that of the Judahite, although this should not necessarily be interpreted as a measure of disapproval. Rather, the relative status of the two craftsmen reflects the partisan interests of a Judean author. The fact that a Danite is remembered by name at all is significant; there is no hostility against Oholiab in the narrative. The text relates very little about this Danite, indicating little more than that he was noted for his work in textiles. Oholiab seems to be related, in some way, to the Danite craftsman, Huram-abi, who leads the construction of the temple of Solomon in the Chronicler's History (2 Chron. 2; cf. 1 Kgs 7). As the Hebrew Bible stands (in its final form), this positive tradition about Oholiab seems to function as a 'type' for this latter Danite craftsman.

Second, it is my proposal that the anonymous blasphemer in Lev. 24.1-23 is only secondarily linked with the tribe of Dan. That is, the identification of the blasphemer's mother with the Danites is neither original nor integral to the narrative, but may be a secondary addition to the text intended to connect this incident of blasphemy with the blasphemous slogan of Jeroboam I ('Here is/are your god[s], O Israel, who brought you up from the land of Egypt', 1 Kgs 12.28) spoken in reference to the golden calves at the cities of Bethel and Dan.

The third individual Danite about whom a narrative has been preserved in the Hebrew Bible is Samson. However, the tribe of Dan plays no obvious role in the narrative itself, and Samson is identified as a member of the tribe of Dan only in the framework of Judges 13 (vv. 2, 25; see also 16.31). I have argued, on the basis of folklore analysis and the application of the anthropological model of honor/shame, that in their origin the stories about Samson were *positive* stories about a heroic figure whose purpose was to inspire hope and articulate the aspirations of the Danites, who were, at the time, a marginalized group in Israel, subject (apparently) not only to the Philistines but to their Judahite brethren (Judg. 15.9-13). It is the canonical context of Judges 13–16 that results in making Samson appear to be a faithless Nazirite and poor judge, although (and it is worth repeating) references to Samson's judgeship occur only in the framework (which may be editorial) and *he* is nowhere unequivocally identified as a Nazirite in the text. It is difficult to determine the degree to which Samson represents a typical Danite; my conclusion, however, is that this degree is probably very low—it is unlikely that the interpreter should correlate every detail narrated in the Samson story with the historical reality of the tribe of Dan. The significance of Samson is that, as a heroic figure, he represents the dreams and unrealized expectations of the marginalized tribe of Dan vis-à-vis Judahites (Judg. 15) and Philistines (chs. 14–16). Similarly, according to the present analysis, the blasphemer in Leviticus 24 hardly represents the historical character of the tribe of Dan. The reader must always move beyond narrowly historical concerns to consideration of the literary and theological interests of the editors who have handed on and, often, reshaped these biblical traditions.

4.   Finally: What is there in the Hebrew Bible that led to such an entirely uncomplimentary appraisal of Dan in the later Jewish and Christian traditions? To what degree is this latest, post-biblical Danite material shaped by the tribal traditions in the Hebrew Bible? That is, how do these late materials cohere with the biblical texts themselves?

The survey of the later biblical and post-biblical writings in the Introduction showed that Dan, whether in texts concerning the city, the ancestor, or the tribe, is almost everywhere disparaged. It is clear, however, that much of the early post-biblical interpretation of the Dan traditions (rabbinic midrash, early Church Fathers) is not actually supported by the biblical text. Rather, it is my conclusion that the theological interests of the Deuteronomistic movement exercised an exceptional influence over these subsequent interpreters. The vast majority of these post-biblical texts locate Dan (city or tribe) in the north, and have as part of their message a criticism of Jeroboam's cult center and its antecedent tribal sanctuary. It is clear, however, in light of the present study, that the Deuteronomistic evaluation of Dan was only one among many. For example, in the postexilic period, the Chronicler has a more favorable opinion of Dan. Indeed, there is no polemic against Dan in 1–2 Chronicles.

In the Introduction I noted that, for example, in the case of Irenaeus' interpretation of Dan in Jeremiah 8, we learn more about Irenaeus than about Dan (while the biblical text clearly refers to the city of Dan, Irenaeus interprets the passage in terms of the tribe). I have also, on numerous occasions in the present study, raised the question about the ability to reconstruct, with any degree of confidence, the history of the tribe of Dan based on little more than the biblical traditions. In particular, I have challenged the use of Judges 1, 13–16, and even Judges 17–18 for such an undertaking. One of the more significant contributions of the present study is the conclusion that there is not a *single* 'Danite tradition' that runs through the entire Hebrew Bible, is continued in the New Testament, and may be traced into the post-biblical material. While the vast majority of references to Dan in the latter documents are negative, the portrayal of Dan in the Hebrew Bible is more ambiguous. Some texts are clearly negative (e.g. 1 Kgs 12), while others are neutral or even positive. In every instance, however, one must be sensitive to the redaction history of the text and theological interests of the authors. That is, I have suggested that in certain cases an originally positive tradition about Dan has been recast as a negative tradition by a later redactor (Judg. 13–16; 17–18). The latest biblical and post-biblical traditions surveyed here apparently have been influenced most heavily by the Deuteronomistic movement in ancient Israel. It is my conclusion that the idea of linking Dan with apostasy emerges within the biblical tradition only in the Deuteronomistic presentation of Jeroboam's political and cultic activity.

It is possible that the present study may be characterized by some as an effort at rewriting history, and that an unstated objective of the writer has been to redeem Dan and the Danites from the usual interpretation of the biblical traditions. I resist such a judgment on the work, while readily conceding that I have been interested in questioning the typical interpretations of Dan, always asking if there is another way to understand the stories or portrayals of Dan in the Hebrew Bible. In this way, I have sought, perhaps, to reclaim more fully the richness of the Dan traditions in the Hebrew Bible. I agree with the presumption that there is more to the biblical traditions than history, especially 'history' as we understand that term today; and that in large measure the biblical authors and editors, and their communities, were more inclined toward the genre of story than history.[4] It is partly for this reason that I continue to hold that it is difficult to reconstruct a 'history of an old Israelite tribe', such as Nieman attempted to do for Dan. Rather, the interpreter (indeed, the historian as well) must be attentive to the literary character of the biblical text, the theological interests of its authors and editors, and to the text's history of transmission. I have attempted to do just this. In addition, where appropriate, I have pursued alternative interpretations of the biblical material in light of certain social considerations and anthropological models. Thus, I have sought to test Carney's observation that 'models provide a source from which new views of a long familiar reality can be drawn'.[5] While not limited to the texts in Joshua–2 Kings, my analysis of the Dan traditions included in the DH has, perhaps, benefitted the most from the application of these models.

On the basis of the present, comprehensive study of Dan in the biblical traditions, I conclude that the portrayal of Dan in the Hebrew Bible is ambivalent. The disparaging image of Dan that one gets from reading the latest biblical and post-biblical material is not derived from a singular depiction of Dan in the Hebrew Bible. That is, there is not a single strand of Danite tradition that moves all the way through the Hebrew Bible, and then from the pages of the Hebrew Bible to the post-biblical documents. Most traditions about Dan in the Hebrew Bible are either positive, or were positive in origin but have been reshaped by a subsequent editor (or editors) into their final form. In fact, outside of the DH, Dan is, more often than not, positively depicted. And within this well-defined corpus, Jeroboam's activity at the city of Dan plays a significant role in the overall impression left of Dan. It is due to the influence of this perspective on not only other parts of the biblical tradition and the post-biblical writers and

4. See again the remark of Matthews and Benjamin in 'Social Sciences and Biblical Studies', p. 10.
5. Carney, *The Shape of the Past*, p. 9.

their audiences, but also on the Jewish and Christian communities through the years, that the casual reader today may still come away from the Bible with a negative impression of Dan in the biblical traditions. Nevertheless, the conclusion offered here is that the evidence from the Hebrew Bible does not completely justify the negative appraisal of Dan in these later traditions, but that the overall picture of Dan in the Hebrew Bible is mixed.

BIBLIOGRAPHY

Ackroyd, Peter R., 'The Composition of the Song of Deborah', *VT* 2 (1952), pp. 160-62.
Aharoni, Yohanan, *The Land of the Bible: A Historical Geography* (Philadelphia: Westminster Press, rev. and enlarged edn, 1979).
Ahlström, G.W., 'Judges 5:20f. and History', *JNES* 36 (1977), pp. 287-88.
—*Royal Administration and National Religion in Ancient Palestine* (SHANE, 1; Leiden: E.J. Brill, 1982).
—*Who Were the Israelites?* (Winona Lake, IN: Eisenbrauns, 1986).
Akers, Ronald L., *Criminological Theories: Introduction and Evaluation* (Los Angeles: Roxbury, 2nd edn, 1997).
Albertz, Rainer, *A History of Israelite Religion in the Old Testament Period*. I. *From the Beginnings to the End of the Monarchy* (OTL; 2 vols.; Louisville, KY: Westminster/John Knox Press, 1994).
—Review of *Die Daniten: Studien zur Geschichte eines altisraelitischen Stammes*, by Hermann Michael Niemann, *BZ* 31 (1987), pp. 299-301.
Albright, William Foxwell, *Archaeology and the Religion of Israel* (Baltimore: The Johns Hopkins University Press, 1942).
—'The List of Levitic Cities', in American Academy for Jewish Research, *Louis Ginzberg Jubilee Volume: On the Occasion of His Seventieth Birthday* (New York: American Academy for Jewish Research, 1945), pp. 49-73.
—'The Moabite Stone', in *ANET*, pp. 320-21.
—'Some Additional Notes on the Song of Deborah', *JPOS* 2 (1922), pp. 284-85.
—'The Song of Deborah in the Light of Archaeology', *BASOR* 62 (1936), pp. 26-31.
—*Yahweh and the Gods of Canaan: A Historical Analysis of Two Contrasting Faiths* (repr., Winona Lake, IN: Eisenbrauns, 1990 [1968]).
Allen, Leslie C., *Ezekiel 20–48* (WBC, 29; Dallas: Word Books, 1990).
—'The First and Second Books of Chronicles: Introduction, Commentary, and Reflections', in Leander E. Keck *et al.* (eds.), *New Interpreter's Bible* (Nashville: Abingdon Press, 1999), III, pp. 297-659.
Alt, Albrecht, 'Bemerkungen zu einigen judäischen Ortslisten des Alten Testaments', in *idem*, *Kliene Schriften zur Geschichte des Volkes Israel*, II, pp. 289-305.
—'Das System der Stammesgrenzen im Buche Josua', in W.F. Albright (ed.), *Beiträge zur Religionsgeschichte und Archäologie Palestinas. Ernst Sellin zum 60. Geburtstage* (Leipzig: Deichert, 1927), pp. 13-24 (reprinted in *idem*, *Kliene Schriften zur Geschichte des Volkes Israel*, I, pp. 193-202).
—'Judas Gaue unter Josia', *PJ* 21 (1925), pp. 100-16 (reprinted in *idem*, *Kliene Schriften zur Geschichte des Volkes Israel*, II, pp. 276-88).
— *Kliene Schriften zur Geschichte des Volkes Israel* (3 vols.; Munich: C.H. Beck, 1959).
Anderson, Francis I., and David Noel Freedman, *Amos: A New Translation with Introduction and Commentary* (AB, 24A; New York: Doubleday, 1989).

Ashley, Timothy R., *The Book of Numbers* (NICOT; Grand Rapids: Eerdmans, 1993).

Bal, Mieke, *Death and Dissymetry: The Politics of Coherence in the Book of Judges* (Chicago: University of Chicago Press, 1988).

Barnett, R.D., 'Early Shipping in the Near East', *Antiquity* 32 (1958), pp. 220-30.

Barstad, Hans M., *The Religious Polemics of Amos* (VTSup, 34; Leiden: E.J. Brill, 1984).

Bauckham, Richard, 'The List of the Tribes in Revelation 7 Again', *JSNT* 42 (1991), pp. 99-115.

Beasley-Murray, G.R., *The Book of Revelation* (NCB; Grand Rapids: Eerdmans, rev. edn, 1978).

Bechmann, Ulrike, *Das Deboralied zwischen Geschichte und Fiktion: Eine Exegetische Untersuchung zu Richter 5* (Dissertation Theologische Reihe, 33; St Ottilien: EOS Verlag Erzabtei, 1989).

Bechtel, Lyn M., 'Shame as a Sanction of Social Control in Biblical Israel: Judicial, Political, and Social Shaming', *JSOT* 49 (1991), pp. 47-76.

Becker-Spörl, Silvia, *Und sang Debora an jenem Tag: Untersuchung zu Sprache und Intention des Deboraliedes (Ri 5)* (Europäische Hochschulschriften Reihe, 23; Theologie, 620; Frankfurt am Main: Peter Lang, 1998).

Ben Zvi, Ehud, 'The List of the Levitical Cities', *JSOT* 54 (1992), pp. 77-106.

Bendor, S., *The Social Structure of Ancient Israel: The Institution of the Family (Beit 'Ab) from the Settlement to the End of the Monarchy* (Jerusalem Biblical Studies, 7; Jerusalem: Simor, 1996).

Benoit, P., 'Editing the Manuscript Fragments from Qumran', *BA* 19 (1956), pp. 75-96.

Berridge, Maclennan, *Prophet, People, and the Word of Yahweh: An Examination of Form and Content in the Proclamation of the Prophet Isaiah* (Basel Studies of Theology, 4; Zürich: EVZ-Verlag, 1970).

Bezold, C., and E.A. Wallis Budge, *The Tell El-Amarna Tablets in the British Museum with Autotype Facsimiles* (London: Harrison & Sons, 1892).

Biran, Avraham, *Biblical Dan* (Jerusalem: Israel Exploration Society, 1994).

—'Tel Dan: Biblical Texts and Archaeological Data', in Michael David Coogan, J. Cheryl Exum and Lawrence E. Stager (eds.), *Scripture and Other Artifacts: Essays on the Bible and Archaeology in Honor of Philip J. King* (Louisville, KY: Westminster/John Knox Press, 1994), pp. 1-17.

—'"To the God who is in Dan"', in Avraham Biran (ed.), *Temples and High Places in Ancient Israel* (Jerusalem: Nelson Glueck School of Biblical Archaeology of Hebrew Union College/Jewish Institute of Religion, 1981), pp. 142-51.

Biran, Avraham, and Joseph Naveh, 'An Aramaic Stele Fragment from Tel Dan', *IEJ* 43 (1993), pp. 81-98.

—'The Tel Dan Inscription: A New Fragment', *IEJ* 45 (1995), pp. 1-18.

Blenkinsopp, Joseph, *Ezra–Nehemiah: A Commentary* (OTL; Philadelphia: Westminster Press, 1988).

—'Structure and Style in Judges 13–16', *JBL* 82 (1963), pp. 65-76.

Boissevain, Jeremy, *Friends of Friends: Networks, Manipulators and Coalitions* (New York: St Martin's, 1974).

Boling, Robert G., '"In Those Days There Was No King in Israel"', in Howard N. Brean, Ralph D. Helm and Carey A. Moore (eds.), *A Light Unto My Path: Old Testament Studies in Honor of Jacob M. Myers* (Gettysburg Theological Studies, 4; Philadelphia: Temple University Press, 1974), pp. 33-48.

—*Judges: Introduction, Translation, and Commentary* (AB, 6A; Garden City, NY: Doubleday, 1975).

—'Levitical Cities: Archaeology and Texts', in Ann Kort and Scott Morschauser (eds.), *Biblical and Related Studies Presented to Samuel Iwry* (repr., Winona Lake, IN: Eisenbrauns, 1985 [1978]), pp. 23-32.

Boling, Robert G., and G. Ernest Wright, *Joshua: A New Translation with Notes and Commentary* (AB, 6; Garden City, NY: Doubleday, 1982).

Botterweck, G. Johannes, 'אֲרִי *'arî', TDOT*, I, pp. 374-88.

Bourdieu, Pierre, 'The Sentiment of Honour in Kabyle Society', in J.G. Peristiany (ed.), *Honour and Shame: The Values of Mediterranean Society* (Chicago: University of Chicago Press, 1966), pp. 191-241.

Braun, Roddy, *1 Chronicles* (WBC, 14; Waco, TX: Word Books, 1986).

Brettler, Marc, 'The Book of Judges: Literature as Politics', *JBL* 108 (1989), pp. 395-418.

Brueggemann, Walter, *To Pluck Up, To Tear Down: A Commentary on the Book of Jeremiah 1–25* (International Theological Commentary; Grand Rapids: Eerdmans, 1988).

Brunet, Adrien-M., 'Le Chroniste et ses Sources', *RB* 60 (1953), pp. 481-508.

Budd, Phillip J., *Numbers* (WBC, 5; Waco, TX: Word Books, 1984).

Burney, C.F., *The Book of Judges, with Introduction and Notes, and Notes on the Hebrew Text of the Books of Kings, with an Introduction and Appendix* (The Library of Biblical Studies; repr., New York: Ktav, 2nd edn, 1970 [1930]).

Burns, Thomas A., 'Riddling: Occasion to Act', *Journal of American Folklore* 89 (1976), pp. 139-65.

Butler, Trent C., *Joshua* (WBC, 7; Waco, TX: Word Books, 1983).

Bynum, David E., 'Samson as a Biblical φὴρ ὀρεσκῷος', in Susan Niditch (ed.), *Text and Tradition: The Hebrew Bible and Folklore* (Atlanta: Scholars Press, 1990), pp. 57-73.

Caird, G.B., *The Language and Imagery of the Bible* (Philadelphia: Westminster Press, 1980).

Campbell, Anthony F., 'Martin Noth and the Deuteronomistic History', in Steven L. McKenzie and M. Patrick Graham (eds.), *The History of Israel's Traditions: The Heritage of Martin Noth* (JSOTSup, 182; Sheffield: Sheffield Academic Press, 1994), pp. 31-62.

Carney, T.F., *The Shape of the Past: Models and Antiquity* (Lawrence, KS: Coronado, 1975).

Carroll, Robert P., *Jeremiah: A Commentary* (OTL; Philadelphia: Westminster Press, 1986).

Casson, Lionel, *The Ancient Mariners: Seafarers and Sea Fighters of the Mediterranean in Ancient Times* (New York: Macmillan, 1959).

Chalcraft, David J. (ed.), *Social-Scientific Old Testament Criticism: A Sheffield Reader* (The Biblical Seminar, 47; Sheffield: Sheffield Academic Press, 1997).

Chaney, Marvin L., '*ḤDL*-II and the "Song of Deborah": Textual, Philological, and Sociological Studies in Judges 5, with Special Reference to the Verbal Occurrences of *ḤDL* in Biblical Hebrew' (unpublished PhD dissertation, Harvard University, 1976).

Charles, R.H., *The Apocrypha and Pseudepigrapha of the Old Testament in English, with Introductions and Critical and Explanatory Notes to the Several Books*. II. *Pseudepigrapha* (2 vols.; Oxford: Clarendon Press, 1913).

—*A Critical and Exegetical Commentary on the Revelation of St. John* (ICC; Edinburgh: T. & T. Clark, 1920).

—*The Testaments of the Twelve Patriarchs: Transated from the Editor's Greek Text and Edited with Introduction, Notes, and Indices* (London: A. & C. Black, 1908).

Childs, Brevard S., *Introduction to the Old Testament as Scripture* (Philadelphia: Fortress Press, 1979).

Clines, D.J.A., *Ezra, Nehemiah, Esther* (NCB; Grand Rapids: Eerdmans, 1984).

Coogan, Michael David, 'A Structural and Literary Analysis of the Song of Deborah', *CBQ* 40 (1978), pp. 143-66.

Cooke, G.A., *A Critical and Exegetical Commentary on the Book of Ezekiel* (ICC; Edinburgh: T. & T. Clark, 1951).

Craigie, Peter C., *The Book of Deuteronomy* (NICOT; Grand Rapids: Eerdmans, 1976).

—'The Song of Deborah and the Epic of Tukulti-Ninurta', *JBL* 88 (1969), pp. 253-65.

—'Three Ugaritic Notes on the Song of Deborah', *JSOT* 2 (1977), pp. 33-49.

Crenshaw, James L., *Samson: A Secret Betrayed, A Vow Ignored* (Atlanta: John Knox Press, 1978).

Cross, Frank Moore, Jr, *Canaanite Myth and Hebrew Epic: Essays in the History of the Religion of Israel* (Cambridge, MA: Harvard University Press, 1973).

—'Reuben, First-Born of Jacob', *ZAW* 100 (1988), pp. 46-65.

—'The Tabernacle: A Study from an Archaeological and Historical Approach', *BA* 10 (1947), pp. 45-68.

Cross, Frank Moore, Jr, and David Noel Freedman, *Studies in Ancient Yahwistic Poetry* (SBLDS, 21; Missoula, MT: Scholars Press, 1975).

Cross, Frank Moore, Jr, and G. Ernest Wright, 'The Boundary and Province Lists of the Kingdom of Judah', *JBL* 75 (1956), pp. 202-26.

Curtis, Edward Louis, and Albert Alonzo Madsen, *A Critical and Exegetical Commentary on the Books of Chronicles* (ICC; New York: Charles Scribner's Sons, 1910).

Dahood, Mitchell J., *Psalms. II. 51–100: Introduction, Commentary, and Notes* (AB, 17; 3 vols.; Garden City, NY: Doubleday, 2nd edn, 1973).

—*Psalms. III. 101–150: Introduction, Translation, and Notes, with an Appendix, The Grammar of the Psalter* (AB, 17A; 3 vols.; Garden City, NY: Doubleday, 1970).

Davies, Eryl W., 'A Mathematical Conundrum: The Problem of the Large Numbers in Numbers I and XXVI', *VT* 45 (1995), pp. 449-69.

—*Numbers* (NCB; Grand Rapids: Eerdmans, 1995).

de Geus, C.H.J., *The Tribes of Israel: An Investigation into Some of the Presuppositions of Martin Noth's Amphictyony Hypothesis* (Studia Semitica Nederlandica, 18; Assen: Van Gorcum, 1976).

de Jonge, M., *Testamenta XII Patriarcharum* (Pseudepigrapha Veterii Testamenti, 1; Leiden: E.J. Brill, 2nd edn, 1970).

—*The Testaments of the Twelve Patriarchs: A Study of their Text, Composition and Origin* (Assen: Van Gorcum, 2nd edn, 1975).

de Moor, Johannes C., 'The Twelve Tribes in the Song of Deborah', *VT* 43 (1993), pp. 483-94.

de Vaux, Roland, *Ancient Israel. II. Religious Institutions* (2 vols.; New York: McGraw–Hill, 1961).

DeVries, LeMoine F., *Cities of the Biblical World: An Introduction to the Archaeology, Geography, and History of Biblical Sites* (Peabody, MA: Hendrickson, 1997).

Dillard, Raymond B., *2 Chronicles* (WBC, 15; Waco, TX: Word Books, 1987).

Dommershausen, W., 'גּוֹרָל *gôral*', *TDOT*, II, pp. 450-56.

Dossin, G., 'La route de l'étain en Mésopotamie au temps de Zimri-Lim', *Revue d'Assyriologie* 64 (1970), pp. 97-106.

Dothan, Moshe, 'Ashdod', in *ABD*, I, pp. 477-82.

—*Ashdod II-III: The Second and Third Seasons of Excavations 1963, 1965* (ed. A. Biran, Inna Pommerantz and J.L. Swauger; 'Atiqot English Series, 9-10; Jerusalem: Israel Exploration Society, 1971).

—'The Foundations of Tel Mor and Tel Ashdod', *IEJ* 23 (1973), pp. 1-17.

Dothan, Trude, and Moshe Dothan, *People of the Sea: The Search for the Philistines* (New York: Macmillan, 1992).

Dothan, Trude, and Seymour Gitin, 'Miqne, Tel (Ekron)', in *NEAEHL*, III, pp. 1051-59.

Douglas, Jack D., and Frances Chaput Waksler, *The Sociology of Deviance: An Introduction* (Boston: Little, Brown & Co., 1982).

Driver, Samuel Rolles, *A Critical and Exegetical Commentary on Deuteronomy* (ICC; New York: Charles Scribner's Sons, 1895).

—*Notes on the Hebrew Text of the Books of Samuel* (Oxford: Clarendon Press, 1890).

—*An Introduction to the Literature of the Old Testament* (New York: Charles Scribner's Sons, new rev. edn, 1931 [1913]).

Dumbrell, W.J., '"In Those Days There Was No King in Israel; Every Man Did What Was Right in his Own Eyes": The Purpose of the Book of Judges Reconsidered', *JSOT* 25 (1983), pp. 23-33.

Edelman, Diana, 'The Asherite Genealogy in 1 Chronicles 7:3-40', *BR* 33 (1988), pp. 13-23.

Edgerton, William F., and John A. Wilson, *Historical Records of Ramses III: The Texts in Medinet Habu, I and II* (Studies in Ancient Civilization; Chicago: University of Chicago Press, 1936).

Eichrodt, Walther, *Ezekiel: A Commentary* (OTL; Philadelphia: Westminster Press, 1970).

Eisenstadt, N., and L. Roniger, *Patrons, Clients, and Friends: Interpersonal Relations and the Structure of Trust in Society* (New York: Cambridge University Press, 1984).

Eissfeldt, Otto, *The Old Testament: An Introduction* (trans. Peter R. Ackroyd; Oxford: Basil Blackwell, 1965).

Elliger, Karl, 'Sinn und Ursprung der priestlichen Geschichtserzählung', *ZTK* 49 (1952), pp. 121-43.

Elliott, John H., 'Patronage and Clientage', in Rohrbaugh (ed.), *The Social Sciences and New Testament Interpretation*, pp. 144-56.

—*What is Social-Scientific Criticism?* (GBS; Minneapolis: Fortress Press, 1993).

Engel, Helmut, Review of *Die Daniten: Studien zur Geschichte eines altisraelitischen Stammes*, by Hermann Michael Niemann, *Bib* 67 (1986), pp. 292-95.

Exum, J. Cheryl, 'The Centre Cannot Hold: Thematic and Textual Instabilities in Judges', *CBQ* 52 (1990), pp. 410-31.

—'Promise and Fulfillment: Narrative Art in Judges 13', *JBL* 99 (1980), pp. 43-59.

Fichtner, J., 'Die etymologische Ätiologie in der Namengebung der geschichtlichen Bücher des Alten Testaments', *VT* 6 (1965), pp. 372-96.

Finkelstein, Israel (ed.), *Shiloh: The Archaeology of a Biblical Site* (Tel Aviv: Institute of Archaeology, 1993).

Finkelstein, Israel, and Nadav Na'aman (eds.), *From Nomadism to Monarchy: Archaeological and Historical Aspects of Early Israel* (Washington: Biblical Archaeology Society, 1994).

Fohrer, Georg, *Introduction to the Old Testament* (trans. David Green; Nashville: Abingdon Press, 1968).

Ford, J. Massyngberde, *Revelation: Introduction, Translation and Commentary* (AB, 38; Garden City, NY: Doubleday, 1975).

Freedman, David Noel, 'Early Israelite History in the Light of Early Israelite Poetry', in *idem* (ed.), *Pottery, Poetry, and Prophecy: Studies in Early Hebrew Poetry* (Winona Lake, IN: Eisenbrauns, 1980), pp. 131-66.

Freedman, H., and Maurice Simon (eds.), *Midrash Rabbah: Translated in English with Notes, Glossary and Indices* (10 vols.; London: Soncino Press, 1939) (Genesis = I-II, Leviticus = IV, Numbers = V-VI).

Frick, Frank S., *The City in Ancient Israel* (SBLDS, 36; Missoula, MT: Scholars Press, 1977).

Fried, Morton H., *The Notion of Tribe* (Menlo Park: Cummings, 1975).

Friedman, Richard Elliott, 'The Tabernacle in the Temple', *BA* 43 (1980), pp. 241-48.

—*Who Wrote the Bible?* (New York: Harper & Row, 1987).

Garbini, Giovani, '*Parzon* "Iron" in the Song of Deborah?', *JSS* 23 (1978) pp. 23-24.

Gervitz, Stanley, 'Adumbrations of Dan in Jacob's Blessing on Judah', *ZAW* 93 (1981), pp. 21-37.

Ginzberg, Louis, *The Legends of the Jews* (Philadelphia: Jewish Publication Society of America, 1909) (*Bible Times and Characters from the Creation to Jacob* = I, *Bible Times and Characters from the Exodus to the Death of Moses* = III).

Golka, Friedemann W., 'The Aetiologies in the Old Testament: Part 1', *VT* 26 (1976), pp. 410-28.

Gordon, Robert P., 'The Variable Wisdom of Abel: The MT and Versions at 2 Samuel XX 18-19', *VT* 43 (1993), pp. 215-26.

Gottwald, Norman K., *The Hebrew Bible—A Socio-Literary Introduction* (Philadelphia: Fortress Press, 1985).

—*The Tribes of Yahweh: A Sociology of the Religion of Liberated Israel, 1250–1050 B.C.E.* (Maryknoll, NY: Orbis Books, 1979).

Gray, George Buchanan, *A Critical and Exegetical Commentary on Numbers* (ICC; New York: Charles Scribners Sons, 1903).

Gray, John, *I & II Kings, A Commentary* (OTL; London: SCM Press, 1964).

—'Israel in the Song of Deborah', in Lyle Eslinger and Glen Taylor (eds.), *Ascribe to the Lord: Biblical and Other Essays in Memory of Peter C. Craigie* (JSOTSup, 67; Sheffield: JSOT Press, 1988), pp. 421-55.

—*Joshua, Judges, Ruth* (NCB; Grand Rapids: Eerdmans, 1986).

Greenspoon, Leonard, 'The Qumran Fragments of Joshua: Which Puzzle are They Part of and Where Do They Fit?', in George J. Brooke and Barnabas Lindars (eds.), *Septuagint, Scrolls and Cognate Studies: Papers Presented to the International Symposium on the Septuagint and Its Relations to the Dead Sea Scrolls and Other Writings (Manchester 1990)* (SBLSCS, 33; Atlanta: Scholars Press, 1992), pp. 159-94.

Gunkel, Hermann, *The Folktale in the Old Testament* (trans. Michael D. Rutter; Historic Texts and Interpreters in Biblical Scholarship; Sheffield: Sheffield Academic Press, 1987 [German original 1917]).

—*Genesis* (trans. Mark E. Biddle; Mercer Library of Biblical Studies; Macon: Mercer University Press, 1997).

Gunn, David M., 'Narrative Criticism', in McKenzie and Haynes (eds.), *To Each Its Own Meaning*, pp. 171-95.

Gunneweg, A.H.J., 'Über den Sitz im Leben der sogenannten Stammessprüche (Gen 49 Dtn 33 Jdc 5)', *ZAW* 76 (1964), pp. 245-55.

Habel, Norman C., *The Land is Mine: Six Biblical Land Ideologies* (Overtures to Biblical Theology; Minneapolis: Fortress Press, 1995).

Halpern, Baruch, 'Levitic Participation in the Reform Cult of Jeroboam I', *JBL* 95 (1976), pp. 31-42 (36).

—'Shiloh', in *ABD*, V, pp. 1213-15.

—'The Stela from Dan: Epigraphic and Historical Considerations', *BASOR* 296 (1994), pp. 63-80.

Hammerschaimb, Erling, *The Book of Amos: A Commentary* (New York: Schocken Books, 1970).

Hamp, V., 'חָצֵר *ḥāṣēr*', *TDOT*, V, pp. 131-33.

Hamp, V., and G.J. Botterweck, 'דִּין *dîn*', *TDOT*, III, pp. 187-94.

Haran, Menahem, 'Studies in the Account of the Levitical Cities', *JBL* 80 (1961), pp. 45-54, 156-65.

—*Temples and Temple-Service in Ancient Israel: An Inquiry into Biblical Cult Phenomena and the Historical Setting of the Priestly School* (repr., Winona Lake, IN: Eisenbrauns, 1985 [1978]).

Harper, William Rainey, *A Critical and Exegetical Commentary on Amos and Hosea* (ICC; New York: Charles Scribner's Sons, 1905).

Herzog, Zeev, 'Gerisa, Tel', in *NEAEHL*, II, pp. 480-84.

Heschel, Abraham J., *The Prophets* (New York: Harper & Row, 1962).

Hess, Richard, 'Asking Historical Questions of Joshua 13–19: Recent Discussion Concerning the Date of the Boundary Lists', in A.R. Millard, James K. Hoffmeier and David W. Baker (eds.), *Faith, Tradition, and History: Old Testament Historiography in Its Near Eastern Context* (Winona Lake, IN: Eisenbrauns, 1994), pp. 191-205.

—'Late Bronze Age and Biblical Boundary Descriptions of the West Semitic World', in George J. Brooke, Adrian H.W. Curtis and John F. Healey (eds.), *Ugarit and the Bible: Proceedings of the International Symposium on Ugarit and the Bible, Manchester, September 1992* (UBL, 11; Münster: Ugarit-Verlag, 1994), pp. 123-38.

—'Tribes, Territories of the', *ISBE*, IV, pp. 907-13.

Hiebert, Paula S, '"Whence Shall Help Come to Me?": The Biblical Widow', in Peggy Day (ed.), *Gender and Difference in Ancient Israel* (Minneapolis: Fortress Press, 1989), pp. 125-41.

Hippolytus, 'Appendix to the Works of Hippolytus, Containing Dubius and Spurious Pieces', in Roberts and Donaldson (eds.), *The Ante-Nicene Fathers*, pp. 242-58.

—'Fragments from Commentaries on Various Books of Scripture', in Roberts and Donaldson (eds.), *The Ante-Nicene Fathers*, pp. 163-203.

Holladay, William L., *Jeremiah. I. A Commentary on the Book of the Prophet Jeremiah, Chapters 1–25* (Hermeneia; 2 vols.; Philadelphia: Fortress Press, 1986).

Holmes, S., *Joshua: The Hebrew and Greek Texts* (Cambridge: Cambridge University Press, 1914).

Hopkins, David C., 'Life on the Land: The Subsistence Struggles of Early Israel', *BA* 50 (1987), pp. 178-91.

Huehnergard, John, *A Grammar of Akkadian* (Harvard Semitic Studies, 45; Atlanta: Scholars Press, 1997).

Hurvitz, A., '"Diachronic Chiasm" in Biblical Hebrew', in Benjamin Uffenheimer (ed.), *Bible and Jewish History: Studies in Bible and Jewish History Dedicated to the Memory of Jacob Liver* (Tel Aviv: University of Tel Aviv Press, 1972), pp. 253-54 (Hebrew).

Hutton, Rodney R., 'Narrative in Leviticus: The Case of the Blaspheming Son (Lev 24, 10-23)', *Zeitschrift für Altorientalische und Biblische Rechtsgeschichte* 3 (1997), pp. 145-63.

Irenaeus, 'Against Heresies', in Roberts and Donaldson (eds.), *The Ante-Nicene Fathers*, pp. 315-562.

Irwin, William H., Review of *Die Daniten: Studien zur Geschichte eines altisraelitischen Stammes*, by Hermann Michael Niemann, *CBQ* 51 (1989), pp. 724-25.

Ishida, Tomoo, 'The Structure of the Lists of Pre-Israelite Nations', *Bib* 60 (1979), pp. 461-90.

Japhet, Sara, *I and II Chronicles: A Commentary* (OTL; Louisville, KY: Westminster/John Knox Press, 1993).

—*The Ideology of the Book of Chronicles and Its Place in Biblical Thought* (Beiträge zur Erforschung des Alten Testaments und des Antiken Judentums, 9; New York: Peter Lang, 1989).

Jeremias, Jörg, *The Book of Amos: A Commentary* (OTL; Louisville, KY: Westminster John Knox Press, 1998).

Jones, Allen H., *Bronze Age Civilization: The Philistines and the Danites* (Washington: Public Affairs Press, 1975).

Jones, Gwilym H., *1 and 2 Kings* (2 vols.; NCB; Grand Rapids: Eerdmans, 1984).

Josephus, *Josephus with an English Translation by H.St.J. Thackeray and Ralph Mareus, in Eight Volumes* (LCL; Cambridge, MA: Harvard University Press, 1934).

Kallai, Zecharia, *Historical Geography of the Bible: The Tribal Territories of Israel* (Leiden: E.J. Brill, 1986).

—'The Twelve-Tribe Systems of Israel', *VT* 47 (1997), pp. 53-90.

Kaplan, Jacob, 'Bene-Barak and Vicinity', in *NEAEHL*, I, pp. 186-87.

Kardimon, Samson, 'Adoption as a Remedy for Infertility in the Period of the Patriarchs', *JSS* 3 (1958), pp. 123-26.

Kaufmann, Yehezkel, *The Biblical Account of the Conquest of Palestine* (Jerusalem: Magnes Press/Hebrew University Press, 1953).

Keil, C.F., *The Books of Chronicles* (Edinburgh: T. & T. Clark, 1878).

Kellermann, D., 'גּוּר *gûr*', *TDOT*, II, pp. 439-49.

Kenyon, Kathleen M., *Amorites and Canaanites* (Schweich Lectures, 1963; London: Oxford University Press, 1966).

King, Philip J., *Amos, Hosea, Micah—An Archaeological Commentary* (Philadelphia: Westminster Press, 1988).

Klapp, Orrin E., 'The Clever Hero', *Journal of American Folklore* 67 (1954), pp. 21-34.

Klein, Lillian R., *The Triumph of Irony in the Book of Judges* (JSOTSup, 68; Sheffield: Almond Press, 1988).

Klein, Ralph W., *1 Samuel* (WBC, 10; Waco, TX: Word Books, 1983).

—*Ezekiel: The Prophet and His Message* (Studies on Personalities of the Old Testament; Columbia: University of South Carolina Press, 1988).

—'How Many in a Thousand?', in M. Patrick Graham, Kenneth G. Hoglund and Steven L. McKenzie (eds.), *The Chronicler as Historian* (JSOTSup, 238; Sheffield: Sheffield Academic Press, 1997), pp. 270-82.

—'Reflections on Historiography in the Account of Jehoshaphat', in David P. Wright, David Noel Freedman and Avi Hurvitz (eds.), *Pomegranates and Golden Bells: Studies in Biblical, Jewish, and Near Eastern Ritual, Law, and Literature in Honor of Jacob Milgrom* (Winona Lake, IN: Eisenbrauns, 1995), pp. 643-57.

Klostermann, A., 'Chronik, die Bücher der', in Johan Jacob Herzog (ed.), *Realencyklopädie für protestantische Theologie und Kirche* (Leipzig: J.C. Hinrichs, 1898), pp. 84-98.

Knoblach, Frederick W., 'Adoption', in *ABD*, I, pp. 76-79.

Knoppers, Gary N., *Two Nations Under God: The Deuteronomistic History of Solomon and the Dual Monarchies. II. The Reign of Jeroboam, the Fall of Israel, and the Reign of Josiah* (HSM, 53; 2 vols.; Atlanta: Scholars Press, 1994).

Krentz, Edgar, *The Historical-Critical Method* (GBS; Philadelphia: Fortress Press, 1975).

Krodel, Gerhard A., *Revelation* (Augsburg Commentary on the New Testament; Minneapolis: Augsburg, 1989).

Lapp, Paul W., 'The 1968 Excavations at Tell Ta'annek', *BASOR* 195 (1969), pp. 2-49.

Lemche, Niels Peter, *Early Israel: Anthropolgical and Historical Studies on the Israelite Society Before the Monarchy* (VTSup, 37; Leiden: E.J. Brill, 1985).

Lenski, Gerhard E., *Human Societies: A Macrolevel Introduction to Sociology* (New York: McGraw–Hill, 1970).

—*Power and Privilege: A Theory of Social Stratification* (New York: McGraw–Hill, 1966).

Levenson, Jon Douglas, *Theology of the Program of Restoration of Ezekiel 40–48* (HSM, 10; Missoula, MT: Scholars Press, 1976).

Levine, Baruch A., *The JPS Torah Commentary: Leviticus, The Traditional Hebrew Text with the New JPS Translation* (Philadelphia: Jewish Publication Society of America, 5749/ 1989).

—*Numbers 1–20: A New Translation with Introduction and Commentary* (AB, 4; New York: Doubleday, 1993).

Lindars, Barnabas, *Judges 1–5: A New Translation and Commentary* (Edinburgh: T. & T. Clark, 1995).

Liverani, M., 'The Amorites', in D.J. Wiseman (ed.), *Peoples of Old Testament Times* (Oxford: Clarendon Press, 1973), pp. 100-33.

Long, Burke O., *1 Kings, with an Introduction to Historical Literature* (FOTL, 9; Grand Rapids: Eerdmans, 1984).

—*The Problem of Etiological Narrative in the Old Testament* (BZAW, 108; Berlin: Alfred Töpelmann, 1968).

Lundbom, Jack R., *Jeremiah 1–20: A New Translation with Introduction and Commentary* (AB, 21A; New York: Doubleday, 1999).

Malamat, Abraham, 'The Danite Migration and the Pan-Israelite Exodus-Conquest: A Biblical Narrative Pattern', *Bib* 51 (1970), pp. 1-16.

—'Syro-Palestinian Destinations in Mari Tin Inventory', *IEJ* 21 (1971), pp. 31-38.

Malina, Bruce J., *The New Testament World: Insights from Cultural Anthropology* (Louisville, KY: Westminster/John Knox Press, rev. edn, 1993).

—'Patronage', in Pilch and Malina (eds.), *Biblical Social Values and Their Meaning*, pp. 133-37.

Malina, Bruce J., and Jerome H. Neyrey, 'Conflict in Luke–Acts: Labelling and Deviance Theory', in Neyrey (ed.), *The Social World of Luke–Acts*, pp. 97-122.

—*Calling Jesus Names: The Social Values of Labels in Matthew* (Sonoma: Poleridge, 1988).

—'Honor and Shame in Luke–Acts: Pivotal Values of the Mediterranean World', in Neyrey (ed.), *The Social World of Luke–Act*, pp. 25-65.

Malina, Bruce J., and Richard L. Rohrbaugh, *Social-Science Commentary on the Synoptic Gospels* (Minneapolis: Fortress Press, 1992).

Margalith, Othniel, *The Sea Peoples in the Bible* (Wiesbaden: Otto Harrassowitz, 1994).

Martin, Dale B., 'Social-Scientific Criticism', in McKenzie and Haynes (eds.), *To Each Its Own Meaning*, pp. 103-19.

Matthews, Victor H., and Don C. Benjamin, 'Social Sciences and Biblical Studies', *Semeia* 68 (1994), pp. 7-21.

May, Herbert G. (ed.), *Oxford Bible Atlas* (New York: Oxford University Press, 3rd edn, 1984).

Mays, James Luther, *Amos: A Commentary* (OTL; Philadelphia: Westminster Press, 1969).

Mayes, A.D.H., *Deuteronomy* (NCB; Grand Rapids: Eerdmans, 1979).

Mazar, Ahimai, *Archaeology of the Land of the Bible: 10,000–586 B.C.E.* (Anchor Bible Reference Library; New York: Doubleday, 1990).

Mazar, Benjamin, 'The Cities of the Priests and the Levites', in The Board of the Quarterly (eds.), *Congress Volume, Oxford 1959* (VTSup, 7; Leiden: E.J. Brill, 1960), pp. 193-205.

—'The Cities of the Territory of Dan', in Shmuel Ahituv and Baruch A. Levine (eds.), *The Early Biblical Period: Historical Studies* (Jerusalem: Israel Exploration Society, 1986), pp. 104-12.

McCarter, P. Kyle, Jr, *I Samuel: A New Translation with Introduction, Notes & Commentary* (AB, 8; Garden City, NY: Doubleday, 1980).

—*II Samuel: A New Translation with Introduction and Commentary* (AB, 9; Garden City, NY: Doubleday, 1984).

—*Textual Criticism: Recovering the Text of the Hebrew Bible* (GBS; Philadelphia: Fortress Press, 1986).

McKenzie, John L., *The World of the Judges* (Backgrounds in the Bible Series; Englewood Cliffs, NJ: Prentice–Hall, 1966).

McKenzie, Steven L., 'Deuteronomistic History', in *ABD*, II, pp. 160-68.

McKenzie, Steven L., and Stephen R. Haynes (eds.), *To Each Its Own Meaning: An Introduction to Biblical Criticisms and Their Application* (Louisville, KY: Westminster/John Knox Press, 1993).

McNutt, Paula, *Reconstructing the Society of Ancient Israel* (Library of Ancient Israel; Louisville, KY: Westminster/John Knox Press, 1999).

McVann, Mark, 'Family-Centeredness', in Pilch and Malina (eds.), *Biblical Social Values and Their Meaning*, pp. 70-73.

Mendenhall, George E., 'Amorites', in *ABD*, I, pp. 199-202.

—'The Census Lists of Numbers 1 and 26', *JBL* 77 (1958), pp. 52-66.

Meshel, Ze'ev, 'Kuntillet 'Ajrud: An Israelite Religious Center in Northern Sinai', *Expedition* 20 (1978), pp. 50-54.

—'Teman, Horvat', in *NEAEHL*, IV, pp. 1459-64.

Meyers, Carol, *Discovering Eve: Ancient Israelite Women in Context* (New York: Oxford University Press, 1988).

Milgrom, Jacob, *The JPS Torah Commentary: Numbers, The Traditional Hebrew Text with the New JPS Translation* (Philadelphia: Jewish Publication Society of America, 5750/1990).

Miller, J. Maxwell, 'Reading the Bible Historically: The Historian's Approach', in McKenzie and Haynes (eds.), *To Each Its Own Meaning*, pp. 11-28.

—'Rehoboam's Cities of Defense and the Levitical City List', in Leo G. Perdue, Lawrence E. Toombs and Gary L. Johnson (eds.), *Archaeology and Biblical Interpretation: Essays in Memory of D. Glenn Rose* (Atlanta: John Knox Press, 1987), pp. 273-86.

Miller, J. Maxwell, and John H. Hayes, *A History of Ancient Israel and Judah* (Philadelphia: Westminster Press, 1986).

Miller, Patrick D., Jr, 'Animal Names as Designations in Ugaritic and Hebrew', *UF* 2 (1970), pp. 177-86.

Mittwoch, H., 'The Story of the Blasphemer Seen in a Wider Context', *VT* 15 (1965), pp. 386-89.

Mobley, Gregory, 'The Wild Man in the Bible and the Ancient Near East', *JBL* 116 (1997), pp. 217-33.

Montgomery, James A., *A Critical and Exegetical Commentary on the Books of Kings* (ICC; New York: Charles Scribner's Sons, 1951).

Moore, George F., *A Critical and Exegetical Commentary on Judges* (ICC; New York: Charles Scribner's Sons, 1901).

Moran, William L., *The Amarna Letters* (Baltimore: The Johns Hopkins University Press, 1992).

Motzki, Harald, 'Ein Beitrag zum Problem des Stierkultes in der Religionsgeschichte Israels', *VT* 25 (1975), pp. 475-76.

Mowinckel, Sigmund, *Tetrateuch—Pentateuch—Hexateuch: Die Berichte über die Landmahme in den drei altisraelitischen Geschichtswerken* (BZAW, 90; Berlin: Alfred Töpelmann, 1964).

—*Zur Frage nach dokumentarischen Quellen in Josua 13–19* (Oslo: I. Kommisjon hos J. Dybwad, 1946).

Moxness, Halvor, 'Honor and Shame', in Richard Rohrbaugh (ed.), *The Social Sciences and New Testament Interpretation* (Peabody, MA: Hendrickson, 1996), pp. 19-40.

—'Patron-Client Relations and the New Community in Luke–Acts', in Neyrey (ed.), *The Social World of Luke–Acts*, pp. 241-68.

Mullen, E. Theodore, 'Judges 1:1-36: The Deuteronomistic Reintroduction of the Book of Judges', *HTR* 77 (1984), pp. 33-54.

Myers, Jacob M., *I Chronicles: Introduction, Translation, and Notes* (AB, 12; Garden City, NY: Doubleday, 1965).

—*II Chronicles: Translation and Notes* (AB, 13; Garden City, NY: Doubleday, 1965).

Na'aman, Nadav, *Borders and Districts in Biblical Historiography: Seven Studies in Biblical Geographical Lists* (Jerusalem Biblical Studies, 4; Jerusalem: Simor, 1986).

—'The "Conquest of Canaan" in the Book of Joshua and History', in Israel Finkelstein and Nadav Na'aman (eds.), *From Nomadism to Monarchy: Archaeological and Historical Aspects of Early Israel* (Washington, DC: Biblical Archaeology Society of America, 1994), pp. 218-81.

Nakhai, Beth Alpert, 'The Meaning of Religious Centralization for the Israelite Monarchy', an unpublished paper presented to the 'Archaeological Excavations and Discoveries: Illuminating the Biblical World Section' at the Annual Meeting of the Society of Biblical Literature, Boston, MA (22 November 1999).

Nelson, H.H., *Medinet Habu I: Early Historical Records of Ramses III* (Chicago: University of Chicago Press, 1930).

Nelson, Richard D., *Joshua: A Commentary* (OTL; Louisville, KY: Westminster Press, 1997).

Newsome, James D., Jr, *A Synoptic Harmony of Samuel, Kings, and Chronicles, With Related Passages from Psalms, Isaiah, Jeremiah, and Ezra* (Grand Rapids: Baker Book House, 1986).

Neyrey, Jerome H., 'The Symbolic Universe of Luke–Acts: "They Turn the World Upside Down"', in Neyrey (ed.), *The Social World of Luke–Acts*, pp. 271-304.

Neyrey, Jerome H. (ed.), *The Social World of Luke–Acts: Models for Interpretation* (Peabody, MA: Hendrickson, 1991).

Nicholas, Ralph W., 'Factions: A Comparative Analysis', in Steffen W. Schmidt *et al.* (eds.), *Friends, Followers, and Factions: A Reader in Political Clientalism* (Berkeley. University of Califormia Press, 1977), pp. 55-73.

Nicholson, Ernest W., *Deuteronomy and Tradition* (Philadelphia: Fortress Press, 1967).

Niditch, Susan, *Folklore and the Hebrew Bible* (GBS; Minneapolis: Fortress Press, 1993).

—'Samson as Culture Hero, Trickster, and Bandit: The Empowerment of the Weak', *CBQ* 52 (1990), pp. 608-24.

—*Underdogs and Tricksters: A Prelude to Biblical Folklore* (New Voices in Biblical Studies; San Francisco: Harper & Row, 1987).

Nielsen, Eduard, *Shechem: A Traditio-Historical Investigation* (Copenhagen: G.E.C. Gad, 1959).

Niemann, Hermann Michael, *Die Daniten: Studien zur Geschichte eines altisraelitischen Stammes* (FRLANT, 135; Göttingen: Vandenhoeck & Ruprecht, 1985).

—'Zorah, Eshtaol, Beth Shemesh and Dan's Migration to the South: A Region and its Traditions in the Late Bronze Age and Iron Ages', *JSOT* 86 (1999), pp. 25-48.

Noll, K.L., 'The God Who is Among the Danites', *JSOT* 80 (1998), pp. 3-23.

Noth, Martin, 'The Background of Judges 17–18', in Bernhard W. Anderson and Walter Harrelson (eds.), *Israel's Prophetic Heritage: Essays in Honor of James Muilenburg* (New York: Harper & Brothers, 1962), pp. 68-85.

—*Das Buch Josua* (HAT, 7; Tübingen: J.C.B. Mohr [Paul Siebeck], 2nd edn, 1953).

—*The Chronicler's History* (JSOTSup, 50; Sheffield: JSOT Press, 1987 [1943]).

—*The Deuteronomistic History* (JSOTSup, 15; Sheffield: JSOT Press, 2nd edn, 1991 [trans. from the German 2nd edn = *Überlieferungsgeschichtliche Studien: Die sammelnden und bearbeitenden Geschichtswerke im Alten Testament* (Tübingen: Max Niemeyer Verlag/ Zweite Unveränderte Auflage, 1957]).

—*A History of Pentateuchal Traditions* (trans. with an Introduction by Bernhard W. Anderson; Scholars Press Reprints and Translations Series, 5; Atlanta: Scholars Press, 1981 [1972]).

—*Numbers: A Commentary* (London: SCM Press, 1968).

—'Studien zu den historisch-geographischen Dokumenten des Josuabuches', *ZDPV* 58 (1935), pp. 185-255.

Oakman, Douglas E., 'The Countryside in Luke–Acts', in Neyrey (ed.), *The Social World of Luke–Acts*, pp. 151-79.

O'Brien, Mark A., *The Deuteronomistic History Hypothesis: A Reassessment* (OBO, 92; Göttingen: Vandenhoeck & Ruprecht, 1989).

—'Judges and the Deuteronomistic History', in Steven L. McKenzie and M. Patrick Graham (eds.), *The History of Israel's Traditions: The Heritage of Martin Noth* (JSOTSup, 182; Sheffield: Sheffield Academic Press, 1994), pp. 235-59.

Olson, Dennis T., 'The Book of Judges: Introduction, Commentary, and Reflections', in Leander E. Keck *et al.* (eds.), *New Interpreter's Bible* (Nashville: Abingdon Press, 1998), II, pp. 235-59.

Olyan, Saul M., 'Honor, Shame, and Covenant Relations in Ancient Israel and Its Environment', *JBL* 115 (1996), pp. 201-18.

—'The Oaths of Amos 8.14', in Gary A. Anderson and Saul M. Olyan (eds.), *Priesthood and Cult in Ancient Israel* (JSOTSup, 125; Sheffield: JSOT Press, 1991), pp. 121-49.

Oppenheim, A.L., 'Trade in the Ancient Near East', in Hermann Van der Wee, Vladimir A. Vinogradov and Grigorii G. Kotovsky (eds.), *Fifth International Congress of Economic History, Leningrad 1970* (8 vols.; Leningrad: Mockba, 1976), V, pp. 125-49.

Orlinsky, Harry M., 'The Hebrew Vorlage of the Septuagint of the Book of Joshua', in the Board of the Quarterly (eds.), *Congress Volume, Rome 1968* (VTSup, 17; Leiden: E.J. Brill, 1969), pp. 187-95.

Osiek, Carolyn, *What Are They Saying About the Social Setting of the New Testament?* (New York: Paulist, rev. and exp. edn, 1992).

Paul, Shalom M., *Amos: A Commentary on the Book of Amos* (Hermeneia; Mineapolis: Fortress Press, 1991).

Peristiany, J.G., 'Introduction', in J.G. Peristiany (ed.), *Honour and Shame: The Values of Mediterranean Society* (Chicago: University of Chicago Press, 1966), pp. 9-18.

Peterson, John L., 'Aijalon', in *ABD*, I, p. 131.

—'Eltekeh', in *ABD*, II, pp. 483-84.

—'Gibbethon', in *ABD*, II, pp. 1006-1007.

—'A Topographical Surface Survey of the Levitical "Cities" of Joshua 21 and 1 Chronicles 6: Studies in the Levites in Israelite Life and Religion' (unpublished ThD dissertation, Chicago Institute of Advanced Theological Studies and Seabury-Western Theological Seminary, 1977).

Petrie, W.M. Flinders, *Egypt and Israel* (London: SPCK, 1911).

Pfeiffer, Robert H., *Introduction to the Old Testament* (New York: Harper & Brothers, 1941).

Pilch, John J., and Bruce J. Malina (eds.), *Biblical Social Values and Their Meaning: A Handbook* (Peabody, MA: Hendrickson, 1993).

Pitt-Rivers, Julian, *The Fate of Shechem, or The Politics of Sex: Essays in the Anthropology of the Mediterranean* (Cambridge Studies in Social Anthropology, 19; New York: Cambridge University Press, 1977).

Plevnick, Joseph, 'Honor/Shame', in Pilch and Malina (eds.), *Biblical Social Values and Their Meaning*, pp. 95-104.

Polley, Max E., *Amos and the Davidic Empire: A Socio-Historical Approach* (New York: Oxford University Press, 1989).

Pritchard, James B. (ed.), *Harper Atlas of the Bible* (New York: Harper & Row, 1987).

Rast, Walter E., 'Bab edh-Dhra and the Origin of the Sodom Saga', in Leo G. Perdue, Lawrence E. Toombs and Gary L. Johnson (eds.), *Archaeology and Biblical Interpretation: Essays in Memory of D. Glenn Rose* (Atlanta: John Knox Press, 1987), pp. 185-201.

Reider, Joseph, *The Holy Scriptures: Deuteronomy, with Commentary* (Philadelphia: Jewish Publication Society of America, 1937).

Reimer, David J., 'The "Foe" and the "North" in Jeremiah', *ZAW* 101 (1989), pp. 223-32.

Reindl, J., 'לָחַץ *lāḥaṣ*', *TDOT*, VII, pp. 529-33.

Reventlow, Henning Graf, *Liturgie und prophetisches Ich bei Jeremia* (Gütersloh: Gütersloher Verlagshauser [Gerd Mohn], 1963).

Rhoads, David, and Donald Michie, *Mark as Story: An Introduction to the Narrative of a Gospel* (Philadelphia: Fortress Press, 1982).

Roberts, Alexander, and James Donaldson (eds.), *The Ante-Nicene Fathers: Translations of the Writings of the Fathers down to A.D. 325*, V (10 vols.; Grand Rapids: Eerdmans, 1981 [1885]).

Robertson, D.A., *Linguistic Evidence in Dating Early Hebrew Poetry* (SBLDS, 3; Missoula, MT: Scholars Press, 1972).

Rohrbaugh, Richard, 'Agrarian Society', in Pilch and Malina (eds.), *Biblical Social Values and Their Meaning*, pp. 4-8.

Rohrbaugh, Richard (ed.), *The Social Sciences and New Testament Interpretation* (Peabody, MA: Hendrickson, 1996).

Rook, John, 'When is a Widow Not a Widow? Guardianship Provides an Answer', *BTB* 28 (1998), pp. 4-6.

Rudolph, Wilhelm, *Chronickbücher* (HAT, 21; Tübingen: J.C.B. Mohr [Paul Siebeck], 1955).

Sahlins, Marshall D., *Tribesmen* (Foundations of Modern Anthropology Series; Engelwood Cliffs: Prentice–Hall, 1968).

Sanderson, G.V., 'In Defence of Dan', *Scripture* 3/4 (1948), pp. 114-15.

Sarna, Nahum, *The JPS Torah Commentary: Genesis, The Traditional Hebrew Text with the New JPS Translation* (Philadelphia: Jewish Publication Society of America, 5749/1989).

Sasson, Jack M., 'Canaanite Maritime Involvement in the Second Millennium B.C.', *JAOS* 86 (1966), pp. 126-38.

—'A Genealogical "Convention" in Biblical Chronography?', *ZAW* 90 (1978), pp. 171-85.

Schipper, Jeremy, 'Narrative Obscurity of Samson's חידה in Judges 14.15 and 18', *JSOT* 27.3 (2003), pp. 339-53.

Schley, Donald G., *Shiloh: A Biblical City in Tradition and History* (JSOTSup, 63; Sheffield: JSOT Press, 1989).

Schloen, J. David, 'Caravans, Kenites, and *Casus belli*: Enmity and Alliance in the Song of Deborah', *CBQ* 55 (1993), pp. 18-38.

Schmid, H.H., 'גּוֹרָל *gôral* lot', in *TLOT*, I, pp. 310-12.

Schoville, Keith N., 'Canaanites and Amorites', in Alfred J. Hoerth, Gerald L. Mattingly and Edwin M. Yamauchi (eds.), *Peoples of the Old Testament World* (Cambridge: Lutterworth; Grand Rapids: Baker Book House, 1994), pp. 157-82.

Segert, Stanislav, 'Paronomasia in the Samson Narrative in Judges 13–16', *VT* 34 (1984), pp. 454-61.

Seow, Choon-Leong, 'The First and Second Books of Kings: Introduction, Commentary, and Reflections', in Leander E. Keck *et al.* (eds), *New Interpreter's Bible* (12 vols.; Nashville: Abingdon Press, 1999), III, pp. 1-295.

Simkins, Ronald A., '"Return to Yahweh": Honor and Shame in Joel', *Semeia* 68 (1996), pp. 41-54.

Sjoberg, Gideon, *The Preindustrial City: Past and Present* (New York: Free Press, 1966).

Skinner, John, *A Critical and Exegetical Commentary on Genesis* (ICC; New York: Charles Scribner's Sons, 1910).

Smend, Rudolf, 'Das Gesetz und die Völker: Ein Beitrag zur deuteronomistischen Redaktionsgeschichte', in Hans Walter Wolff (ed.), *Probleme biblischer Theologie: Gerhard von Rad zum 70. Geburtstag* (Munich: Chr. Kaiser Verlag, 1971), pp. 494-509.

Smith, Christopher R., 'The Portrayal of the Church as the New Israel in the Names and Order of the Tribes in Revelation 7.5-8', *JSNT* 39 (1990), pp. 111-18.

Smith, Daniel L., *The Religion of the Landless: The Social Context of the Babylonian Exile* (Bloomington, IN: Meyer-Stone, 1989).

Smith, Henry Preserved, *A Critical and Exegetical Commentary on the Books of Samuel* (ICC; Edinburgh: T. & T. Clark, 1899).

Soggin, J. Alberto, 'Abraham and the Eastern Kings: On Genesis 14', in Ziony Zevit, Seymour Gitin and Michael Sokoloff (eds.), *Solving Riddles an Untying Knots: Biblical, Epigraphic, and Semitic Studies in Honor Jonas C. Greenfield* (Winona Lake, IN: Eisenbrauns, 1995), pp. 283-91.

Soggin, J. Alberto, *Joshua: A Commentary* (OTL; London: SCM Press, 1972).

—*Judges: A Commentary* (OTL; London: SCM Press, 1981).

—*The Prophet Amos: A Translation and Commentary* (London: SCM Press, 1987).

Speiser, Ephraim Avigdor, *Genesis: Introduction, Translation, and Notes* (AB, 1; Garden City, NY: Doubleday, 1964).

Spencer, John R., 'Levitical Cities', in *ABD*, IV, pp. 310-11.

—'The Levitical Cities: A Study of the Role and Function of the Levites in the History of Israel' (unpublished PhD dissertation, University of Chicago, 1980).

—'Sojourner', in *ABD*, VI, pp. 103-104.

Stager, Lawrence E., 'Archaeology, Ecology, and Social History: Background Themes to the Song of Deborah', in J.A. Emerton (ed.), *Congress Volume 1986, Jerusalem* (VTSup, 40; Leiden: E.J. Brill, 1988), pp. 221-34.

—'The Archaeology of the Family in Ancient Israel', *BASOR* 260 (1985), pp. 1-35.

Steinthal, H., 'The Legend of Samson', in Ignaz Goldhizer (ed.), *Mythology Among the Hebrews and Its Historical Development* (New York: Cooper Square Publishers, 1967), pp. 392-446.

Stone, Ken, 'Gender and Homosexuality in Judges 19: Subject—Honor, Object—Shame?', *JSOT* 67 (1995), pp. 87-107.

Strange, John, 'The Inheritance of Dan', *ST* 20 (1966), pp. 120-39.

Stuart, Douglas, *Hosea–Jonah* (WBC, 31; Waco, TX: Word Books, 1987).

Swete, Henry Barclay, *The Apocalypse of St John: The Greek Text with Introduction, Notes, and Indices* (New York: MacMillan, 2nd edn, 1907).

Talmon, Shemaryahu, 'The Textual Study of the Bible—New Outlook', in Frank Moore Cross and Shemaryahu Talmon (eds.), *Qumran and the History of the Biblical Text* (Cambridge, MA: Harvard University Press, 1975), pp. 321-400.

Thompson, Stith, *Motif-Index of Folk-Literature: A Classification of Narrative Elements in Folktales, Ballads, Myths, Fables, Mediaeval Romances, Exempla, Fabliaux, Jest-Books and Local Legends* (6 vols.; Bloomington: Indiana University Press, rev. and enlarged edn, 1989).

Thompson, Thomas L., *The Historicity of the Patriarchal Narratives: The Quest for the Historical Abraham* (BZAW, 133; New York: W. de Gruyter, 1974).

Tigay, Jeffrey H., 'Adoption', *EncJud*, II, pp. 298-301.

—*The JPS Torah Commentary: Deuteronomy, The Traditional Hebrew Text with the New JPS Translation* (Philadelphia: Jewish Publication Society of America, 5756/1996).

Toews, Wesley I., *Monarchy and Religious Institution in Israel under Jeroboam I* (SBLMS, 47; Atlanta: Scholars Press, 1993).

Tov, Emanuel, 'The Growth of the Book of Joshua in the Light of the Evidence of the LXX Translation', *ScrHier* 31 (1986), pp. 321-39.

—'Midrash-Type Exegesis in the LXX of Joshua', *RB* 85 (1978), pp. 50-61.

Tristram, H.B., *The Natural History of the Bible* (New York: Pott, Young, & Co., 1867).

Tuell, Steven Shawn, *The Law of the Temple in Ezekiel 40–48* (HSM, 49; Atlanta: Scholars Press, 1992).

Ussishkin, David, 'Lachish', in *NEAEHL*, III, pp. 897-911.

van der Toorn, Karel, 'Torn Between Vice and Virtue: Stereotypes of the Widow in Israel and Mesopotamia', in Ria Kloppenborg and Wouter J. Hanegraaff (eds.), *Female Stereotypes in Religious Traditions* (Studies in the History of Religion, 65; Leiden: E.J. Brill, 1995), pp. 1-13.

Van Seters, John, *Abraham in History and Tradition* (New Haven: Yale University Press, 1975).

—'The Problem of Childlessness in Near Eastern Law and the Patriarchs of Israel', *JBL* 87 (1968), pp. 401-408.

Vannutelli, Primus, *Libri Synoptici Veteris Testamenti seu Librorum Regum et Chronicorum Loci Paralleli* (2 vols.; Rome: Pontificio Instituto Biblico, 1931, 1934).

Veijola, Timo, *Das Königtum in der Beurteilung der deuteronomistischen Historiographie: Eine redaktionsgeschichtliche Untersuchung* (Annales Academie Scientiarum Fennicae, Series B, 198; Helsinki: Suomalainen Tiedeakatemia, 1977).

von Rad, Gerhard, 'The Deuteronomistic Theology of History in the Books of Kings', in *idem*, *Studies in Deuteronomy*, pp. 74-91.

—'Deuteronomy's "Name" Theology and the Priestly Document's "Kabod" Theology', in *idem*, *Studies in Deuteronomy*, pp. 37-44.

—*Genesis: A Commentary* (OTL; Philadelphia: Westminster Press, rev. edn, 1972).

—*Studies in Deuteronomy* (SBT; Chicago: Henry Regnery Company, 1953 [German edn 1948]).

Wapnish, Paula, Brian Hesse and Anne Ogilvy, 'The 1974 Collection of Faunal Remains from Tell Dan', *BASOR* 227 (1977), pp. 35-62.

Watson, Wilfred G.E., *Classical Hebrew Poetry: A Guide to Its Techniques* (JSOTSup, 26; Sheffield: Sheffield Academic Press, 2nd edn, 1995).

Weinberg, Joel, *The Citizen–Temple Community* (JSOTSup, 151; Sheffield: JSOT Press, 1992).

Weinfeld, M., 'Judges 1.1–2.5: The Conquest Under the Leadership of the House of Judah', in A. Graeme Auld (ed.), *Understanding Poets and Prophets: Essays in Honour of George Wishart Anderson* (JSOTSup, 152; Sheffield: JSOT Press, 1993), pp. 388-400.

—'The Period of the Conquest and of the Judges as Seen by Earlier and Later Sources', *VT* 17 (1967), pp. 93-113.

Wellhausen, Julius, *Prolegomena to the History of Israel* (Scholars Press Reprints and Translations Series; Atlanta: Scholars Press, 1994 [1885]).

Wenham, Gordon J., *Genesis 1–15* (WBC, 1; Waco, TX: Word Books, 1987).

—*The Book of Leviticus* (NICOT, 3; Grand Rapids: Eerdmans, 1979).

Westermann, Claus, 'Arten der Erzählung in der Genesis', in *idem*, *Forschung am Alten Testament: Gesammelte Studien* (TBü 24; Munich: Chr. Kaiser Verlag, 1964), pp. 9-91.

—*Genesis 12–36: A Commentary* (Minneapolis: Augsburg, 1985 [German original 1981]).

—*Genesis 37–50: A Commentary* (Minneapolis: Augsburg, 1986 [German original 1982]).

Willi, Thomas, *Chronik* (BKAT, 24.1; Neukirchen–Vluyn: Neukirchner Verlag, 1991).

Williamson, H.G.M., *1 and 2 Chronicles* (NCB; Grand Rapids: Eerdmans, 1982).

—*Ezra, Nehemiah* (WBC, 16; Waco, TX: Word Books, 1985).

—'A Note on 1 Chronicles VII 12', *VT* 23 (1973), pp. 375-79.

Willoughby, Bruce E., 'Amos, Book of', in *ABD*, I, pp. 203-12.

Wilson, Robert R., *Genealogy and History in the Biblical World* (Yale Near Eastern Researches, 7; New Haven: Yale University Press, 1977).

Wolf, Eric R., *Peasants* (Foundations of Modern Anthropology Series; Englewood Cliffs, NJ: Prentice–Hall, 1966).

Wolff, Hans Walter, *Joel and Amos: A Commentary on the Books of the Prophets Joel and Amos* (Hermeneia; Philadelphia: Fortress Press, 1977).

—'The Kerygma of the Deuteronomic Historical Work', in Walter Brueggemann and Hans Walter Wolff (eds.), *The Vitality of Old Testament Traditions* (Atlanta: John Knox Press, 1975 [German original 1961]), pp. 83-100.

Woudstra, Marten H., *The Book of Joshua* (NICOT; Grand Rapids: Eerdmans, 1981).

Wright, G. Ernest, 'The Literary and Historical Problem of Joshua 10 and Judges 1', *JNES* 5 (1946), pp. 105-14.

Würthwein, Ernst, *Das Erste Buch der Könige, Kapital 1–16* (ATD, 11.1; Göttingen: Vandenhoeck & Ruprecht, 1977).

Yadin, Yigael, '"And Dan, why did he remain in Ships?": Judges, V, 17', *AJBA* 1 (1968), pp. 9-23.

Yadin, Yigael, *et al.*, *Hazor I: An Account of the First Season of Excavations, 1955* (Jerusalem: Magnes Press, 1958).

Yellin, Joseph, and Jan Gunneweg, 'Instrumental Neutron Activation Analysis and the Origin of Iron Age I Collared-Rim Jars and Pithoi from Tel Dan', in Seymour Gitin and William G. Dever (eds.), *Recent Excavations in Israel: Studies in Iron Age Archaeology* (AASOR, 49; Winona Lake, IN: Eisenbrauns, 1989), pp. 133-41.

Younger, K. Lawson, Jr, 'The Configuring of Judicial Preliminaries: Judges 1.1–2.5 and Its Dependence on the Book of Joshua', *JSOT* 68 (1995), pp. 75-92.

Zimmerli, Walther, *Ezekiel*. II. *A Commentary on the Book of the Prophet Ezekiel, Chapters 25–48* (Hermeneia; 2 vols.; Philadelphia: Fortress Press, 1983).

Zobel, H.-J., *Stammesspruch und Geschichte. Die Angaben der Stammesspruche von Gen 49, Dtn 33 und Jdc 5 über die politischen und kultischen Zustände im damalgin 'Israel'* (BZAW, 95; Berlin: Alfred Töpelmann, 1965).

INDEXES

INDEX OF REFERENCES

OLD TESTAMENT

Genesis					
1–11	24	29.1-30	26	36	31
1.12-24	24	29.30	25	37–50	31
1.18-20	24	29.31-35	67, 116	37	5
3.1-2	41	29.31-32	59	37.28-36	42
3.4	41	29.31	26	39.1	42
4.17	177	29.32-25	28	42.23	245
8.1	26	29.32	26	42.24	245
9.20-27	150	29.33	26	46	26, 27, 31,
13.12	23	29.35–30.5	178		32, 56, 75,
14	5, 22-25,	29.35	26		76, 247
	74, 75,	30	262	46.1	242
	263	30.1-8	31	46.5	242
14.1-9	23	30.1-6	18, 27, 28,	46.8-27	22, 31, 59
14.2	74		30, 31, 60,	46.20	60
14.14	9, 22, 23		68, 247,	46.23-25	31
16	28		253, 260	46.23	30, 64,
16.15	30	30.3	27, 28, 30,		245, 246
20.13	213		154, 230	46.27	31
21.14	242	30.7-8	247	48.12-20	29, 60
21.32-33	242	30.14-18	67	49	4, 22, 26,
22.1-3	58	30.23	31		32-34, 38,
22.2	52	34	26, 33,		39, 73,
22.19	242		116, 150		226, 262,
26.23-25	242	35	22, 27, 31,		264
26.31-33	242		32, 42, 56,	49.1-2	1, 32
28.10-22	183		59, 75,	49.1	32
28.10	242		228, 243	49.2-27	32
28.20-22	190	35.1-15	183	49.9	4, 33, 39,
29–30	19, 22,	35.7	213		69, 261
	25-28, 30,	35.22-26	22, 31	49.14	33, 39
	60, 75,	35.22	116	49.16-21	56
	228, 260,	35.23-26	243	49.16-17	9, 34, 38,
	262	35.24-25	244		71, 226
29	33	35.24	250	49.16	30, 33-35,
		35.25	30		38, 40, 75

13.4-15	62, 63	34.17	65	33.26-29	68
13.7-10	62	34.22	55, 66	34	66, 74, 75
13.8-11	62	34.25-26	62	34.1-4	74
13.12	55, 63	35.1-8	98	34.1	22, 74
13.14	63	35.3	99	34.4	74
13.17	62			35	67
13.22	62	*Deuteronomy*		35.22	67
13.25	165	1	62		
14.26-35	65	1.4	113	*Joshua*	
15.16	49	3.8	113	1.7-9	120
16.31	165	4.46-47	113	2–12	122
21	40	5.8-10	196, 199	6.9	62
21.8-9	41	6.4	35, 38	6.13	62
21.9	197	7.1-2	51	7	166
21.13	113	7.1	113	7.14	166
21.26	113	9.14	51	10	113
22.25	114	10.18	134	12	81, 120
25.5	35	12.8	182	13–22	79, 80
26	58, 63-65,	14.29	134	13–21	121, 122
	75, 76,	16.11	134	13–19	19, 20, 26,
	178	16.14	134		33, 77,
26.2	63	22.13–23.1	150		80-88, 90,
26.12	64	24.17	134		92, 98,
26.15	64	24.19	134		104, 106,
26.20	64	26.7	114		122, 198,
26.22	64	26.11-13	134		217, 218
26.23-27	62	27	66, 68, 75	13–16	92
26.23	64	27.1-2	66	13	81
26.26	64	27.11-14	77, 80	13.1-6	120
26.28	64	27.19	134	13.2-3	122
26.35	64	28.58	51	13.17-18	92
26.37-38	64	29–30	67	14	81
26.39	245	29.19	51	14.3-4	71
26.42-43	64	30.19-20	67	15	81, 118
26.42	55, 64,	32.36	38	15.6-10	83
	245, 246	33	22, 26, 34,	15.11	93
26.43	64		41, 66, 68,	15.19	261
26.44	64		69, 71-73,	15.33	168, 178
26.48	64, 245		178, 263	15.45	88
26.50	64	33.1	68	15.47	88
26.52-56	63	33.2-5	68	15.63	117, 122
32	65	33.4	68	16–17	81
32.33	113	33.7	72	16.1-3	81, 83
33.50-56	117	33.13-17	72	16.6-7	83
34	65	33.22	4, 9, 66,	16.10	122
34.1-12	65, 102		68-73,	17.7-9	83
34.9	93		261, 263,	17.12	122
34.13-15	65		264	17.15	93
34.16-29	65	33.24	68	18–21	201

NEW TESTAMENT

ANCIENT AND CLASSICAL REFERENCES

INDEX OF AUTHORS

Robertson, D.A. 72
Rohrbaugh, R.L. 15-17, 19, 28, 103, 105, 210, 248
Roniger, L. 135
Rook, J. 45
Rudolph, W. 243, 244, 246, 250

Sahlins, M.D. 84, 85
Sanderson, G.V. 2
Sarna, N. 25, 28, 29, 32
Sasson, J.M. 131, 132, 244
Schipper, J. 146
Schley, D.G. 176
Schloen, J.D. 125-27
Schmid, H.H. 89
Schoville, K.N. 112
Segert, S. 12
Seow, C.-L. 211
Simkins, R.A. 16
Simon, M. 5-7, 38, 50
Sjoberg, G. 88
Skinner, J. 23-27, 29, 35, 36, 69
Smend, R. 120
Smith, C.R. 2
Smith, D.L. 165
Smith, H.P. 203
Soggin, J.A. 24, 82, 124, 138, 160, 199, 200, 232, 236
Speiser, E.A. 23, 32, 69
Spencer, J.R. 103, 134
Stager, L.E. 11, 16, 19, 37, 124-27, 129, 132-34
Steinthal, H. 12
Stone, K. 15, 111
Strange, J. 91
Stuart, D. 232
Swete, H.B. 3

Talmon, S. 203
Thompson, S. 139
Thompson, T.L. 30
Tigay, J.H. 30, 67-69, 71
Toews, W.I. 107, 182-84, 199, 200, 208, 209
Tov, E. 96

Tristram, H.B. 39
Tuell, S.S. 227, 228

Ussishkin, D. 97

van der Toorn, K. 46
Van Seters, J. 24, 28, 30
Vannutelli, P. 253, 254
Veijola, T. 80, 170
von Rad, G. 24, 35, 51, 78

Waksler, F.C. 53
Wallis Budge, E.A. 132
Wapnish, P. 69
Watson, W.G.E. 35, 52
Weinberg, J. 108
Weinfeld, M. 116, 117
Wellhausen, J. 44, 103, 208, 209
Wenham, G.J. 23, 24, 26, 27, 29, 32, 34, 36, 39, 50
Westermann, C. 23-27, 29, 34, 36, 40, 69, 189
Willi, T. 243, 244
Williamson, H.G.M. 47, 50, 243-48, 250, 252, 253, 256
Willoughby, B.E. 239
Wilson, J.A. 36
Wilson, R.R. 26
Wolf, E.R. 88, 199
Wolff, H.W. 79, 108, 232, 234, 237
Woudstra, M.H. 93
Wright, G.E. 81, 82, 87, 93, 96, 97, 101, 113, 121
Würthwein, E. 213

Yadin, Y. 36, 37, 180
Yellin, J. 180
Younger, K.L., Jr 116

Zimmerli, W. 228
Zobel, H.-J. 123

This JSOTS book forms part of the *Journal for the Study of the Old Testament* series

We also publish

Journal for the Study of the Old Testament
Edited by
John Jarick, *University of Oxford, UK*
Keith Whitelam, *University of Sheffield, UK*

You can read about the most up-to-date scholarship and research on the Old Testament by subscribing to the *Journal for the Study of the Old Testament*, which is published five times a year. The fifth issue comprises of the *Society for Old Testament Study Book List*, a book containing reviews of the most important works being published on the Old Testament from authors and publishers world-wide.

The *Journal for the Study of the Old Testament* is published by Sheffield Academic Press, a Continuum imprint and you can find out more including current subscription prices by visiting:

www.continuumjournals.com/jsot

FREE Sample Copy
Please request a no obligation sample copy by contacting:

Orca Journals
FREEPOST (SWB 20951)
3 Fleets Lane, Stanley House
Poole, Dorset BH15 3ZZ
United Kingdom

Tel: +44 (0)1202 785712
Fax: +44 (0)1202 666219
Email: journals@orcabookservices.co.uk

OR

Visit **www.continuumjournals.com/jsot** and request a FREE sample copy from our website

SHEFFIELD ACADEMIC PRESS
A Continuum imprint
www.continuumjournals.com

JOURNAL FOR THE STUDY OF THE OLD TESTAMENT
SUPPLEMENT SERIES